After taking a B.A. in War Studies and an M.A. in Strategic Studies at King's College, London, Roger Parkinson was for seven years Defence Correspondent of the *Scotsman*. He acted as War Correspondent in Vietnam, Biafra, Aden and Malaysia before becoming a full-time author. His previously published books include: *Clausewitz* (1970); *The Peninsular War* (1973); *Peace for our Time*; *Blood, Toil, Tears and Sweat*, and *A Day's March Nearer Home*, which form a trilogy based on the Second World War Cabinet papers (1972–4); *The Hussar General: The Life of Blücher* (1975); *The Fox of the North: The Life of Kutuzov* (1976); and *The War in the Desert* (1976).

Roger Parkinson died in 1978

Roger Parkinson

Encyclopedia of Modern War

PALADIN
GRANADA PUBLISHING
London Toronto Sydney New York

Published by Granada Publishing Limited
in Paladin Books 1979

ISBN 0 586 08321 9

First published in Great Britain by
Routledge & Kegan Paul Ltd 1977
Copyright © Roger Parkinson 1977

Granada Publishing Limited
Frogmore, St Albans, Herts AL2 2NF
and
3 Upper James Street, London W1R 4BP
1221 Avenue of the Americas, New York, NY 10020, USA
117 York Street, Sydney, NSW 2000, Australia
100 Skyway Avenue, Toronto, Ontario, Canada M9W 3A6
110 Northpark Centre, 2193 Johannesburg, South Africa
CML Centre, Queen & Wyndham, Auckland 1, New Zealand

Made and printed in Great Britain by
Richard Clay (The Chaucer Press) Ltd
Bungay, Suffolk
Set in Monotype Ehrhardt

Granada Publishing ®

only 1 vessel had been lost, sunk by a U-boat. But in January 1942 Germany transferred the battleship 'Tirpitz' to the Norwegian port of Trondheim. The existence of this ship in northern waters, together with similar threats offered by other surface raiders such as 'Hipper', 'Scharnhost' and 'Gneisenau', severely complicated sailings: ships in a concentrated convoy were highly vulnerable to attack from surface vessels, yet if the convoy scattered the vessels became easy targets for U-boats. This dilemma resulted in the tragedy of Convoy PQ17, July 1942. Air reconnaissance revealed the disappearance of the 'Tirpitz' and 'Hipper' from Trondheim; the Admiralty, believing these massive warships might soon intercept PQ17, ordered the convoy to scatter on 5 July. The destroyer escort left the merchantmen in order to block the approach of the German surface vessels. The 'Tirpitz' and 'Hipper' were in fact returning to Norway. German U-boats and aircraft struck the scattered merchantmen: of 36 vessels which started the voyage, 2 had turned back, 13 and 1 rescue ship were sunk by aircraft and 10 by U-boats. By the end of 1942 24 ships had been sunk by U-boats during the year and 36 by aircraft, from a total of 13 convoys to and from Russia. Only the destruction of the German surface ships gave real protection, although ironically these warships caused no direct casualties. 'Gneisenau' was severely damaged in February 1942, 'Hipper' was sunk in December 1942, 'Scharnhorst' in December 1943 and 'Tirpitz' in

November 1944. Only 4 ships were lost in 1943, all by U-boats – but only 6 convoys sailed; 9 convoys sailed in 1944 with a loss of 7 ships, by U-boats; 4 convoys sailed in 1945 for a loss of 5 ships to U-boats and 1 to aircraft.

Ardennes, German offensive in, December 1944 *Second World War* (Maps 12, 13). Known as the 'Battle of the Bulge'. *Hitler* apparently sought a modern version of the March 1918 offensive by *Ludendorff* in the *Somme* region. Ludendorff had thrown 40 divisions against 21 British; Hitler assembled 30 which would strike against only 4 American. But Hitler had virtually no reserves. The Fuhrer chose the Ardennes as the battle area, the same difficult terrain which had brought such success in the battle for *France* in May 1940, and he had a similar battle plan – to thrust for Antwerp, thus cornering allied forces north of the Antwerp–Brussels–Bastogne line. The attack began early on 16 December. Rain and fog had reduced allied reconnaissance for the past 36 hours and panzer units now jabbed through the mists: only 4 days before, *Eisenhower* had described these units as 'weak' and 'badly trained'. Neither Eisenhower nor *Bradley*, Commander of the 12th Army Group, seemed to appreciate the extent of the German offensive. Realization came to Eisenhower late on the 17th, but by then the panzers were pushing towards Stavelot, where the allies held large supply stocks, and farther south had prised a gap in the allied lines between St Vith and Bastogne. The US 1st

Army, commanded by General Courtney Hodge, was forced back on a 50-mile front, but farther north the US 5th Corps, under General Leonard Gerow, stood firm near Malmédy and halted the advance on Liège. By 19 December the allies had begun to recover. To the south the US 4th Infantry and 9th Armoured Divisions stopped the Germans near Echternach in Luxembourg, and the US 101st Airborne Division bolstered Bastogne, which was almost surrounded. On 18 December Bradley had ordered General *Patton* to halt his 3rd Army advance on the Saar and to undertake a 90 degree northern shift in direction to hit the enemy's southern flank. The German advance south of St Vith had, however, split the US 1st and 9th Armies north of the bulge from Bradley's 12th Army Group HQ; to clarify communications Eisenhower decided on 20 December to pass command of the two US armies in the north to *Montgomery*, Commander of the 21st Army; this only left Patton's force under Bradley. On Boxing Day Patton's 3rd Army reached Bastogne. Battle raged around this town until 2 January, but better weather in the last days of December enabled about 5,000 allied aircraft to inflict heavy damage. The allied counter-offensive began on 3 January, with Montgomery ordering Hodge's 1st US Army down from the north and with Patton maintaining his pressure from the south. By 16 January the bulge had been eliminated. About 120,000 German casualties were suffered, 600 tanks and guns destroyed, 1,600 aircraft and 7,000 vehicles; allied casualties were 40,000 men and about 730 tanks. The allied invasion of *Germany*, delayed about 6 weeks, could now begin.

Armstrong, William George, Baron Armstrong of Cragside, 1810–1900 British inventor. A Newcastle solicitor turned hydraulic engineer, Armstrong invented a hydro-electric machine in the early 1840s and a hydraulic crane in 1846. In July 1855, after merely 9 months' design work, he produced a steel-tubed built-up rifled breech-loading gun, employing all contemporary resources of metallurgy and technology: the 8-pounder displayed far better accuracy than the existing smooth-bores in the British Army – according to a contemporary study 'the accuracy of the Armstrong gun at 7,000 yards was as seven to one compared with the common gun at 3,000 yards'. But the British Army refused to adopt the gun on a wide scale and retained existing smooth-bore muzzle-loaders for a further 14 years. Armstrong, working from his Elswick Ordnance Company, sold to other nations. He produced a breech-loading gun with a wire-wound cylinder in 1880. The Elswick Engineering Works merged in 1927 with *Vickers*' Sons and Co. to form Vickers Armstrong.

Arnhem operation, September 1944 *Second World War* (Maps 12, 13). *Montgomery*, Commander of the 21st Army Group, proposed to *Eisenhower* in early September that the allied advance should be hastened by an airborne offensive against Arnhem, Holland. German defences blocked the northern advance over the Meuse and Rhine, and also hindered a thrust towards Rotterdam, Antwerp and the *V-bomber* sites. Eisenhower agreed to the scheme, code-named 'Market Garden'. The plan envisaged an advance by ground forces towards Arnhem, in conjunction with airborne attacks on bridges over the Maas, Waal and Rhine at Grave, Nijmegen and Arnhem itself. The air drops were carried out during daylight on 17 September, intended to provide stepping-stones over the rivers for the advancing British 2nd Army led by the 30th Corps. Troops of the 1st British Airborne Division, supported by a Polish brigade, dropped on the north bank of the Rhine to move forward and seize Arnhem bridge; airborne units of the US 82nd Division parachuted down to capture the bridges at Nijmegen and Grave, whilst the US 101st Airborne aimed to secure the road from Grave to Eindhoven. Aircraft shortages meant the drop had to be spread over 3 days, allowing the Germans to recover. The two US airborne divisions achieved their objective to the north of Eindhoven and at Grave and Nijmegen, but the British element spearheading the attack at Arnhem were dropped 7 miles from the Rhine bridge. Bad weather hampered the fly-in of reinforcements and supplies. The British 1st Airborne troops were left isolated; gallant fighting continued until 25 September, but Montgomery was then obliged to order the survivors to pull back. This attempt

was made during the night of 25–26 September, with only 2,400 men escaping out of the original 10,000.

Arnold, Henry Harley, 1886–1950 US General of the Air Force. Graduated West Point, 1907; joined Army Aviation, 1911; appointed Chief of US Army Air Corps, 1938; Chief of US Army Air Forces, June 1941, remaining in this position throughout the *Second World War*, and a member of the US *Joint Chiefs of Staff*. Arnold proved more flexible than his superior, *Marshall*, in the acute Anglo-US debate over the Second Front in Europe, but he criticized the lack of effective use of bombers being sent to Britain in late 1943, urging greater intensification of the *strategic bombing* campaign; General of the Air Force, May 1949.

Arras, Battles of, April 1917, June 1940 *First and Second World Wars* (Maps 10, 13). *Nivelle* aimed to batter through the German lines in the Aisne region. But essential to the *Nivelle offensive* was a diversionary attack by the British in the Arras region. The new British Prime Minister, *Lloyd George*, arranged to place the BEF commander, *Haig*, under Nivelle's orders; Haig reacted with horror, as did the new British Chief of the Imperial General Staff, *Robertson*. Arrangements were eventually made whereby Haig retained absolute command of the British Army and had the right to appeal against the French orders, although he would follow these for the coming offensive. On 9

April the British diversionary attack was launched 8 miles south of Arras to 7 miles north of the town after a heavy preliminary artillery and gas bombardment. The British offensive comprised General *Allenby*'s 3rd Army on the right and General Sir Henry Sinclair Horne's 1st Army on the left. Included in the British attack were a number of *tanks*. British-Canadian forces totalled 14 divisions; German strength comprised 6 divisions in the front line and 6 in close reserve, commanded by General Baron Ludwig von Falkenhausen. The initial attack was successful, although the tanks either broke down or were destroyed through being committed piecemeal. To the north the British pushed forward 3 miles, with the attack commanded by General Sir Charles Fergusson – the deepest penetration since trench warfare solidified after the *Race to the Sea* in autumn 1914. Canadian troops stormed and took the greater part of the famous feature known as Vimy Ridge. Farther south the supporting British 5th Army under General Hubert Gough made little progress. The battle had a final spasm on 3 May, when Haig sought to lend support to the *Nivelle offensive* which had now begun. British casualties at Arras were about 84,000; the German total was probably about 75,000. Arras became the scene of critical fighting in May 1940, and a comparison underlines the revolution brought about by *blitzkrieg*. The Second World War engagement came after the German drive on the Channel wheeled northwards in the battle for *France*. French and British

units were sent reeling backwards by the swift-moving German panzers and motorized infantry; a task force sent by *Gort*, BEF commander, attempted to counter-attack German armour at Arras, but was beaten off by *Rommel*'s 7th Panzer Division on 21 May. During Rommel's subsequent strike for the coast he moved his division 150 miles in one day; his casualties amounted to 3,000 men – as compared with the British losses of 80,000 in 1918 merely to gain a handful of miles.

Artillery, general Artillery in the *Napoleonic Wars* was divided into light and heavy, defined by the weight of solid shot fired. Light guns, deployed at battalion level, were usually 4–6 pounders. Heavy guns, 8–12 pounders, were grouped in batteries: the latter were termed redoubts if they enjoyed all-round breastwork protection, or 'flèches' or redans if the positions were open at the rear. A distinction had already emerged between conventional field-guns with a low to medium angle of fire – trajectory – and the high-angle howitzers and *mortars* which lobbed the missile. A further distinction would later become apparent between the mortar as an infantry weapon and the howitzer as an artillery piece. In the Napoleonic era guns fired roundshot, with a maximum range of up to a mile including the bounce and roll of the missile, or *grape-shot* for bombardments of up to about 400 yards; shells had a varying range, but so far only the British had developed *shrapnel*. Guns were limited in close support use through slow rate of fire, inaccuracy and recoil problems – valuable time had to be spent realigning after the gun jerked back with each discharge. Efforts had however been made, especially by *Gribeauval*, to improve mobility through reducing the length and weight of the barrel and gun carriage. *Napoleon*, who declared 'it is only with artillery that one makes war', used this weapon en masse to punch a hole through the enemy lines, as at *Wagram* in 1808; *Wellington* employed his artillery in a more selective fashion, aiming at specific targets. Post-Napoleonic development centres on the adoption of *rifling*, the change to *breech-loading*, improvements in *ballistics* and the introduction of better recoil mechanisms. During the *Crimean War* a number of muzzle-loading smooth-bore guns were converted into rifled weapons, giving greater range and accuracy; the first successful breech-loading cannon had in fact appeared in 1851 with the *Krupp* 6-pounder, rapidly followed by a version made by Armstrong and Whitworth in Britain. By the 1860s almost every principle embodied in the modern gun had been introduced, although often in crude form – considerable difficulties arose in 1866 through burst barrels on the Krupp guns. At the start of the *Franco-Prussian War* the French Army was completely equipped with rifled cannon, although many were still muzzle-loaders and manufactured from bronze – this material had been chosen since it resulted in fewer flaws during manufacture, thus reducing chances of burst barrels. The Prussians, on the other hand, were armed with the Krupp gun made from steel, with Krupp having recently introduced radical improvements in the casting process. This gun, being a breech-loader, proved far superior to the French weapon, and the Prussians added to this advantage through their better artillery employment. Detailed study of the tactical use of artillery had been made in Prussia and this weapon was utilized in devastating form especially by the Guards artillery commander Prince Kraft zu *Hohenlohe*. Artillery was massed in highly effective fashion, notably at *Sedan*. Development in the late nineteenth century in Germany, Austria, France, Britain and the USA led to heavy guns with ranges of up to 15,000 yards and field-guns with ranges of up to 9,000. Rates of fire were vastly improved through the absorption of recoil, with Krupp again leading the way: a Krupp hydraulic system soaked up recoil. The system was adapted in the French 75 mm and the 1897 model òf this gun was the most famous French artillery piece of the *First World War*: it had a rate of fire of 6 rounds per minute and threw a 16-pound shell over 7,500 yards. The main German guns included the 42 cm which could fire a 1-ton shell 16,000 yards, the 75 mm Model 1906 firing a 15-pound shrapnel shell or a combined HE and shrapnel missile; the Germans had also developed a better variety of howitzers. On average each German army corps had about 160 guns of all types; the French total was 126 and the British 154. The heaviest gun was the German Big Bertha, 75 tons, which had a crew of 280 and a rate of fire 10 rounds per hour: this weapon was used against the forts of Liège, Maubeuge and Antwerp. Massed artillery bombardments initially allowed the infantry to sweep forward and occupy the enemy front trenches; this advantage was removed after the first six months of war, when trenches were extended in area. The next step was the rolling barrage, moving steadily forward ahead of the infantry to allow the latter to advance deeper; this tactical move was introduced at the *Somme*, 1916, preceded by a general bombardment in which 1,738,000 shells were blasted into the German defences. But the rolling barrage still failed to achieve the breakthrough. *Messines*, 1917, was preceded by a 17-day bombardment of $3\frac{1}{2}$ million shells; the Third Battle of *Ypres*, soon after, began with a 19-day bombardment using 4,300,000 shells – 321 trainloads amounting to a year's production for 55,000 war workers. The barrage and the downpours of rain turned the area into a wilderness of water-logged shell craters, hampering the movement of advancing troops. Ypres marked the last great artillery battle of the Western Front. Inter-war development was mainly concerned with achieving greater mobility for artillery weapons and with the production of specific types for definite functions. Self-propelled guns were advanced, together with specially designed tracked vehicles for towing. Warhead improvements included the introduction of shaped Armour Piercing (AP)

shot, demonstrated by the Swiss in 1938: this 'shaped charge', consisting of explosive and shot, had better capabilities for cutting through armour. Other developments followed, including the British projectile known as the Armour Piercing Discarding Sabot (APDS), used in the latter stages of the *Second World War*. To aid mobility and to make weapons airportable for *airborne* operations, guns were reduced in weight: the US 75 mm pack howitzer, for example, weighed only 1,340 pounds, compared with 1·5 tons for the 75 mm gun, and could be easily dismantled. Guns were further diversified, with *anti-tank* and *anti-aircraft* categories becoming increasingly important. The most famous German gun in the Second World War was the 88 mm, designed as an anti-aircraft weapon but used – especially by *Rommel* – as a highly effective anti-tank field-gun with a range of about 12,000 yards. Other German guns included the monstrous Karl siege weapon which fired a shell weighing 4,850 pounds – this had a crew of 250 men and could only fire twice an hour. The main British artillery piece was the 25-pounder which replaced the old 18-pounder, able to be used as a howitzer, long-distance or anti-tank gun. US guns included the 37 mm anti-tank weapon. The Russians were probably the most effective artillery users: weapons included the 122 mm howitzer, range 22,000 yards; the Red Army also utilized *rockets*. Russian artillery tactics primarily depended upon mass barrages, but the Red Army, in common with all other forces, developed close co-ordination between artillery and tanks. Improved *wireless* communication enabled better central direction of heavy artillery groups: this technique was first developed by US General Charles *Summerall* in the closing months of the First World War: a single Fire Direction Centre rapidly and accurately shifted the barrages from a number of batteries across a wide front, thus increasing fire power effectiveness. In *Montgomery*'s 8th Army a senior artillery commander was appointed at every level of infantry or armoured formation command, responsible for the co-ordination of the fire from that formation with adjacent groups. Postwar developments have increased this co-operation, especially through computers. Thus the British FACE system – Field Artillery Computer Equipment – processes all information required to place a shell accurately on target within a few seconds; information includes earth rotational effects, muzzle velocity of each gun for each charge, temperature of the ammunition charges and even meteorological data. The system, introduced into the British Army in 1969, is for use with the latest 105 mm, 155 mm and 175 mm guns: these are all multi-charge weapons, having both high and low angle fire capability, and each employs many projectile types. Modern US guns range from the 8-inch self-propelled howitzer M-110, introduced in 1962 with a maximum range of 16,800 yards and with nuclear capacity, to the 105 mm towed howitzer which for many years has been the standard general

purpose close support light artillery weapon of the US Army. The largest conventional gun in service with the Soviet Army is the 203 mm howitzer, with the same calibre as the US 8-inch. The Red Army has continued the doctrine of employing artillery fire 'en masse', and the proportion of artillerymen remains at about 25 per cent of the army as a whole – higher than in Western forces.

Atlanta, campaign and Battle of, 1864 *American Civil War* (Map 3). *Sherman* opened the Atlanta campaign on 5 May 1864. The aim was to disrupt the Confederacy while *Grant* launched the second half of a gigantic pincer movement in the Virginian *Wilderness*. Sherman's forces comprised the Army of the Cumberland, 61,000 men, under *Thomas*; the Army of the Tennessee, 24,500 men under General James McPherson; and the Army of the Ohio, 13,500 troops under General John M. Schofield. Against this Union array was General Joseph Johnston's Army of the Tennessee, supported by cavalry under John H. Morgan and *Forrest*. Johnston selected a series of defensive positions – at Dalton on 9 May, Resaca on 15 May, Allatoona on 24 May – which he held until the last moment before slipping to the next. Sherman declined to attack in frontal fashion; instead he attempted to outflank the enemy, vainly inviting Johnston to attack. Only once did Sherman throw his Union troops forward in frontal assault, at the Battle of Kenesaw Mountain, 27 June; he lost about 3,000 men to Johnston's

800 with no appreciable gains. Johnston withdrew to positions north of the Chattahoochie River, 25 miles north-east of Atlanta, which Sherman attempted to turn on 9 July; the Confederates pulled back to Peachtree Creek, immediately to the north of Atlanta. Johnston retired on 17 July and was succeeded by *Hood*. Johnston had already prepared plans for a counter-attack, and his successor followed these plans on 20 July in the Battle of Peachtree Creek. This failed to stop the Union advance and the Confederates withdrew into the final Atlanta defences. Hood began the Battle of Atlanta on 22 July by throwing his best troops, under William J. Hardee, against McPherson's section of the Union Army. The assault was repulsed with a loss of about 8,000 Confederates and 3,700 Union troops, the latter including McPherson. Sherman now sent his cavalry, 6,000-strong, to outflank Atlanta and cut rail links; this failed, but so too did a counter-attack at Ezra Church on 28 July. Siege continued until Sherman swung round Atlanta and sliced the Confederate rail links south of the city on 31 August. Hood evacuated during the night; Sherman marched into the city on 1 September. Plans for the next Union move were prepared during September and October, while Hood's Confederate Army moved west and north to attack Sherman's communications. To counter this Sherman divided his forces: he sent Thomas's Army of the Cumberland back to deal with Hood, and he himself prepared to advance further into

the south with 60,000 men. By doing so he would abandon his communications and live off the country until he reached Savannah and the coast. On 12 October Grant wired his approval: 'You will no doubt clean the country where you go of railroad tracks and supplies.' On 15 November Sherman proceeded, in his words, to 'cut a swath through to the sea'. He advanced on a 50-mile front and by 9 December had covered the 300 miles to Savannah. Confederate defenders of the city under Hardee were forced to evacuate on 21 December. Although non-combatants were usually treated with respect, Sherman's march to the sea formed an example of the 'total' form of war which emerged in the final stage of the American Civil War; non-military targets were considered as important as the opposing army.

Atlantic, Battle of *First World War*. By 1914 Germany had a *submarine* fleet of about 70 vessels, a number of which were diesel-powered. The submarine war began with the sinking of 3 British cruisers by U-boat 9 off the Dutch coast on 22 September 1914; operations increased after 4 February 1915. German submarines were obliged to use their periscopes rather than undertaking surface attacks, owing to pressure from surface hunters; this made it more difficult to distinguish British vessels from neutrals, and from the beginning the latter were involved: a Norwegian vessel was sunk on 19 February and the US tanker 'Gullflight' torpedoed on 1 May. US public opinion was incensed by the sinking of the liner 'Lusitania' on 7 May: among the 1,198 passengers drowned were 124 Americans. This incident, followed by the sinking of the British liner 'Arabic', 19 August, provoked such an American outcry that Germany announced on 1 September that she would cease unlimited submarine war. The Germans still managed to destroy 1 million tons of shipping in the period 1915–16. Britain equipped merchantment with 12-pounder guns, but the entire Merchant Navy could not be so armed until autumn 1916. This eventual protection forced the German submarines to seek security through depth, with U-boat commanders having to rely to an even greater extent on periscope sightings. The German Naval Command, headed by *Tirpitz* and *Scheer*, therefore began pressing for a return to unrestricted submarine warfare. They calculated that Britain would sue for peace within 5 months – before US intervention could be effective. Unrestricted submarine war reopened on 1 February 1917. Ships lost rose from 181 in January to 259 in February, 325 in March and 423 in April. Britain attempted to retaliate with accelerated mine development, depth charges and detection devices such as the hydrophone, but the convoy system was ruled out by the Admiralty on the grounds that this would present a larger target and would waste vital cruisers and destroyers. America joined the war on 6 April, following the sinking of several US ships, but US troops needed transporting, using up even more tonnage. However, the convoy advocates received a powerful supporter in Admiral William S. Sims, commander of US naval operations in the Atlantic. These advocates, already including the influential *Beatty*, argued that the size of a convoy was still small in proportion to the total sea area, and that every time a convoy slipped through about 40 ships would escape; the concentration of shipping made escort duties easier and convoys could be more easily deflected from danger areas. Opposers of the system included the First Sea Lord, *Jellicoe*, even though he had warned in February 1917 that Britain would run out of food and other raw materials by July. Prime Minister *Lloyd George* insisted upon a convoy trial which began on 10 May. By the end of October 1917, 99 homeward convoys, totalling over 1,500 vessels, had reached safety; only 10 vessels had been lost in convoy formation. In addition, Britain developed better offensive measures, including hunter-vessel packs and wider mine distribution: about 15,700 mines were laid in the Heligoland Bight during 1917 and 21,000 in 1918. By 1918 a U-boat operating from Flanders could only hope for 6 voyages before being destroyed.

Atlantic, Battle of *Second World War*. Britain introduced convoys from the start but lacked escort vessels. In July 1940 Britain had to divert shipping from the approaches south of Ireland to the longer route via Northern Ireland; in the week ending 22 September 1940, 27 vessels were sunk – more than in any 7 days during the

First World War. Already, by 15 August, $2\frac{1}{2}$ million tons of British shipping had been destroyed. German U-boats operated in 'wolf packs' of up to 20 submarines, under the central direction of Admiral *Doenitz*. British losses steadily mounted: by June 1941 about 5·7 million tons of shipping had been sunk, whereas British shipyards could only build 800,000 tons as replacements. Britain tried to retaliate by increased aerial protection, but the U-boats moved beyond aircraft range. In September 1940 Britain attempted to find an answer through the use of an escort aircraft carrier: the first of these, HMS 'Audacity', was a merchant ship modified to carry 6 aircraft. The 'Audacity' was sunk in December. Churchill successfully sought to buy old destroyers from America, but US assistance was restricted through the country's neutral status; she did however undertake limited escort and patrol duties in the western Atlantic. Added to the U-boat menace was the offensive waged by long-range German bombers and the constant threat by Germany's huge capital ships, including the 'Bismarck' until this vessel was sunk in May 1941, and the 'Tirpitz'. The situation remained desperate until America's entry into the war, December 1941. US involvement ultimately tipped the scales through provision of merchant and escort shipping and through the employment of far greater numbers of hunter weapons. Allied merchant losses in the Atlantic and Arctic in 1942 totalled 1,027,000 tons, but during the year 85 U-boats were sunk. The situation shifted back in

Germany's favour during early 1943, with 108 allied merchantmen sunk at a cost of only 15 U-boats up to the end of March, but closer Anglo-US co-operation led to more efficient hunting techniques; production of faster transports and escorts steadily rose. By the end of 1943, allied 'kills' had passed German replacement ability; between May and September, 3,546 merchantmen in 62 convoys had crossed the Atlantic without loss.

Atomic warfare, general development In 1896, Antoine Henri Becquerel, 1852–1908, discovered radioactivity, providing the first evidence of a source of energy within the atom exceeding its chemical energy. In 1919 Ernest Rutherford, 1871–1937, disintegrated the nucleus of the nitrogen atom with alpha particles from radium; by 1940 scientists in Germany, Britain and America were working on the atom bomb project. This weapon, code-named by the allies 'Tube Alloys' and with overall development known as the Manhattan project, became a clear possibility as the war continued. *Churchill* and *Roosevelt* agreed in June 1942 that allied development should take place mainly in the USA. Anglo-US co-operation suffered setbacks: General Leslie Groves, executive agent of the US Military Policy Committee, which handled all atomic research construction work, became increasingly concerned over security aspects, and Dr James Conant, Chairman of the National Defense Research Committee, deplored the fact that the US effort amounted to 90 per cent of the whole. On 13 January 1943, Dr Conant completed a paper which proposed the British should be given no more information about electromagnetic separation, about heavy water production, fast neutron reaction or about the actual manufacture of the bomb. More harmonious relations were restored after the Quebec Summit Conference, August 1943. The first live test of the atomic bomb was made in New Mexico on 16 July 1945: on 6 and 9 August the bombs were dropped on *Hiroshima and Nagasaki*. Russian scientists exploded their first atomic bomb in 1949; on 16 October 1964 the Chinese exploded a low-yield atomic device. Developments to increase destructive power had already resulted in the first *hydrogen*-bomb explosion in 1953, undertaken by the Russians in Siberia. Nuclear research also led to atomic power: the US *submarine* 'Nautilus', completed in 1954, was the world's first nuclear-powered ship.

Auchinleck, Sir Claude John Eyre, 'The Auk', 1884– British Field-Marshal. Served in *First World War*; served for long periods in India between the wars; C-in-C India at outbreak of *Second World War*, but returned to England in late 1939; GOC Northern *Norway*, 1940; C-in-C India, January 1941, after period as GOC-in-C Southern Command, England; chosen by *Churchill* to replace *Wavell* as Middle East Commander, July 1941 (Map 14). Auchinleck withstood pressure from *Churchill* to launch a premature offensive in the North African *Desert Campaign*; he began his 'Crusader' offensive against *Rommel* south of *Tobruk* on 18 November. The battle lasted until 20 December, with Auchinleck displaying the utmost determination, and with Rommel finally falling back to El Agheila. But Rommel's victory at Gazala, May 1942, led to the withdrawal of the 8th Army to the El *Alamein* positions. Auchinleck assumed personal command of the 8th Army and rallied the troops at Alam al Halfa ridge, July. His defensive techniques were later largely adopted by *Montgomery*. Auchinleck was replaced by *Alexander*, 15 August. He returned to India as C-in-C, 20 June 1943; appointed Field-Marshal 1946 and Supreme Commander, India and Pakistan, 1947.

Auerstedt and Jena, Battles of, 1806 *Napoleonic Wars* (Map 1). Both were fought on 14 October. Prussia's army was outdated, with officers largely ignoring the new flexible tactics introduced by the French, preferring the oldfashioned methods of Frederick the Great – rigid lines relying upon massed volleys. Prussia stood apart while *Napoleon* defeated the Austrians at Ulm and *Austerlitz* in 1805. Napoleon increased his pressure on Prussia during the following months, and finally, in September 1806, Frederick William ordered full mobilization, even though Prussia would now have to fight without allies. Moreover, the Prussians allowed Napoleon the initiative: the 100,000 Prussian troops would be outnumbered; Napoleon advanced into Prussian territory with 160,000, and by 3 October had deployed his regiments in south Prussia ready for a move on Berlin. The Prussian Army, spread between the French and Berlin, comprised 3 main field corps. The first, about 20,000 strong, was commanded by the Duke of Brunswick; the second, under Frederick Louis, Prince of Hohenlohe, totalled about 65,000 men; and the third, about 25,000, was led by General von Rüchel. *Scharnhorst*, Brunswick's able Chief of Staff, complained on 7 October: 'What we ought to do I know right well. What we shall do, God only knows.' Finally, after a clash between Hohenlohe's advance guard and French regiments on 10 October, the Prussians decided on retreat. The route was based on Auerstedt, Freiberg and Merseburg. Hohenlohe was ordered to provide a flank force while the main army under Brunswick moved from Auerstedt. By the evening of the 13th Hohenlohe's army lay east of the forest of Jena. Hohenlohe believed the main French army was moving towards Dresden, away to his east and he neglected to occupy in strength the Landgrafenberg plateau overlooking Jena. Napoleon had guessed Prussian intentions. He planned to lead his main army north over the Saale in the Jena region, while farther to the north-east the French 1st and 3rd Corps under *Davout* would cross the Saale in the Auerstedt area between Kösen and Naumberg. Early on 14 October Brunswick's regiments began to retreat from Auerstedt. Soon after

dawn French cavalry squadrons advanced over the Saale at Kösen and blocked the Prussian advance guard; by 8 a.m. Davout had deployed almost 3 divisions across the river, and the Prussians never recovered from this determined French move. Arguments intensified at the Prussian headquarters, leading regiments were starved of reinforcements and confusion reached a peak when Brunswick fell fatally wounded. By noon a French division under General Morand was moving south of the Prussians; another division under General Gudin pushed at the centre; and a third under *Friant* curved round the north. Frederick William believed Hohenlohe to be still intact at Jena and decided the main army should join this flanking force. Retreat therefore began at about 5 p.m. with the Prussian regiments falling into increasing chaos. By nightfall Frederick William had reached Mattstedt, where he heard the result of the Battle of Jena. Napoleon had attacked Hohenlohe at 6 a.m. under cover of fog. Troops under Marshal Louis Gabriel Suchet, General Gazen and *Soult* pushed forward over the Landgrafenberg plateau; at 9 a.m. Napoleon ordered a halt to allow his forces to regroup, but Marshal *Ney* continued his advance in the centre. Napoleon reinforced Ney with troops under Henri Gratien Bertrand and *Lannes*; the latter's regiments came face to face with 20,000 Prussian infantry under General von Grawert. These Prussians were deployed in rigid close-order lines, extremely vulnerable to the concentrated French fire which they suffered for 2 terrible hours: this senseless sacrifice epitomized Prussia's whole outdated attitude to war. Along the whole battle front the Prussians started to collapse; French skirmishers swarmed forward; Hohenlohe had used all his reserves, while Napoleon still had 42,000 men uncommitted. The 3rd Prussian Army under Rüchel, advancing from the north, came far too slowly. Rüchel reached the battlefield at 2 p.m. and deployed in rigid line; his troops were immediately subjected to concentrated French artillery fire, and within 15 minutes had suffered 50 per cent casualties. Rüchel was fatally wounded. By 4 p.m. the Prussians were in full retreat. In one day each of Prussia's 3 armies had been shattered. The Prussians lost some 22,000 men killed or wounded, 18,000 prisoners and 200 guns. French casualties were about 12,000 killed or captured. The remains of Prussia's forces fled north, with the last survivors surrendering at Lübeck on 6 November after a courageous withdrawal by *Blücher* and Scharnhorst.

Austerlitz, campaign and Battle of, 1805 *Napoleonic Wars* (Map 1). The Austrian, Russian and Swedish allies planned first to destroy *Masséna*'s army in *Italy* – 50,000 men – then to move westwards towards the Rhine and France. Napoleon advanced from the English Channel area with his Grand Army, 200,000 strong, to disrupt such a move, concentrating upon General Mack von Leiberich's Austrian Army of 50,000 men which invaded Bavaria

on 2 September and marched towards Ulm. Napoleon drove forward on a wide front, crossing the Rhine in late September to catch the allies off-balance. His forces reached the Danube on 6 October and, while *Murat*'s cavalry demonstrated in front of Mack at Ulm, 6 great columns of the Grand Army swept north and east of the Austrian commander in a wide concentric arc. On 17 October, his communications severed, Mack surrendered with nearly 30,000 men. Napoleon immediately thrust into Austria, driving 120,000 Russians under *Kutuzov* before him and occupying Vienna at the beginning of November. On 15 November he advanced north in Moravia, leaving 20,000 men to hold Vienna. He now had 65,000 men, positioned in the midst of his enemies. Archduke Ferdinand, with 18,000 Austrians, lay to the north-west at Prague; to the north-east lay Russians and Austrians commanded by Kutuzov; to the south were 80,000 Austrians, under the Archdukes *Charles* and John. Kutuzov wanted the allies to continue withdrawal, thus extending Napoleon's communications, but was overruled. Instead on 28 November the allies began to move upon the French Army, positioned 2 miles west of Austerlitz. Napoleon deliberately overstretched his right wing, to make it appear weak as a further inducement for the enemy to attack. The allies obliged, attempting to move between Napoleon and Vienna. Battle began early on 2 December; by 9 a.m., one-third of the allied army was pressing against this sector, despite warnings from Kutuzov that the offensive was premature. While the battered French right continued to draw enemy strength, *Soult*'s corps in the French centre was ordered forward to split the weakened allied front. Soult then encircled the allied left and drove it back, assisted by *Davout*. Meanwhile, further French troops hammered through the gap made by Soult and *Lanne*'s corps struck against the allied right. By nightfall the French victory was complete, at a loss of 9,000 men. Austro-Russian losses were 26,000 plus 185 guns. Austria abandoned the coalition against Napoleon after the Treaty of Pressburg, 26 December. France gained domination over western and southern Germany; next year, with the Russians having retired back into Poland, Napoleon turned on Prussia in the *Auerstedt* campaign.

Austro-Prussian 'Seven Weeks' War, 1866 (Map 5) The conflict arose through Austria's determination to block Prussia's growing power in central Europe. On 14 June 1866 Austria condemned Prussia's occupation of Holstein, which had taken place in 1848 following a Prussian-inspired revolt in this Danish province. The Austrian government also objected to a treaty which the Prussian Chancellor, *Bismarck*, had concluded with the French. Bismarck took the Austrian outburst as a declaration of war. Prussian forces were fully prepared as a result of careful planning by the Chief of General Staff, *Moltke*, who had worked out in detail schemes for

mobilization and deployment based on the *railway* network. Four Prussian armies moved forward over a 275-mile front. In the north General Vogel von Falkenstein entered Hanover with 50,000 men; into Saxony and Silesia advanced Crown Prince Frederick William's 2nd Army moving from Landeshut, together with Prince Frederick Karl's 1st Army from Görlitz and General Karl E. Herwarth von Bittenfeld's Army of the Elbe. The point of Prussian concentration was Gitschen. The Austrian Army was believed to be one of the best in the world; its cavalry was considered superb, and its *rifled* field-guns were superior to the Prussian artillery. But the Austrian general staff was inferior to the Prussian, and the Austrian infantry was armed with muzzle-loading rifles which were completely outclassed by the Prussian needle-guns as developed by *Dreyse*. The Prussian Army of the Elbe occupied Dresden on 19 June, then advanced through the Bohemian Mountains to unite with the 1st Army; these two armies reached Gitschen on 29 June. The Prussian 2nd Army reached a point just east of Gitschen on 30 June after surviving stiff Austrian attacks at Trautenau and Nachod on the 27th. Also during these hectic days, Falkenstein's army in Hanover succeeded in outmanoeuvring an Austrian force under General Alexander von Arentschildt, with the latter surrendering on 29 June. In Bohemia the 1st and 2nd Prussian Armies and the Army of the Elbe organized themselves for battle far quicker than their Austrian opponents.

This battle began on 3 July at *Sadowa*: a crushing Prussian victory effectively ended the war. The Treaty of Prague, 23 August, was highly beneficial to Prussia, who became the leader of a new North German Confederation. Moltke's reputation had been established, and he continued to improve the Prussian forces prior to the *Franco-Prussian War*, 1870.

B

Bacteriological warfare – see Chemical and bacteriological warfare (CBW)

Baden-Powell, Robert Stephenson Smyth, 1st Baron, 1857–1941 British General. Served in India, 1878, and thereafter in South Africa. *Wolseley*, appointed C-in-C of British Army in 1895, included Baden-Powell in an expedition to West Africa during the same year. In 1896 he was appointed Chief Staff Officer to Sir Frederick Carrington when the latter's troops dealt with the revolt of the Matabele in the British South African Company territory north of the Transvaal. Baden-Powell commanded the 5th Dragoon Guards in India, 1897 to July 1899, when he returned to South Africa. Hostilities with the *Boers* were clearly imminent (Map 7): Baden-Powell was appointed C-in-C North West Frontier Forces and ordered to raise two regiments from the white settlers in Bechuanaland. Baden-Powell defended Mafeking for 215 days, from 13 October 1899 to 17 May 1900, when he was relieved by a flying column under Major-General Bryan T. Mahon. Later assessments downgraded the defence of Mafeking;

its political significance at the time, when Britain desperately needed some success to outweigh the general humiliations of the Boer War, far outrated its military importance. Baden-Powell claimed he tied up large numbers of Boer troops who would otherwise have been involved elsewhere, but these probably never rose above 6,000. Baden-Powell was appointed Inspector-General of Cavalry in 1903; he left the Army to found the Boy Scouts movement in 1908.

Balaklava, Battle of, October 1854 *Crimean War* (Map 4). The action followed the attempt of the Russian commander, Menshikov, to break between the allied forces besieging Sebastopol and the British base at Balaklava. The battlefield centred on the road running south-east from Sebastopol which crossed Balaklava plain on a narrow ridge known as the Causeway Heights. Beyond the ridge lay North Valley with the Fedioukine Hills rising on the Sebastopol side. Southwards of the ridge was South Valley, with Balaklava base on its southern edge. *Raglan*, commanding the allies jointly with the French

General François Certain Canrobet, had constructed 6 redoubts on the road along Causeway Heights; each had a 12-pounder naval gun manned by Turkish troops. But insufficient account had been taken of a report by a Turkish spy, made the evening before the battle, that 20,000 Russian infantry and 5,000 Russian cavalry were marching on Balaklava. The attack began on the 6 redoubts soon after dawn, 25 October. By mid-morning 4 of the redoubts had fallen and British reinforcements under Sir George Cathcart advanced too slowly. Meanwhile the British cavalry, comprising the Heavy and Light Brigades under Major-General G. C. Bingham, Lord Lucan, had to pull back. Raglan ordered him to take the cavalry to the west of the battlefield, even though Lucan would then be unable to provide fully effective support for the 93rd Highland Division in South Valley, the only remaining force standing between the advancing Russians and the Balaklava base. The division, commanded by Sir Colin *Campbell*, consisted of 550 men of the Argyll and Sutherland Highlanders; against them advanced a section of the Russian cavalry. The subsequent defence by the Highlanders has been immortalized as 'the thin Red Line': this section of the enemy cavalry eventually wheeled away, but the main Russian cavalry continued to advance towards Balaklava base. Lucan ordered a charge by the Heavy Brigade, commanded by Brigadier-General Lord James Scarlett. The latter's force, comprising the Scots Greys, Inniskillings and 5th Dragoon Guards, was heavily outnumbered by the 3,000 enemy cavalrymen, but nevertheless repulsed the Russians. During this action the Light Brigade, under Brigadier-General James Thomas Brudenell, Lord Cardigan, had stood inactive: Cardigan had not been given specific orders to support the Heavy Brigade and declined to use his own initiative. Battle activity dwindled for the moment: Lucan merely moved the Light Brigade to a position across the end of the North Valley, with the Heavy Brigade behind them to the right. The British headquarters, situated behind the Light Brigade on the extreme west of the battlefield, observed that the Russians were dragging away the captured naval guns from the redoubts on the Causeway Heights. Raglan immediately sent an order to Lucan to advance the cavalry and prevent these guns from being carried away. Lucan, unable to see the Causeway Redoubts from his position in North Valley, assumed the order referred to Russian artillery lined at the far end of North Valley; he passed the order to Cardigan, who argued that a charge down the valley would be directly against the Russian guns and would also be exposed to batteries and riflemen on each flank. The disastrous charge of the Light Brigade nevertheless began, against the wrong target. Of the 673 men who rode into the 'Valley of Death', less than 200 returned. The Russians maintained positions on the Causeway Heights; they attacked again 11 days later in the battle of *Inkerman*.

Ballistic Missile Defence (BMD) – see Anti-Ballistic Missile defence (ABM)

Balloon Françoise Rozier became the first man to ascend in a lighter-than-air craft when he made a short journey in a Montgolfier-designed balloon on 15 October 1783. A balloon was first used for military observation at the Battle of *Fleurus*, June 1794. The invention caused widespread interest in France during the Revolution, with schemes being drawn up to carry as many as 3,000 troops. A French balloonist corps was formed for observation duties. Soon after 1800 John Sadler became the first known Englishman to make an ascent. Interest faded after 1814, until 1849 when Venice was besieged by the Austrians: the latter attempted to drop small bombs from balloons, using a time fuse, but the experiment – organized by Lieutenant Franz Uchatius – proved a failure. Balloon development nevertheless continued, stimulated by the introduction of the more effective coal gas. Devices were used during the *Franco-Prussian War*, largely owing to inventor M. Godard: the French dispatched messages by balloon during the siege of Paris, and the political leader Gambetta escaped from the city in one of these craft on 11 October 1870. Observations balloons were used in the *First World War*, but were rendered obsolete by the related *airship* and by the development of *aircraft*.

Battenberg, Prince Louis Alexander of, Marquis of Milford Haven, 1854–1921 German-born nobleman, becoming naturalized British subject. C-in-C Atlantic Fleet, 1908–10; First Sea Lord, 1912–14, during final build-up of Royal Navy prior to hostilities with Germany, with this accumulation of strength centred on the Dreadnought *battleship*; resigned in October 1914 following anti-German protests over his ancestry, and for the same reason renounced title of Battenberg, 1917, with his family choosing instead the surname *Mountbatten*. His eldest son, George Louis Victor Mountbatten (1892–1938), fought at Heligoland, *Dogger Bank* and *Jutland*. For younger son, see Mountbatten.

Battlecruiser Warship designed to combine *battleship* fire power with greater mobility; guns were therefore almost equal to battleship armaments, but armour protection was reduced. HMS 'Indomitable', 1907, represented the prototype of this class; HMS 'Lion', 1910, was an example of the most modern battlecruiser prior to 1914. This vessel, *Beatty*'s flagship at *Jutland*, had eight 13·5-inch guns and sixteen 4-inch; midships armour was 9 inches thick, bow and stern 4 inches thick. By comparison, the Queen Elizabeth class of British battleship, the ultimate Dreadnought type, had eight 15-inch guns and twelve 6-inch; the bulk of her armour was over 6 inches thick, increasing to 13 inches on the hull. Battlecruisers featured at Jutland, 1916, with the British having 9 of these vessels and the Germans 5; the British also had 8, less powerful, armoured cruisers. Production continued after the war, with the lower tonnage being a means of circumventing restrictions imposed by the Treaty of *Versailles* and subsequent naval agreement. In 1939 the British had 18 battleships and battlecruisers; the French total was 11 and German strength comprised 2 battleships being built and 5 'pocket' battleships already operational. The latter fell into battlecruiser specifications; they comprised the 'Scharnhorst' and 'Gneisenau' and the 3 Deutschland-type vessels – 'Deutschland', 'Admiral Scheer' and 'Graf Spee'. The Deutschland class had been started in 1928, officially with a displacement of 10,000 tons, the limit set by the Versailles Treaty, but actually 11,700 tons. 'Scharnhorst' and 'Gneisenau' were started in 1935, when *Hitler* rejected the Versailles clauses; these displaced 31,800 tons. 'Scharnhorst' was sunk in December 1943; 'Gneisenau' was damaged in 1942, putting her out of action for the rest of the war. Pride of the British battlecruiser fleet was 'Hood', built in 1918; she was destroyed in the fighting with the German battleship 'Bismarck', May 1941. Already the navies of the major powers were turning towards faster and lighter armed ships such as heavy cruisers, which had 8-inch guns, light cruisers, with 6-inch guns and the smaller and lighter armed destroyers.

Battleship Origins can be seen in the *ironclads* such as the '*Merrimack*' and '*Monitor*' and in Britain's '*Minotaur*' of 1863: the latter was armed with 9-inch muzzle-loading guns. As guns increased in power, so armour became thicker and stronger. Germany's 'Fuerst Bismarck' of 1898 represented a new concentration of power: this 10,000-ton vessel was armed with 9-inch breech-loading guns, plus smaller guns, 6 *torpedo* tubes, and had an extensive armour belt. Warships were rapidly becoming ponderous gun platforms. By now the Anglo-German *naval race* was beginning; in 1897 *Tirpitz* had become head of the German Navy; the 'big-ship' ideas of the US naval theorist *Mahan* became increasingly influential. In December 1905 the keel of the first British Dreadnought was laid at Portsmouth, and this massive warship was completed in record time by October 1906: she had ten 12-inch guns and twenty-seven 12-pounders – the previous most heavily-armed battleship had only had four 12-inch guns. The Dreadnought design was influenced by work being undertaken in Italy, for example studies made by Vittorio Cuniberti for guns with all-round arcs of fire – Cuniberti's advanced ideas were incorporated into the Italian battleship 'Leonardo da Vinci' eventually launched in 1911. Britain, stimulated by the race with the Germans, went ahead at an accelerating pace. Three battleships of the Dreadnought class were laid down in 1907 and 2 in 1908. The size of guns was increased from 12-inch to 13·5-inch in 1909, thus raising the British shell from 850 to 1,400 pounds; *Churchill* insisted the size should be further increased to 15·75 inches, accomplished in the ultimate Dreadnought development represented by HMS 'Queen Elizabeth'. This warship had eight 15-inch guns, each capable of firing a 1,920-pound projectile 35,000 yards: a broadside from the 'Queen Elizabeth's' eight guns totalled 16,000 pounds. By 1914 Britain had 5 of these super-Dreadnoughts and 35 other Dreadnoughts and older battleships; Germany had a total battleship fleet of 35. The two main fleets met at *Jutland*, 1916, but all battleships except one old German vessel survived. The Treaty of *Versailles*, June 1919, limited the number of German battleships to 6 old vessels; when these became unfit for further service they would have to be replaced by cruiser-size ships of 10,000 tons with 11-inch guns maximum. The Washington Treaty of 1922 agreed not to build capital ships for 10 years and to apportion capital ship tonnage at the ratio of 5 American and British to 3 Japanese to 1·7 French and Italian. In 1931 the first of 3 German 'pocket' battleships was launched – the 'Deutschland'. Officially designated as displacing 10,000 tons, she was actually 1,700 tons over the Versailles limit. In March 1935 *Hitler* repudiated the Versailles Treaty, but in June an Anglo-German Naval Treaty was drawn up, with Germany limiting herself to 35 per cent of British naval power. The treaty allowed each country 5 battleships. In 1936 a German building programme was started, based on the last 2 battleships to be built with conventional-power engines – the 'Bismarck' and the 'Tirpitz'. Neither was completed by 1939. Each had 15-inch guns and they displaced

41,700 tons and 42,900 tons respectively; the British and US capital ships were still limited to 35,000 tons as laid down at the Washington Conference. But battleships proved more of a threat than a positive destructive force during the *Second World War*. Air power reduced their effectiveness; *aircraft carriers* assumed the role of the most powerful capital ships. At the start of the war Britain had 18 battleships and battlecruisers, the most powerful being the 'Prince of Wales' and 'Repulse' – both sunk by Japanese aircraft in December 1941. The 'Bismarck' was sunk on her maiden voyage in May 1941, the 'Tirpitz' in November 1944. The Japanese battleships 'Yamato' and 'Musashi' were the largest ever built, with lengths of 863 feet, beam 127 feet, standard displacement 64,000 tons; the main armaments consisted of nine 18·1-inch guns. The 'Yamato', built from 1937 to 1941, was sunk during the Battle of Leyte Gulf, October 1944, in the *Philippines* campaign. The major powers laid up surviving battleships after 1945: one of the 4 'mothball' battleships in the US Navy was temporarily brought back into service during the *Vietnam War* to act as a gun platform for off-coast shelling.

Bautzen, Battle of, May 1813
Napoleonic Wars (Map 1). The Prussian and Russian Allied Armies withdrew eastwards after the Battle of *Lützen* had opened the 1813 campaign, despite complaints from the Prussian commander, *Blücher*, that they should stand and fight. The overall com-

mander, Prince Wittgenstein, allowed *Napoleon* to enter Dresden on 11 May. Allied disagreements continued: Frederick William III of Prussia insisted Berlin must be defended; Alexander, Tsar of Russia, wished to keep his army as close to the homeland as possible. The Allied Army reached Bautzen on 14 May but remained inactive. Preliminary French manoeuvring began on 19 May. *Ney* was first ordered to advance on Berlin but Napoleon later instructed him to move on Bautzen from the north. The allied position spread along the eastern bank of the Spree, with Blücher's 32,000 Prussians forming the right, or northern, flank around the village of Kreckwitz, and with the Russians deployed farther south around Lobau. Napoleon ordered a frontal attack to be launched from Bautzen on the 20th; Ney would be in a position to undertake a flanking attack from the north on the 21st. The French established a firm foothold over the Spree during the 20th, with the fighting fiercest in the Russian sector. Battle began again early on the 21st with a French artillery bombardment along an 8-mile front, followed by a determined infantry advance. Blücher received reports of Ney's advance and urged a cavalry offensive; Wittgenstein refused, and instead ordered withdrawal late in the afternoon, much to Blücher's disgust. Lack of cavalry prevented a firm French pursuit, and French casualties were higher than those of the allies: about 22,500 against 11,000. Vigorous allied counter-attacks shattered the French advance guard at Reichenbach and at Haynau. General Barclay de Tolly took over from Wittgenstein on 26 May, but followed the same withdrawal policy. Napoleon needed time to recover strength and the two sides agreed to a truce on 1 June. This armistice was extended until 20 July and later to 16 August, when the gigantic *Leipzig* campaign began.

Bayonet The name of this infantry weapon originated from the city of Bayonne, southern France, famous for its cutlery. Initially the bayonet was over a foot long, inserted into the muzzle of the *musket* – hence known later as a 'plug bayonet': this had the obvious drawback of preventing the musket from being fired whilst it was in place. The socket bayonet was introduced by the French towards the end of the seventeenth century: this contained a sleeve fitting round the barrel and locking into place with a slot and stud. The socket version became standard for most European armies shortly after 1800 and remained so for about 150 years although with the size of the blade decreasing. Bayonets were extremely valuable for use during the long reloading period, and they could also be used as a 'hedge' around the infantry *square* to give added protection, especially against *cavalry* charges. They could be effective in an infantry advance, although actual bayonet charges were rarely attempted unless the enemy was already in flight or appeared about to be. In a line advance the unprotected left arm of each infantryman was protected by the bayonet of his left-hand man; bayonet thrusts took less time than sword slashes and resulted in less disturbance to the rigid line. Thrusts were also considered more injurious, in that they penetrated into the body of the victim rather than cutting the exterior as with sword wounds. Moreover the techniques of bayonet fighting were relatively simple, able to be acquired in minimum time by recruits. This weapon decreased rapidly in importance with the introduction of repeating *rifles* and *machine-guns*, after which bayonets were only used for extremely close-quarter fighting – especially when silence was essential – or when all ammunition had been expended.

Beatty, Sir David, 1st Earl, 1871–1936 British Admiral of the Fleet. Served in the *Sudan*, 1885, operating on the Nile close to *Omdurman* battlefield. Naval Secretary to First Lord of the Admiralty *Churchill*, 1911–13; Commander, *battlecruiser* squadron, 1913–17. Beatty led the action at Heligoland, January 1915, and was engaged heavily at *Jutland*, 1916; appointed Commander of the British Grand Fleet, 1917, after *Jellicoe* became First Sea Lord. Beatty was among those who advocated the convoy system in the Battle of the *Atlantic*. First Sea Lord, 1919–27.

Beaverbrook, Lord William Maxwell Aitken, 1st Baron, 1879–1964 Canadian-born British Minister. Chosen by *Churchill* to be Minister of Aircraft Production, May 1940. Production soared from 325 aircraft in May to 446 in June, 496 in July and 476 in August, giving a total of 1,745 aircraft when the Air Ministry had only believed 1,164 to be possible. But this accomplishment, whilst vital to the Battle of *Britain*, damaged other aspects of aircraft production including the development and supply of bombers. Beaverbrook was succeeded by John Moore-Brabazon, May 1941; he acted as Minister of State until June, when he was appointed Minister of Supply, remaining in this position until appointed first Minister of Production, February 1942. Uneasy relations with Churchill, despite their long friendship, led Beaverbrook to abandon this post 15 days later, with Oliver Lyttelton his successor. Beaverbrook journeyed to Russia and the USA, urging an early Second Front in Europe; he served as Lord Privy Seal from September 1943 to July 1945.

Berlin Airlift, June 1948 to May 1949 Relations between the four powers who had occupied Berlin since 1945 – America, Russia, Britain and France – deteriorated during 1948, with the Western allies preparing to create the Federal Republic of (West) Germany and to introduce a new currency, the D-mark. The Soviets ordered Berlin's mayor to accept their own new East German mark as currency for the entire city; deadline for acceptance was 6 a.m., 23 June 1948. The Berlin City Parliament refused. During the evening of 23 June the Soviets switched off electricity supplies; 'technical difficulties' halted passenger and freight traffic along road and rail links to Berlin. West Berlin had only enough food to last a month and coal for 10 days. General Lucius D. Clay, commander of the US occupation forces in West Germany, flew to the city on 25 June; President *Truman* supported his policy of full defiance of the blockade; so too did Britain's Prime Minister, Clement Attlee. Next day the first C-54 Skymasters landed, beginning the airlift; supervising the operation was General Albert C. Wedemeyer. Eventually 277,264 flights were made; the record day's lift was 16 April 1949, when 1,398 flights brought 12,940 tons, with landings every 63 seconds. The D-mark became the only legal tender of the western sector on 20 March 1949. The blockade was officially lifted on 12 May 1949, although the lift continued until 30 September. Over 2,300,000 tons were brought into the city; 79 pilots were killed in air crashes.

Berthier, Marshal Louis Alexandre, Prince of Neuchâtel, 1753-1815 Served under Lafayette on the colonialist side in the American Revolution; acted as a staff officer in the French Army prior to the Revolution, becoming an 'Ingénieur-Géographe' officer, with this branch of the engineers entrusted with drawing up deployment memoranda. He continued such service in the Army of the French Revolution. Berthier joined *Napoleon* during the *Italian* campaign, 1796, and became his closest staff officer, staying with him for the *Egyptian* campaign, 1798-1800. He acted as War Minister, 1800-8, then

became Napoleon's Chief of Staff. His capabilities often fell short of Bonaparte's requirements but he rendered loyal service; he was named Prince of *Wagram* after the battle of that name in 1809; he accompanied Napoleon to *Russia*, 1812, attempting to deter the Emperor from advancing beyond Smolensk. After 1814 Berthier supported the cause of Louis XVIII.

Bismarck, Prince Otto Eduard Leopold von, known as the 'Iron Chancellor', 1815-98 German Minister. President of the Prussian Cabinet and Foreign Minister from 1862. He declared in 1862 that German problems must be solved by 'blood and iron'. These problems centred on the formation of the Germanic state. Prussia had occupied Schleswig-Holstein in 1848, but the Treaty of Berlin, 1850, restored full Danish rights in the disputed provinces; in 1864 Bismarck once again precipitated Prussian involvement in the area in order to obtain full Prussian ascendancy in north Germany. Prussian troops entered the provinces in 1864; Denmark sued for peace in August, renouncing her rights in favour of Prussia and Austria. Bismarck now moved to create a 'casus belli' with Austria, and the *Austro-Prussian 'Seven Weeks' War* began in June 1866 (Map 5). Prussia's shattering victory under *Moltke* enabled Bismarck to accept peace under his own terms: the Treaty of Prague, 23 August, excluded Austria from German affairs, with the German states north of the Main forming a new confederation under Prussian leadership. France reacted against Prussia's growing power, and the *Franco-Prussian War* began in July 1870 (Map 6). Bismarck's strong civilian leadership was well matched by Moltke's brilliant organization of the Prussian forces, and the French armies were defeated at *Sedan*, 1 September. Relations between Moltke and Bismarck, never very close, deteriorated over the question of a bombardment of Paris; Moltke objected to Bismarck's interference in military affairs, while the political leader criticized publicly the conduct of the war. Moltke submitted to political dictates, and the bombardment began on 5 January 1871. The city capitulated on the 28th; once again Bismarck and Moltke found themselves in opposition: Moltke saw the fall of the city as offering the opportunity of prosecuting the war in the provinces with greater effort; Bismarck wanted negotiations to begin, concerning himself with strict diplomatic objectives. His negotiations led to the Treaty of Frankfurt, 10 May: France agreed to cede Alsace and north-western Lorraine to Prussia and to pay an indemnity of 5 billion francs. Bismarck had succeeded in establishing Prussia's predominance. In 1871 he became the first Chancellor of the new Germanic Empire. He presided over the International Congress of Berlin, 1878, and joined with Italy and Austro-Hungary in the Triple Alliance aimed at protecting Germany against France and Russia. He quarrelled with Kaiser William II and resigned in 1890.

Blitz, the *Second World War*. Concentrated German bombing against Britain began on 7 September 1940, with a raid on London by 300 bombers. Over 430 civilians died; over 600 tons of bombs were dropped – the highest total during the Blitz was to be 1,026 tons and 4,252 incendiary containers on 19 April 1941. London received another major attack on the 9th and the capital was hit in varying degrees each day until 3 November. The number of homeless Londoners rose to 17,000. In mid-October the Germans switched to mainly night raids. About 70,000 incendiaries were dropped on 15 October, the first time so many had been used, and nearly 1,000 fires were started; 400 civilians died. In early November the Germans turned from concentrated raids on London to attacks on a succession of provincial centres: Coventry was hit on 14 November, suffering widespread damage; the House of Commons was severely damaged on 6 December and on the 29th another massive incendiary raid struck the capital, causing 1,500 fires. During the 12 weeks from 19 February to 12 May 1941, only 7 out of 61 raids involving more than 50 aircraft were directed against London, the majority, 39, being aimed at Britain's western ports. The Chief of the Air Staff, *Portal*, claimed in March that air defence was improving: in December 1 bomber in every 326 had been brought down; in January 1 in every 110; in February 1 in every 95, and in the first 12 days of March 1 in every 63. Yet London suffered heavy damage on 16 April, known as 'The

Wednesday', resulting in the death of over 1,000 civilians; 3 days later came the heaviest onslaught of the war on the capital, with another 1,000 civilians killed and 1,026 tons and 4,252 incendiary containers dropped. About 150,000 houses were destroyed or damaged in these two raids. Saturday 10 May saw the last and possibly the worst night of the main London Blitz, when the number of deaths reached their highest total, 1,436, and 2,200 fires were started. Sixteen enemy aircraft were destroyed, the maximum yet in night fighting. A second Blitz on London began in June 1944 with the *V-bomb* offensive. In all, about 60,000 British civilians died during the war; the German casualty figure from *strategic bombing* was over 600,000.

Blitzkrieg, 'Lightning War' A German form of armoured and aerial warfare devised prior to the *Second World War*, which reasserted the supremacy of the offensive. In essence, it depended upon a breakthrough and deep penetration by an armoured force, close supported from the air. *Aircraft* would inflict severe damage upon enemy communications and installations, would help the field artillery during the advance by attacking ground targets, and would keep the attacking force supplied. *Tanks*, backed by motorized infantry, would strike forward under this aerial shield. Concentration and speed would throw the enemy off-balance; surprise would breed shock; shock would lead to enemy disintegration, collapse of morale and retreat. The strategy

reflected ideas put forward by the British theorists *Fuller* and Liddell *Hart*. Blitzkrieg showed its ruthless effectiveness in the invasion of *Poland*, 1939, and in the battle for *France*, May–June 1940; the greatest exponents were *Guderian* and *Rommel*.

Bloch, Jean de, 1836–1902 Polish banker and author. His 6-volume 'The War of the Future in its Technical, Economic and Political Relations' appeared in 1897; in 1899 the 6th volume was translated into English with the title 'Is War Impossible?', reprinted in 1900 with the title 'Modern Weapons and Modern War'. Many of Bloch's predictions proved accurate: future war would result in slaughter on such terrible scale that neither side would be able to force the issue; trench stalemate would ensue; decision would be reached through economic, non-military factors; victory would be hollow. Bloch, in direct contrast to military leaders prior to 1914 who insisted upon the continuing supremacy of the offensive, such as *Foch*, therefore gave an exact picture of the defensive deadlock of 1914–18.

Blomberg, Werner von, 1878–1946 German General. Minister of War, 1933–8. Blomberg provided *Hitler* with enthusiastic support; on the day of President *Hindenburg*'s death, 2 August 1934, Blomberg made the whole *Reichswehr* swear allegiance to the person of the new President and Supreme Commander, Hitler. He was thrown out by Hitler, 4 February 1938, on charges of having married a prostitute; Hitler himself took over Blomberg's position.

Blücher, Gebhard Leberecht von, 1742–1819 Prussian Marshal. Blücher first served with the Swedes fighting against the Prussians in the Seven Years' War; taken captive, he entered Prussian service in 1760; he served on the Rhine, 1793–5 (Map 1); he attempted to rally the Prussian advance guard at *Auerstedt*, 14 October 1806, and played a leading role in the retreat of the remains of Prussia's army, with *Scharnhorst* his Chief of Staff. He was eventually obliged to surrender at Lübeck, 6 November. He encouraged Scharnhorst, *Gneisenau* and others in their reforms of the Prussian Army. Blücher was appointed to command the Prussian Army of Silesia in 1813, with Scharnhorst and then Gneisenau his Chiefs of Staff, and displayed aggressive bravery at *Lützen* and *Bautzen* in May, after which the war became one of manoeuvre until in October the allied armies converged on *Napoleon* at *Leipzig*. He urged relentless pursuit to Paris, but the allied monarchs hesitated and Napoleon was allowed time to recover. Blücher spearheaded the advance on New Year's Day 1814. The overall commander, *Schwarzenberg*, preferred a cautious approach and Napoleon seized upon the splintered allied advance. But the pressure became too great; Blücher entered Paris at the beginning of April. During the *Waterloo* campaign Blücher commanded the Prussian Army on the left of *Wellington*'s Anglo-Dutch force; he prevented Napoleon from stabbing between the two armies at *Ligny*, 16 June 1815, during which battle Blücher was thrown from his horse and severely concussed. The 72-year-old Prussian commander recovered in time to lead his troops across country to assist Wellington at Waterloo, 18 June: without his help the Anglo-Dutch Army might well have been defeated. Blücher took Paris on 3 July. His primary attribute as a commander lay in his instinctive realization that the new, massive Napoleonic form of warfare necessitated maximum force being inflicted in minimum time at the most decisive point. Blücher relied heavily on the *staff* system; he provided the figurehead and inspiration while his Chief of Staff provided the planning background and forged the means for putting his ideas into operation.

Boer War, 1899–1902, general (Map 7) The conflict was preceded by the Transvaal Revolt or First Boer War, 1880–1. On 30 December 1880 the Boer Republic was proclaimed by Paul Krüger and Petrus Jacobus Joubert, covering the area between the Orange and Limpopo Rivers in South Africa. Joubert inflicted defeat on the British under General Sir George Colley at Laing's Nek, 28 January, and Majuba Hill, 27 February. These victories, resulting from a vast underrating of Boer skill, led to the Treaty of Pretoria, 5 April: independence was granted to the South African Republic under British suzerainty. On 16 April Krüger became Boer President. In 1886 gold was discovered in the Boer

Republic and foreigners – Uitlanders – swept in. These newcomers were denied full citizenship by Krüger, and appealed to Britain. Boer–British relations deteriorated, especially after the British fanatic Dr L. Starr Jameson led an abortive raid into Boer territory in 1895, attempting to spark an uprising among the Uitlanders. Boer–British talks took place during 1899, with the Boer delegation – led by *Smuts* – attempting to gain time for military preparations. By autumn 1899 vast quantities of *Mauser* rifles and considerable numbers of *Krupp* guns had been brought into the country; on 9 October Krüger issued an ultimatum for the withdrawal of British troops from the Boer borders. War began on 11 October. Boer forces totalled about 50,000 men; British forces at the outbreak only numbered about 14,700. The British clung to the old line formation in battle, men standing shoulder to shoulder; by contrast, the Boers were highly mobile mounted marksmen, armed with the modern repeating rifle and making maximum use of terrain; they struck quickly, then scattered before the unwieldy British forces could recover. *Kitchener* complained: 'The Boers are not like the Sudanese who stood up to a fair fight. They are always running away on their little ponies.' The Boers gained advantage from the British strategic reluctance to move far from rail communications, and from the British tactical method of attacking in massed ranks direct at the opposing force. The investment of British forces under *Baden-Powell* at Mafeking, and the besieging of Kimberley, led to the dispatch of British relief forces which could easily be attacked by the mobile Boers. A relief force under *Methuen*, aiming for Kimberley, managed to reach the Modder River, November 1899, but was defeated at *Magersfontein* in December after making a frontal assault. *Buller*, leading a relief column towards Ladysmith, suffered similar defeat at *Colenso*, also in December, and was replaced by *Roberts*. The latter, with Kitchener his Chief of Staff, undertook an extensive reorganization of the Army. With these changes and the adoption of far more mobile British strategy and tactics, the second stage of the war began. This phase proved more successful, despite setbacks at Spion Kop and Vaal Kranz in January–February 1900. Ladysmith was relieved in late February and Mafeking in May. The Boer leader *Cronje* had already been obliged to surrender. Roberts returned home in December 1900 leaving Kitchener in command. Victory was eventually obtained through the use of overwhelming numbers of British forces – the final total reached about 450,000 – and through Kitchener's policies. The proportion of mounted infantry was increased; combined with added mobility was Kitchener's ruthless method of rounding up the elusive Boer enemy: the country was divided up by nearly 4,000 miles of barbed wire and 8,000 block-houses; each section was then swept by the mounted columns; farms were burnt and women and children herded into concentration camps – where some 20,000 people died of disease. Peace was signed on 31 May 1902. Total British casualties were nearly 6,000 dead and 23,000 wounded. Boer troop losses were nearly 4,000 killed. The inadequate performance of the British Army led to the 'Report of HM Commissioners on the War in South Africa', published in 1903, which condemned aspects of the whole British military machine ranging from the C-in-C, then Wolseley, down to the man in the ranks. From this condemnation sprang the *Esher* Committee recommendations, 1904, and the movement under *Haldane* to create an army better fitted for service in a European war.

Bolshevik Revolution, 1917 – see Russian Revolution, 1917–21

Borodino, Battle of, October 1812; also known as the Battle of Moscow or the Moskva *Napoleonic Wars* (Map 1). The battle marked the turning point in *Napoleon*'s attempted conquest of *Russia* and, in turn, the failure of this campaign represented the beginning of Napoleon's downfall. *Kutuzov* had taken over command of the retreating Russian Army at the end of August, replacing Barclay de Tolly. The latter was in disgrace through failing to stop Napoleon, but his successor was also reluctant to fight a battle: Kutuzov believed that retreat into Russia would be the best means of defeating Napoleon, by overextending the French forces. However, under pressure from Tsar Alexander, Kutuzov reluctantly made a defensive

stand near the small village of Borodino, 70 miles west of Moscow. Total Russian strength was about 128,000 men, with 640 guns; opposing them were about 130,000 French with 587 guns. Napoleon began the battle at 6 a.m., 7 October, with a heavy artillery bombardment followed by an infantry advance. The battle centred on the Russian Great Redoubt, with Napoleon eventually concentrating over two-thirds of his total artillery on bombarding this defensive position. Despite terrible casualties, the French forced back the Russians on the left; General Pyotr Bagration, commanding the flank, ordered a counter-attack against French forces under *Davout*, but the offensive failed to make ground and Bagration was himself fatally wounded. The French focused even more attention on the Great Redoubt; this fell at 3 p.m., but was retaken by the Russian Guard. The French attacked again with 200 guns, and although repeated assaults resulted in appalling losses, they took the Redoubt with cavalry support. The Russians made counter-attacks, but in the late afternoon retired to a ridge slightly to the rear. Casualty estimates are unreliable, but the Russians probably lost 44,000 dead and wounded, amounting to about 34 per cent of the forces committed to battle. The French probably lost more than 30,000 killed or wounded, making the battle one of the bloodiest one-day clashes in history. Many expected the struggle to be resumed next day, but Kutuzov decided to continue the retreat. He withdrew next day, leaving the battlefield – and Moscow – in Napoleon's hands. His strategy was to prove correct.

Botha, Louis, 1862–1919 *Boer War* General and political leader (Map 7). He was appointed to command Boer forces blocking the British advance on Ladysmith, December 1899, following the illness of Lukas Meyer. Botha, aged 37, immediately organized his forces for the Battle of *Colenso*, and after this victory he played a part in the successful Boer action at Spion Kop, 23 January 1900; he became the Boer C-in-C later in 1900 following the death of General Joubert. By this time the British had over 100,000 troops active in the war, against whom Botha could only muster about 30,000, but he continued to wage guerrilla warfare until early 1902. He took part in the peace talks which led to the Treaty of Vereeniging, 31 May 1902. Botha became the first Prime Minister of the Transvaal, 1907, and the first Prime Minister of the Union of South Africa, 1910, holding the latter position until 1919. In late 1914 and early 1915 he suppressed an uprising of Boer extremists, led by the former Boer General Christian De Wet, who were protesting over the Union of South Africa's declaration of war against Germany. Botha was helped in this suppression by *Smuts*. He obtained the surrender of German forces in south-west Africa, 1915.

Bradley, Omar Nelson, 1893– US General. Instructor at West Point, 1934–8; Commandant Infantry School, Fort Benning, 1941–2; Commander 82nd Infantry Division, 1942; Deputy Commander then Commander US 2nd Corps, *Tunisia* and *Sicily*, 1943; Commander US 1st Army in *Normandy* landings, 1944 (Map 13). Bradley broke out from the bridgehead at St Lô, 25 July, and on 1 August was appointed to command the newly formed US 12th Army Group which breached the German Siegfried Line, 21 October. He ordered *Patton* to make his dramatic shift in direction against the German southern flank in the *Ardennes* offensive during December; his troops took the Remagen bridge over the Rhine, 7 March 1945, and invaded south Germany to reach Prague by the end of the war. Bradley was Chief of Staff, US Army, 1948–9; on 16 August 1949 he became the first formally appointed Chairman of the US *Joint Chiefs of Staff*, and he remained at this post until his retirement, 14 August 1953.

Brauchitsch, Heinrich Alfred Hermann Walther von, 1881–1948 German General. Chief of Artillery, 1933; C-in-C German High Command, 1939; responsible for planning occupation of Austria and Czechoslovakia, the invasion of Poland and the offensive against France, May 1940; he opposed *Hitler*'s direction of the *Russian* campaign, arguing against the proposal to seize the Ukraine before Moscow, summer 1941. Brauchitsch, suffering from ill-health, repeatedly sought to resign; Hitler agreed in late 1941 and took over as C-in-C German High Command himself. Brauchitsch was interned in 1945 and died in British captivity.

Breech-loading Loading from the breech end of a weapon had obvious advantages compared with loading from the muzzle: firing would be faster and it reduced the exposure time of the user during the recharging procedure; breech-loading infantry weapons would more easily enable the troops to lie behind cover. The main obstacle to be overcome was the prevention of escaping gas – obduration – round the joint between the breech and breech-block. British troops had their first breech-loaders during the American Revolution, when a special corps under the command of Patrick Ferguson was equipped with weapons which he himself had invented. His device used a modification of the screw breech: a threaded plug which could be removed for inserting a new charge. This weapon still leaked gas and had the disadvantage of only allowing loose powder and ball to be fired. Meanwhile, Giuseppe Crespi of Milan invented a weapon with a tip-up breech; this allowed paper cartridges to be inserted. Improvements of this mechanism were made by the American John H. Hall; his weapon was adopted by the USA in 1819. But real advance could only come with the introduction of more efficient cartridges. This step was made by Johannes Samuel Pauly in Paris in 1812. He invented a cartridge with a brass head and a paper body: the soft head of the cartridge expanded with the detonation of powder, thus forming its own seal against the escape of gas. One of Pauly's workmen, *Dreyse*, used this cartridge principle for his famous needle-gun, although his first models were muzzle-loaders. In 1839 Dreyse produced a breech-loader, the first bolt-action weapon. *Chassepot* of France improved on Dreyse's design in 1866, and both the chassepot and needle-gun were used in the *Franco-Prussian War* They were superseded by the French *Gras* rifle in 1874, the true forerunner of the modern infantry *rifle*. The development of breech-loading *artillery* followed a similar line, although progress was slower. Again, the introduction of the breech mechanism was aided by the development of better casing for the projectile: the introduction of later shells, for example the type invented by *Paixhans*, increased the calibre of the guns and made muzzle-loading not only difficult, but also dangerous. The *Krupp* works at Essen invented a suitable breech device shortly after the Crimean War; this was in the form of a sliding, tapering steel wedge, incorporated into the Krupp 1851 model and employed extensively in the Franco-Prussian War.

Britain, Battle of, July–October 1940 *Second World War* (Map 13). *Hitler* needed air supremacy over England as an essential requirement for his proposed invasion, Operation *Sealion*. The preliminary phase, lasting until 13 August, centred on *Luftwaffe* attacks on Channel convoys and coastal towns which would be important invasion objectives. The Germans hoped also to draw off *RAF* Fighter Command strength; *Dowding*, head of Fighter Command, soon criticized the Admiralty's demand that fighter escorts should be provided for the mass of Channel shipping. RAF casualties mounted and on 26 July discussions between Dowding and the First Sea Lord, *Pound*, resulted in cessation of merchant ship sailings until better night convoys could be arranged. The heaviest engagement so far took place on 8 August, when a night convoy was detected by the Germans and was attacked by aircraft and E-boats: fighting probably cost the *Luftwaffe* 31 aircraft to the RAF's 20. The offensive on 13 August, named by *Göring* as Eagle Day, was preceded by attacks against RAF *radar* stations: continuation of these strikes would probably have been more effective for the Germans than the policy now started – a campaign against Fighter Command itself by striking at airfields. Total German air strength for this main phase of the battle numbered about 2,800 aircraft organized into 3 main fleets: *Kesselring*'s Air Fleet Two, based in northern France; Marshal Hugo Sperrle's Fleet Three, operating from Belgium and Holland; and General Hans-Jurgen Stumpff's Fleet Four, based in Norway and consisting mainly of bombers. Fighter Command had a front-line strength of only about 650 aircraft. Respective aircraft chiefly consisted of the German Messerschmitt Bf 109 and the British Spitfire and Hurricane. The Me 109 equalled the Spitfire in fighting performance and was superior to

the Hurricane; the latter aircraft, older than the Spitfire, accounted for two-thirds of the RAF's fighters. But the Me 109 could only operate for 90 minutes before having to refuel, thus reducing the time over the target area. The other main German fighter aircraft, the twin-engined Me 110, was unwieldy, while the Stuka dive-bomber was slow in dog-fights and weakly armed. RAF pilots operated near to base, thus enabling a greater number of sorties; the British also enjoyed the early-warning benefits of *radar*. Göring intended a combination of bombing and high-level fighter sweeps on 13 August, but thick cloud prevented liaison between the bombers and fighters: 45 German aircraft were shot down, against the RAF total of 13. Göring tried again on 15 August, this time also using aircraft from Fleet Four in Norway: 75 German aircraft were destroyed compared with the RAF total of 34, with Dowding using his available resources with brilliant efficiency. Another major attack was launched next day, 16 August; Göring seriously underestimated the number of serviceable aircraft left to the RAF, especially at Biggin Hill, Kenley, West Malling and Croydon. On the 19th Göring told the Luftwaffe: 'We have reached the decisive period of the air war.' On the 20th *Churchill* declared in the House of Commons: 'Never in the field of human conflict has so much been owed by so many to so few.' These 'few' were dwindling fast: shortages of pilots, rather than aircraft, always caused Dowding most concern. The offensive was resumed on 24 August, mainly against Kent and the south coast: German losses were 40, Fighter Command 20. During the night German bombers struck at south England – and some bombs fell on London for the first time. The battle reached a critical stage at the end of August. Over 1,000 Fighter Command sorties were flown on the 30th, and the battle was maintained at peak intensity on the 31st. By nightfall on the 31st the British had lost about 50 aircraft, compared with the German total of 41. Many Fighter Command bases had been severely damaged, especially Biggin Hill. Air activity dwindled during the next few days. Then, 7 September, the Germans launched a massive bomber and fighter raid totalling nearly 1,000 aircraft: of these about 250 bombers managed to reach London. The *Blitz* had begun, aimed at British cities. By conceding defeat in the attempt to eliminate Fighter Command, Hitler's chances of achieving air supremacy over southern England were reduced. On the 15th Kesselring used all his available aircraft in an assault on London, while Sperrle sent a diversionary force against Portsmouth. Once again Dowding deployed his resources with extreme skill. At times during the day almost all Fighter Command squadrons were committed, but by nightfall the Luftwaffe had suffered about 60 losses, compared with an RAF total of 25 aircraft with 13 pilots killed or missing. The RAF had retained air supremacy. The Blitz would continue, but the Battle of Britain had been won; on 12 October

Hitler called off his invasion preparations. Total losses during the battle were about 1,733 German aircraft destroyed and 915 British. Britain owed her success in the battle to three main factors: first, the inadequacy of the Luftwaffe to perform the role thrust upon it; second, the skill and tenacity of RAF Fighter Command; third, and perhaps most important, the astonishing replacement rate of RAF aircraft. With the first, the Luftwaffe had been designed primarily for a close support role in conjunction with ground forces: both training and aircraft had not been directed towards the strategic, front-line task involved with the Battle of Britain. With the second, Dowding directed his resources with admirable dexterity, and RAF pilots themselves learnt from earlier mistakes – notably the folly of being lured too far out to sea. With the third, replacement figures, postwar statistics reveal that the RAF Fighter Command was in fact farther from defeat at the climax of the Battle of Britain than it had been after the fall of Dunkirk. On 3 June 1940, Fighter Command operational strength stood at 79 Blenheims, 162 Spitfires, 163 Hurricanes and 9 Defiants, giving a total of 413; on 1 August, just before the most active period of the battle, these figures had risen respectively to 63, 329, 348, 25, a total of 675. Despite subsequent losses in the intense aerial struggle by 20 September the figure still stood at 55, 237, 391, 31, a total of 704. RAF Fighter Command therefore had almost 300 aircraft more after the battle than at the time of

Dunkirk, largely due to the incredible efforts in the production factories under Lord *Beaverbrook*'s leadership. Pilot losses always caused anxiety, yet these also can be exaggerated. More men were killed and wounded on average each day during the battle for *France*: 361 men in June, compared with only 7 more for the 5 weeks 7 August to 15 September. With hindsight it can be seen that, despite later assessments that the Luftwaffe came near to obtaining air superiority, in fact the RAF enjoyed such advantages to render a German victory completely non-feasible.

Brooke, Sir Alan Francis, 1st Viscount Alanbrooke, 1883–1963 British Field-Marshal. Artillery officer during *First World War*; Commandant, School of Artillery, 1929–32; Instructor, Imperial Defence College, 1932–4; Commander, Mobile Division, 1937–8; Commander, Anti-Aircraft Corps, 1938–9; GOC-in-C Southern Command, July–September, 1939; Commander, 2nd Corps British Expeditionary Force (BEF) in France, September 1939 to June 1940. Brooke withdrew at the time of *Dunkirk*, but returned on 12 June 1940 to command remaining British troops on the Continent; he withdrew with them from Cherbourg on 18 June; C-in-C, Southern Command, June–July 1940; C-in-C Home Forces, July 1940–December 1941, when he replaced *Dill* as Chief of the Imperial General Staff. He remained in this position until June 1946, combining the function of CIGS with that of Chairman of the British *Chiefs of Staff* Committee from March 1942 onwards. His partnership with *Churchill* was fundamental to the British and even allied strategy. He often opposed Churchill, but the Prime Minister always agreed to his military point of view, even though much argument preceded this concurrence. Brooke's task was to translate Churchill's ambitious, far-seeing projects into hard reality in terms of military resources available.

Browning, John, 1855–1926 American firearms inventor. Born the son of a gunsmith, he patented a single-shot dropping-block action in 1879 which he sold to Winchester; in 1884 he secured patents on a lever-action *rifle* which he also sold to Winchester and which became the 1886 Winchester rifle – the first lever-action rifle strong enough to use the latest high-power cartridges. Other pump and lever-action rifles followed, and Browning's interest in automatic weapons led him to the development of a gas-operated *machine-gun* in 1895. Further models were produced in 1917 and 1919; the Browning was used extensively by US forces in the *First World War*. Over 65 different models of the Browning recoil-operated machine-guns have been produced. He also undertook considerable development of pistols, which again continued as standard models for many years. He worked for a while at the famous Belgian armaments factory Fabrique Nationale (FN), at Herstal lez Liège, where he died.

Brusilov, Alexei Alekseevich, 1853–1926 Russian General. Led the army invading Galicia in 1914 (Map 9) and Volhynia in 1915; in early 1916 he succeeded General Nikolai Ivanov as commander of the Russian armies south of the Pripet marshes. Brusilov aimed to achieve surprise through a highly mobile attack. The offensive began on 4 June 1916 north of the Carpathian Mountains. The Russian armies surged forward on a 300-mile front without any prior massing of troops or artillery bombardment which would have destroyed secrecy. This Brusilov offensive achieved spectacular initial results. Up to 70,000 prisoners were taken. German reinforcements were rushed from the Western Front. Brusilov soon found he was receiving insufficient support from the two other Russian army groups in this front, and shortage of ammunition finally halted his offensive in late summer 1916. The operation was the most competent Russian effort in the war: it caused the Germans to bring valuable material from *Verdun*, and it eliminated Austria as a major military power. But the offensive cost 1 million Russian casualties, and this toll helped prepare the way for the *Russian Revolution*. Brusilov was appointed to the supreme command by the Russian coalition government, 1917, and on 1 July attacked towards Lemberg. This Kerensky, or Second, Brusilov offensive made good progress, but broke down on 5 July through lack of supplies; the Germans successfully counter-attacked on the 19th.

Bull Run, First Battle of, July 1861; Second Battle of, August 1862 *American Civil War* (Map 3). The First Bull Run Battle, also known as Manassas, represented the first major engagement in the war. The Union commander, Brevet-Major Irvin McDowell, moved south from Washington with 38,000 men on 19 July, but less than 2,000 of his men were professional soldiers and the Union staff was inexperienced. McDowell advanced against the Confederate force of 20,000 positioned near Centerville, 20 miles south-east of Washington. The Confederate Army, under Major-General Pierre G. T. Beauregard, was deployed along the Bull Run River. McDowell believed he outnumbered the Confederates, but was unaware that General Joseph Johnston arrived at the last moment with 12,000 men from the lower Shenandoah, bringing the southern strength to about 32,000. McDowell began the battle on 21 July by attempting to turn the Confederate left, checked by Brigadier-General Thomas *Jackson*'s Virginian troops. Jackson was henceforth known as 'Stonewall'. Johnston's newly arrived force outflanked the Union enveloping movement; many of the Union recruits fled, and retreat spread along the Union line. Union losses were just under 3,000, Confederate casualties nearly 2,000. President Jefferson *Davis* resisted pressure for a major advance on Washington after this southern victory, preferring to fight the war on defensive lines. In Washington, Major-General *McClellan* replaced McDowell. Bull Run again became the focus of military activity 13 months later. *Lee* learnt in August that the Union Army under McClellan was moving south to join Major-General John Pope's Army of Virginia: this would result in a Union force of 150,000 facing the Confederate Army of only 55,000. Lee therefore undertook a daring operation to defeat Pope before the junction of the Union armies. Confederate forces under Jackson were ordered to manoeuvre behind Pope's army; Lee would follow with a force under *Longstreet*, and once the Confederates were united they would strike against Pope in the Bull Run region. Jackson began his advance on 25 August and marched 54 miles in 2 days to fall upon Pope's supply depot at Manassas. Pope turned against him and Jackson goaded him with an offensive action near Groveton on 26 August, aimed at diverting attention from Longstreet's advance proceeding along Thoroughfare Gap. Pope suffered a flanking attack from Longstreet on the 30th in the Second Battle of Bull Run. The Union Army was thrown back across the Bull Run but withdrew in reasonable order towards Washington. On 4 September Lee invaded the north in the *Antietam* campaign.

Buller, Sir Redvers Henry, 1839–1908 British General. Served in the Zulu War of 1879; appointed Commander of the Army of Natal in *Boer War*, late 1900, despite his total lack of experience in commanding large bodies of men and despite his own reluctance for the task. He took the unwise decision to split the British Army strength into three sections: one was dispatched in an attempt to relieve Kimberley; another was intended to occupy the centre of the war area; Buller himself led the third in a relief expedition towards Ladysmith. On 15 December Buller threw his forces across the River Tugela into the Boer trap at *Colenso*; he himself was wounded in this suicidal frontal attack, and his inept handling of the battle may have been aggravated by shell-shock. Buller was so badly shaken by the setbacks of this 'Black Week' that he declared it would be best 'to let Ladysmith go'; he was immediately replaced as C-in-C by *Roberts*. Buller retained command of the 30,000 British troops in the Tugela–Ladysmith area (Map 7).

Bülow, Friedrich Wilhelm von, Count Bülow von Dennewitz, 1755–1816 Prussian General. Served as Colonel in the fusiliers during early stage of *Napoleonic Wars* (Map 1), and soon became involved in attempted reforms in the Prussian Army; in the period after 1806, after Prussia's disastrous defeats at Jena and Auerstedt, he joined with other influential officers urging a drastic reorganization of tactics and training methods. In June 1808 he joined a committee to draft new training instructions, chaired by *Yorck*, which stressed speed and flexibility rather than the previous precision demanded by *close order* formations. In general, Bülow gave maximum support to the notable reformers

Scharnhorst and *Gneisenau*. He acted as Governor of West and East Prussia in 1812, supporting *Blücher* in plans for Prussia's resumption of hostilities against France. He displayed high tactical ability during the 1813 campaign, commanding troops blocking French attempts to reach Berlin prior to the battle of *Leipzig*; he defeated Nicolas Oudinot at Luckau and again at Grossbeeren, and Michel *Ney* at Dennewitz, all in September and early October. He served with distinction at Leipzig and as a corps commander under Blücher in the *Waterloo* campaign: his regiments were the first Prussians to reach Waterloo on 18 June, and his pressure on the French right flank played a significant part in the battle. His brother Baron Dietrich Adam Heinrich von Bülow (1757–1807) was an extremely outspoken critic of Prussian tactics prior to 1806 – so much so that he was jailed for a short period.

Bülow, Karl von, 1846–1921 German Field-Marshal. Commander, 3rd Army Corps, 1903–12; Commander German 2nd Army, 1914–15, joining with Alexander von Kluck's 1st Army in invasion of Belgium, 3–20 August 1914 (Map 10), defeating the French at the Sambre, 22–23 August, but with advance falling behind Kluck during September. Bülow was engaged at the *Marne*, 5–10 September, suffering heavy losses. He was appointed Field-Marshal in 1915 and was succeeded as 2nd Army Commander by General Georg von der Marwitz, retiring from active service.

Burma, campaign in, 1942–5 *Second World War* against *Japan* (Map 16). The Japanese 15th Army under General Shojiro Iida invaded south Burma from Thailand in January 1942, advancing north over the Sittang in February. The British commander, General Thomas Hutton, was replaced by Alexander on 5 March, but the Japanese seized Rangoon on the 7th and the British continued to fall back. The Chinese 5th and 6th Armies marched south down the Burma Road, sent by *Chiang Kai-shek* to assist the reeling British, commanded by Chiang's US Chief of Staff, *Stilwell*. The Japanese advance retained momentum; Mandalay fell on 30 April. *Slim*, now commanding the British corps, withdrew to the Indian border; the Japanese halted at the Chindwin. Slim established his HQ at Imphal, just over the Indian border, where he was joined by Stilwell. British casualties in this disastrous campaign totalled about 30,000, two-thirds of the original force. *Wavell*, C-in-C India, tried to build up strength to defend the Indian border, while Stilwell organized a supply system to China: this involved flying over the eastern Himalayas – known by pilots as 'the Hump'. The allies advanced into Arakan, the north-west coastal province of Burma, in December 1942, but were repulsed by the Japanese north of the key town in the province, Akyab, in operations lasting until May 1943. Meanwhile, in February 1943 *Wingate*'s Long-Range Penetration Groups, the *Chindits*, launched an attack across the Irrawaddy in an attempt to cut the Mandalay–Lashio railroad. Stilwell opened an offensive from Ledo in north Burma in October; this campaign in the Hukowing valley region continued into 1944. Among the features of the fighting were the operations of a new US infantry regiment under Brigadier-General Frank D. Merrill – these Chindit-type troops were thus known as Merrill's Marauders. In December 1943 a second allied campaign began in Arakan, but in April 1944 allied strength had to be taken from this front to support defences farther north, following a Japanese invasion attempt in India launched on 6 March under General Renya Mutaguchi. This offensive advanced over the Chindwin and moved rapidly towards Imphal and Kohima, besieging both in April. Kohima was relieved, 20 April, but the siege of Imphal continued, with Slim flying all available reinforcements to the defending 4th Corps. Relief forces broke through on 22 June, and the Japanese were pushed back to the Chindwin during the next 3 months. The Japanese 15th Army probably suffered 65,000 dead during the campaign, over half through disease and starvation. Meanwhile the British had continued to maintain a presence in Arakan, preparing for renewed fighting when the monsoon ended in December, and another Chindit operation had been launched, with these troops flying into north-central Burma to disrupt Japanese communications. Wingate was killed in an air crash on 25 March, and the Chindits failed to make large-scale progress; some moved north to operate with Stilwell's forces. Stilwell resumed his offensive in north Burma on 15 October, using 5 Chinese divisions, plus the mixed US–Chinese forces known as the 'Mars' Brigade, and the British 36th Division. This army outnumbered the enemy, which comprised General Masaki Honda's 33rd Army. Stilwell aimed to trap the Japanese between his advance and Chinese troops moving from the Yunnan. Progress against fierce Japanese opposition was made during October–November, but then the Chinese were severely shaken by a Japanese offensive in the Yunnan; Roosevelt sought to have Stilwell made commander of the entire Chinese Army to restore the situation, but Chiang instead demanded Stilwell's recall. Roosevelt had to oblige: *Wedemeyer* replaced Stilwell as Chiang's Chief of Staff on 18 October, and General Dan Sultan took over from Stilwell as commander in the North Burma area. Main attention switched to the area farther south, where the British launched an offensive into Burma on 19 November. Slim's forces pushed back Japanese armies under General Hoyotaro Kimura, with the latter hoping to destroy the British as they crossed the Irrawaddy in the Mandalay region. Slim, guessing this plan, ordered a diversionary crossing of the Irrawaddy on his left flank, while the main force swerved south to cross the river 100 miles below Mandalay. This was accomplished with brilliant success on 12–13 February 1945; Slim's forces darted forward to seize Meiktila and Mandalay at the beginning of March; Japanese forces were defeated at the Battle of Meiktila, 15–31 March. Meanwhile, in north Burma, British and American troops slogged through appalling terrain to reach the Burma Road. Slim turned south at the beginning of April; allied troops entered Rangoon on 2 May, and the Japanese withdrew in disorder towards Thailand. Burma had been reconquered. The war in this region was characterized by terrible conditions suffered by both sides, by the courage and endurance shown by troops of a variety of nations, and by the constant struggle by Wavell, Slim and *Mountbatten* – Supreme Allied Commander in South-East Asia after October 1943 – for adequate supplies, manpower and equipment.

Burnside, Ambrose Everett, 1824–81   Union General in *American Civil War* (Map 3). Graduated West Point, 1847; took part in coastal operations in North Carolina, February–April 1862, capturing New Bern and Beaufort; commanded corps at *Antietam*, September 1862; replaced *McClellan* as Commander of the Army of the Potomac, 7 November, but reluctant to assume this role, declaring: 'I am not competent to command such a large army.' His defeat at *Fredericksburg*, 13 December, justified his words, and he was replaced by *Hooker* on 26 January 1863. Burnside was assigned to the Department of the Ohio; he was besieged at Knoxville in November 1863, during the *Chattanooga* campaign; he fought under *Grant* with the Army of the Potomac in 1864, during the siege of *Petersburg*, but failed to follow up advantage after Union mine explosion, 30 July. He was blamed for his conduct by a court of inquiry and resigned his commission, 1865.

C

Cambodia (Map 18) Independence from France, proclaimed 9 November 1953, was formally recognized at the Geneva Conference, April–July 1954. But from the start this 'neutral' nation was affected by the war in *Vietnam* on its eastern border. The National Liberation Front forces fighting the South Vietnamese used Cambodia as a sanctuary and as a supply route south from Hanoi. The Cambodian Head of State, ex-king Prince Norodom Sihanouk, increasingly veered towards the communist bloc, accepting communist aid and renouncing SEATO protection on 18 February 1956. By 1970 he was tolerating the presence of some 40,000 North Vietnamese troops on Cambodian soil. He attempted to redress the balance in March 1970 during a visit to Paris, when he accused the North Vietnamese and NLF of intrusion; fighting immediately broke out in Cambodia between communists and non-communists. Sihanouk, visiting Moscow after his Paris episode, was dismissed by the Cambodian National Assembly, 18 March, with power passing to General Lon Nol, Prime Minister since 1969. Sihanouk fled to Peking and proclaimed a counter-revolution. Fighting intensified in Cambodia, between Lon Nol's troops and communist 'Red Khmer' insurgents. The former received support from the USA and South Vietnamese, especially through an operation into Cambodia launched in April 1970: US combat troops restricted their activity to an area extending no farther than 30 kilometres from the South Vietnamese border and withdrew on 29 June. Lon Nol declared a state of emergency on 20 October 1971. US forces in Cambodia, operating in a support and advisory capacity, were withdrawn as part of the general retirement from South-East Asia undertaken by *Nixon*. On 22 November about 40,000 South Vietnamese troops began a major offensive into Cambodia in support of Lon Nol, attacking the communists on four major fronts. The ebbing and flowing fighting continued through 1972. The communists crept forward but suffered heavily from air strikes whenever they attempted to concentrate. A major communist offensive against the capital, Phnom Penh, began at the beginning of February 1973, and by April the Red Khmer troops were within a few miles of the city. President Nixon was forced by Congress to halt bombing in Cambodia on

15 August 1973. Lon Nol managed to maintain slender access to the capital during 1974, but remaining land links were severed by the communists in early 1975. Phnom Penh fell in April 1975, with the rest of the country under firm communist control, and with Lon Nol fleeing abroad. This last offensive coincided closely with similar communist gains in neighbouring Vietnam.

Cambrai, Battle of, November–December 1917 *First World War* (Map 10). This British-fought battle, like *Messines* and *Ypres*, was primarily intended to distract the German armies while the French struggled to rebuild their shattered forces. Surprise at Cambrai would be achieved by dispensing with the initial artillery bombardment. New artillery methods, including sound ranging and flash spotting, enabled German batteries to be pinpointed and dealt with during the actual battle. The main feature was the use of the *tank*: 9 battalions, 378 machines, led 2 infantry corps against the German defences. This was the first time that tanks were used in mass, rather than in piecemeal deployment. The assault was launched at 6 a.m., 20 November, over ground which had not been churned up by the usual artillery salvoes, and the massed tanks battered a way through the German lines, followed by waves of infantry from General J. H. Byng's 3rd Army. The Germans fell back, and by 4 p.m. a penetration of 10,000 yards had been achieved: an equivalent advance at the Third Battle of Ypres had taken 3

months. But the British lacked reserves; the advance slowed. The Germans counter-attacked the salient on 30 November and on 3 December *Haig* ordered a partial withdrawal which abandoned about half the penetration. Both sides suffered about 45,000 casualties. But the valuable offensive lessons of Cambrai would be used in the decisive battle of *Amiens*, August 1918.

Cambridge, George William Frederick Charles, 2nd Duke of, 1819–1904 British Field-Marshal. Served in the Hanoverian Army, 1837, but first saw action at *Alma* in the *Crimean War*, 20 September 1854, when he commanded a division (Map 4); he delayed in lending support to the Light Infantry Division whilst awaiting more precise orders from *Raglan*, so causing the Light Division to suffer extra heavy casualties. He commanded the 1st Division at *Balaklava*, 25 October. He succeeded Lord Hardinge as C-in-C of the British Army, 1856, and was created Field-Marshal in 1862. He remained C-in-C until his retirement in 1895. During his period of power Cambridge opposed many of the Army reforms attempted after the Crimean War, for example short service, the formation of the Army Reserve, linked battalions and the reorganization of the War Office; he was suspicious of politicians and the 'new school' represented by men such as *Wolseley*, and feared the royal prerogative might be threatened. Cambridge also opposed reforms put forward at the instigation of Florence *Nightingale*.

Campbell, Sir Colin, Lord Clyde,
1792–1863 British Field-Marshal.
Served in the *Peninsular War*, 1810–
13; West Indies, 1819–26; China,
1842–6; fought in Second Sikh War,
1848–9, remaining as a divisional commander in India until the outbreak of
the *Crimean War*, 1853, when he received command of the Highland
Brigade. This comprised the Cameron
Highlanders, the 93rd (Argyll and
Sutherland Highlanders) and the
Black Watch. Campbell led them in a
magnificent advance at the Battle of
Alma. The stand of his troops against
a section of the Russian cavalry at
Balaklava has been immortalized as
'the thin Red Line'. In the summer of
1857 Campbell arrived in India to be
C-in-C during the *Indian Mutiny*, succeeding Sir Patrick Grant. On 12
November he advanced with 4,500
men from Cawnpore for the relief of
Lucknow, succeeding on 16 November. On 6 December he decisively
defeated a large rebel force outside
Cawnpore and on 16 March the following year, 1858, he finally drove the
dissidents from the Lucknow area.

Cape St Vincent, Battle of, Feb-
ruary 1797 *French Revolutionary*
Wars (Map 1). Spain joined France in
the war against Britain on 19 August
1796, thus threatening the British position in the Mediterranean. Corsica and
Elba were evacuated and the Mediterranean Fleet moved to Gibraltar on
1 December under *Jervis*. Early in
February 1797 the Spanish Fleet was
sighted moving towards the Atlantic.
This Fleet, under Admiral José de

Córdova, consisted of 7 three-deck
ships of the line, carrying over 112
guns each, and other vessels totalling
27. Jervis's strength amounted to 15
warships with only 2 having 100 guns.
The Spanish commander aimed to
join the French Fleet at Brest for a
proposed invasion of England. At day-
break on 14 February the Spanish and
British Fleets were positioned 25 miles
west of Cape St Vincent. The Spanish
Fleet was separated into two groups
with the first, of 6 vessels, about 7
miles ahead of the rest. Jervis succeeded in slicing between the two sections, although 3 more Spanish vessels
from the larger group managed to join
the foremost 6. Jervis turned on the
remaining 18. Eventually, the British
had to tack about, and the Spanish
Admiral attempted to use this lull to
break away behind the British column.
Jervis's subordinate *Nelson* forestalled
this move by sweeping round to engage the leading Spanish ships without
waiting for orders. Joined by another
British vessel, he blocked the Spanish
retreat until the rest of the British
Fleet could come up. The Spanish
Fleet was shattered, with the loss of
4 vessels and severe damage to many
others. The British lost 74 men killed.

Cardwell, Edward, Viscount, 1813–
86 British statesman. From 1868 to
1874 Cardwell was Secretary for War,
under Gladstone. His ministry included the Cardwell Reforms of the
Army, with the need for reform having
been revealed by the *Crimean War* but
with innovations resisted by conservatives such as the Duke of *Cambridge*,

Army C-in-C 1856–95. Cardwell started by reducing the number of soldiers in the colonies: by 1870 this number had been cut from 49,000 to 18,000. He reorganized the War Office, establishing three departments under the C-in-C, the Surveyor-General of the Ordnance and the Financial Secretary. All three were brought under the control of the Secretary of State for War, and the subordination of the C-in-C to the Parliamentary Minister was further emphasized by the removal of the HQ staff from the Horse Guards to the War Office. This also terminated the sovereign's dominance over the Army: Queen Victoria signed the Order in Council, with some reluctance, in June 1870. Prussia's success in the *Franco-Prussian War* stimulated the search for greater efficiency. Army Estimates of 1871 involved an increased expenditure of £3 million: for this sum the country was to have 497,000 men under arms, including 135,000 regulars of whom 108,000 would be in England. The rest of the army manpower comprised militia and yeomanry reserves; the latter would no longer be controlled by provincial lord lieutenants but by the central government. Also included in Cardwell's measures was the abolition of purchase of commissions. Enlistment would be for 12 years, half with the colours and half in a special reserve. Each regiment, associated with a territorial district, consisted of two battalions, one of which served at home whilst the other went abroad. This 'linked battalion' system was intended to introduce continuity of service, better conditions for the men by allowing them to return home sooner, and better local patriotism. Cardwell's reforms were sufficient for the small colonial wars, but inadequate for a modern army fighting with, and against, modern weapons. The *Boer War*, 1889–1902, would reveal continuing deficiencies.

Carnot, Lazare Nicolas Marguerite, 1753–1823 French military reformer. Became a member of Committee of Public Safety, August 1793. Carnot was made responsible for the direction of French military operations. The *Levée en masse*, introduced 23 August, resulted in a flood of raw recruits into the Army: Carnot merged these conscripts with remnants of the old professional Army, and during the next 2 years he introduced further measures to make the best use of French patriotic fervour. French successes at Menin on 13 September and Hondschoote in the same month, followed by victory at *Wattignies*, 15–16 October, established Carnot's reputation as the central organizer of the French armies: he was soon titled the 'Organizer of Victory'. Carnot forged the weapon which *Napoleon* would soon use to such dramatic effect. He developed the French *column*, involving the deployment of units in depth and providing flexibility and firm control; he also developed the *division*, with this formation comprising all arms and being capable of carrying out independent operations. The system opened the way for the grouping of units into the larger formation, the *corps*. Carnot became President of the Convention in 1795 and was a member of the Directory 1795-7. He acted as War Minister for a short time in 1800-1, and was a member of the Tribunate 1802-7. Napoleon appointed him Minister of the Interior during the Hundred Days, 1815. He was exiled by Louis XVIII in 1815.

Cassino, Battle of, January–May 1944 *Second World War* (Map 14). By the end of 1943 German forces in *Italy* had been pushed back to the 'Gustav' defensive line, running from the Garigliano River estuary on the west, along the Rapido, to just south of Pescara on the Adriatic. *Kesselring* held this line with 9 divisions. Facing them, under *Alexander*'s command, were the 7 Commonwealth divisions of the 8th Army and the US 5th Army, comprising 5 US, 5 British, 2 French and 1 Polish divisions. The 8th Army route lay along the Adriatic Coast, while the 5th Army pushed against the Gustav Line in the centre. Monte Cassino was the key obstacle in the 5th Army advance. Allied discussions eventually led to a plan for an amphibious assault on *Anzio*, some 60 miles behind the Rapido, combined with a frontal attack at Cassino by the 5th Army. The latter attacked on 17 January, and made some gains. The Anzio operation was launched on 21 January, but soon bogged down. Repeated attempts to take Cassino were also unsuccessful and costly, including an operation on 12 February by the US 34th Division and an offensive on the 15th by the New Zealand Corps. The latter was co-ordinated with an aerial bombardment on the historic monastery of St Benedict, situated on the summit of Mount Cassino and mistakenly believed by the New Zealand commander, Freyberg, to be used by the Germans. The New Zealand assault ended on 18 February; stalemate continued. An attempt by British, Indian and New Zealand troops on 15 March resulted in a foothold in the monastery ruins, but this attack was also halted. Finally, on 11 May Alexander launched a full-scale surprise assault in the 20-mile area between Cassino and the sea, aimed at outflanking the Germans. This succeeded, with the Polish Corps taking Cassino from the rear on 17-18 May. The Anzio force linked with the 5th Army on the 25th for the advance on Rome. Allied casualties during this operation numbered 42,000; the German total was similar.

Cavalry, general Three forms of cavalry were used in the *Napoleonic Wars*: heavy (cuirassiers and carabiniers); medium (dragoons); and light (chasseurs, hussars, lancers). The types overlapped one another, but basically the heavy cavalry was intended for shock battlefield tactics, forming a throwback to the medieval knights; medium cavalrymen often acted in the role of mounted infantry, using their horses for transport in order to reach the fighting area, where they would operate on foot; light cavalry were primarily concerned with screening and skirmishing – they were also responsible for the main reconnaissance role, reporting on enemy movements and on suitable routes, including fords and mountain passes; light cavalrymen undertook much of the foraging duties. The Russian Cossacks carried out both medium and light cavalry duties: these famous horsemen, most of whom originated from the lower reaches of the Don or Volga Rivers, were able to move long distances over the harshest terrain. The use of cavalry in rough terrain in fact continued after other roles had been superseded by later weapons developments. During the Napoleonic Wars the French made more use of cavalry as a whole than did their allies and opponents: *Napoleon*'s Grand Army in *Russia*, 1812, contained 48 cavalry regiments of up to 1,200 men in each. French and Prussian cavalry usually charged against enemy infantry already shaken by artillery fire or by infantry attacks, and rapid cavalry action against a faltering enemy could best exploit victory. On the other hand unshaken infantrymen standing in square formation could withstand most cavalry charges alone. The British undertook fewer decisive cavalry charges, with *Wellington* restricting their roles to screening, reconnaissance, foraging and less formal attacks, largely because of the British cavalry's tendency to become disorganized after a charge. British cavalry strength was therefore usually lower than the French; nevertheless the British Army contained some excellent cavalry commanders, notably

Paget. Charges were rarely attempted in the *American Civil War*; raiding and reconnaissance were however still carried out by the cavalry in this conflict, often with brilliant success when led by men such as 'JEB' *Stuart*. The largest cavalry duel in the war took place in June 1863 at Brandy Station, with Stuart's 10,000 Confederate cavalrymen clashing with, and eventually overcoming, 12,000 Union cavalrymen under Brigadier Alfred Pleasanton. In the *Crimean War* the decimation of the Light Brigade at *Balaklava* showed the danger of advancing unsupported against enemy guns, but the charge of the Heavy Brigade in the same battle proved that cavalry could still be used effectively against other cavalry regiments. The *Franco-Prussian War* revealed an almost total lack of direct charges. Only one successful charge was made, by General von Bredow's Prussian brigade at Vionville in August 1870: the brigade suffered 50 per cent casualties even though the enemy was short of ammunition. A charge by the French General Gallifet at *Sedan* resulted in almost total destruction of his 'Chasseurs d'Afrique'. Cavalry continued to be useful against ill-armed opponents in the British colonial wars, for example at Omdurman in 1897, although these successes tended to obscure the fact that this weapon had become outdated. The British Expeditionary Force, 1914, possessed one cavalry division of 9,269 officers and men, but this force was also well equipped with field guns and machine-guns – four times more machine-guns than in a German cavalry division – and the men had been trained to fight dismounted with modern weapons, as the Boers had done in the *Boer War*. British cavalry rode into a gap in the German second line at the battle of the *Somme*, July 1916 – the last time horse cavalry was employed on a large scale in Western Europe. The mounted arm did however prove valuable in the *Middle East* during the *First World War*, in operations conducted by *Allenby* against the Turks. Cavalry units played an important part in the *Russian Revolution*, notably those commanded by Semen Budenny in the campaign against White forces under Deniken and Wrangel, 1919. But the inter-World War years saw the final struggle between cavalry exponents and those of the *tank*. The cavalry were gradually switched to the light tank role: in 1934 tentative agreement was reached that the British Cavalry Division should be replaced by a Mobile Armoured Division. Some of the most famous old British cavalry regiments re-emerged in an equally famous armoured role, including the 7th, 8th and 11th Hussars as the original Desert Rats in the *Desert Campaign*. The last US cavalry units were merged into the armoured forces on 4 April 1946. The Chinese Army still retained 4 cavalry divisions in 1976.

Chancellorsville, campaign and Battle of, April–May 1863 *American Civil War* (Map 3). *Hooker*, appointed to command the Union Army of the Potomac on 26 January 1863, planned to reverse the Union defeat at *Fredericksburg* the previous December. Hooker aimed to drive across the Rapidan with 73,000 men to circle *Lee*'s left, while Major-General John Sedgwick, with 40,000 troops, fixed Lee's attention by crossing direct from Fredericksburg. Lee's Army of Northern Virginia was short of equipment and had been reduced to only 60,000 men. But Lee, skilfully screened by 'JEB' *Stuart*'s cavalry, was fully informed of Hooker's movements, and in the last days of April he marched to meet the main Union offensive, leaving 10,000 men under Major-General Jubal Early positioned on Marye's Heights outside Fredericksburg to block Sedgwick's secondary thrust. The main armies clashed on 1 May, 1 mile east of Chancellorsville. Hooker, despite numerical superiority, displayed typical caution and moved on to the defensive. Early on 2 May Lee dispatched 'Stonewall' *Jackson* with 26,000 men on an encircling mission, while he himself remained with only 17,000 men to hold the front. Jackson moved quickly and attacked the Union right flank just before dusk. Then Jackson fell, mortally wounded by fire from his own men. The Confederates attacked in full strength next day, but met strong resistance and reports reached Lee that Sedgwick's force was driving Early's hard-pressed men from Marye's Heights. Lee, his rear threatened, left Stuart to hold Hooker and rushed back to defeat Sedgwick at Salem Church, 4 May. Hooker failed to make use of his opportunity at Chancellorsville and the triumphant Confederate Army withdrew across the Rappahannock during 5–6 May. Chancellorsville marked the high-water of the south's success. The Union Army lost 17,000 men, the Confederates 13,000.

Charles Louis, Archduke of Austria, Duke of Teschen, 1771–1847

The Archduke Charles, son of Emperor Leopold II of Austria, was one of the most competent generals of the *Napoleonic Wars* (Map 1): according to *Clausewitz* only Charles and *Wellington* were worthy of being compared with the French commander. He first saw action at *Jemappes*, 1792, but obtained renown as the Austrian commander in the campaign east of the Rhine, 1796, when he outwitted superior French numbers commanded by Jean Baptiste Jourdan and Jean Victor Moreau. The former was defeated at Amberg, 24 August, and again at Würzburg, 3 September – at the latter battle both French flanks were enveloped after skilled manoeuvring by the Archduke. Charles was then sent into *Italy* (Map 1) to help deal with the threat posed by Napoleon, but was obliged to fall back in March 1797; Bonaparte invaded Austria to bring about the Treaty of Campo Formio. During the Italian campaign of 1799 Charles was caught off-balance by Jourdan, in March, but recovered to check the enemy at Stockach on the 25th, obliging the French to pull back to the Rhine. *Masséna*, Jourdan's successor, defeated Charles's left wing in mountain fighting near Zurich, August, and

thereafter Charles was ordered to march north to fight the French in the Netherlands. This move was however cancelled soon after his march began: the withdrawal of Charles's forces none the less allowed Masséna to take Zurich, 25 September, thus ending the 1799 campaign. Charles fought again in Italy in 1805, once more opposing Masséna, and blocked French forces from moving north through the Alps to join Napoleon in the early stage of the *Austerlitz* campaign. In 1809 Charles marched on *Ratisbon*, but was forced back by Napoleon at Eggmühl, 22 April. He managed to escape the French at Ratisbon itself the following day; he defeated Napoleon at Aspern-Essling, 21–22 May, at the start of the *Wagram* campaign – the first time that the French Emperor had lost a battle. Napoleon recovered to make a surprise crossing of the Danube, 4–5 July; Charles's army suffered heavy loss at Wagram itself, 5–6 July. Charles retired from military life soon afterwards, and thereafter wrote a number of books on the theory and art of war.

Chassepot, Antonie Alphonse, 1833–1905

French firearms inventor. Chassepot was made famous by the breech-loading rifle which bore his name. An employee of the St Thomas d'Aquin artillery works, Chassepot developed this weapon over a period of 10 years; it was designed to outperform the *Dreyse* gun adopted by the Prussians in 1848. The French authorities considered introducing the Chassepot from 1863 onwards, but critics – headed by War Minister

Marshal Comte Randon – said the rifle was untried and would use too much ammunition. Prussia's success at *Sadowa* against the Austrians in 1866 swept away this bureaucratic obstacle: Napoleon III ordered the chassepot to be put into immediate production. The French Army embarked on the *Franco-Prussian War*, 1870, confident that their rifle was superior. The Dreyse lacked a gastight breech; Chassepot solved this defect by incorporating a rubber ring seal. His rifle also had a smaller calibre than the Dreyse, giving the French weapon a range of 1,600 yards compared with 600 yards for the Dreyse, and reducing ammunition weight which the infantryman had to carry. But the small calibre fouled more quickly, and the light weight increased the recoil. In 1874 the chassepot was modified for use with the new metallic *percussion* cartridges and became the *Gras* rifle.

Chattanooga, campaign and Battle of, September–December 1863
American Civil War (Map 3). Confederate hopes had received a serious setback in July 1863, with the defeats at *Gettysburg* and *Vicksburg*, and now Union pressure was increased in the Chattanooga area of Tennessee. In mid-August General William Rosecrans advanced on this town from Tullahoma, while *Burnside*'s Army of the Ohio moved from Lexington towards Knoxville, 100 miles northeast of Chattanooga; the latter was abandoned by the Confederates on 7 September. Rosecrans pursued the enemy into north-west Georgia. Union forces totalled 60,000; the Confederate Army of Tennessee, under Brayton Bragg, reinforced by *Longstreet*'s corps, numbered 70,000; Bragg turned on his pursuers at Chickamauga Creek on 19 September. The Union Army was disorganized and a Confederate attempt to thrust through the centre almost succeeded on the 20th; determined defence by troops under *Thomas*, commanding the left wing, saved the Union Army from disaster. This battle of Chickamauga cost over 15,000 Union casualties and a similar Confederate number. Bragg maintained his Confederate pressure and drove Rosecrans back to Chattanooga, investing this town and preventing the arrival of Union reinforcements under Burnside and *Hooker*. On 17 October *Lincoln* placed *Grant* in command of all Union forces between the Mississippi and the Alleghenies; Grant immediately rushed to relieve Chattanooga, using the telegraph link with the town to replace Rosecrans with Thomas. Between 23 and 27 October Grant prised open a gap in the Confederate line near Lookout Mountain, 2 miles south-west of the town by the bank of the Tennessee and Hooker's troops advanced through this temporary breach. The Confederates held strong positions on Lookout Mountain and Missionary Ridge, encircling Chattanooga to the south, and Confederate troops under Longstreet were also besieging Burnside at Knoxville. Grant, on the other hand, had ordered *Sherman* to bring up his Union army

from Memphis; this arrived on 24 November, and Grant immediately ordered an assault. Sherman's exhausted troops were repulsed, but Union troops under Hooker took Lookout Mountain late on the 24th; this battle was the first day of the Battle of Chattanooga. The second day, also known as the Battle of Missionary Ridge, opened with Sherman renewing assaults against the right wing of Bragg's Confederate army, while Hooker pushed against the left. During the afternoon a third Union attack began with Thomas's troops advancing against Missionary Ridge from Chattanooga: these troops reached the summit of the feature. The Confederates fled. Casualties suffered during the 2 days were about 5,700 Union troops and 6,500 Confederates. Longstreet abandoned the siege of Knoxville on 4 December on the approach of Sherman's force. The Gettysburg and Vicksburg disasters had already split the south vertically, and now the Confederacy could also be cut horizontally through a Union advance into Georgia and to the sea: Sherman began his famous march to *Atlanta* and then to the coast at Savannah on 5 May 1864.

Chemical and Bacteriological (or Biological) Warfare (CBW) A form of conflict identified by the use of chemicals depending upon toxicity for their effect: this strict definition excludes weapons such as flamethrowers and *napalm*. Wells were deliberately poisoned by throwing in corpses during the *Napoleonic Wars*; this

method of striking at the enemy was also employed in the *American Civil War* during the retreat from *Vicksburg* in July 1863. The suggestion was also raised during the American Civil War that chlorine should be used; this was rejected, as was a proposal in 1855 that sulphur dioxide should be introduced by the allies against the Russians at Sebastopol in the *Crimean War*. Also in 1855 the British produced prototype shells filled with cacodyl and cacodyl oxide, substances containing arsenic. The French were the first to use toxic weapons in the *First World War*, firing tear-gas grenades from rifles in August 1914. On 27 October 1914 the Germans bombarded the British at Neuve Chapelle with shrapnel shells containing a chemical irritant known as dianisidine chlorsulphonate. In January 1915 the Germans fired shells containing xylyl bromide at the Russians. Neither operation proved a success due to difficulties experienced with the chemicals concerned. But on 22 April 1915 the Germans opened over 500 cylinders containing 168 tons of pressurized chlorine gas, which was swept by the wind on to the French positions over a 4-mile front, causing 15,000 casualties, 5,000 of them fatal. Choking chlorine gas causes intense irritation of the lungs and results in death if inhaled over a short period – 1 or 2 minutes – in a concentration of over 1 part in 10,000. On 25 September 1915 the British released chlorine on the Germans at *Loos*, and from this date onwards chlorine was used frequently by both sides. Canisters were discarded for the more effective method of enclosing chlorine in a shell, used by the Germans in July 1915 in the Argonne. Chemical escalation started, in a race against constantly improving respirators: phosgene was introduced by the Germans in December 1915, soon with a vomiting gas such as diphenyl chlorasine added to the mixture. Phosgene is also a choking gas, but more toxic than chlorine; symptoms are delayed. Mustard-gas – dichloroethylsulphide – was first used by the Germans in July 1917, and became the most common substance. This gas is virtually colourless and without smell; it evaporates slowly; it causes intense burning in liquid form and results in severe vomiting. An estimated 800,000 casualties were caused by chemical warfare between 1914 and 1918, although this figure might be far too low. Concern with this new trend of CW led to the Geneva Protocol of 1925 forbidding the use of chemical or biological offensive weapons; 29 nations signed the treaty, excluding the USA and Japan. The Geneva Protocol was considered at a UN General Assembly in December 1966, with a resolution calling on all member states to observe the Protocol and inviting them to accede to it. Both the USA and Japan voted for the resolution. The First World War remains the only conflict in which toxic weapons have been used on a large scale. Biological or bacteriological weapons were probably not employed, although there is a possibility that anthrax was inoculated into horses and cattle at Bucharest in 1916 and on the French Front

in 1917. Anthrax, like glanders, is an animal disease which can be passed to humans and which leads to death in extreme form. Bacteriological weapons are far more difficult to control and have since been less developed than chemical forms. Since 1918 nations have refrained from extensive involvement in CBW apart from isolated instances: mustard-gas was used by the Italians against the Abyssinians in January 1936; the Japanese made repeated small gas attacks against the Chinese 1937–43. Nevertheless, the potential power of these weapons had been vastly increased by 1939, both through the development of new delivery systems, especially aircraft, and the development of new toxic weapons. The latter included nervegas, notably sarin, produced in Germany after about 1936. Britain contemplated the use of both chemical and bacteriological forms during the Second World War. On 2 October 1941 the *Defence Committee* discussed a proposal to use mustard-gas in an operation to capture Trondheim; the *Chiefs of Staff* believed that the operation would be militarily unfeasible, with or without the use of gas. In July 1944 the COS were asked by *Churchill* to consider the use of mustard-gas 'or any other method of warfare which we have hitherto refrained from using against the Germans'; this would be in retaliation for the *V-bomb* attacks and in the event of a stalemate in *Normandy*. The COS ruled out gas through fear of German retaliation; bacteriological warfare was considered more favourably, especially a strain code-named N – probably anthrax – because German stocks were lower than British. But British supplies were insufficient to launch a sustained attack and the proposal was abandoned. During the war the British tested anthrax on Gruinard Island, Scotland: this small island will probably still be contaminated in another 100 years. Development in CBW has continued since 1945, for instance at Britain's Microbiological Research Establishment, Porton, Wiltshire, and on a far larger scale at Camp Detrick, Maryland, USA. The threat of CBW has remained: for example the Israelis purchased 20,000 gas masks from West Germany in 1967. Mustard-gas and phosgene were used by Egyptian forces in the Yemen during 1966 and 1967. Earlier, in 1965, the US forces in *Vietnam* began employing incapacitating chemicals; US authorities stated that these tear- or nausea-producing gases were standard riot control chemicals. These referred to tear-gas of the DM, CN and CS varieties. DM, or Adamsite, is the strongest, incapacitating for up to an hour and causing sneezing, coughing, nausea and vomiting. The US authorities claimed these 'benevolent incapacitators' resulted in less severe casualties than would otherwise have been incurred. The Americans also used defoliants in Vietnam, designed to kill vegetation which screened enemy movement and to deny the enemy food. Vast areas of countryside around Saigon were sprayed from the air, with consequent fears for seriously disturbing the ecological balance in the regions involved; during 1967 a total area of 965,000 acres was sprayed. Chemicals used included dichlorophen and trichlorophen oxyacetic acid, together with cacodylic acid, which rely for their effect on boosting the growth of plants to such an extent that they literally burn themselves out.

Chiang Kai-shek, real name Chiang Chung-cheng, 1887–1975 Chinese generalissimo and statesman. Engaged in minor civil wars, 1911–17; became influential in the Kuomintang Army, military wing of the National People's Party announced by Sun Yat-sen, January 1924. After Sun's death, 1925, Chiang became generalissimo of the Kuomintang. He occupied Peking, 1928, and waged aggressive civil war against the communists, 1927–36. His campaign forced the communists to make their *Long March*, 1934–5. War began with Japan following invasion on 7 July 1937; Chiang, his forces ill-equipped and inadequately trained, was obliged to retreat to Hankow. The closing of the *Burma* Road in early 1942 restricted allied aid to China, where, in January, Chiang was named Supreme Commander of allied air and land forces. *Chennault*'s 14th Air Force managed to gain air supremacy over most of China in 1943, but disagreements between Chiang and his US Chief of Staff *Stilwell*, combined with worsening relations with the communists, restricted Chinese participation in Burma operations. Japan launched a vigorous offensive in east China in May 1944 and in south and central China in early 1945, but

Chinese counter-attacks plus Japanese setbacks elsewhere began to turn the tide. With the defeat of Japan, the *China Communist Civil War* again became intense, leading to Chiang's withdrawal to Formosa, 7 December 1949.

China, Communist Civil War, 1945–9 Sporadic civil war had waged in China since the mid-1920s between the communists under *Mao Tse-tung* and the nationalist government of the Kuomintang Party under *Chiang Kai-shek*. The highlight of this early struggle was the communist *Long March*, 1934–5. Mao used the *Second World War* period to gather strength. In August 1945 the communists moved in behind the retreating Japanese to take over the abandoned countryside; US Marines occupied Peiping, Tientsin and coastal areas in late September 1945 in an endeavour to keep the two sides apart. The nationalists began a large offensive in south-west Manchuria on 15 November, while the communists moved forward in Santung at the end of the month. By the end of 1946 a stalemate had arisen in Manchuria, with the communists controlling the countryside but unable to mount effective sustained attacks against the regular nationalist troops. In north China the nationalists launched a major offensive in July 1947 and by November had gained large areas. Mao embarked on a highly skilled *guerrilla warfare* campaign and gradually these guerrilla groups regained control over the countryside, even though the nationalists captured

Mao's capital of Yenan on 19 March 1947. The guerrillas developed into regular forces for offensives in Manchuria, in the Yangtse River area and in Shensi; they won a major victory at Hawai Hai, east of Kaifeng, in a battle lasting from November 1948 to January 1949 and which resulted in 250,000 nationalist casualties. Peking fell after a long siege on 22 January 1949, Nanking on 22 April, Canton on 15 October. Chiang established a new capital at Changtu after his existing base at Chungking was seized on 30 November but almost immediately afterwards withdrew to Formosa.

China–Tibetan War, 1950 In November 1949 Peking radio broadcast an appeal by the Panchen Lama, refugee rival of the Tibetan ruler, the Dalai Lama, for a communist 'liberation' of Tibet; on 1 January 1950 the Chinese communist government declared it would assist this 'liberation'. In October a large Chinese force of unspecified size swept over the mountain frontier. Tibet was unable to prevent the Chinese from overrunning the country; the Dalai Lama was allowed to remain as a figurehead. Guerrilla warfare continued in the mountains, leading to a widespread revolt in early 1954. By summer 1954 the Chinese had suppressed this uprising, killing an estimated 40,000 Tibetans. Unrest continued, and rebellion again broke out on 10 March 1959. This was put down by 27 March, with the Dalai Lama fleeing to India. He accused the Chinese of genocide and claimed that 65,000 Tibetans had been killed, 10,000 young people deported to China and 5 million Chinese had settled in Tibet. Guerrilla warfare continued, mainly undertaken by Kambah tribesmen in the mountains along the border with Nepal.

China, invasion of India, 1962 – see India–China War, 1962

Chindits name given to *Wingate*'s Long Range Penetration Groups in *Burma* (Map 16) during Second World War; the title has two origins, one being the mythical Burmese animal known as the 'chinthe' which served as the Chindit emblem, and the other being the Chindwin River. Wingate's plan, approved by the C-in-C India, *Wavell*, was to send small parties behind Japanese lines; these troops, from Wingate's 77th Indian Division, would be mainly air-supplied. The first Chindit operation began on 18 February 1943, when 3,000 men in several small columns crossed the Chindwin, temporarily interrupted the Mandalay–Myitkyina railroad, then crossed the Irrawaddy in an attempt to cut the Mandalay–Lashio rail link. Japanese opposition increased and the Chindits withdrew; casualties totalled about 1,000 men. Another operation was launched on 5 March 1944, with Wingate now able to use manpower from 6 infantry brigades. Five of these landed in north-central Burma and blocked Mandalay–Myitkyina communications at Mawlu. Wingate was killed in an air crash, 25 March, and was succeeded by General W. D. A. Lentaigne. Japanese opposi-

tion mounted, and Lentaigne withdrew westwards, with Chindits suffering considerable casualties. The least damaged groups moved north and took part in *Stilwell*'s operations, but relations between Lentaigne and Stilwell were unsatisfactory: the US officer believed the Chindits could have fought harder, while Lentaigne criticized the misuse of the Chindits in Stilwell's offensive.

Churchill, Sir Winston Spencer, 1874–1965 British political leader. Entered British Army 1895, serving thereafter in Cuba, India, *Egypt*, *Boer War*. President, Board of Trade, 1908–10; Home Secretary, 1910–11; First Lord of the Admiralty, 1911–15, during which period he gave ardent support for the *Dardanelles* operation: succeeded by Arthur Balfour during the political upheaval following the failure of this campaign. Churchill acted as Chancellor of the Duchy of Lancaster in 1915, still with a seat on the War Council. Subsequent appointments were: Minister for Munitions 1917, Secretary of State for War and Air 1919–21, for Air and Colonies 1921, for Colonies 1922, Chancellor of the Exchequer 1924–9; during the 1930s he was most famous among those who warned of perils of nazism. Prime Minister Neville Chamberlain included Churchill in his *War Cabinet*, September 1939, as First Lord of the Admiralty and Chairman of the Military Co-ordination Committee. He succeeded Chamberlain on 10 May 1940; Churchill also held appointments of First Lord of the Treasury and *Defence* Minister. His principal assets as a war leader were his optimism, expressed in magnificent speeches, especially during 1940, his resilience in the face of repeated setbacks during 1940, 1941 and up to *Alamein* in October–November 1942, his astonishing energy – he travelled over 40,000 miles in 1943, aged 70. Churchill's vision, dramatically simplified, enabled a framework for strategic planning upon which his *Chiefs of Staff* under *Brooke*, and the *Combined Chiefs of Staff*, could laboriously build. Churchill was defeated in the General Election, July 1945, and was succeeded by Clement Attlee, who had worked closely with him in the wartime coalition government.

Clark, Mark Wayne, 1896– US General. Graduated West Point, 1917; battalion commander in First World War, and thereafter served on the staff; appointed Chief of Staff, under *Eisenhower*, for Ground Forces in Europe, July 1942; in October 1942 he held secret talks with French officers in French North Africa, attempting to enlist support prior to allied '*Torch*' landings the following month. Clark commanded the US 5th Army in 1943, landing at *Salerno* in the invasion of *Italy*, 9 September; he relieved General John P. Lucas as commander of the *Anzio* force, February 1944; he then returned to the 5th Army and entered Rome on 4 June. Clark commanded US forces in Austria, 1945–7, leaving to become Deputy US Secretary of State for a short while. He commanded the US 6th Army, 1947–9. In

May 1952 he replaced *Ridgway* as commander in *Korea* for the final stages of the war.

Clausewitz, Carl Marie von, 1780–1831 Prussian General and military theorist. His writing stemmed from his experiences during the *French Revolutionary* and *Napoleonic Wars* (Map 1). He entered Prussian service in 1792 and was engaged at Mainz in 1793 and on the Rhine in 1794. After the Peace of Basel, 1795, he entered the military school in Berlin. Clausewitz fought at *Auerstedt* in October 1806, after which he spent some months as a French prisoner of war. He returned to Prussia in November 1807 and worked closely with *Scharnhorst* and *Gneisenau* when they undertook military reforms. He left Prussia to fight the French in *Russia*, 1812, serving as a Russian staff officer; he played a part in convincing General *Yorck*, commander of the Prussian forces allied with the French, to change allegiance: this resulted in the Treaty of Tauroggen, 30 December. Clausewitz held a staff post as liaison officer between Prussian and Russian forces at *Lützen* and *Bautzen*, 2 May and 21 May 1813; after the armistice ended in August he served as Chief of Staff to General Count Walmoden. During the *Waterloo* campaign, 1815, he acted as Chief of Staff to General von Thielman, fighting at *Ligny* on 16 June, and being responsible for organizing rearguard defences at Wavre on the day of Waterloo, 18 June. In September 1818, now a Major-General, Clausewitz was appointed Director of the

General War School, Berlin, holding this office until 1830. He then undertook inspection duties in Poland until his death in November 1831. His great treatise 'On War', written mainly during his time at the Berlin War School, was unfinished; his wife Marie assembled the manuscripts for publication. 'On War' comprises the first 3 volumes of Clausewitz's 10-volume 'Hinterlasse Werke über Krieg und Kriegführung'. Volume 4 dealt with a study of the Italian campaign, 1796–7; Volumes 5 and 6 with the 1799 campaign in Switzerland and Italy; Volume 7 with the wars of 1812, 1813 and 1814; Volume 8 with the Waterloo campaign. Volumes 9 and 10, which followed after Marie's death, covered a variety of campaigns by leading generals. 'On War' describes the traumatic transition of warfare which had taken place during Clausewitz's lifetime. He examined the old and the new and exposed the implications of the Napoleonic developments. He described the old as artificial, largely consisting of manoeuvre between small armies each seeking to avoid battle; they fought 'algebraic actions'. During the Napoleonic era war had changed to a vast outpouring of energy using all national resources. 'The element of War, freed from all conventional restrictions, broke loose with all its natural force,' Clausewitz wrote. 'Superiority in numbers becomes every day more decisive.' Such statements earned Clausewitz the titles of the 'Mahdi of Mass' and the 'Apostle of Violence', and he was quoted by those who sought increased

militarism, including massive preparations for war in time of peace. Yet 'On War' developed another theme, more sophisticated and important; unfortunately this failed to receive full expression in Clausewitz's writings, perhaps because his work was unfinished. Clausewitz believed that war could be studied on two distinct levels: the abstract and the reality. To the abstract belonged the unceasing escalation of violence, the attempt to destroy the enemy completely, the total disregard of bloodshed. In reality war should be very different: the threat of battle might be sufficient. 'The decision may either be a battle or a series of great combats – but it may also consist of the result of mere relations, which arise from the situation of the opposing forces, that is, possible combats.' Moreover, everything depended upon the war's political objective. If the political aims were restricted, then military activity should not be pursued to the utter end. This matching of military to political marked the fundamental distinction between abstract and real war. The abstract represented 'blind passion'. The reality turned war into a calculated political act. From this emerged Clausewitz's most famous statement: 'War is not merely a political act, but also a real political instrument, a continuation of political commerce, a carrying out of the same by other means.' This message in 'On War' was only half-digested. Clausewitz's military disciples concentrated on his comments concerning abstract, unreal war. They overlooked his belief that the defensive was the strongest form of strategy; instead, they declared that, according to Clausewitz, the side with the largest army must win and that the state could only survive with massive forces always ready for use. Clausewitz's dictum that 'War is a continuation of policy by other means' was taken to mean generals should supersede politicians when war began, the very reverse of Clausewitz's belief. *Moltke* declared: 'The politician should fall silent the moment that mobilization begins.' Moltke's successes in the *Austro-Prussian War*, of 1866 and the *Franco-Prussian War*, 1870-1, seemed the final vindication for Clausewitz's teachings – or the teachings as the generals understood them. As Liddell *Hart* commented, military leaders were 'intoxicated with the blood-red wine of Clausewitzian growth'. So, fed on their misinterpretation of 'On War', the generals rode out with their monstrous armies in 1914 to senseless slaughter. The *First World War* confirmed Clausewitz's comments on useless, unpolitical, abstract conflict.

Close order Infantry system which epitomized the pre-*French Revolution* form of battle, especially in Prussia under Frederick the Great. The latter based his battle tactics on the infantry attack, with *cavalry* and *artillery* of secondary importance. The infantry volley was considered the most powerful weapon. Indeed, these could be highly effective: at the Battle of Crefeld in 1758 the first Prussian volley slaughtered 75 per cent of the enemy front line. But such effectiveness depended upon two fundamental factors: first, the ability to concentrate fire in a volley; second, the presence of the enemy in a formation large and vulnerable enough to be subjected to such mass fire. From the first factor stemmed close order. To achieve maximum concentrated fire from a volley, infantrymen had to stand shoulder-to-shoulder in as long and as narrow a line as possible. By the 1740s a Prussian battalion of about 700 men formed a line of 3 ranks spreading over a 150-yard front. But this close order necessitated precisive manoeuvring. Battalions had to be placed closely together, to prevent the enemy breaking through the thin front; hence close order referred not only to the formation within a battalion but also to the relation between one battalion and another. The system had far-reaching implications within an army. Close order drill meant that the different units had to be organized long before battle took place, since the movements were too complicated to be undertaken once fighting began. One side could easily outmanoeuvre another into defeat, simply by being ready first. The result was a cumbersome, inflexible system relying upon persistent supervision, perfect drill and unimaginative tactics. Infantrymen were expected to display no individual initiative; often they were even instructed to avoid aiming their muskets since this took time and resulted in ragged fire. Harsh discipline was imposed to obtain the drill precision. The system proved to be extremely vulnerable to the new form of tactics introduced by the French, especially through the *tirailleur* skirmishers and through the far more flexible *column* formation. The skirmishers, swarming over the battlefield and making use of natural cover, could create havoc with the rigid Prussian lines, while the latter were denied a massed target for their volleys and offered themselves as prime targets for *Napoleon*'s artillery as, for example, at *Auerstedt*, 1806. Moreover the extended line, whilst allowing maximum volleys, did not provide adequate defence against cavalry. For the latter the *square* proved more suitable.

Colenso, Battle of, December 1899 *Boer War* (Map 7). The culmination of Britain's 'Black Week' when British forces suffered a series of setbacks in attempts to relieve Ladysmith and Kimberley; during this week troops under *Methuen* were defeated at Magersfontein, and others under General Sir William Gatacre were ambushed at Stormberg. Meanwhile, the British commander, *Buller*, advanced towards besieged Ladysmith. He crossed the Tugela River and launched a frontal attack on 6,000 Boers under *Botha* entrenched on the northern bank. British guns, unlimbering to fire, were surprised by a concealed Boer force. Inept generalship by Buller may have resulted from shell-shock – Buller was wounded during the battle. He squandered lives both during the advance and in the subsequent retreat. British losses amounted to 1,119; Boer casualties were 6 killed and 21 wounded. Buller was so demoralized that he advocated surrender of Lady-

smith; he was immediately relieved by *Roberts*.

Colt, Samuel, 1814–62 US firearms inventor. His 1835 patent for a hand revolving cylinder gun included the ability to rotate the 5-shot cylinder simultaneously upon bringing the hammer to full cock. The Colt Patent Arms Manufacturing Company was established at Peterson, New Jersey, in 1836; the company received a small government order for 50 Paterson 8-shot rifles in 1838, but it was liquidated in 1842. Colt began production again in 1847. The new company received increased orders as a result of the *American–Mexican War*, 1846–8, and from the westwards expansion. In the *American Civil War* the revolver became more important than the sabre in *cavalry* actions.

Column Infantry formation which became prominent during the *French Revolution* and *Napoleonic Wars*. It showed a significant improvement from the previous close order lines, still used by the Prussians in their fateful *Auerstedt* campaign, 1806: this old system was based on a thin line of men facing the enemy, usually 3 ranks deep; a battalion of 700 men thus extended over a 150-yard front. Disadvantages stemmed from the extreme inflexibility, combined with the length of time required to organize such a line for battle. In addition, cavalry and artillery were kept separate from the infantry. The column overcame these drawbacks, with this formation being developed in France during the 1780s from tactical experiments undertaken by Marshal Saxe over a century before. Instead of an extended line, the column was a 'brick' formation of up to 18 ranks deep, with each rank comprising 40 men. This gave a compact mass of men, far more easily directed on the approach to the battlefield and in the battle itself: the column could be moved at speed through a gap in the enemy formation, or could be thrown at a particular point to pierce the thin, close order opposition. Originally the column was intended as a formation for movement of men to the battlefield; once there, they would reform into the usual 3-rank line. But with further developments carried out by *Carnot* and perfected by *Napoleon*, it became far more common for the men to fight in columns, although a distinction existed between the marching and the attack column, the former having a narrower front and greater depth. Loss of fire power of the attack column was more than outweighed by speed and impetus gained; untrained men in a column felt far less exposed than in a thin line, and this made the formation especially suitable for the raw French recruits of the *Levée en masse*. The column could move into line or into squares if necessary, and one unit could be joined with another in building-brick fashion.

Combined Chiefs of Staff (CCS) Committee *Second World War*. The CCS was created at the Washington Conference held in December 1941 and attended by Roosevelt, Churchill and the respective staffs. The aim was to provide a permanent Anglo-US staff link and at the same time to form a suitable body for top-level staff meetings at summit conferences. It was therefore decided that during summits the US *Joint Chiefs of Staff* (JCS) and their British equivalent, the *Chiefs of Staff* (COS), should meet in joint session under the title of CCS, with these meetings discussing matters of grand strategy. Detailed considerations would then continue between summits with US and special British representatives joining at frequent CCS working meetings in Washington. Britain's chief representatives at these sessions was *Dill*, succeeded by Sir Henry Maitland Wilson in November 1944. The CCS did not themselves make strategic decisions; instead they put forward recommendations to their respective governments. The first CCS meeting took place on 23 January 1942; 54 meetings were held in 1942, 85 in 1943, 60 in 1944 and 1945 up to 24 July.

Combined operations Military activity designed to co-ordinate the efforts of more than one service. Army and naval forces combined in amphibious attacks have long been attempted, with historical examples from the last two centuries including the British landings in Corsica, 1794, in Holland, 1799, and at Aboukir in the *Egyptian* campaign of 1801. Later examples include the *Dardanelles* operation, 1915–16. The latter also underlined the difficulties involved in obtaining smooth inter-service co-operation and emphasized the need for a more formalized and integrated system. Such a system was created in June 1940 in Britain, after *Churchill's* plea for sudden amphibious strikes against German occupied France and Belgium. Already, in 1938, an Inter-Service Training and Development Centre had been established near Portsmouth, aimed at studying the subject of combined operations in all aspects, including aircraft support, parachute descents and the use of amphibious tanks. The centre had been disbanded on the outbreak of war, but was soon revived; on 11 June the British *Chiefs of Staff* proposed to the Prime Minister the appointment of a Commander, Offensive Operations, with a small inter-service staff. Lieutenant-General A. G. B. Bourne, Royal Marines, was accordingly selected; on 20 June the Chiefs of Staff approved Bourne's scheme for the organization and equipment of a Directorate of Combined Operations. Two raids were carried out during early summer, at Le Touquet in June and Guernsey in July; in August Bourne was succeeded by Admiral of the Fleet Sir Roger Keyes, who had carried out the famous raid on *Zeebrugge*, 1918. Keyes intensified the raising and training of *commandos* and created the beginnings of a landing-craft force; he was succeeded by *Mountbatten* in October 1941, who had the title Adviser, Combined Operations, until March 1942: on that date Mountbatten became Chief of Combined Operations with a seat on the Chiefs of Staff Committee. Mountbatten's first raiding venture com-

prised attacks on the Vaagso and Maaloy islands, south Norway, and the Lofoten islands in the north, undertaken successfully on 26 December 1941; another raid took place against a special radar station near Le Havre, February 1942; on 28 March took place the dramatic raid on St Nazaire to destroy the dry dock. Thereafter Mountbatten and his Combined Operations Command became heavily involved in planning and preparations for large-scale allied landings. Work covered the design and testing of landing craft and amphibious vehicles and a multitude of other schemes such as PLUTO – the Pipe-Line Under the Ocean – which eventually carried petrol to the Normandy beach-head. Detailed plans were drawn up for the allied landings against North Africa – ultimately undertaken in late 1942 as *'Torch'*, together with the *Normandy* landings themselves. Meanwhile other raids took place, among the most famous being that on *Dieppe*, August 1942. Mountbatten left to become Supreme Allied Commander, South-East Asia, October 1943, succeeded by General R. E. Laycock. At the same time the Americans were gaining vast experience of combined operations in the Pacific, especially through the development of *marines*: from this experience emerged better means of ship-shore communication and more sophisticated landing-craft. Development continued after the war, helped by the emergence of the *helicopter* and also by the trend towards unified command structures throughout the service as a whole.

Commando, Royal Marine The name commando was adapted from Boer mounted groups active in the *Boer War*. Churchill, in early 1940, sought the formation of a mobile specialist corps of '*storm troopers*', and the commandos resulted from this proposal. Critics complained that the new élite force would attract the best men from other services, precipitating a decline in morale amongst these regular forces. The first commandos were drawn from Army and Royal Marine volunteers but they soon became an integral part of the latter force. The original units were based on 12 companies raised in 1940 for the Narvik operation in the *Norway* campaign, April–June. The commandos were controlled by Combined Operations, head of which was Sir Roger Keyes until October 1941, when *Mountbatten* took over until October 1943. Eventually the number of trained commandos reached 25,000 of whom 1,760 were killed in action during the war. The Americans based their *Rangers* on the commando concept. The Royal Marine Commandos continued to be active in the post-war period, especially in the multiple small-scale operations accompanying Britain's withdrawal from her Empire role. Examples included the *Malaysian–Indonesian* hostilities in Borneo, April 1963 to June 1966. No. 42 Royal Marine Commando was the last unit to leave *Aden*, November 1967. A valuable addition to the commando role was the special commando carrier: converted aircraft carriers able to house 16 helicopters and vehicles.

HMS 'Bulwark', the first vessel of this kind, completed her conversion in 1960, followed by HMS 'Fearless'.

Committee of Imperial Defence (CID) British politico-military body charged with presentation of military planning prior to final cabinet decision; established 1902 to supersede the previous Colonial Defence Committee. The latter, which had been revived in 1885, lacked an efficient secretariat and had inadequate powers; its deficiencies were fully revealed in the *Boer War*. The CID was strengthened by the recommendations of the *Esher* Committee, 1903. Lord Maurice Hankey, 1877–1962, the CID Secretary 1912–38, further increased the influence of this body after the *First World War*, although during the war itself Prime Minister Asquith abandoned the CID with disastrous results: a gap existed between the military and political leadership. The Salisbury Committee, reporting in November 1924, successfully recommended the creation of the *Chiefs of Staff* (COS) Sub-Committee, which gradually became the core of the CID system. A further development took place with the appointment of a Minister for the Co-ordination of Defence, charged with day-to-day supervision and control of the CID on behalf of the Prime Minister, thus giving the CID a full-time manager at Cabinet level. The first holder of this post was Lord Thomas Inskip, 1876–1947, who took up his position in 1936, succeeded in January 1939 by Lord Alfred Chatfield, 1873–1967. But by 1939 the

CID had declined in effectiveness; it had grown unwieldy, with 18 members; during 1938 a total of 876 people worked in one way or another on CID tasks. Prime Minister Neville Chamberlain attempted to introduce a more streamlined system: in April 1940 he appointed *Churchill* as Chairman of a new Ministerial Committee on Military Co-ordination, charging him with the direction of the Chiefs of Staff and daily military operations. With Churchill's appointment Chatfield resigned as Minister of Co-ordination of Defence and this office lapsed completely; so too did the CID. Churchill, becoming Prime Minister on 10 May, abandoned the newly formed Ministerial Committee on Military Co-ordination in favour of his *Defence Committee*, which he, as Defence Minister, also chaired.

Condor Legion, the Name given to German forces participating in the *Spanish Civil War* (Map 11) to aid the Nationalists under *Franco*. The Legion eventually numbered about 6,000 troops and pilots and just over 60,000 non-combatants. Formed in November 1936, the force was commanded by General Hugo Sperrle, later commander of the *Luftwaffe*'s Air Fleet Three in the Battle of *Britain*. His Chief of Staff was the then Colonel Wolfram von Richthofen, cousin of Manfred von Richthofen, the First World War air ace. Wolfram von Richthofen was a keen student of the air theorist *Douhet* and convinced of the power of the bomber in destroying the morale of the opposing forces:

such a conviction probably lay behind the raid on *Guernica*, April 1937, undertaken by the Condor Legion. During the war German pilots flew about 200 aircraft of all types, including Stuka dive-bombers; army and air officers who gained experience in Spain included the later Ritter von Thoma, a *blitzkrieg* expert, *Keitel*, *Jodl* and the fighter aces Adolf Galland and Werner Molders.

Congo, civil war in, 1960–4 Belgium granted independence to the Congo on 30 June 1960. The new nation, under Joseph Kasavubu as President and Patrice Lumumba as Prime Minister, fell into chaos. Moise Tshombe declared separate independence for the Katanga region on 11 July and sought increased Belgian assistance – about 8,000 Belgian troops were already in Katanga protecting manufacturing investments. Lumumba appealed for UN assistance; the first UN troops arrived 15 July; the number eventually rose to about 20,000 men. On 30 August Belgium declared that all her combat troops had departed, but the UN Secretary-General, Dag Hammerskjöld, insisted some remained. Lumumba was overthrown on 14 September by Colonel Joseph Mobutu, Army Chief of Staff; he escaped but was murdered on 9 February 1961. Tshombe was suspected of organizing this killing. Meanwhile, on 14 December, another revolt had broken out, this time at Stanleyville, led by Antoine Gizenga, but this dissident agreed on 1 August 1961 to become Vice-President in a new Congolese government, with Cyrilla Adoulla as Prime Minister. UN troops prepared to move against Katanga; the campaign began in September 1961. Hammerskjöld was killed in an air crash trying to arrange a ceasefire. At the end of 1962 UN troops defeated the Katangan rebels and Tshombe went into exile; UN troops withdrew from the Congo, with the last units departing on 30 June 1964. Chaos again erupted. In an effort to obtain unity the government named Tshombe as President on 9 July; Tshombe returned and organized forces to deal with the rebels, including mercenaries. During autumn 1964 the rebels made significant gains in central Congo helped by the supply of communist weapons, establishing a strong base at Stanleyville; they threatened to kill 2,000 white hostages at this town if Congolese troops approached. On 25–27 November Belgian paratroops, flown by US air units, made a surprise landing at Stanleyville, seized the town and rescued two-thirds of the hostages. Other hostages were massacred and African states opposed to Tshombe issued protests at the Belgian–US intervention. Other rescue plans were therefore abandoned. But the government managed to exert steadily increasing control during the next 12 months and greater stability was achieved by the assumption of power in November 1965 of Colonel Mobutu.

Congreve, Sir William, 1772–1828 British artillery officer and rocket specialist. Congreve transformed the rocket into a lethal weapon; he also designed a new gun for frigates in 1813. His rocket found use in Europe and the USA as a middle-range weapon between the infantry musket or rifle and the 12-pounder gun. Soon after 1800 Congreve introduced rockets to Western battlefields, first as incendiary weapons and later including explosive and shrapnel warheads. Their chief value was that one or two men could discharge missiles equivalent in power to those projected by the heaviest cannon of the day. Rockets were best fired in salvo, as at *Copenhagen*, 1807. Congreve served with *Wellington* in southern France in the closing stages of the *Peninsular War*, but his rockets failed to find favour with the British Commander: Wellington complained they were inaccurate and frightened the horses. Their inaccuracy was in fact notorious, and these weapons had a maximum effective range of only about 1,500 yards. Congreve rockets were used at *Leipzig*, 1813, *Waterloo*, 1815, and in the *American War of 1812*.

Conscription Forms of compulsory military service have long been evident: both the Romans and Greeks employed forced enlistment; in England the Anglo-Saxon fyrd comprised a military-type force created by levy; the Italian Ordinanza of 1506, composed by Niccolo Macchiavelli, established obligatory military service for all men between 18 and 30. But Revolutionary France introduced conscription on modern scale with the *Levée en masse*, 1793. This had wide-ranging implications on the art and practice of war. With full conscription, war was rendered far more total: armed hordes returned to the battlefield. One almost immediate effect was to decrease the value of the individual soldier's life – with more replacements available than ever before, the single soldier became expendable. *Napoleon* boasted in 1805 that he could afford to lose 30,000 men a month. Armies could be engaged in battle with less regard for casualties. In turn the system of campaigning seasons was affected: in previous times warfare had dwindled during the winter, because the small-size volunteer armies had to move into cantonments or even to disband, partly to avoid loss of life in the harsh weather and partly to allow new recruits to be obtained. Conscription led to the continuance of fighting throughout the year: deaths through exposure could be made up by fresh levies. With conscription, war also became more national – the *nation-in-arms* was being created. The wars of kings, fought often with *mercenaries*, were ending; the wars of peoples had begun. In the twentieth century this aspect had obvious appeal to socialist and communist doctrines. Friedrich Engels wrote in 1891: 'Contrary to appearance, compulsory military service surpasses general franchise as a democratic agency.' At the same time, conscription led to intense opposition within affected nations, on the grounds that domestic economy would be severely damaged through the absence of manpower and through the need to supply such huge armies, and also on the grounds of the infringements of human liberties. Conscription spread its influence on all sections of population: women, for example, were obliged to undertake previously excluded roles through the absence of the men, and this became especially noticeable in the *First World War*. Conscription therefore resulted in profound social, political and economic upheavals. Compulsory service could be expensive and unwieldy; the existence of the system in times of peace made it more difficult for the peace to endure in stable fashion, since nations remained equipped for war, with the economy and means of production geared to the maintenance of the large standing army – and with this situation always seen as a potential threat by rivals and neighbours. Conscription has often been opposed by regular soldiers themselves, who considered that the system diluted the professionalism of the army and diverted energy to the training of raw civilians. On the other hand the existence of a large standing army in peacetime, either through volunteers or enlisted men, often aroused suspicions that such a permanent force might become a rival to the central authority. This latter fear has been especially strong in Britain, following the trauma of the Civil War. Supporters of conscription argued that a semiprofessional standing army would be less likely to seize power and would be firmly rooted in the democracy; opposers of conscription, notably army officers, argued that the system allowed the infiltration of unwelcome and undesirable elements.

Yet reliance on volunteers raised in time of emergency could mean insufficient strength with which to oppose a conscripted enemy; in 1807 Britain could only find 35,000 men to fight the French in the *Peninsular War*. Britain continued to oppose the principle of conscription after the Napoleonic conflict, and such a system was not fully introduced until the Military Service Act of 27 January 1916, when unmarried men between 18 and 41 were made liable for call-up if not in a reserved occupation. Obligatory service was again abandoned in Britain at the end of the First World War, until the Military Training Act of May 1939 called up men for 6 months' training. Immediately after the outbreak of war the May 1939 Act was superseded by the National Service Act, affecting men of 20 and 21 years old and gradually extended as the war progressed: the National Service (No. 2) Act of December 1941 also conscripted unmarried women between the ages of 20 and 30, with these females being given a choice between the auxiliary services and industry. Two-year National Service for young males was continued after the war, but its end was announced by Defence Minister Duncan *Sandys* in 1957: the last call-ups were made in 1960. In his 1957 statement Sandys declared that 'Britain has a long and honourable tradition of voluntary service': the same tradition has existed in the USA, despite pressure from some advocates of conscription. Amongst the most influential of the latter was Alexander Hamilton, who argued in 1813 for 'the

necessity of obliging every citizen to be a soldier; this was the case with the Greeks and Romans, and must be that of every free State'. The American Militia Act of 1792 included provision for compulsory service, but on an extremely restricted local basis. Conscription was introduced during the US Civil War, with a Confederate system beginning in April 1862 and a Federal programme starting the following year, but the principle of a volunteer army soon returned. *Root*, US War Secretary 1899–1904, even abolished the 1792 Militia Act. The realities of total conflict in the First World War led to the US Selective Service Act of 19 May 1917, which helped swell the Army to over 4 million men for the country's intervention in the European struggle. Peace again ended the draft, but compulsory service returned with the Selective Service Act of 16 September 1941: this legislation, violently opposed by US isolationists and other anti-conscription groups, was only passed by the House of Representatives by one vote. The Act expired on 31 March 1947, only to be replaced by fresh legislation on 19 June 1948. The *Korean War* began on 25 June 1950; 5 days later President *Truman* signed a bill extending the Selective Service Act, yet opposition to compulsory service continued: on 4 March 1952 the House of Representatives defeated a proposed Bill for universal military training, and conscription fell out of favour again with the ending of the Korean hostilities in 1953 – only to become necessary once more with

Vietnam. The 2-year conscripts served for about 1 year in the Vietnam battle area. On 27 January 1973 Defense Secretary Melvin Laird announced plans to end the draft, with a target date set at 1 July, since which time the US Army and other services have relied on volunteers. Similar see-saw struggles have taken place in other countries over this controversial issue, even in France where the modern system was introduced. Compulsory service was ended by Louis XVIII upon the restoration of the French monarchy in 1815, but was reintroduced in 1818 although enforced as leniently as possible: Frenchmen were selected by ballot and even those chosen were allowed substitutes. The system was clearly inadequate and was strongly criticized by Marshal Niel when he became War Minister in 1867; conscription formed part of the debate following the shock of Prussia's victory over the Austrians at *Sadowa*, 1866. Nevertheless full-scale compulsory service in France was opposed not only on political grounds, but by many officers themselves. Niel's proposals were diluted, yet succeeded in strengthening the conscription system especially through the enlistment of men in the National Guard as a reserve for the main Army. Thereafter France experienced the same demand for conscripts in the two World Wars, and even retained short compulsory service after 1945 to the present. Prussia followed France's Napoleonic example, through reforms advocated by *Scharnhorst* and especially through the Defence Law of 3 September 1814

and the *Landwehr* Law of 21 November 1815. Both did much to create the Prussian nation-in-arms. The first bound every Prussian from the age of 20 to a 3-year service obligation with the Army, followed by 2 years with the reserve and then possible Landwehr service until the 40th year. The Landwehr covered all able-bodied men who had not been called up with their annual contingent. The system of compulsory service remained in being in Prussia, although in practice suffered decline during the years of peace until reforms introduced by *Roon* in 1867-8. The First World War again demanded a vast influx of German conscripts, but the compulsory system was banned by the *Versailles Treaty*, 1919. The dictates of the treaty were rejected by *Hitler* on 16 March 1935 when he issued a decree for universal military service. The demilitarization of Germany was announced in the allied Potsdam Agreement of 2 August 1945, but compulsory military service for West Germans was introduced in July 1956, and an obligatory 15-month period remains at present. Of the *NATO* countries, 5 rely entirely upon volunteers – the USA, Britain, Canada, Denmark and Luxembourg; the remainder have some system of conscription, ranging from 12 months in Belgium and France to 2 years in Greece and Portugal. All Warsaw Pact countries employ conscripted men.

Copenhagen, Battle of, April 1801
Napoleonic Wars (Map 1). In early 1801 Russia, Denmark and Sweden formed a Confederacy of the North to

protect their shipping from British claims and closed the Baltic to British trade. The British government reacted in March with the assembly of a 53-vessel fleet under Admiral Sir Hyde Parker. *Nelson* was second in command. The fleet arrived at the Skaw, the most northerly point of Denmark, on 19 March. Nelson urged immediate action but Parker hesitated: Danish guns covering the Elsinore Straits to Copenhagen were strong, and the Danes were technically neutral. The Danes rejected a British ultimatum on 22 March, but Parker only moved forward as far as the Kattegat, between the Skaw and Zealand Island upon which Copenhagen lies. Eventually Nelson persuaded him to advance and the British Fleet entered Elsinore Straits on the 30th. The passage proved easier than feared: Swedish guns on the opposite shore were still unprepared. Eighteen British ships of the line and 35 smaller vessels therefore anchored 5 miles south of Copenhagen. Parker believed the city's defences to be too formidable, but Nelson persuaded the Admiral to allow him to move forward with 12 ships: he made secret soundings of the Middle Ground shoals to the east of Copenhagen, passage of which would enable his ships to sweep with the current into the enemy fleet. The battle began on 2 April. Three British vessels went aground, but Nelson pressed on. The warships encountered heavy Danish fire and an exchange continued for nearly 4 hours. Parker, seeing the battle from a distance, flew the signal 'Cease Action',

which Nelson disregarded. Danish fire eventually slackened. Nelson, who would have had difficulty in withdrawing through the channel, bluffed the Danes by demanding an armistice; this was arranged. The Russians also signed a convention, 17 June, terminating hostilities.

Copenhagen, Battle of, September 1807 *Napoleonic Wars* (Map 1). The Treaty of Tilsit, July 1807, allowed *Napoleon* rule of virtually the whole of west and central Europe. Already, in 1806, Napoleon had decreed the closure of all Continental ports to British trade; after Tilsit it appeared likely he might take the further step of seizing Europe's remaining neutral fleets, those of Portugal and Denmark. George Canning, British Foreign Secretary, therefore ordered Denmark to place her fleet in British 'custody' until the end of the war; the Danes refused, and Britain dispatched a combined naval and army force under Admiral James Gambier and General Lord William Cathcart. British troops landed near Copenhagen on 16 August under Sir Arthur Wellesley (*Wellington*). Copenhagen refused to surrender, and on 2 September the British began bombarding the city, with the artillery barrage stiffened by *Congreve* rockets. The bombardment continued in sporadic fashion until the garrison surrendered on 5 September, after which the British took possession of the Danish fleet. The action helped further Wellesley's career; in turn Britain's belligerence increased Napoleon's resolve to block Portugal to

British trade, precipitating the *Peninsular War*.

Coral Sea, Battle of, May 1942

Second World War (Map 16), against *Japan*. The engagement opened a new era of naval warfare – a naval battle during which no surface warships sighted the enemy; the first large-scale *aircraft carrier* clash. It also marked the opening of the US naval offensive to revenge the disaster of *Pearl Harbor* the previous December. The US Carrier Fleet had been absent from Pearl Harbor and now 2 of these 3 carriers were sent with a task force under Admiral Frank Fletcher to block a Japanese Fleet moving from the central Pacific towards the Coral Sea. This Japanese Fleet, commanded by Rear-Admiral Tekeo Takagi, was built around the carriers 'Shokaku' and 'Zuikaku'. A secondary Japanese force, based on the small carrier 'Shoho', sailed north towards Takagi's main fleet. These Japanese warships were intended to cover a large assault force leaving Rabaul for an invasion of Port Moresby. Opposing aircraft sighted respective US and Japanese warships during the evening. Both sides flew air strikes against each other the following day: the 'Lexington' was sunk and the 'Yorktown' damaged; the 'Shokaku' was severely damaged. A squadron of US and Australian warships under Rear-Admiral J. O. Crace, RN, had meanwhile begun to move against the Japanese Invasion Fleet heading for Port Moresby and the Japanese commander at Rabaul, Vice-Admiral Shigeyoshi Inouye, called off the planned assault. Admiral *Yamamoto*, Combined Fleet Commander, believed both the 'Yorktown' and 'Lexington' had been sunk, and therefore pushed ahead with plans for the seizure of *Midway*.

Corbett, Sir Julian, 1854–1922

British naval historian. His books included 'Drake and the Tudor Navy', 1898; 'The Successors of Drake', 1900; 'The Campaign of Trafalgar', 1910; 'Principles of Maritime Strategy', 1911; and the 3-volume 'Naval Operations', 1920–3. Corbett discussed the main naval issues of his time, notably the Two-Power Standard – the principle that the British navy should equal the two strongest European navies combined. This principle contributed to the *naval race* spiral and to the British Dreadnought *battleship* programme. Another major issue was the controversy over whether the Royal Navy should be separate, as a 'fleet in being' propounded by *Mahan*, or should be designed primarily to co-operate with the army in defence against invasion. Respective schools of thought were termed 'Blue Water' and 'Bolt from the Blue'. Corbett, although avoiding extreme views, supported the First Sea Lord *Fisher* in his advocacy of the Dreadnought programme. Among Corbett's chief values was his attempt to co-ordinate strategic planning, stemming from his belief that great conquests were not the result of military accident but from the 'ordered combination of naval, military and diplomatic force'.

In this respect Corbett's writing was almost *Clausewitzian*.

Corps Before the *French Revolutionary* wars and the '*levée en masse*', armies were small enough to be controlled in their entirety, composed merely of regiments grouped in brigades. As armies became larger, the *division* was introduced as a grouping of brigades; as armies swelled even further, approaching 200,000 men, they had to be split into corps for administration and control. Each corps became a virtual army in itself. The first corps appeared in 1800, when *Moreau* brought together the 11 divisions of the French Army of the Rhine into 4 corps, each commanded by a general. *Napoleon* made full use of the 'corps d'armée' after 1804; *Wellington* lagged behind, only turning to such delegated formations in the closing stage of the war. A corps varied in manpower during the Napoleonic age from 20,000 to 75,000 soldiers, and a similar composition and variety in strength has continued.

Corunna, retreat to and battle of, December 1808–January 1809. The *Peninsular War* (Map 1). This campaign followed the desperate attempt by *Moore* to ease pressure on the Spanish allies by moving north from Lisbon to Salamanca, and thereafter further north to draw the French from Madrid. Retreat was inevitable for Moore's 17,000 men – outnumbered, inadequately supplied, without Spanish support. Withdrawal through the mountains of Galacia therefore began

from the Saldaña area on 25 December, hard pressed by French under *Soult* and *Napoleon*. The British fought rearguard actions, especially at the Esla, 29 December, and Lugo, 7–8 January, with cavalry led by Lord Paget and the Light Brigade under Sir Robert Craufurd displaying extreme bravery. Napoleon handed over direction of the pursuit to Soult on 1 January. Corunna was reached by the British on 11 January with about 5,000 men lost during the retreat. Moore hastily organized embarkation, but had to fight the delaying battle at Corunna on the 16th. The British repulsed Soult's 20,000 men; Moore was fatally wounded. The British returned in March under Sir Arthur Wellesley (*Wellington*).

Crazy Horse, 1849?–77 North American Indian, chief of the Oglala tribe of Sioux. Crazy Horse defeated General Custer's 7th Cavalry at *Little Big Horn*, 25 June 1876, and eluded all attempts to capture him until his village was finally located by Colonel Nelson Miles, 8 January 1877; the Indians were shelled and scattered. Many surrendered during the following weeks. Crazy Horse allowed himself to be arrested in September; he died on 8 September from a bayonet wound, caused attempting to resist being thrown into a cell.

Crete, fall of, May 1941 *Second World War* (Map 14). About 15,500 British and New Zealand troops were landed on Crete at the end of April following evacuation from *Greece*;

these were reinforced by 12,000 men from Egypt and, together with the 14,000-strong Greek garrison, were placed under the New Zealand General, Sir Bernard Freyberg. *Hitler* selected the island as a prime target for the élite 11th 'Fliegerkorps' *airborne* troops under General Kurt Student. Both Freyberg and the British Middle East Commander, *Wavell*, warned that the island would be difficult to defend against airborne attack. Before dawn on 20 May heavy aerial bombardment began, followed by a massed glider and parachute assault. Student ordered late on the 20th that all resources should be concentrated on the vital Maleme airstrip; during the 21st a German foothold was gained at this point. On the 23rd German troop transports began to land at Maleme, reaching a rate of 1 every 3 minutes, and a New Zealand counter-attack was repulsed. Freyberg cabled on the 26th that the position was hopeless. On the 27th Wavell ordered evacuation; this began on the night of the 28th and continued until the 31st. About 18,000 men were rescued; 9 British warships were sunk, 17 seriously damaged. German casualties were probably nearly 10,000. Hitler could claim victory, but insufficient airborne troops remained for an attack on *Malta*.

Crimean War, 1853–6 (Map 4) Relations between Russia and Turkey deteriorated over jurisdiction within the Holy Places of Turkish-ruled Jerusalem. France, protector of Catholic interests, was drawn in. British

fears were aroused of a Russian partition of the Turkish Empire: this would allow Russian command of the Bosporus and Dardanelles, with consequent danger to the British Imperial route to India. Turkey declared war on 4 October 1853, and an army under Omar Pasha defeated Russian forces at Oltenitza near the Danube on 4 November. A Turkish naval flotilla was destroyed at *Sinope* (Sinop) on the 30th. Russian forces under Marshal Ivan Paskievich invaded Turkey's Balkan provinces, besieging Silistria in March 1854, but this army withdrew after Austria joined a defensive alliance with Prussia against Russia on 20 April. Despite this withdrawal an Anglo-French expeditionary force prepared to attack the Russian naval base at Sebastopol in the Crimea, aimed at destroying Russian naval power in the Black Sea area. This expeditionary force had landed at Scutari in March–April and moved to Varna, 50 miles south-east of Silistria, 2 weeks before the Russians withdrew from the area. The British Army, which had not been involved in a European conflict since 1815, was soon shown to be outdated, resting on the laurels of *Waterloo*; this archaic aspect spread from the central administration in London to the command system, equipment and training of the ordinary soldiers. In joint command of the Anglo-French force were the French Marshal Armand J. L. de Saint-Arnaud, and British Major-General Lord *Raglan*; the latter, aged 66, was brave and honourable, but had never commanded men in the field. The supply system to the expeditionary force was completely inadequate and already, at Scutari and Varna, casualties from cholera were rising at an appalling rate. The weakened allied troops left Varna for Sebastopol in early September: no prior reconnaissance had been attempted, the point of debarkation had not been decided, and the troops were ill-equipped. Landings were eventually completed about 30 miles north of Sebastopol on 18 September and the allied force, 51,000 men, began their march on the Russian base. Opposing them were 36,500 Russian troops under Prince Menshikov. The two armies clashed at *Alma*, 20 September. The siege of Sebastopol opened in October, with the French contingent now commanded by General François Certain Canrobert following Saint-Arnaud's death from cholera on 29 September. On 25 October, Menshikov attempted to drive between the besieging lines and the British base at Balaklava: the Battle of *Balaklava*, followed by *Inkerman* on 5 November, left the Russians astride the only paved road from the port of Balaklava. Raglan insisted the siege must be maintained, rather than allowing the Army to be billeted near their supplies at Balaklava itself, although Raglan did warn the authorities in London that his troops were totally ill-equipped. Available tracks between the positions and the port of Balaklava became almost impassable; cholera raged in the British camp; without adequate clothing, the men froze to death; food was restricted to a semi-starvation diet. By February 1855 British strength had been reduced to about 12,000 men. Accounts of the misery being suffered by the troops were sent home by William Howard *Russell*, correspondent for the London 'Times'. The outcry led to the fall of Lord Aberdeen's government; it also resulted in the mission to the Crimea by Florence *Nightingale*. Allied assaults on Sebastopol continued in 1855, centring on the two principal Russian strong points, the Malakoff and the Redan. Raglan died in June and was succeeded by General Sir James Simpson; the French commander, Canrobert, resigned in April and was succeeded by General Aimable Jean Pelissier; Menshikov had been replaced by Prince Michael Gorchakov in February. Finally, on 8 September 1855, the allies launched a successful offensive: the French took Malakoff, and their fire from this position drove the Russians from the Redan. The Russians evacuated Sebastopol and the allies entered on 9 September. Preliminary peace conditions were agreed to at Vienna on 1 February 1856. Total casualties during the war were 256,000 Russians and 252,600 allies. Of these about 128,700 Russians died in combat and 70,000 allies; the rest died from other causes, mainly cholera. According to the 'Report of the Commission of Inquiry into the Supplies of the British Army in the Crimea', which appeared in late 1855, mortality was 35 per cent of the active strength of the British Army between 1 October 1854 and 30 April 1855, with this rate caused by 'over-work, exposure to wet and cold, improper food, insufficient clothing during part of the winter, insufficient shelter'. Sporadic reforms began: in June 1854 the Secretary of State for War was separated from that of the Colonies, thus giving a full-time Secretary of State for military affairs; in December 1854 supply and transport were transferred from the Treasury to the War Secretary; in February 1855 the post of Secretary-at-War was amalgamated with that of Secretary of War. Despite opposition from conservatives such as the Duke of *Cambridge*, Commander-in-Chief of the Army 1862–95, reforms were continued over the next decades, leading to *Cardwell*'s innovations.

Cronjé, Piet Arnoldus, 1840?–1911
Boer War (Map 7). General Cronjé saw action in the Transvaal insurrection (1st Boer War), 1880–1, and he forced the surrender of the Jameson raiders in 1896. He made one of the first moves in the Boer War, investing Mafeking on 13 October 1899. He opposed *Methuen* at the Modder River, 28 November, and defeated him at Magersfontein, 10 December. In February 1900 *Roberts* bypassed Cronjé's position at Magersfontein and threatened his communications, and the Boers were obliged to withdraw. *Kitchener* attacked frontally at Paardeberg Drift, 18 February, and was repulsed, but Roberts resumed command and organized the encirclement of the Boer positions; Cronjé refused to leave his wounded and surrendered on 27 February. He was imprisoned on St Helena until the end of the war, 1902.

Crook, George, 1829–90 US General. Commanded a Union cavalry division at Chattanooga, November 1864, in *American Civil War*; fought in *Wilderness* campaign, spring 1864, as an army corps commander. After war Crook fought the Indians in the far north-west, 1866–72, in Arizona against the Apaches, 1873, and in the Sioux War, 1876–7. During the latter he made a long, rapid march to surprise *Crazy Horse*'s winter camp on 17 March, but was forced to withdraw; he clashed with Crazy Horse again at the Battle of Rosebud, 17 June. Crook pulled back to reorganize and was therefore absent from the *Little Big Horn*. He revived the action on 25 November when he discovered and destroyed a large Indian camp; after Crazy Horse's surrender, 1877, Crook continued Indian fighting elsewhere, including operations against Apaches under Geronimo, 1882–95.

Cuba, 1952–75 A coup on 10 March 1952 brought to power the dictator Fulgencio Batista. On 26 July 1953 about 150 rebels under Fidel Castro attacked the Santiago de Cuba barracks; this operation, although unsuccessful, started the impetus of the Cuban Revolution, later known as the 'Movement of 26 July'. Eleven months later Castro was freed from prison under an amnesty and went into exile in the USA. On 2 December 1956 he landed on the coast of Cuba's Oriente province, but was attacked by Batista's troops; all but 12 of his 82 guerrillas were killed or captured. Castro escaped to the Sierra Maestra Mountains and with *Guevara* began to build up a powerful insurgent force. Operations increased during 1958 and on 5 November Castro began a major military campaign. Batista fled on 1 January 1959 and Castro became premier on 16 February. Tension rose between Cuba and the USA over the 'export' of Cuban revolutionary ideas to other Latin American states, over the nationalization of US-owned oil refineries on 29 June 1959, and over the question of the US naval base at Guantánamo. On 12 April 1961 about 1,200 anti-Castro Cubans, trained by the US Central Intelligence Agency, landed with US military supplies at the Bay of Pigs, Cuba; most were killed or captured within a few days. On 1 May 1961 Castro proclaimed Cuba a socialist nation. On 22 October 1962 President *Kennedy* demanded the withdrawal of Soviet missiles from the island; US forces were alerted as this 'missile crisis' developed, and Kennedy announced the right to quarantine Soviet shipments to Cuba, one of which was en route. On 27 October Kennedy rejected a Soviet counterproposal that the missiles would be withdrawn if US missiles were likewise removed from Turkey. Next day Khrushchev finally agreed to remove Soviet rockets. Cuba has, however, continued to encourage close military co-operation with the Soviet Union and in 1975 there were probably over 1,000 Soviet technicians on the island.

Cunningham, Sir Andrew Browne, 1st Viscount of Hyndhope, 1883-1963 British Admiral of the Fleet. Vice-Admiral commanding *battle-cruiser* squadron, 1937-8; appointed Admiral and C-in-C Mediterranean Fleet, 1 June 1939; disarmed the French squadron at Alexandria, July 1940, in the British attempt to save these vessels from sailing into German hands; in November 1940 he executed the successful raid against the Italian Fleet at *Taranto*, and he defeated Italian warships at Cape Matapan, March 1941; he evacuated British troops from *Greece*, then *Crete*, April-June 1941. Cunningham acted as chief of allied naval operations in the '*Torch*' invasion of French North Africa, November 1942; from December 1942 to February 1943 he was a member of the British Military Mission to Washington and the *Combined Chiefs of Staff*, returning to the Mediterranean to be allied naval C-in-C until October 1943. He then became First Sea Lord and Chief of Naval Staff, succeeding *Pound*, until 1946. His brother Sir Alan Cordon commanded British forces in Kenya and Somaliland in 1940, and the 8th Army on the *Desert Campaign* under Wavell, until November 1941 when he was replaced by General Neil Ritchie.

Cyprus, 1955-75 Agitation for independence for Cyprus, a British Crown colony since 1925, reached a climax in 1952. The independence movement was complicated by the strong support amongst the Greek population on the island for 'enosis' – union with Greece – bitterly opposed by the Turkish/Cypriot minority.

Conflict between Greek and Turkish sections broke out in 1952. British troops, eventually rising to a total of 30,000, were a prime target of these attacks. The Greek guerrilla leader was *Grivas*; full support to enosis was given by Archbishop Makarios, head of the Greek Orthodox Church on the island. Makarios was exiled to the Seychelles by the British in 1956, but the struggle continued. The British Governor, Sir John Harding, resigned in October 1957 and was succeeded by Sir Hugh Foot. A ceasfire was eventually arranged on 13 March 1959, following an agreement on 19 February: Cyprus was to be an independent republic, in which Turkish Cypriot rights would be protected. On 14 December 1959 Makarios was elected first President of Cyprus. Within a few months disturbances had once again broken out between the Greek and Turkish Cypriots, complicated by a split in the Greek Cypriot section: Grivas denounced the London agreement of February 1959, and Greek Cypriots were divided between supporters of Grivas and Makarios. Conflict between the Turkish and Greek communities increased in December 1963, following efforts by Makarios to reform the constitution. In March 1964 a UN *peacekeeping* force arrived in an effort to keep the two sections apart. This attempt continued with some success until 1974, despite threats by both Greece and Turkey to intervene directly on the island – Turkish air intervention did take place in August 1964, but the UN managed to avert full-scale war. The UN proved powerless in the face of a large Turkish invasion of Cyprus in 1974. On 15 July a coup staged with the active involvement of Greek officers in Cyprus forced Makarios to flee from the island; Turkey regarded this coup, and the subsequent nomination of former guerrilla Nicos Sampson as new President, to be a violation of a Treaty of Guarantee signed in 1960 to protect Turkish Cypriot interests. The Turkish government began to land forces on 20 July, building this invasion strength to about 40,000 men during August. Turkish troops ultimately occupied the northern third of Cyprus. The situation calmed after the return of Makarios later in the year, but a de facto partition had been obtained.

Czechoslovakia, crisis in, 1968

Opposition to the Czech political leader Antonin Novotný, in power since 1957, led to his overthrow in January 1968 and his replacement by the Slovak party leader Alexander Dubček. The country began a bold liberal programme 'to give communism a human face'. On the night of 20–1 August 1968, 40,000 invasion troops from the Soviet Union, East Germany, Poland, Bulgaria and Hungary occupied the Czech capital. NATO troups were alerted and Western nations issued strong protests; opposition also came from Romania and Yugoslavia. The Soviet Union allowed the Dubček régime to continue in nominal power until spring 1969, when pro-Soviet Czech politicians assumed control.

D

Dardanelles and Gallipoli, February 1915 to January 1916 *First World War.* On 1 January 1915 *Lloyd George*, then Chancellor of the Exchequer, drew attention to the increasing difficulties being faced by Russia and to the need for action in the Balkan area to rally Greece and Bulgaria to the allied cause. Next day a telegram from Moscow revealed that the Russian position in the Caucasus gave cause for concern in view of a Turkish enveloping movement; the Russian C-in-C, Grand Duke Nicholas, asked *Kitchener*, British War Secretary, if he could assist. On 3 January the First Sea Lord, *Fisher*, suggested to *Churchill*, First Lord of the Admiralty, that an operation should be launched with troops and that warships should force the Dardanelles Straits. On the 13th the War Cabinet approved a scheme based merely on the naval aspects of Fisher's proposal: the Admiralty was told to 'prepare for a naval expedition in February to bombard and take the Gallipoli peninsula' with Constantinople the ultimate objective. Fisher reacted strongly against this plan for a purely naval operation and threatened to resign on 28 January; also on the 28th the War Cabinet took the final

decision for the naval plan. Fisher was persuaded to stay, and in the event the scheme was almost immediately enlarged to include army action; on 16 February the War Cabinet considered the possibility of massing troops on the Greek island of Lemnos and in Egypt, ready to help in the Dardanelles if needed. These troops included the 29th Division, then in France, and this body of men became the focal point in the subsequent controversy over the relative needs of the Western Front or the Balkans. Advocates of operations in the latter area, led by Churchill and known as 'Easterners', did not deny the primary importance of the Western Front, but sought to break the trench deadlock, raise morale and stimulate the Russians. Kitchener swung disastrously between the two schools. An Anglo-French Fleet under Admiral Sackville Carden, RN, opened a long-range bombardment on the outer line of Turkish fortifications lining the narrow Dardanelle Straits; first shots were fired on 19 February. Not until 10 March did Kitchener consent to the 29th Division being used, and the delay proved serious. On 18 March the naval forces in the Straits switched their bombardment on to the second, inner line of Turkish fortifications, the outer line having been silenced on 25 February. By the afternoon of the 18th all Turkish guns had ceased to fire. But then 3 old battleships in the Anglo-French Fleet struck an undetected minefield and were sunk; others were disabled. Admiral John de Robeck, who had taken over command following the illness of Carden, called off the operation. At this moment the army expeditionary force, 78,000 men under General Ian Hamilton, was moving towards the Gallipoli peninsula just north of the opening to the Dardanelles Straits. The force had been hastily gathered and naval transports were inefficiently packed. Two main landing areas were planned: one by the 29th Division at Cape Helles at the tip of the Gallipoli peninsula; the second, an assault by the Australian and New Zealand Army Corps at Ari Burun, about 25 miles north up the peninsula coast. Opposing the landings were about 60,000 Turkish troops commanded by a German General, Liman von Sanders. The British landings at Cape Helles proved disastrous. Four assaults were attempted; one was repulsed completely; another was soon abandoned. Part of the 29th Division managed to advance towards the dominant hill feature, Achi Baba, but halted at the foot of the rise; this delay allowed the Turks to move in reinforcements. Farther north troops landed a mile from their planned assault point: determined advance threatened to slice the Turkish defences, but a junior Turkish divisional officer, Mustafa *Kemal*, secured the vital Chunuk Bair height and the attackers were obliged to dig in. Without the two critical features of Achi Baba and Chunuk Bair, both landings were doomed to failure. The handling of the situation had immediate repercussions in London: the need to send reinforcements caused increasing tensions; Fisher handed in his resignation on 15 May; the Asquith government fell to be replaced by a coalition, although with Asquith still Prime Minister; Churchill handed over the office of First Lord to Arthur Balfour. Another landing was made at Suvla Bay, north of the Anzac position, on 6 August; the 2 British divisions failed to move inland. Hamilton was replaced as commander by General Sir Charles Monro on 15 October. Troops suffered increasing casualties; Monro recommended evacuation, and this was approved on 23 November after a visit to the area by Kitchener. The last troops left on 8 January 1916. Allied casualties totalled over 250,000; the Turks lost a similar number, including about 21,000 through disease.

Davis, Jefferson, 1808–89 Confederate President in the *American Civil War* (Map 3). Graduated from West Point, 1828, and served on the frontier until 1835 when he resigned from the Army; elected to Congress, 1845, but resigned the following year to serve in the *American–Mexican War*; served as Secretary of War, 1853–7. On 18 February 1861 he was chosen by the provisional congress to be President of the Confederacy. Davis never wished to be President, and would probably never have been elected except for the political muddle. He advocated a defensive policy, based on hopes that the north would not fight and that European recognition would be forthcoming. The First Battle of *Bull Run* seemed to indicate that Union forces were weak; hopes still remained that foreign recognition of the Confederacy might persuade *Lincoln* to abandon the struggle. Davis therefore rejected demands for a major advance on Washington after *Bull Run* and the opportunity passed. Davis's chief failure was probably his inability to create a nation in the southern states: conflicting interests and war aims among the various factions resulted in a dissipation of effort. Davis was captured on 10 May 1865. He was imprisoned and indicted for treason, but was released on 14 May 1867.

Davout, Louis Nicolas, 1770–1823 French Marshal. Served under *Dumouriez* in Belgium, 1792, and under *Napoleon* in *Egypt*, 1798–9; Austerlitz (Map 1), 1805; commanded French troops at *Auerstedt*, 1806; attacked the Russian left at Preusich-*Eylau*, 1807; in 1809 joined with Napoleon to crush the Austrian left at Eggmühl in *Ratisbon* campaign; launched decisive attack on Austrian left at *Wagram*, July 1809; commanded the largest French corps in the invasion of *Russia*, 1812. His reconstituted corps was stationed at Hamburg in 1813 and 1814. Napoleon entrusted Davout with the defence of Paris during the 1815 *Waterloo* campaign, as Minister of War, although he would have been of far greater use in the field.

Dayan, Moshe, 1915– Israeli General and politician. Trained with Jewish underground in Palestine; imprisoned by British, 1939; fought for allies in Syria during *Second World War*, losing an eye in battle; Israeli Chief of Staff, 1953–7, introducing army improvements; displayed military skill during the Sinai campaign at the time of the *Suez* invasion, 1956. Dayan was appointed Defence Minister, June 1958; he organized the forces for, and the campaigns in, the Israeli *Six Day War*, 1967. He suffered loss of prestige after Israel's apparent unpreparedness at the start of renewed war in 1973; he resigned in 1974.

Defence Committee, British *Churchill* became both Prime Minister and Defence Minister on 10 May 1940. He had no Defence Ministry; instead he altered the existing Military Co-ordination Committe, an offshoot of the previous *Committee of Imperial Defence* (CID), splitting it into Defence Committee (Operations) and Defence Committee (Supply). Meetings dealing with operations were attended by the three Service Ministers and the *Chiefs of Staff*, plus other ministers involved with specific items. Meetings of the Supply section were attended by leading representatives of the Supply Ministry and by service departments immediately concerned.

The Defence Committee (Operations) acquired important influence during 1941, taking over much of the *War Cabinet* discussion on strategic matters; 52 meetings of this committee were held in 1940, 77 in 1941, falling to 20 in 1942, as Churchill began to deal more directly with the Chiefs of Staff. The Defence Committee was replaced by the Defence and Overseas Policy Committee under the reorganization announced in 1963, leading to the unified *Defence Ministry* in 1964.

Defense Department, US (Pentagon) Created in effect by President *Truman*'s National Security Act, 1947, although titled the National Military Establishment until 1949. *Forrestal* was the first Secretary. The department was formed in the recognition that in future conflicts the respective service combat forces would have to be employed under unified strategic direction. Thus operational direction was made the responsibility of the unified command reporting to the Secretary through the *Joint Chiefs of Staff*. The 1947 Act provided for a National Military Establishment comprising the Departments of the Army, Navy and Air Force and, in addition, the War Council, the JCS and other bodies. The Defense Secretary was to be a non-military person appointed by the President; he would be Chairman of the War Council, with other members of this body being the Secretaries of the Army, Navy and Air Force, and the Chiefs of Staff of the Army, Navy and Air Force.

Defence, Ministry, British The 1946 Labour government under Clement Attlee established the first Defence Ministry, with its principal task being to allot resources to the 3 services. A Conservative government White Paper of 1963 announced plans for a unified Defence Ministry, to come into existence on 1 April 1964, which would bring under one roof the existing Defence Ministry, Admiralty, War Office and RAF administration. The Board of the Admiralty, Army Council and Air Council, previously the highest decision-making bodies in their respective services, ceased to exist; instead a single Defence Council was established to formulate major policy. The Navy, General and Air Staffs were brought together in the Defence Staff and a Defence Operations Centre was established together with other unified bodies. The old political titles of First Lord of the Admiralty, Secretary for War and Secretary for Air were abolished; instead the political heads of the 3 services became ministers of state under an overall Secretary of State for Defence. The first holder of the latter appointment was Peter Thorneycroft, soon replaced by Denis *Healey*.

De Gaulle, Charles André Joseph Marie, 1890–1970 French General and President. Prisoner of war, 1916–18; Professor of Military History at St Cyr Military Academy, 1921; entered L'école Supérieure de Guerre, 1924. De Gaulle urged the development of mechanization in the French Army and explained his theories of armoured warfare in 'Le Fil de l'Epée', 1932; 'Vers l'Armée de Métier', 1934; 'La France et son Armée', 1938. French strategic thinking remained based on the static defence of the *Maginot Line*, and his ideas were more closely studied in Germany and Russia. In May 1940 De Gaulle commanded the 4th Motorized Division; he fought well in the attempt to stop the German drive on the Channel in the Battle of *France*, making three attacks against the German south flank from Laôn, 17–19 May. Lacking support, he had to pull back. On 5 June De Gaulle was appointed Under-Secretary of State for National Defence in Paul *Reynaud*'s short-lived Cabinet; he fled to England when France capitulated and headed the French National Committee, acting as C-in-C of the Free French Forces. He became President of the French Committee of National Liberation, 1943–4, and of the French provisional government after his return to Paris, 25 August 1944, until 1946. He returned to power in 1959 during the *Algerian* conflict, being President of the Fifth Republic until 1969.

Desert Campaign, North Africa, 1940–3 *Second World War* (Map 14). Italy declared war on Britain on 10 June 1940. British commander in the Middle East, based on Cairo, was General Sir Archibald *Wavell*; he had about 36,000 badly-equipped men in Egypt. Marshal Graziani, the Italian commander, had about 1 million men in Cyrenaica and Tripolitania. Wavell was constantly under pressure from elsewhere in his area – the Sudan,

Palestine and Transjordan, Cyprus, British Somaliland, Aden, Iraq and the Persian Gulf. Nevertheless, Wavell's subordinate, General Richard O'Connor, attacked on 11 June, taking Forts Maddalena and Capuzzo. But the Italians launched an offensive on 13 September; the British pulled back from Sidi Barrani, with Wavell gathering all available strength for a general advance. This began on 8 December with British forces taking Bardia at the beginning of January 1941. Troops had now to be taken from North Africa to help *Greece*, but *Tobruk* fell on 22 January and Benghazi at the beginning of February. In 2 months British divisions had advanced 500 miles, routing an army of 10 divisions. German troops under *Rommel* began to arrive to bolster the Italians; Rommel attacked on 31 March, taking the weakened British by surprise and seizing Benghazi, 4 April. O'Connor was captured on 6 April and the depleted British forces were unable to prevent Rommel advancing to Sollum. Tobruk nevertheless held out. Wavell attempted to counter-attack on 15 May and again on 14 June – operation Battleaxe – on the Capuzzo–Sollum front. Rommel's counter-attack on the 16th threatened to outflank the British forces; the latter withdrew. Wavell was replaced by *Auchinleck*. Both sides struggled to build up strength. Auchinleck attacked first with operation Crusader launched on 18 November 1941. General Sir Alan Cunningham, commander of the 8th Army, achieved initial surprise when Rommel, preoccupied with Tobruk, failed to react with sufficient speed. Hard fighting continued south-east of Tobruk until 7 December when Rommel was obliged to retreat to Agheila. Rommel resumed the offensive on 21 January 1942. He surprised the 8th Army, now under General N. M. Ritchie, and the British evacuated Benghazi on 28 January. In 17 days Rommel pushed the British almost to Tobruk. He attacked again on 26 May, sweeping south round the British line which stretched to Bir Hacheim. On 15 June the 8th Army began to retreat; Tobruk fell on the 21st. The 8th Army pulled back to Mersa Matruh and then to El Alamein only 60 miles from Alexandria. Auchinleck repulsed the enemy at the First Battle of El *Alamein*, beginning 1 July, but was relieved on 8 August by *Alexander* with *Montgomery* taking over 8th Army command. The Second Battle of El Alamein began on 23 October, after Rommel's attempt to break through at Alam al Halfa on 30 August had been repulsed. On 4 November Rommel started his retreat across the desert, and on 7 November the allied '*Torch*' landings took place in French North Africa. The German and Italian forces were now threatened from east and west. Tripoli fell to the 8th Army on 23 January 1943 and the enemy withdrew into Tunisia. The battle for *Tunisia* opened in February. About 620,000 German and Italian troops were killed or wounded during the 3-year struggle in the desert and in Tunisia; British losses totalled 220,000. Both sides had experienced the same difficulties of supply, especially at the moment of victory when they were advancing from their bases; this in turn resulted in the violent pendulum swings which characterized the campaign.

Dienbienphu, siege of, November 1953 to May 1954 *Indochina War* (Map 18). General Henri Navarre, French commander, hoped to lure communist troops under *Giap* into a trap, where they could be crushed by superior French fire power: this trap was set at the small village of Dienbienphu near the Vietnam–Laos border. Troops under General Christian de la Croix de Castries took up position at the end of November 1953, but it became clear that the Viet Minh enemy were embarking on a siege policy. French defences included an outer and inner ring of fortifications, each carefully co-ordinated with the others. Giap increased pressure during the second week of March 1954. On 13 March his men overran one of the outer positions, 'Beatrice', and on the 15th the French were forced to abandon nearby 'Gabrielle'. Two days later a third outer post, 'Anne-Marie', was also abandoned. Airstrips were put out of action; all supplies had to be dropped and over 20 per cent fell into enemy hands. Giap's troops dug a long trench, almost surrounding the French positions, from which other trenches were dug inwards towards the centre. From these vantage points the Viet Minh launched savage assaults on the French inner fortifications, starting 30 March. By 1 May almost the entire inner system had been taken;

after a pause for regrouping the last offensive began on the morning of 7 May; by noon the French Command HQ was taken. French casualties totalled over 7,000; prisoners numbered 11,000. Viet Minh casualties were over 20,000.

Dieppe, allied raid on, August 1942 *Second World War* (Map 13). Codenamed 'Rutter' then 'Jubilee', this raid on German-held Dieppe was primarily intended to soothe Soviet apprehensions over the lack of a 'Second Front' in Europe. About 6,100 troops took part in the raid, 19 August, nearly 5,000 of them Canadians. German units had been warned to expect attacks, especially at certain alert periods, one of which ended on the 19th. The operation aimed to effect landings on 8 beaches, after which installations would be destroyed before forces withdrew. Only the assault on the western flank achieved success; some progress was made in the east; in the centre resistance was far stiffer than expected. Casualties totalled 3,350, including 68 per cent of the Canadians. A total of 107 RAF aircraft were lost; enemy aircraft losses were 96 certain, 40 probable and 140 damaged. Churchill called the raid 'a mine of experience': it confirmed British views regarding German defensive capabilities along the Channel Coast and reinforced arguments with the USA over the dangers of a premature mass invasion attempt.

Dill, Sir John Greer, 1881–1944 British Field-Marshal. Entered Army 1901; served in final stage of *Boer War*, 1901–2; in *First World War*; Commander, 1st Army Corps in France, 1939; appointed Vice-Chief of the Imperial General Staff, 1940; replaced Field-Marshal Sir William Ironside as CIGS, 10 June 1940. Despite his conscientious and efficient handling of army affairs, and his quiet, unassuming personality, Dill failed to achieve a close working relationship with *Churchill*; he was replaced as CIGS by *Brooke*, December 1941. He became head of the British Military Mission to Washington and a member of the *Combined Chiefs of Staff*. He died on 4 November 1944 and was accorded the unique honour of being buried in the US Arlington National Cemetery; he was succeeded by Maitland *Wilson*.

Division First appearing in France during the eighteenth century, the divisional system became increasingly important during the *French Revolutionary* and *Napoleonic Wars*, when large armies had to be controlled. Carnot developed the division in 1794 into a section of the Army comprising all three arms – infantry, cavalry and artillery – and by 1796 the system had become universal in the French forces. *Napoleon*'s infantry division, over 6,000 men, consisted of 2–3 infantry brigades, each comprising 2 regiments, and 1 artillery brigade of 2 batteries. The British did not adopt the division until 1807. The larger *corps* structure, appearing in France in 1800, was a progression from the divisional system caused by the ever-growing size of the armies. By 1914 the normal Continental infantry division totalled about 16,000 men, organized in 2 infantry brigades of 4 three-battalion regiments, 1 artillery brigade and supporting units.

Doenitz, Karl, 1891– German Admiral. Joined German submarine service 1916, operating against British shipping in the *First World War* Battle of the *Atlantic*; he studied *submarine* warfare techniques between the World Wars, publishing his theories in 1939. Doenitz commanded German U-boats from 1939 to January 1943 and was responsible for the renewed Battle of the *Atlantic*. On 30 January 1943 he replaced *Raeder* as C-in-C of the German Navy, and soon afterwards stepped up his wolf-pack campaign, causing extensive damage before the allies swung the balance. Hitler nominated Doenitz as his successor, 29 April 1945. On 4 May he sent an emissary, Admiral Friedeburg, to Montgomery's HQ and surrendered German forces in the north-west and other areas. Doenitz, who wished to make peace with the Western allies whilst continuing to fight the Russians, was arrested on 23 May and sentenced to 10 years' imprisonment at the Nuremberg trials.

Dogger Bank, Battle of, January 1915 *First World War*. On 16 December 1914 German *battlecruisers* bombarded Scarborough, Hartlepool and Whitby on the English east coast, hoping to draw out and engage British naval forces. Another German sweep was made on 24 January 1915, but the Royal Navy obtained advance information through the recent capture of a German codebook. The British battlecruiser squadron, under *Beatty*, therefore steamed to intercept. Beatty's force consisted of 5 battlecruisers and a light cruiser squadron. The German force, under Hipper, comprised 3 battlecruisers and 1 armoured cruiser. The two fleets met at 7 a.m. on the 24th. Hipper withdrew, but 2 hours later the pursuing British warships fatally damaged the armoured cruiser 'Blücher' and the battlecruiser 'Seydlitz', Hipper's flagship. The Germans inflicted sufficient damage on Beatty's flagship, HMS 'Lion', to cause her to swerve out of line. Through signals confusion the remainder of the British squadron concentrated on the stricken 'Blücher', which sank, enabling the rest of Hipper's squadron to escape.

Dominican Republic, US intervention in; 1916–24; 1965 US Marines landed in May 1916, following internal disorder which threatened national bankruptcy; US officials took over fiscal affairs. Full military occupation began on 29 November and continued until 1924. A pro-US dictator, Rafael Leonidas Trujillo, came to power in 1930; he was assassinated, 30 May 1961, and internal disorders increased. The situation formed an example of US fears of a *Domino theory* scenario in Latin America, with the Dominican Republic following *Cuba*'s experience. Disorders were indeed fanned by Cuban involvement. A popular revolt, with rebels including junior officers under Colonel Francisco Denó, overthrew the conservative Cahral régime on 24 April 1965, and increased still further the US fears of 'another Castro'. US Marines landed on the 28th, with the number of US servicemen rising to about 20,000. This force remained 4 months. On 6 May a peace force created by the Organization of American States came into being, requested by the USA, and on 1 March 1966 the OAS supervised a presidential election which placed Joaquin Balaguer in power.

Domino theory Argument originally put forward by *Eisenhower* during his presidential administration, 1953–61, as a reason for US involvement in South-East Asia and especially *Vietnam*. This theory, strongly supported by *Dulles*, assumed that if South Vietnam fell to communism, then other countries in the area would topple one after the other – *Laos*, *Cambodia*, Thailand, Malaysia, even perhaps India. Each acquisition would give insurgents added encouragement and bases for the next. The so-called 'domino theory' received fresh attention each time communist successes were reported, for example after Pathet Lao victories in Laos, spring 1970; the notable North Vietnamese politician *Truong Chinh* insisted that the Vietnamese form of revolution could be exported. But Western critics of the theory argued that fears were exaggerated and that the theory was invalidated by historical examples: in 1945 Poland and Hungary became communist, but Finland did not, and

all the Balkan States became communist, but *Greece* and Turkey did not; the example of *Cuba* was not followed by other Latin American countries despite the efforts of *Guevara*. Nevertheless, communist victories in Vietnam in 1975, simultaneous with those in Laos and especially Cambodia, obviously revived the theory; in 1976 the principle was also applied by its supporters to the situation in Africa, following the success of communist forces in *Angola*.

Doolittle, James Harold, 1896– US General. Conceived, planned and led a dramatic raid on Tokyo, 18 April 1942, when 16 B-25s took off from the US carrier 'Hornet' and flew 800 miles to the Japanese capital and other cities. The attack had strong psychological value. Doolittle led the 12th Air Force in the '*Torch*' landings, French North Africa, November 1942, then commanded strategic air forces in long-range raids on Italy; he later commanded the US 8th Air Force against Germany and against Japan.

Douhet, Giulio, 1869–1930 Italian soldier and aviation theorist. Entered Italian Army as an artillery officer, rising to rank of Colonel; he became interested in air power in 1909. Douhet was court-martialled in late 1916 for criticizing the air policy of the Italian staff; the court-martial decision was formally repudiated in 1920, but Douhet had already been recalled to service, February 1918, as head of the Central Aeronautical Bureau; he was promoted General in 1921. Also in 1921 his first book on air power was published, 'Il Dominio dell'Aria'. He believed no defence against aircraft would be possible. Command of the air was therefore critical, with this weapon being directed against civilian rather than military targets; ground forces would merely adopt a defensive role. Douhet declared that if London were subjected to raids by 1,000 bombers, 50 areas of 500 metres in diameter could be devastated daily.

Dowding, Sir Hugh Caswall, 1st Baron Dowding, 1882–1970 British Air Chief Marshal. Transferred to *RFC* from Royal Artillery, 1914; AOC-in-C RAF Fighter Command, July 1936 to 25 November 1940; succeeded by Sholto Douglas. Dowding is rightly called the architect of victory in the Battle of *Britain*, through his efficient handling of slender resources. From November 1940 to 1941 he undertook a special mission to the USA; in 1941 he reviewed the RAF manpower establishment, and he retired in 1942.

Dresden, Battle of, August, 1813 *Napoleonic Wars* (Map 1). Dresden was the pivot for French operations against the Prussian, Austrian, Russian and Swedish allies, under the command of *Schwarzenberg*. These allied armies were deployed south of Berlin, following a policy of avoiding direct battle with *Napoleon* but attempting to strike at his subordinate commanders. Dresden, defended by a French corps under St Cyr, was attacked by

Schwarzenberg on 26 August with 150,000 men. Napoleon rushed to the city with reinforcements and repulsed the hesitant assault, then counter-attacked next day, 27 August, even though he had only about 70,000 men. The main French assault, under *Murat*, was directed against the allied left flank: this was separated from the Austrian centre by a ravine into which allied troops were driven with heavy losses. French pressure was simultaneously exerted on the allied centre and right. Schwarzenberg retreated, having suffered 38,000 casualties; French losses were about 10,000. But Dominique Vandamme, in charge of the French pursuit, was attacked by the allies at Kulm on 29 August, and his men suffered heavy casualties. Napoleon won a brilliant tactical victory at Dresden, yet allied pressure remained intense and this pressure would eventually lead to the Battle of *Leipzig*.

Dreyse, Johann von, 1787–1867 Prussian firearms inventor. The first man to interest the authorities in the manufacture of a self-contained cartridge, with bullet, powder and *percussion* cap in one packet. This cartridge was adopted by Prussia in 1827, fired initially from a muzzle-loaded gun. In 1837 Dreyse developed his 'needle-gun', the first true *breechloader*, using his cartridge. The firing pin was a long needle which detonated the fulminate powder at the base of the bullet when driven through the charge. In this way less gas escaped. The Dreyse gun was tested by the

Prussian authorities in 1841 and adopted in 1848; it proved its value in the *Austro-Prussian War*, 1866, and the *Franco-Prussian War*, 1870.

Dulles, John Foster, 1888–1959 US lawyer and statesman. Law counsellor to US commission in peace negotiations, 1918–19; US delegation adviser at UN Conference, San Francisco, 1945; member of US delegation to UN assembly meetings, 1947–50; consultant to Secretary of State, 1950–2; Secretary of State under Eisenhower, 1953–9, during the period of US and Russian acquisition of growing nuclear power. He caused consternation in 1955 when he declared that 'small tactical atomic weapons probably would be used if the US became involved in any major military action anywhere'. The theory of *massive retaliation* originated from a speech by Dulles, January 1954.

Dumouriez, Charles François, 1739–1823 French General. Appointed Foreign Minister, 1792, but took a field command in the autumn as Commander of the Army of the North; he joined forces with the Army of the Centre, commanded by General François Kellermann, to block the Prussian advance at Valmy, 20 September (Map 1). He then returned north and defeated the Austrians at *Jemappes*, 6 November. He attacked Austrian troops under Frederick Josias, Prince of Saxe-Coburg, at Neerwinden, 18 March 1793, but was repulsed. In April Dumouriez was falsely accused of treason; he lived in exile in Hamburg until 1804, when he accepted asylum in England.

Dunkirk, 1940 *Second World War* (Map 13). Contingency plans were drawn up by *Ramsay*, Flag Officer at Dover, for possible evacuation on 20 May, as the British Expeditionary Force and French troops were falling back in the Battle of *France*. The operation, 'Dynamo', was approved by the British *War Cabinet* on the evening of the 26th when *Gort*, BEF commander, was already withdrawing to the Channel ports; in London there were fears that only about 35,000 men would be saved. Evacuation began on the night of 27–28 May, when 11,000 troops were taken off. On 29 May the number of men rescued reached 40,000 and evacuation was proceeding at the rate of 2,000 an hour. Gort handed over command to *Brooke* on 31 May. 'Dynamo' ended on the night of 2 June. Troops saved totalled 338,226, of whom 225,000 were British. About 860 small boats were involved, of which 240 were sunk. Vast quantities of equipment were abandoned, including 90,000 rifles, 2,300 guns, 120,000 vehicles. No British troops remained on the beaches, although 40,000 French troops were left owing to late orders for French evacuation.

E

Egypt, campaigns in 1798–9; 1800–1; 1882 *French Revolutionary, Napoleonic* and British colonial Wars (Map 1). *Napoleon* landed near Alexandria with his 40,000-strong Army of the Orient in June 1798, and took Alexandria on 2 July; on 21 July he defeated Turkish troops under Ibrahim Bey and Murad Bey in the Battle of the Pyramids. Then, on 1 August, *Nelson* disrupted Napoleon's plans by destroying the French Fleet in the Battle of the *Nile*. The French Army in Egypt was isolated, and Turkish forces gathered in Syria and at Rhodes. Napoleon advanced into Syria and defeated the Turks at the battle of Mount Tabor, 17 April 1799, but was obliged to pull back into Egypt. The Turks struck to take advantage of his apparent weakness: on 15 July 18,000 Turks landed at Aboukir under Mustapha Pasha IV, vastly outnumbering Napoleon's available force of 6,000 men. Napoleon advanced, and pushed the enemy back to the sea in the Battle of Aboukir, 25 July, with vigorous attacks by *Lannes* and *Murat* piercing the Turkish defensive lines. Turkish losses were over 10,000, French about 900. Napoleon returned to France in August. On 8 March 1801 a British-Turkish force of 18,000 men landed at Aboukir under Sir Ralph Abercromby and pushed aside French opposition commanded by Friant; the allies then advanced inland to defeat the main French army under Jacques Menou near Alexandria on the 20th. About 3,000 French were killed or wounded, about 1,300 British, in this Second Battle of Aboukir (Alexandria). Abercromby, wounded in the fighting, died 8 days later. The allies took Cairo in July and Alexandria in August; Menou capitulated on 31 August. From 1863 to 1879 the country was ruled by Khedive Ismail, nominally a vassal of the Sultan of Turkey but enjoying virtual autonomy. Ismail fell into crippling debt, and in November 1875 was compelled to sell to Britain his shares in the Suez Canal Company: the canal had been completed in 1869. British and French influence over Ismail inflamed the growing nationalist movement, and violence broke out in 1882. British warships, commanded by Admiral Sir Frederick B. P. Seymour, bombarded Alexandria on 11 July after nationalists had massacred about 50 Europeans, and troops under *Wolseley* were landed at Ismailia. His 25,000-strong force defeated 38,000 nationalists under Ahmad Urabi in a surprise night attack at Tell el-Kebir, 13 September. This involvement precipitated British entanglement in neighbouring *Sudan*, 1883.

Eisenhower, Dwight David, 1890–1960 US General and 34th President. Commissioned in US infantry, 1915; assistant to the military adviser (*MacArthur*) in the Philippines, 1935–40; Chief of War Plans Division, War Department, February–June 1942, when he laid first plans for the invasion of north-west Europe – plans he eventually executed in the *Normandy* landings (Map 13); Commanding-General US Forces European Theatre, until November 1942, when he was appointed C-in-C Allied Forces North Africa for the '*Torch*' operation and subsequent *Tunisia* campaign (Map 14); on 20 January 1943 his title was elevated to Supreme Allied Commander, Mediterranean. In December 1943 Eisenhower was appointed Supreme Commander, Allied Forces Europe, after *Roosevelt* had considered *Marshall* was too indispensable for this post. Eisenhower was responsible for the *Normandy* operations in June 1944, subsequent operations in France, and the final invasion of *Germany*. He accepted unconditional surrender from the Germans, 7 May 1945. Eisenhower, an excellent organizer and managerial commander, succeeded Marshall as US Army Chief of Staff in late 1945, holding this position until 1948; he acted as Supreme Allied Commander Europe (SACEUR) 1950–2, and was US President 1953–61

after *Truman*, succeeded by *Kennedy*. A notable feature of his presidency was the formulation of the doctrine of *massive retaliation*, as propounded by his Secretary of State, *Dulles*.

Enfield The Royal Small Arms factory was established at Enfield Lock, Middlesex, England, in 1804, mainly assembling weapon parts received from private manufacturers. In early 1854, when arms contractors failed to deliver weapons urgently required for the Crimean War, a total of £315,000 was spent on land, equipment and buildings for the creation of a mechanized production unit. The new Enfield machinery first produced the Pattern 1853 *rifled* musket, known as the Enfield. By 1900 the factory had manufactured at least 50 different types of arms, and had given its name to the system of rifling used in the *Martini*-Enfield and *Lee*-Enfield weapons. Enfield arms continued to be famous, including the ·303 used by the British in the Second World War.

Ericsson, John, 1803–89 Swedish-born engineer. Built up his reputation in London, introducing the first *steam-powered* screw propeller, 1836; lived in the USA after 1839, and was responsible for much of the *Monitor* design, which used his propeller and revolving turret; he also improved heavy gun designs, invented an underwater dynamite gun, and attempted to develop an electric *torpedo*, 1873.

Esher, Lord Reginald Baliol, 1852–1930 British parliamentarian. Chairman of the Committee appointed by Prime Minister Balfour, 7 November 1903, as a result of inferior Army performance in the *Boer War*. Other members of the Esher Committee were the soldier Sir George Clarke and Admiral *Fisher*. The Committee reported on 11 January 1904; it recommended the formation of a Defence Committee; the replacement of the Commander-in-Chief post with that of the Chief of the General Staff; the placing of the Secretary of State for War on the same footing as the First Lord of the Admiralty; the creation of an Army Council. These most important recommendations led to the establishment of the modern War Office. The new Army Council was to provide a single body for policy questions, in place of the existing vague responsibilities of the War Secretary, C-in-C, Adjutant-General and Quartermaster-General. The Army Council pressed ahead with the formation of a permanent general *staff* and the Esher Committee gave added strength to the *Committee of Imperial Defence* (CID).

Explosives During the Napoleonic Wars the British and Prussian ratio of saltpetre to sulphur to charcoal was about 75:10:15; the French had a greater charcoal content, giving heavier smoke. The thick billowing smoke obscured vision and hindered army control: this situation remained until the advent of *smokeless powder* in the 1890s. Most of the common military explosives – TNT, tetryl, picric acid, PETN and cyclonite – were discovered in the nineteenth century, but were only utilized after the technique of detonating high explosives (HE) was better understood. *Nobel* was responsible for much of this increased knowledge. Picric acid (lyddite) was used in the Russo-Japanese War, 1904–5, but this explosive corroded shell casings and was soon replaced by TNT (trinitrotoluene). Amatol, a derivative of TNT containing added oxygen, was first used by the British in 1915.

Eylau, campaign and Battle of, **January–February 1807** *Napoleonic Wars* (Map 1). Only a few Prussian units remained intact after *Napoleon*'s shattering *Auerstedt* campaign, October 1806; these merged with Russian forces under Count Levin A. Bennigsen deployed around Pultusk. Napoleon moved east with 80,000 men, but after a brief clash on 26 December both sides went into winter quarters. The Russians suddenly resumed the offensive in the first days of 1807, attacking French troops under *Ney* south of Königsberg (Kaliningrad) and forcing the enemy to withdraw. Napoleon counter-attacked at Preussisch-Eylau 8 February, even though the 2 corps under Ney and *Davout* had still to arrive. Napoleon therefore had only 50,000 troops against the Russian strength of 67,000, and Bennigsen expected the arrival of 10,000 Prussians under General Anton Lestocq and *Scharnhorst*. The Russians checked Napoleon's initial assault, but then Davout reached the battlefield – amidst a blinding snowstorm –

and turned the Russian left flank. He in turn was blocked by the arrival of the Prussians, and neither side could gain an advantage. Bennigsen withdrew, having suffered about 25,000 casualties. French losses totalled over 18,000. Both sides returned to winter quarters; the spring campaign would lead to *Friedland* in June.

F

Falkenhayn, Erich von, 1861–1922
German General. Replaced *Moltke* as
Chief of Staff, 14 September 1914, and
ordered extension of German line
northwards, thus precipitating the
Race to the Sea; he believed that the
war must be won in the west, rather
than devoting all effort to the defeat of
Russia as urged by *Hindenburg* and
Ludendorff, but the Germans nevertheless moved on to the defensive in
the west during 1915. The main effort
swung back to the west in 1916, with
Falkenhayn's offensive at *Verdun*. The
German commander aimed at a war of
attrition against France, but was
thwarted by the need to shift resources
from this battle to check the allies at
the *Somme*. Failure resulted in Falkenhayn's replacement by Hindenburg,
29 August 1916, after which he commanded forces in Romania, 1916, and
in the Caucasus and Palestine, 1917–
18.

**Falkland Islands, Battle of, Dec-
ember 1914** *First World War*.
British shipping in the Indian and
Pacific Oceans was threatened by the
German China Squadron, lying off
Chile and commanded by Admiral
Maximilian von Spee. In October a
British squadron under Admiral Sir
Christopher Cradock began searching
for the enemy, and the 2 squadrons
met off Coronel, Chile, 1 November.
Spee used superior fire power to batter
the British at long range, sinking 2
heavy cruisers; the rest pulled away.
The British Admiralty dispatched the
battlecruisers 'Invincible' and 'Inflexible', fearing Spee would sail
round the Horn to raid the Atlantic.
These British warships were joined by
4 other cruisers, and the British force,
commanded by Admiral Sir F. D.
Sturdee, steamed into the Falkland
Islands early in December to refuel.
Spee, unaware of their presence, raided
the base on 8 December. The Germans tried to escape when confronted
by the British warships but were pursued and engaged. Only the light
cruiser 'Dresden' survived out of 5
warships; up to 1,800 German sailors
were lost.

Farragut, David Glasgow, 1810–70
US Admiral. Commanded the sloop
'Saratoga' in the *American–Mexican
War*, 1846–8; joined the Union Navy
at the outbreak of the *American Civil
War* (Map 3), and commanded the
West Gulf Blockading Squadron. He

advanced past Forts Jackson and St Philip, 24 April 1862, sinking 9 out of 11 Confederate gunboats, and he took New Orleans on the 25th. In March 1863 he steamed upriver past Port Hudson and proceeded to sweep Confederate shipping off the central Mississippi. In 1864 Farragut returned to the Gulf. Ordered to capture Forts Morgan and Gaines, the defences of Mobile Bay, he led his flagship 'Hartford' into the thick Confederate minefield on 5 August. His ships broke through and battered the Confederate *ironclad* 'Tennessee' into submission. The forts surrendered; Farragut's victory virtually ended Confederate blockade running in the Gulf.

Fatah, Al Started action, 1965, as a revolutionary movement to recover Israeli-occupied Palestine for the Arabs, eclipsing older groups such as the Palestinian Liberation Organization. Fatah received a massive increase of support after the Arab defeat in the *Israeli–Arab War* of 1967, offering an attractive alternative to unprofitable conventional struggle. Moreover, unlike a conventional war, guerrilla fighting did not need complete harmony among various Arab countries – which was difficult to achieve. Fatah declared that as long as Israel existed, there would be no Arab unity, because Israel's existence was the cause of disunity. Fatah was therefore given considerable freedom of action. Reaction occurred in autumn 1969 when Jordan attempted to move against widespread Fatah presence; a compromise was reached. Since then Fatah has achieved even greater recognition, with the leader of the organization, Yasser Arafat, winning prestige through his address to the UN General Assembly, 1974.

Finnish–Russian War, 1939–40 *Stalin*, anxious to regain Baltic territories lost after the First World War, invaded Finland on 30 November 1939. Russian forces crossed the border from east and south-east, totalling almost 1 million men, while amphibious operations were launched across the Gulf of Finland. Finnish forces, numbering about 300,000, were commanded by the elderly but brilliant *Mannerheim*. The main Russian offensive was aimed at Finnish defensive positions in the Karelian Isthmus, the so-called 'Mannerheim' Line built in the First World War. The Finns fought well, despite equipment shortages: Russian attacks were thrown back with heavy casualties. Finland requested help from Britain on 13 December, and a limited number of aircraft arrived. Meanwhile an advance by the Russian 163rd Division in east Finland was encircled by the Finnish 9th at Suomussalmi, and another Russian division, the 44th, was surrounded when attempting to bring relief. Both were annihilated in the period 27 December to 9 January 1940, with Russian losses of over 27,500. Finnish casualties were under 3,000, but the Finns remained outnumbered and ill-armed. The British War Cabinet agreed on 25 December to send further aid, and late in January plans were discussed for military intervention using British and French 'volunteers'. On 1 February 54 Russian divisions began to exert heavy pressure on the Mannerheim Line, and despite terrible casualties a breakthrough was achieved near Summa on 13 February; by 1 March the Finns had been pushed back to Viipuri. Finland capitulated on 12 March; British forces assembling to help Finland were instead used in the *Norway* campaign. Russia's weak performances inflated *Hitler*'s hopes for a successful invasion of *Russia*, 1941.

First World War, 1914-18, general

(Maps 9, 10). A conflict dominated by, in *Fuller*'s words, the combination of 'bullet, spade and barbed wire'. Both the German modified *Schlieffen* Plan and the French *Plan XVII* relied upon a rapid, overwhelming offensive; military leaders – especially Schlieffen and *Moltke* in Germany and *Joffre* and *Foch* in France – believed the offence still to be superior to the defence; they failed to appreciate the lesson of the *Russo-Japanese War* that modern fire power, especially the *machine-gun*, favoured the attacked rather than the attacker. Neither side gained decisive advantage in the Battles of the *Frontiers*, and although the Anglo-French allies obtained victory at the *Marne* in early September, this proved insufficient to gain supremacy in the 'Race to the Sea'; by the end of 1914 the British Expeditionary Force (BEF) had been virtually annihilated at *Ypres*; trench stalemate began. By 1915 an average of 19,000 British soldiers alone were struck down each

month; by 1916 this had risen to 44,000, to 56,000 in 1917, and to 75,000 in 1918. The yearly battles were ghastly repeats of each other. The allied offensive in Artois and Champagne, January–March 1915, led to the Second Battle of *Ypres*, followed by renewed allied attacks in Artois and Champagne which included terrible French casualties at Vimy Ridge and British carnage at *Loos*. Failure at the latter resulted in a change in the British command, with *Haig* replacing *French*. The year 1916 saw two gigantic convulsions: the German offensive under *Falkenhayn* at *Verdun*, lasting from February to December, and the British offensive at the *Somme*, June–November. Total allied casualties were over 1,100,000, German almost as many. In early 1917 the allies gained additional strength: President *Wilson* declared war on Germany in April and the first US troops under *Pershing* were shipped to France in June. Meanwhile the British attacked at *Arras* in April, prior to the French *Nivelle* offensive; failure of the latter led to widespread mutiny in the French Army; the British successfully diverted German attention from this internal French collapse through the Battle of *Messines*, June, a preliminary to the Third Battle of *Ypres*, July–November, also called Passchendaele. The British attacked again in November, this time at *Cambrai*. Germany's *Hindenburg* and *Ludendorff* realized they must win a victory before US intervention smothered them. A series of offensives therefore began in March 1918: at the

Somme pushing to 75 miles from Paris; at *Lys-Aisne*, April–May; at Noyon-*Marne*, June–July. German troops were exhausted; US troops were arriving at the rate of 300,000 a month. The allies began their counter-attacks in July–August, centred on *Amiens*; the Americans displayed their strength at *St Mihiel*, September; the allies pushed forward against the *Hindenburg Line* in the final offensive. Germany sought an armistice on 6 October via *Wilson*: negotiations, spurred by revolution inside Germany and by a mutiny of the High Seas Fleet, began on 7 November. The armistice was signed on the 11th. In the east, the Germans had won their brilliant victory at *Tannenberg* and the Masurian Lakes in September 1914, but their Austrian allies had failed to defeat the Serbs; German troops were obliged to assist the Austrians in west Poland in late 1914 yet managed to push back the Russians in 1915; the Russians counter-attacked in 1916 with the *Brusilov* offensive. But internal unrest flared inside Russia – the *Russian Revolution* began in 1917. German pressure increased with the *Hutier* tactics. In December the Russians signed the armistice of Brest Litovsk. Other campaigns were in *Italy*, the *Middle East*, covering Egypt, Palestine and Arabia, and in *Mesopotamia*. None was decisive. Nor, contrary to hopes of advocates such as *Lloyd George* and *Churchill*, was the campaign in the *Dardanelles*. The trenches remained the centre of the holocaust, with both sides attempting a variety of means to achieve penetra-

tion. *Artillery* first seemed the answer. Massed bombardment enabled infantry to surge forward and occupy the enemy's foremost trenches in the 1915 battles. The defensive reply soon followed – deeper trenches both in the distance dug down into the ground and in area coverage. Rolling barrages were first tried on a large scale at the Somme, 1916, with the infantry advancing behind this moving bombardment to sweep further into the enemy trench area. But the infantry wallowed in the shell craters, and casualties per yard gained were still colossal. Another means used in the endeavour to break the defensive hold was *chemical warfare*. Other weapons arrived too late to be of decisive effect: the *tank*, first used in effective fashion at Cambrai, and the *aircraft* – already, by the end of the war, men like *Trenchard* were advocating the use of *strategic bombing* against Germany, and the idea of *airborne forces* had been raised. The tank, aircraft and airborne unit, combined with Hutier's infiltration methods, provided the base for future *blitzkrieg*. At sea the *submarine* appeared with almost devastating effect in the Battle of the *Atlantic*; the age of the large capital ship, the *battleship*, was almost at an end, and despite the frantic pre-war Anglo-German *naval race*, the use of the great fleets was confined mainly to threats and to *Jutland*. Nearly 5 million allied soldiers died in the First World War, including almost 1,400,000 French, 1,700,000 Russians, nearly 1 million from the British Empire and over 50,000 Americans; deaths for the central powers, totalling over 3 million, included more than 1,800,000 Germans.

Fisher, John Arbuthnot, 1st Baron Fisher of Kilverstone, 1841–1920 British Admiral. Served in China, 1859–60; in *Egypt*, 1882; member of *Esher* Committee, 1903–4; First Sea Lord 1904–10. He pushed forward the great *naval race* programmes of 1908 and 1909, advanced the size of naval guns from 12 to 13·5 inches, developed *submarines* on the one hand and the huge Dreadnought *battleships* on the other; he also introduced better naval education and established nucleus crews for reserve ships. Fisher resigned in early 1910 following opposition to some of his reforms, but *Churchill*, First Lord of the Admiralty from 1911, recalled Fisher to be First Sea Lord in November 1914, after *Battenburg* had resigned. Fisher worked well with Churchill until the *Dardanelles* operation in 1915, the failure of which led to his resignation, 15 May; succeeded by Sir Henry Jackson.

Fleurus, campaign and Battle of, June 1794 *French Revolutionary Wars* (Map 1). French fortunes were revived at the end of 1793 with the successes at Hondschoote, Menin and *Wattignies*; the effect of *Carnot*'s reorganization began to be felt. A renewed French offensive began on 18 May 1794 with a French victory over Austrian, Hanoverian and British troops under Frederick Josias, Prince of Saxe-Coburg, at Tourcoing. Five days later the opposing forces clashed at Tournai. Both retreated, but the French renewed pressure and forced the allies northwards. *Jourdan* merged his Army of the Moselle with that of General Pichegru's Army of the North, creating the 80,000-strong Army of the Sambre and Meuse, and invested Charleroi on 12 June. Saxe-Coburg moved south to relieve the town, unaware it had fallen on 25 June; battle took place at Fleurus on the 26th. Five allied columns struck the French, but strong counter-attacks against the allied right and centre reversed the balance. The allies retreated, 27 June; the French pursued, taking Brussels on 10 July and Antwerp on the 27th. The British contingent sailed home. Jourdan crossed the Roer and cleared the left bank of the Rhine. Farther south the newly formed Army of the Rhine and Moselle, under *Moreau*, suffered defeat at Kaiserslautern in September and withdrew to Saarbrücken, but Moreau resumed the offensive in October to force the Austrians and Prussians back over the Rhine and besiege Mainz. French successes led to the Treaty of Basel, April.

Flexible response Strategic policy evolved under President *Kennedy* and especially by *McNamara*, US Defense Secretary 1961–8. This policy envisaged the creation of military forces able to be used in a variety of ways to meet a variety of problems. The concept recognized the need for protection against guerrilla, conventional and nuclear war; the policy also involved tight civilian control over the use of armed forces, to ensure the correct response to the particular threat. Flexible response led to increased development of US anti-guerrilla forces – under Kennedy the US involvement in *Vietnam* was accelerated. At the other extreme, nuclear warfare, the strategy resulted in a move away from the *Eisenhower–Dulles* policy of *massive retaliation*. Instead of this effort to deter attack through the threat of overwhelming nuclear reply – a policy no longer feasible in view of Soviet nuclear development – there would be an attempt to introduce controlled nuclear response. In the late 1960s this policy was extended down to weapons of a nuclear tactical range.

Foch, Ferdinand, 1851–1929 French Marshal. Entered École de Guerre 1885; Professor of Strategy at this college, 1894, Commandant, 1907. At the outbreak of the *First World War* (Map 10) Foch was Commander of the 20th Corps, playing a decisive part in holding Nancy in August; he was appointed Commander of the newly-formed 9th Army in September, fighting at the *Marne* then aiding the British at *Ypres*. In 1915 he commanded the Army Group of the North, engaged in the Artois offensive and at the *Somme* in 1916. Foch became technical adviser to the French government and President of the Inter-Allied Council at Versailles, 1917; he was appointed Allied Co-ordinator for the Western Front, 26 March 1918 and Supreme Commander, 3 April. Foch had far-reaching influence before and during the First World War. In his 'Principles of War', 1903, he stated his belief in the supremacy of manoeuvre and advocated an offensive rather than defensive policy. He underestimated the power of modern firearms to strengthen the defence; he believed the moral factor in war to be more important. His beliefs, taken to their extreme, resulted in the French theory of 'l'offensive à l'outrance' – a blind doctrine of attack at all costs.

'Force de frappe' Title given to French nuclear forces, later changed to the less belligerent name of 'force de dissuasion'. The French nuclear programme, made public 1955, arose from doubts over the reliability of the US 'nuclear umbrella' protection and from the desire for greater French independence. Development up to early 1975 resulted in a nuclear strength of 9 squadrons of Mirage IVA bombers, each aircraft being able to carry an atomic bomb of 60 kilotons or more; 2 squadrons of intermediate range land-based ballistic missiles, and 2 submarines, each with 16 missiles.

Foreign Legion, French Founded 9 March 1831 as a means of using unemployed foreign soldiers in the newly acquired French territory of Algeria; Frenchmen have always been refused admittance. The Legion's fighting history began against Algerian dissidents; service outside North Africa soon followed: the Legion, about 5,000 men, fought in Spain from 1835 but was disbanded in 1838 having lost all but 500 men. Another Legion had already been created in 1835 for Algerian service. For the next 40 years troops served in Algeria, elsewhere in Africa, in the *Crimean War* where they showed especial bravery at *Alma* and *Inkerman*, in Italy in 1859, the *Franco-Prussian War*, and in Indochina, 1883–95. Nearly 43,000 légionnaires fought in Europe during the *First World War*, suffering 5,250 dead. During the *Second World War* the 13th Demi-Brigade of the Foreign Legion was created from escapees from Vichy France and from North African recruits: this unit fought in the Middle East, including against a Vichy France regiment of the Foreign Legion. The latter was dissolved after the conquest of Syria, and many of its members joined the 13th Demi-Brigade, which fought throughout the *Desert Campaign* – showing especial courage at Bir Hacheim, May 1942 – followed by the campaign in Italy and Germany. The Foreign Legion featured prominently in the *Indochina War*, 1945–54, during which Legion strength rose to 65,000. The tradition of mixed nationalities remained, with about 100 different nations represented at varying times. Recruiting was restricted after 1954, but rose again during the fighting in *Algeria*. With the abandonment of French North African possessions the Legion lost its original purpose, and the force has been reduced to bare existence level.

Foreign Legion, Spanish Organized in Spanish Morocco in September 1920 by Colonel José Millan Astray and his young Major, *Franco*. The latter acted as Deputy Commander, 1920–3, and Commander 1923–7. The Legion fought extensively in North Africa, and its success aided Franco's promotion to Brigadier-General, 1926. The force became a valuable weapon for Franco in the *Spanish Civil War*, 1936–9, and was expanded to 20 battalions. But it suffered heavily, losing almost half its officers and over a third of the enlisted men. It returned to Africa in 1939, and remained in Morocco until the independence of this territory in 1956, when the Legion was merged with the regular Spanish Army.

Forrest, Nathan Bedford, 1821–77 Confederate cavalry commander, *American Civil War* (Map 3). In November 1862 he began his cavalry raids against Union communications in north-west Tennessee. Forrest's troops fought as infantry in the Battle of Chickamauga, September 1863, but reverted to their mounted role in early 1864: Forrest took less than 3,000 men into the northern Mississippi region, repulsing 9,000 Union troops under General W. Smith at Okolona, 22 February. His campaign continued with deep raids into Kentucky during March–April, capturing Fort Pillow, 12 April. *Sherman* sent 3,400 cavalry, 2,000 infantry and 12 guns under General Samuel D. Sturgis to destroy Forrest, and the two sides met at Brice's Cross Road, 10 June. Forrest encircled and routed the Union troops. In early July General A. J. Smith led 14,000 Union soldiers against him; battle took place at Tupelo, 14–15 July, and this time Forrest was repulsed, suffering over 1,300 casualties; he himself was wounded. He recovered to strike against the Union defences at Memphis, 21 August. Following the seizure of *Atlanta* by Sherman in late August, Forrest moved north-east to attack Union communications. He again distinguished himself through his vigorous raiding during the *Nashville* campaign, November–December 1864, although Union troops won final victory at Nashville, 15–16 December. Forrest suffered final defeat at Selma, 2 April 1865.

Forrestal, James Vincent, 1892–1949 US politician. Under-Secretary of the Navy, 1940–4, Secretary 1944–7; became first US Secretary of Defense, 1947, under *Truman*, when *Defense Department* created by the National Security Act; succeeded by Louis A. Johnson, March 1949. Forrestal's death by suicide led to doubts over the state of his mental health during the latter period of his life.

France, Battle and fall of, May–June 1940 *Second World War* (Maps 12, 13). The 'phoney' or 'Twilight' war, existing since Germany's victorious *Poland* campaign in September 1939, was abruptly ended by the German invasion of the Low Countries, 10 May 1940. The allies, and especially the British, had wanted to assume forward defensive positions in Belgium: requests for such a movement were refused by the Belgians on the grounds that this would violate the country's neutrality and would per-

haps provoke the Germans. Not until 22 April did a Supreme War Council meeting in Paris decide that Anglo-French forces should advance into Belgium in the event of German invasion, with or without Belgian permission. On 10 May, the allied armies were still deployed in three army groups behind the French frontier. The 1st Army Group, under General Gaston Billottee and including the British Expeditionary Force under *Gort*, stretched from the Channel to Montmedy; the 2nd Army Group, under General Prételat, extended behind the *Maginot Line* from Montmedy to Epinal; General Besson's small 3rd Army Group continued the Maginot Line defences down behind the Rhine. Commanding these allied forces in the north-east was General A. J. Georges, with General Maurice *Gamelin* the allied C-in-C. Allied strength totalled 103 divisions, including the BEF's 10 divisions; the allies had about 3,600 tanks and over 1,600 combat aircraft. The German Army Group B, under General Fedor von Bock, stretched from the North Sea to Aachen; Army Group B, under *Rundstedt*, was concentrated on a narrow front between Aachen and Sarrebourg; Army Group C, under *Leeb*, lay opposite eastern Lorraine and the Rhine. The Germans had fewer tanks than the allies, about 2,574, but they were mostly concentrated in the Army Group A sector. German combat aircraft totalled about 3,500. Overall command was exercised by *Hitler* with *Keitel* his Chief of Staff. The offensive began at about 4 a.m. on 10 May;

Army Groups A and B stabbed across the Belgian, Dutch and Luxembourg borders. The allies attempted to move into Belgium, but could advance no farther than the River Dyle. *Blitzkrieg* pressure from Bock's Army Group B brought the surrender of the Dutch Army on 14 May. The Belgian Army fell back to join the BEF and 1st French Army at the Dyle. The German plan was actually a revised version of the *Schlieffen* concept; instead of maximum pressure being maintained in the north through Belgium and Holland, as the allies expected, the main thrust would now come farther south by the concentrated power of Rundstedt's Army Group A. This hammer blow hit through the Ardennes region towards Sedan; the allies had considered the countryside in this area to be too difficult for tanks. Rundstedt's leading units – the panzer group led by Kleist – reached the Meuse on 12 May; *Guderian*'s corps crossed at Sedan on the 13th; the Germans began to sweep north to trap Anglo-French troops in the Belgium– north France region. Efforts to stop this drive, for example *De Gaulle*'s attacks at Lâon, were brushed aside. Meanwhile, the Anglo-French forces in Belgium were coming under increasing pressure from Army Group B. Gamelin was replaced by Weygand on 19 May. Arras fell to *Rommel*'s 7th Panzer Division on 21 May; on 22 and 23 May Guderian took Boulogne and isolated Calais, but on the 26th the allies gained some respite through Hitler's inexplicable order to Guderian to halt the advance. The order was

rescinded on the 28th; on that day the Belgian Army ceased to fight and the British evacuation from *Dunkirk* began. This withdrawal continued until 4 June. The second phase of the offensive began on 5 June. Bock's Army Group B opened the way, striking for the Somme and reaching the Seine on the 9th. Also on the 9th the main German attack was launched by Rundstedt's Army Group A. The French government abandoned Paris on the 10th; Prime Minister *Reynaud* resigned on the 17th; his successor, *Pétain*, signed an armistice on the 21st; hostilities ended on the 25th. Hitler began planning for an invasion of Britain, operation '*Sealion*'.

Franco, Bahamonde Francisco, 1892–1975 Spanish General and dictator. Fought in Spanish Morocco, 1912–17, and continued to serve in this territory, helping to form the *Spanish Foreign Legion*, 1920; commanded this Legion, 1923–7; subsequent appointments included C-in-C Moroccan Army, 1934; Chief of Spanish General Staff, 1935; C-in-C Canary Isles, 1936. Franco was dispatched to this latter post partly to remove him from the Spanish domestic front in view of the General's political views. But in July 1936, at the outbreak of the *Spanish Civil War* (Map 11), Franco flew to Morocco to organize the transport of légionnaires and Moorish troops to fight on the nationalist side in Spain. He struck northwards from southern Spain in late July. Franco became insurgent leader in October 1936, and his gradual control over the country led to the surrender of Madrid and Valencia, 28 March 1939, whereupon he assumed dictatorial powers which he afterwards maintained. He adopted a neutral policy in the Second World War, but his possible entry on the German side remained a constant source of allied anxiety, and some Spanish troops fought in Russia, 1941. The Spanish monarchy was restored on Franco's death, with King Juan Carlos taking the throne.

Franco-Prussian War, 1870-1 (Map 6) The conflict confirmed *Moltke*'s brilliance as Prussian Chief of General Staff, already indicated with his handling of forces in the *Austro-Prussian War*, 1866. Moltke's use of modern developments such as *railways* provided his armies with new mobility; French war plans were smothered. The French relied upon their *chassepot* rifles to obtain victory over the Prussian needle-guns developed by *Dreyse*. But French muzzle-loading *artillery* was inferior to Prussian *breech-loaders* produced by *Krupp*, and this advantage more than outbalanced the new French infantry weapon. French tactics were based on the longer chassepot range, with troops awaiting the enemy in defensive positions; Moltke answered by holding the French with frontal fire then overwhelming them from the flanks: above all, the Prussians battered the French with well-directed artillery fire from beyond chassepot range. Hostilities began in July 1870. Three well-equipped Prussian armies, 475,000

men, immediately thrust over the frontier aiming at the destruction of French armies in the field followed by the seizure of Paris. Initial manoeuvring engagements took place at Fröschwiller (Worth) and Spichern, 6 August, Borny, 15 August, Mars-la-Tour, Vionville and Rezonville, 16 August, and Gravelotte-St Privat on the 18th. The French were pressed against the Belgian frontier; destruction of the main French forces was achieved at the great Battle of *Sedan*, 1 September. French mistakes at the battle were compounded by command confusion when argument arose as to whether Auguste Ducrot or Emmanuel Wimpffen should replace the injured *MacMahon* as Commander. The siege of *Paris* began on the 19th. Yet the French refused to submit and resistance continued under Leon Gambetta and General Jules Trochu. The bombardment of Paris began on 5 January 1871; after desperate resistance at Belfort the main surviving French army under General Justin Clinchant retreated into Switzerland, 1 February; Paris capitulated on 28 January. A notable feature of French resistance was the part played by the irregular *franc-tireur*.

Francs-tireurs *Franco-Prussian War* (Map 6). On 21 September 1870 the French authorities issued instructions to irregular partisans fighting the Prussian invaders. These francs-tireurs resistance fighters were 'to harass the enemy ... To obstruct him in his requisitions ... Above all to carry out coups de main, to capture convoys, cut roads and railways, destroy bridges.' Companies were raised locally and eventually numbered 57,000 men, grouped into an auxiliary army under a decree issued on 14 October. A number of units were commanded by Giuseppe Garibaldi, the Italian patriot. These irregulars were most effective against communications, isolated detachments and patrols, operating at their best in difficult countryside especially in the Vosges region. Guerrilla operations and Prussian counter-moves increased during the winter of 1870 with mounting terror. *Moltke* denied belligerent rights to the partisans, burnt villages and ordered captives to be summarily shot.

Fredericksburg, campaign and Battle of, October–December 1862 *American Civil War* (Map 3). *Lee* withdrew south towards Fredericksburg after *Antietam*, September 1862; the Union Commander, *McClellan*, delayed pursuit until 5 October, and his Army of the Potomac continued to move slowly. *Lincoln* finally replaced McClellan with *Burnside*, despite the latter's reluctance. Lee's Confederate Army was now positioned on the Fredericksburg bank of the Rappahannock; Burnside launched two assaults on 13 December. One crossed the river and into Fredericksburg, only to meet devastating artillery and infantry fire from *Longstreet*'s corps when attempting to advance from the town: 14 successive Union charges were repulsed with the loss of about 6,000 men. Farther south *Jackson*'s

corps threw back the second Union assault. The Union Army withdrew on the 15th, leaving 12,500 casualties. Confederate losses were under 5,500. Burnside was replaced by *Hooker* on 26 January; the *Chancellorsville* campaign opened in April.

French, Sir John Denton Pinkstone, 1st Earl of Ypres, 1852–1925 British Field-Marshal. Served in Egypt, 1884–5, and in *Boer War* during which he relieved Kimberley, February 1900; CIGS, 1912–14. French commanded the British Expeditionary Force in France at the opening of the *First World War* (Map 10). His forces suffered heavily at Mons, 23 August 1914, in the Battle of the *Frontiers*, and he criticized the withdrawal of General Charles Lanrezac's French 5th Army from the Sambre during the battle. The BEF continued to fight well under his leadership, especially at Le Cateau, 25–27 August, and at the *Marne*, September, but weak relations with Lanrezac persisted. The BEF suffered further deplorable casualties, especially at *Ypres* and *Loos*. Blamed for failure at the latter, French was relieved on 17 December 1915 and replaced by *Haig*, becoming C-in-C in the United Kingdom.

French Revolutionary Wars, 1792–1800 (Map 1) European monarchs felt increasingly threatened as they watched the revolutionary upheaval in France: on 2 August 1791 Prussia's King Frederick William II signed a defensive alliance with Austria's

Leopold II, and Russia and Sweden agreed to raise contingents in an allied effort to restore Louis XVI to power. A full Austro-Prussian alliance was signed on 7 February 1792; troops began to move towards the French frontier. On 20 April the French Assembly declared war on Austria. The allied army of 80,000 men under Carl William, Duke of Brunswick, invaded France on 19 August but was thrown back at Valmy in September. French troops under General Custine besieged Mainz; *Dumouriez*, victor at Valmy, defeated the Austrians at *Jemappes* in November. King Louis was guillotined in January 1793. Then came a series of French reverses along the Rhine; the allies retook Mainz in August, and France appeared on the verge of collapse. Recovery was accomplished under *Carnot*'s reorganization, especially his development of the '*Levée en masse*'. A powerful new force had been created; victories at Hondschoote, Menin and *Wattignies* were the result. In the Mediterranean the siege of Toulon, undertaken by the British under *Hood*, was lifted with the help of young *Napoleon*. Another French victory came at *Fleurus*, June 1794. Prussia made peace with the Treaty of Basel, April 1795, so enabling the French to devote greater resources to the defeat of Austria. Napoleon surged to prominence with his victories over the Austrians in *Italy*, 1796–7; after the Treaty of Campo Formio, October 1797, only Britain remained as a major opponent. Napoleon turned to *Egypt* in 1798, but Britain remained unsubdued and the

young *Nelson*, who with *Jervis* had shattered the Spanish Fleet at *Cape St Vincent* in February 1797, destroyed the French Fleet at the Battle of the *Nile* in August 1798; Russia signed an alliance with Britain in December 1798, which Austria joined, and the War of the Second Coalition had begun. Napoleon rushed back to Paris. A Russian–Austrian Army under *Suvorov* entered *Italy* to defeat the French at Trebbia and Novi, June and August 1799. The allies failed to take full adantage; *Masséna* gained Switzerland for the French by his victory at Zurich in September. Apparent stalemate had been reached. But in November 1799 Napoleon became virtual dictator of France: the age of the *Napoleonic Wars* now began.

Friedland, campaign and Battle of, March–July 1807 *Napoleonic Wars* (Map 1). Opposing French and Russian Armies retired to winter quarters after *Eylau*, February 1807. *Napoleon* planned a spring offensive to start on 10 June. The Russian Commander, Count Levin Bennigsen, opened his offensive 5 days earlier, striking at French troops under Ney. Ney withdrew, and Napoleon counter-attacked in a brief clash at Reilsburg, 10 June. The Russians retreated north, with Napoleon attempting to manoeuvre his Army between Bennigsen and Prussian troops under General Anton Lestocq at Königsberg. Bennigsen, attempting to shatter opposition before Napoleon could arrive with the bulk of his Army, attacked a 17,000-strong French corps under *Lannes* at Friedland, 14 June.

The outnumbered French held firm, enabling Napoleon to rush to the battlefield, and within 2 hours of his arrival the Russians were driven back into their defences at Friedland. These proved untenable and the Russians retreated during the night, having suffered about 28,000 casualties. The French lost between 7,000 and 10,000 men. Napoleon advanced to occupy Tilsit, 19 June; the Russians asked for a truce, resulting in the Treaties of Tilsit, 7–9 July, which established Napoleon as the virtual ruler of western and central Europe.

Frontiers, Battles of, 1914 *First World War* (Map 10). Four great interlocking battles, at Lorraine, Ardennes, Charleroi (Sambre) and Mons, revealed the nature and degree of the new form of warfare created by mass production and technology. Following *Plan XVII*, the French 1st and 2nd Armies advanced into Lorraine on 14 August under Generals Auguste Dubail and Noël de Castelnau. *Moltke*, the German Commander, adhered to his own adaptation of the *Schlieffen* plan and wanted the French to commit themselves so much in this southern sector that they would be unable to switch forces north, where the main German thrust had begun. The Germans therefore undertook planned withdrawals in the south until it appeared on 20 August that the French might be preparing to disengage; the German 6th and 7th Armies thereupon turned and threw back the French to Nancy, defended by the French 20th Corps under *Foch*.

The French managed to hold a front along the line Nancy to Epinal, and would continue to do so until the Battle of the *Marne*, September. The Lorraine situation influenced the battle in the Ardennes immediately to the north. On 21 August the French 3rd and 4th Armies had launched their attack against the German centre in the Ardennes region. After 3 days of heavy fighting the French were beaten back to Verdun, Stenay and Sedan, unable to count upon support from the armies in Lorraine. Farther north, at Charleroi, the Germans thrust forward in their attempt to sweep into France. General von *Bülow*'s 2nd Army crossed the Sambre between Namur and Charleroi on 22–23 August, supported by the 3rd Army under General Max von Hausen. The offensive forced a gap between the French and the British. The French were driven south-west over the Meuse, despite fierce resistance from General Lanrezac's 5th Army. The latter's right wing was unprotected owing to the retreat of the French 4th Army in the Ardennes. Finally, this defeat at Charleroi, itself resulting from the defeat in the Ardennes, had a severe effect on the 70,000-strong British Expeditionary Force deployed in the far north under General *French*. *Joffre* had requested that the BEF should link with Lanrezac's 5th Army, which had now been pushed from the line; the British were left isolated along the Mons Canal, where they were attacked by General von Kluck's 1st Army, 160,000-strong and with 600 guns – twice as many guns as the

BEF possessed. The BEF blocked the German advance for 10 hours, but then had to retreat. The allies suffered about 300,000 casualties in the 4 main battles, and the withdrawals meant that the war would henceforth be fought on French soil. Yet the allies were still undefeated. The Battle of the Marne and the subsequent '*Race to the Sea*' were the results.

Fritsch, Baron Werner von, 1880–1939 German General. Succeeded Kurt von Hammerstein as Chief of the German Army Command in 1933, equivalent to Chief of Staff; he acquiesced, with War Minister *Blomberg*, in *Hitler*'s brutal methods of consolidating power, especially the 'Night of the Long Knives', 30 June 1934. Fritsch played a major part in the dismissal of Blomberg and was his most obvious successor. But Hitler and the SS Chief Heinrich Himmler avoided this choice by demanding Fritsch's resignation on the false charge of homosexuality. The resignations of both Blomberg and Fritsch were announced on 4 February 1938, with Hitler taking over Blomberg's appointment and *Brauchitsch* becoming Army Commander. Fritsch was killed in action before Warsaw, 22 September 1939; he probably committed suicide.

Fuller, John Frederick Charles, 1878–1966 British Colonel and military theorist. Served in Boer War and in the First World War, becoming Chief General Staff Officer in the Tank Corps, 1916–18. After the armistice Fuller struggled to convince

the military hierarchy of the need to develop the *tank*. His appointments included: Chief Instructor, Staff College Camberley, 1923–5; Personal Assistant to CIGS, 1927; Brigade Commander, India, 1928–30. He then resigned in view of the opposition to his outspoken ideas and through his need for increased opportunity to write. His publications included 'Tanks in the Great War', 1920; 'Foundations of the Science of War', 1926; 'On Future Warfare', 1928; 'Memoirs of an Unconventional Soldier', 1936; 'Lectures on Field Service Regulations', 1930 and 1937; 'Decisive Battles of the USA', 1942; 'Armament and History', 1946; 'War and Western Civilization', 1932; 'The Second World War', 1948; 'The Conduct of War', 1961. Fuller believed that the tragedy of the First World War could be prevented from happening again 'by half an inch of steel'. He insisted that the tank was a weapon in its own right, not merely a prop for the infantry; the infantry should instead be relegated to a minor role 'well in the rear, on some anti-tank hill-top', aircraft should operate in support of the tanks, in a similar relationship to cavalry and infantry in the past. Fuller forecast the strategy and even more the tactics of *blitzkrieg*, believing that linear war as in 1914–18 had been replaced by area war through tanks allowing penetration and breakthrough. Defence should be in depth, he claimed. But Fuller, although enlisting Liddell *Hart* as a supporter in 1925, failed to influence the authorities; indeed his most extreme views even made the task of other tank advocates more difficult by turning away potential supporters, especially his apparent plea for an all-tank army. Fuller's 1937 'Lectures on Field Service Regulations' was published in Britain in an edition of only 500 copies, compared with 30,000 copies in Germany and many thousands in Russia.

G

Gallipoli – see **Dardanelles**

Gamelin, Maurice Gustave, 1872–1958 French General. Chief of General Staff, 1931–5; Inspector-General, 1935–7; Vice-President of Higher Council of War, 1935–40; appointed allied Commander-in-Chief, September 1939. Gamelin was a strong supporter of the defensive, epitomized by the *Maginot Line*; he was unable to handle the deteriorating state of military affairs following the German offensive launched 10 May 1940, and he underestimated the German ability to drive through the Ardennes. Gamelin was replaced by Weygand, 19 May, to become Inspector-General; he was arrested by the Germans after the French defeat and liberated by the allied advance in 1945.

Garibaldi, Giuseppe, 1807–82 Italian patriot and soldier of fortune. Engaged in Italian struggle for freedom from Austrian domination, beginning with participation as a sailor in the Sardinian Revolution, 1832–4 (Map 1), fleeing after Austrian and French troops put down the insurrection; formed a volunteer army fighting in the Alps during the Italian War of Independence, 1848–9, with his red-shirted soldiers engaged in the Battle for Rome, 1849; he fled to America after the force had been obliged to retreat, and he lived on Staten Island as a naturalized US citizen. He took part in the defence of Montevideo against Uruguayan invaders under Fructuoso Rivera, 1850–1; returned to Italy, 1854, and commanded corps known as 'Cacciatori delle Alpi' in Sardinian Army, 1859. Thereafter Garibaldi became heavily involved in the further Italian struggles against Austrian rule, leading the forces of Piedmont (the kingdom of Sardinia). He organized an expedition of 1,000 men, his famous Redshirts, and sailed from Genoa on 5 May 1860 to land at Marsala, Sicily; he marched inland, rallying the inhabitants and defeating Neapolitan forces at Calatafimi on 15 May; he took Palermo on the 27th and won a further victory at Milazzo near Messina on 20 July. On 22 August he crossed to the Italian mainland, with British assistance, and marched on Naples, seizing this city against slight opposition on 7 September. His victory at Volturno, 26 October, played a major part in the eventual proclamation of a united

Kingdom of Italy, 17 March 1861, but excluded from this unification were the papal territories around French-held Rome, and these now became Garibaldi's target. Repeated attempts by him to take Rome were thwarted, and the Italian government itself sent forces against his volunteers, leading to his defeat and capture at the battle of Aspromonte, 29 August 1862. Garibaldi, wounded in the battle, was soon released. He organized another expedition against Rome in 1867, but was again defeated. Garibaldi held a command in the French Army during the *Franco-Prussian War*, 1870–1, being given control of *francs-tireurs* in eastern France with his headquarters at Lyons, then Autun. The military effectiveness of the Garibaldians proved considerable, but these irregulars earned unpopularity through the contempt and violence with which they treated the Catholic Church establishments. Garibaldi, gouty and ageing, suffered a decline in his military abilities as the war dragged on; he failed to establish satisfactory liaison with General D. S. Bourbaki in opposition to the Prussian General Wilhelm Werder; the latter defeated Bourbaki at Belfort, January 1871, and Garibaldi's forces failed to halt the arrival of further Prussian reinforcements under General Edwin von Manteuffel. Garibaldi was elected Deputy for Rome in the Italian Parliament, 1874. His two sons, Menotti (1840–1903) and Ricciotti (1847–1924) were also soldiers, fighting in South America and in the French Army during the Franco-Prussian War. Ricciotti served in the Greek Army fighting the Turks, 1897, and organized the Garibaldi Legion to fight for France in the First World War. Other descendants also took up dramatic military careers.

Gatling, Richard Jordan, 1818–1903 US armaments inventor. Gatling invented the first successful *machine-gun*. The Gatling gun arose through the demands of the *American Civil War*, although the first model was designed as early as 1861 as a special weapon to defend specific objectives such as buildings and bridges. In late 1862 Gatling demonstrated his first working model; he worked on improvements during the next 30 years. The Gatling was accepted by the US Army in 1866 after it had been chambered for the ·50 calibre army rifle ammunition. The weapon had up to 10 barrels, revolving round a central axis. Ammunition was fed from a large magazine with each barrel being cranked round in turn. Main drawbacks were weight and clumsiness. But the Gatling encouraged further development, leading to the first truly successful portable machine-gun, the *Maxim*. Hand-operated, the Gatling fired 1,200 rounds per minute; it was later adapted for electric and gas propulsion, achieving a firing rate of 3,000 rounds per minute. It was made obsolete in 1911.

General Staff – see Staff

Germany, allied invasion of, January–April 1945 *Second World War* (Maps 12, 13). Russian armies in the east burst into action in early January, and *Zhukov*'s 1st White Russian Front reached the Oder near Kustrin on the last day of the month after a 300-mile advance. In the west, the allies counter-attacked against German gains in the *Ardennes* on 3 January; by the 16th the bulge had been eliminated. *Montgomery*'s 21st Army Group advanced into the Roermond area in the north; *Bradley*'s 12th Army Group pushed against the Upper Roer in the centre; the US 6th Army Group created from the '*Anvil*/Dragoon' force formed the southern end of the offensive, commanded by General Jacob Devers. On 7 March forward units of the US 1st Army, in Bradley's Group, found the Remagen bridge over the Rhine still standing; troops obtained a foothold on the east bank. On 22 March *Patton*'s 3rd Army in the 12th Army Group swept across the Rhine farther south, at Oppenheim; 24 hours later the British 2nd Army in Montgomery's Group crossed north of the Ruhr at Wesel. *Eisenhower* issued plans for the final phase. These would not be directed against Berlin. Instead, the main thrust would be made by Bradley's 12th Army Group farther south. Eisenhower, rightly, based his plans on military factors: he believed this move would destroy last-ditch Nazi resistance in the German-Austrian Alps. But the scheme aroused immediate opposition from the British *Chiefs of Staff*, who also objected to Eisenhower's transmission of the information direct to Stalin, 28 March, before the British had been consulted. The COS, like Eisenhower, based

their argument on military grounds: they considered Berlin to be the vital objective – once the capital had been taken German resistance would collapse. *Churchill* initially saw no farther than this argument; then on 1 April he added another powerful reason for the earliest possible advance on Berlin – to seize the capital before the Russians as a diplomatic counter in future dealings with the communists. The US *Joint Chiefs of Staff* supported Eisenhower, and the more southerly advance began, while Montgomery continued operations in the far north. In the east, the Red Armies suddenly streaked forward again: Zhukov's troops reached the outskirts of Berlin on 22 April. In the west, the British 2nd Army reached the Elbe on the 26th, and the US 12th Army Group units made contact with the Red Army at Torgau. *Hitler* committed suicide on 30 April; the Russians eliminated last resistance in Berlin on 2 May. German troops in the north surrendered to Montgomery, 5–7 May, and those farther south to Eisenhower on the 7th. Next day *Keitel* ratified the unconditional surrender in Berlin. The Second World War against Germany officially ended at midnight, 8–9 May.

Gettysburg, campaign and Battle of, June–July, 1853 *American Civil War* (Map 3). *Lee* advanced into the Shenandoah valley in early June 1863, attempting to retain Confederate initiative after *Chancellorsville*. His screening force, 10,000 cavalry under *Stuart*, was attacked by 12,000 Union cavalry under Major-General Alfred

Pleasanton at Brandy Station, 9 June, and the Confederates beat off the enemy in the largest purely cavalry action of the war. Lee pushed north with 76,000 men. The Union Commander, *Hooker*, followed with 115,000 men, but dissension in the Union High Command plus Hooker's own hesitation delayed pursuit. *Lincoln* accepted Hooker's resignation and appointed *Meade* to take command of the Army of the Potomac, 28 June. The conflict opened with a clash between Confederate infantry and Union cavalry near Gettysburg, 30 June, but the heavy fighting started on 1 July. Union positions were established on Cemetery Ridge and Culps Hill, ½ mile south of Gettysburg town. The Confederates held the town, and were spread along Seminary Ridge to the south-west; they also threatened to outflank the Union right but throughout the night of 1 July other Union regiments marched into position, facing west. Lee planned an envelopment of the Union left on 2 July, and this attack took place during the afternoon, pushing back the Union 3rd Corps from a peach orchard to the west of Cemetery Ridge. But farther north the Confederates failed in an attack on Culps Hill, aimed at the Union right, and the Union left was saved by vigorous action by an artillery brigade under Brigadier-General Warren. Lee attempted a direct penetration of the Union centre on Cemetery Ridge during the afternoon of 3 July: about 15,000 Confederates swarmed forward in 3 lines over a ½-mile front. The famous assault is known as 'Pickett's charge', although Major-General George Pickett was only 1 of 4 Divisional Commanders involved. Few Confederates reached the objective, and they were overwhelmed by Meade's reserves. Both sides had suffered heavily during the 3-day battle. Confederate casualties totalled over 28,000, Union troops about 23,000. But Lee's supply situation was critical, and he began to withdraw on the 4th. Meade hesitated and the Confederates escaped into Virginia. Yet Lee's repulse at Gettysburg marked the turning-point of the war.

Giap, Vo Nguyen, 1912– North Vietnamese General and politician. Joined the Tan Viet Cach Menh Dang (Revolutionary Party for a Great Vietnam) in 1926 while still a student at Hué; arrested 1930 but emerged from prison after only a few months; probably joined the Communist Party in 1937; escaped French moves against CP but his wife was imprisoned and died in captivity. Giap moved to south China, where his work led to the development of the Vietnam People's Army, VPA; operations against both the French and Japanese invaders began in December 1944. Giap entered Hanoi on 5 August 1945 with the Viet Minh leader *Ho Chi Minh*. He acted as Defence Minister and Army Commander when the *Indochina War* began in 1946. Giap revealed a close understanding of guerrilla doctrines as elaborated by *Mao Tse-tung*, notably the need to move through three stages: first, the clandestine period of preparations, second, open guerrilla warfare and third, the move from guerrilla to conventional forces for the last battle. Giap's handling of his forces in the guerrilla stage prevented the French from obtaining the initiative, but in spring 1951 he made the mistake of moving too early to the third, conventional, effort and his troops suffered heavily when they presented themselves as an easier target. Giap showed his flexibility by reverting to guerrilla warfare; he rebuilt strength and the climax came in November 1954 with the victorious conventional Battle of *Dienbienphu*. He then moved back into the clandestine preparatory stage for the continued struggle aimed at uniting North and South Vietnam in the *Vietnam* war, with Giap acting as Defence Minister in Hanoi. His principle responsibility lay in directing the operations of the regular North Vietnamese forces sent over the border to aid the local guerrillas, but he also supervised the training of these guerrillas and the two types of force worked together in close conjunction. He described his methods in documents translated into English as 'People's War, People's Army', 1962, and 'Big Victory, Great Task', 1968. Giap clearly aimed at the gradual erosion of US and South Vietnamese authority, combined with hammer blows on specific targets and with the constant tying-down of US troops against the regular North Vietnamese around the demilitarized zone. The US withdrawal in the early 1970s allowed Giap to exert increasing pressure on Saigon, reaching its climax in 1975. Giap himself suffered from a serious illness in 1973, obliging him to hand substantial authority to his deputy, General Van Tien Dung.

Gneisenau, August Neithardt von, 1760–1831 Prussian Marshal and military reformer. Born in Saxony and fought against Prussia in the War of Bavarian Succession, 1778; served with British forces in final days of American Revolution; joined Prussian Army, 1783; engaged in *Auerstedt* campaign, 1806 (Map 1), receiving widespread acclaim for his defence of Colberg. On 25 July 1807 Gneisenau was appointed a member of the Prussian Military Reorganization Commission, under *Scharnhorst*'s chairmanship, and the two military reformers worked in close cooperation. Gneisenau urged renewed hostilities to drive the French from Prussia; he formed plans for insurrection in 1808 and in 1809 attempted to organize a 'Free Prussian' Legion to fight alongside the Austrians. In 1811 Gneisenau drew up a memorandum urging Frederick William III to mobilize the Prussian Army; instead the monarch signed an alliance with Napoleon. Gneisenau left the Army in disgust. In 1813 Gneisenau served as Quarter-Master General to *Blücher*, becoming his Chief of Staff in succession to Scharnhorst in May. Blücher relied heavily upon him; together they fought at *Bautzen*, the Katzbach and *Leipzig* in 1813, in the campaign in France in 1814, and at *Ligny* and *Waterloo* in 1815. Unlike Blücher, Gneisenau disliked *Wellington*, and without Blücher's insistence might have refused to support the British at Waterloo.

Gordon, Charles, 1833–85 British General. Served in China in the Second Opium War, 1856–60; detailed in 1863 to command Chinese troops operating against Taiping rebels. From 1874 to 1876 Gordon was employed by Ismail Pasha, Khedive of Egypt, in opening up African equatorial provinces; he acted as Governor of the Sudan, 1877–80, moving to Palestine but returning to the *Sudan*, January 1884, following the Mahdist uprising. Gordon arrived at Khartoum, 18 January, to supervise evacuation, but Mahdist forces invested Khartoum in February, and Gordon's small garrison was besieged for almost a year. The British government believed Gordon should withdraw; he refused because he would have been unable to bring out civilians for whom he felt responsible. A relief force under *Wolseley* reached Khartoum on 28 January 1885, but the town had fallen 48 hours before. Gordon was killed in this final action.

Göring, Hermann William, 1893–1946 German Marshal and politician. Pilot in First World War; involved in *Hitler*'s abortive Munich 'putsch', 1923; joined Reichstag, 1928; appointed Minister for Air Forces in Hitler's Cabinet, 1933, and thereafter built up the *Luftwaffe*; acted as Hitler's first deputy and Minister of the Interior for Prussia; established the Gestapo, the Prussian Secret State Police. Göring convinced Hitler that the Luftwaffe could defeat the RAF in the summer of 1940; after the failure of the Battle of *Britain* and the lack of decisive results from the *Blitz*, Göring became disillusioned with the war. On 23 April 1945 he sought Hitler's permission to open negotiations with the enemy; he was immediately dismissed. He was sentenced to death at Nuremberg but committed suicide by poison, October 1946.

Gort, Lord John Standish, 6th Viscount, 1886–1946 British Field-Marshal. Served in First World War; CIGS 1937–9, succeeded by Sir William Ironside to become Commander of the BEF, 1939–40 (Map 13). His withdrawal to the Channel in May 1940 resulted in the *Dunkirk* evacuation. Gort acted as Governor of Gibraltar, 1941 to April 1942; he replaced General Sir William Dobbie as Governor and C-in-C *Malta*, remaining on the island until he became Governor of Palestine and Transjordan, 1944–5.

Grant, Ulysses S., 1822–85 US General and 18th President. Served in the *American–Mexican War*, 1846–8; resigned from the Army, 1854, and thereafter undertook a variety of business occupations. Grant re-entered the army, 1861, as a Union Colonel. In February 1862, now a Brigadier, he pierced Confederate defences stretching from the Mississippi to the Cumberland Gap, defeating the Confederates at *Shiloh*, 6–7 April (Map 3). He showed a stark contrast to the caution of other Union commanders, and on 11 July *Lincoln* appointed him to command the Army of the Tennessee. He shattered Confederate control of the Mississippi by capturing *Vicksburg*, July 1863, and his success continued with the *Chattanooga* campaign. Disregarding critics who said Grant drank too much, Lincoln appointed him Union General-in-Chief, 9 March 1864, and the epic struggle between Grant and *Lee* reached a climax. Grant dispatched *Sherman* on his march to the sea via *Atlanta* while he accompanied the second pincer movement striking into the *Wilderness*. His strategy proved successful, leading to *Appomattox*, April 1865. Grant's prime ability was to maintain pressure despite setbacks; he fought best when he could keep moving. Military routine bored him. Grant succeeded Andrew Johnson as President, 1869 and was succeeded by Rutherford Hayes, 1877.

Grapeshot (caseshot) One of the three forms of projectile fired by Napoleonic *artillery*, the others being solid shot and shells (*shrapnel*); used for short range, below 400 yards, and consisted of light metal cylinders or canvas bags stuffed with musket balls, iron pieces and even horseshoe nails; rendered obsolete by the continued development of shrapnel.

Gras Designed by Captain Basile Gras, 1836–1904, this *rifle* was a modification of the French *chassepot* adopted in 1866. The Gras 1874 model had an improved barrel and breech mechanism enabling the weapon to fire the latest centre-fire metallic *percussion* cartridge.

Greece, Civil War in, 1944–9 Unrest in Greece broke out as German forces withdrew in late 1944. *Churchill* made a dramatic visit to Athens, 25 December, when heavy fighting was taking place between newly arrived British troops and Greek government forces on the one hand, and the communist-controlled EAM and ELAS groups on the other. Talks held by Churchill resulted in the proposal that Archbishop Damaskinos should be Regent. King George II of Greece, exiled in London, reluctantly gave approval, and in January 1945 the Archbishop formed a government with the Republican General Plastiras being Prime Minister. The monarchy was restored on 1 September following a referendum. Guerrilla warfare again broke out in May 1946, with communist groups led by General Markos Vafiades supported by Albania, Yugoslavia and Bulgaria. British help to the government was overshadowed by massive US aid under the *Truman* doctrine. The Greek Army extended control northwards; fighting was especially heavy in the Vardar and Mount Grammos regions. Rebel leadership passed to John Ioannides in early 1949, but by late August remaining guerrilla strongholds had fallen. Civil War officially ended on 16 October.

Greece, fall of, 1941 *Second World War* (Map 14). British Foreign Secretary Anthony Eden visited Greece in February 1941 and committed Britain to the dispatch of troops to the country from North Africa, even though adequate defence in Greece depended upon Turkish intervention on the allied side, which failed to arrive, and despite the urgent need for these troops in the *desert campaign*. Doubts were expressed by the *War Cabinet* in London, but *Wavell*, Middle East Commander, and *Dill*, the CIGS, approved the plan. On 25 March the Yugoslav Prince Regent Paul reluctantly bowed to German threats and joined the Axis, but anti-German elements seized power in Belgrade. Hitler retaliated with a massive bombardment of the Yugoslav capital, 6 April, followed by invasion. Yugoslav resistance ended on 17 April. Meanwhile the German invasion of Greece had begun. About 59,000 British troops had arrived, under General Maitland *Wilson*, only to find that agreed plans for a defensive position had been altered by the Greeks, and that the latter would now fight farther forward, inviting disaster. The Greek front rapidly collapsed under the German onslaught launched on 6 April. Wilson withdrew to positions north of Mount Olympus. Alexander Papagos, Greek Commander, recommended to Wilson on 16 April that the British should evacuate, and this was decided on 21 April; the Greek Army surrendered on the 23rd. British evacuation was completed on the 27th with the rescue of about 43,000 troops. Casualties numbered about 12,000 British, 5,000 German; the Greeks suffered 70,000 killed and wounded and 270,000 captured. Meanwhile *Rommel* had thrust forward in North Africa. About one-third of the evacuated British troops were landed on *Crete*.

Greece, War of Independence, 1821–32 A revolt by local Greeks against their Turkish rulers resulted in the massacre of the Turkish garrison at Tripolitsa, 5 October 1821. Greek freedom-fighters won the initial advantage, through the naval battle of Chios, 18–19 June 1822, when Constantine Kanaris blew up the Turkish flagship, and through the battle of Karpenizi, 21 August 1822, when a force of only 300 Greeks under Marco Bozzaris surprised and routed 4,000 Turks under Mustai Pasha. But the Greeks threw away this advantage by internal dissension. In February 1825 a strong Egyptian force under Ibrahim landed in Morea in reply to a Turkish appeal. Ibrahim's 5,000 men overran the peninsula, while a Turkish army under Reshid Pasha moved on Missolonghi, north of Corinth, then laid siege to the Acropolis. The Greeks received outside help: Byron had arrived in 1822 but died in 1824; another Englishman, Admiral Lord Cochrane, commanded the Greek Navy, while General Sir George Church commanded the Greek Army. Internal disputes continued to hamper operations, and the Acropolis capitulated on 5 June 1825. On 6 July 1827 the governments of Britain, France and Russia were forced by public opinion to sign the Treaty of London, which demanded the withdrawal of Egyptian troops and the signing of an armistice by the Turks. The three treaty signatories sent naval forces, and the Battle of Navarino took place on 20 October, amounting to a gun duel between the opposing fleets. This resulted in the virtual destruction of the Egyptian–Turkish naval force. The Treaty of London, 7 May 1832, established an independent kingdom of Greece.

Greece, wars with Turkey, 1897; 1919–23 Greek relations with Turkey, ruler of the country until 1832, continued to be unsatisfactory, with frequent border clashes. Fighting on a larger scale broke out in April 1897. Greek forces under Crown Prince Constantine suffered repeated defeats at the hands of Turkish troops led by Edhem Pasha; an armistice was arranged by the Russian Tsar on 19 May, leading to a peace treaty on 18 September. Fighting again erupted in May 1919, in the aftermath of the *First World War* when Western allies attempted to negotiate peace terms following Turkey's alliance with Germany. While the confused negotiations continued, with the allies still occupying Constantinople, a Greek force landed at Smyrna, 15 May, to act as an agent for allied interests. In reply a new Turkish national government was formed in Ankara by General *Kemal*, and hostilities spread. Kemal undertook an extensive reorganization of Turkish forces and under his able leadership the Army showed a dramatic improvement in ability compared with that displayed in the First World War. Kemal negotiated the withdrawal of Italian troops which had landed at the same time as the Greeks, but the latter accelerated their offensives to gain control over western Anatolia and Thrace. A Greek army under General Papoulas was repulsed by Turks under Ismet Pasha in the First Battle of Inönü, January 1921, but in late March Papoulas received large reinforcements and advanced again. Successive Greek attacks were thrown back at the Second Battle of Inönü, 28–30 March. Constantine, King of Greece following the death of Alexander on 25 October 1919, took personal command for another offensive in July 1921, and after arduous fighting managed to defeat Turkish forces at Eskisehir on 17 July. Kemal ordered retirement to the Sakarya River and both sides attempted to build up strength. Constantine advanced on 10 August, but was defeated at the Battle of Sakkaria (Sakarya), 24 August to 16 September, after Kemal had launched a skilled enveloping movement against the enemy left wing. After reorganizing his forces during the rest of 1921 and early 1922, Kemal began a major counter-offensive, starting 18 August. He took Afyon on 30 August, Bursa on 5 September and Smyrna on 9–11 September; he then advanced on Constantinople, still occupied by the allies since 1918. Throughout the conflict the danger had been present of a clash between British and Turkish troops, especially in view of the belligerence displayed by *Lloyd George*, British Prime Minister until November 1922. But the allies finally sought to avoid confrontation and opened negotiations; the Convention of Mudania in

October pledged the restoration of Thrace and Adrianople to Turkey, formalized by the Treaty of Lausanne, 24 July 1923. The Turkish Republic was officially established on 29 October with Kemal the first President. This war between Greece and Turkey was characterized by barbarity displayed by both sides, and the conflict left a legacy of hate and distrust which later re-emerged over the *Cyprus* issue.

Gribeauval, Jean Baptiste de, 1715–89 French General. Appointed Inspector-General of Artillery, 1776, and thereafter introduced multiple improvements in the French *artillery* arm, later used to brilliant effect by *Napoleon*. Gribeauval's innovations, many borrowed from other armies, included standardization through interchangeable parts to ease production and supply problems, and methods to improve mobility. The French field artillery was standardized into 4-, 8- and 12-pounder guns, plus 6-inch howitzers; laying scales and sights were also made uniform and improved. To gain greater mobility, artillery pieces were lightened and carriages improved; caissons (ammunition chests) and limbers (detachable forepart of the gun carriages) were made integral, so that the weapon could be brought into action without having to await the arrival of equipment.

Grivas, George, 1898–1974 Greek General and guerrilla leader. Born in Cyprus; organized his own guerrilla force, 'Xhi', against Germans in *Greece* and against the communists. Grivas visited *Cyprus* in 1951 at the request of Archbishop Makarios, to advise on the formation of a militant youth organization, named PEON. He returned to Cyprus in 1954 to lead the EOKA guerrillas seeking independence from Britain and union with Greece. Full-scale operations began in April 1955, and Grivas led the Greek Cypriot guerrillas until the ending of the conflict in 1959; he gave himself the code-name Dighenis after a legendary Greek hero. After independence his extreme policy led to further clashes with the Turkish Cypriots, and ultimately to disagreement with the more moderate Makarios.

Guadalcanal, naval and land Battles of, August 1942 to February 1943 *Second World War* against *Japan* (Map 16). Japanese control of the Solomon Islands led to the establishment of a base on Guadalcanal. This precipitated US plans for an offensive against Guadalcanal and the nearby island of Tulagi. The US 1st Marine Division under General Alexander Vandegrift began landing on 7 August; the 19,000 troops achieved complete surprise over the 4,000 defenders, but the Japanese began retaliating with heavy air attacks. These air strikes were concentrated on the US naval element of the amphibious invasion forces, based upon a 3-carrier task force under Admiral Frank Fletcher. The whole US operation was commanded by Admiral Richmond K. Turner. A Japanese task force of 7 cruisers and 1 destroyer under Admiral Gunichi Mikawa was approaching the area, and Turner decided on 8 August that he must withdraw to protect his carriers; nevertheless, the two fleets clashed in the battle of Savo Island on the 9th, and excellent Japanese gunnery resulted in 4 US cruisers and 1 destroyer being sunk. Remaining US warships were withdrawn, leaving the US Marines unsupported. Engineers managed to complete the airfield on Guadalcanal, named Henderson Field, on 20 August. On 22 August a Japanese convoy, backed by three carriers under Admiral Nobutake Kondo, approached from Truk, with 1,500 reinforcements. This was intercepted by Fletcher's carrier force in the Battle of the Eastern Solomons, during which the Americans sank 1 Japanese light carrier but suffered damage to the carrier 'Enterprise'. The latter casualty, plus damage to the carrier 'Saratoga' by torpedo attack on 31 August, left the 'Wasp' the only carrier fit for combat in the South Pacific – and the 'Wasp' was sunk by torpedo when covering a convoy to Guadalcanal on 15 September. Meanwhile, land fighting on Guadalcanal had increased, leading to the Battle of 'Bloody Ridge', 12–14 September, when a Japanese attempt to seize ground overlooking the airfield was repulsed. The attempt to send further reinforcements led to another naval battle, Cape Esperance, 11–13 October, when a naval force under Admiral Norman Scott clashed with a Japanese transport force under

Admiral T. Joshima. The latter managed to land his troops. The Americans struggled to repair 'Enterprise', managing to do so by the third week of October; on the 18th Thomas Kinkaid succeeded Fletcher. During intensified land operations Kinkaid attacked Japanese naval forces commanded by Nobutake Kondo in the Battle of the Santa Cruz Islands, 26–27 October: the Japanese inflicted heavy damage on the 'Enterprise' and on a second carrier, the 'Hornet', which had been rushed to the south Pacific; 2 Japanese carriers were damaged in return. The naval campaign reached a climax in mid-November with the naval Battle of Guadalcanal, precipitated by a convoy of 13,000 Japanese under Admiral Raizo Tanaka covered by a squadron under Admiral Hiroaki Abe. This squadron was intercepted by a US carrier force under Admiral Daniel J. Callaghan on the night of 12 November. The interception, in which Callaghan was killed, caused the Japanese convoy to turn back but another attempt to reach Guadalcanal was made next day, 13 November: Admiral Tanaka managed to land troops. The naval battle continued on 14–15 November with a US fleet under Admiral Willis A. Lee clashing with a Japanese covering force in Iron-bottom Sound: 4 US destroyers were quickly put out of action, and 1 battleship was severely damaged, but the remaining US battleship, 'Washington', forced the Japanese to withdraw. The result of this 3-day battle of Guadalcanal, 12–15 November, was

US naval supremacy. On land, the major US offensive began on 10 January 1943. Japanese evacuation began on 1 February, ending on the 7th with about 13,000 troops saved. Japanese casualties during the campaign were about 14,000 killed or wounded, 9,000 dead through disease or starvation and 1,000 captured, in addition to naval losses. US casualties on land were about 1,600 killed, 4,200 wounded, excluding those dying of disease.

Guderian, Heinz, 1886–1954 German General. Prior to 1939 Guderian made an extensive study of tank warfare, especially the writings of Liddell *Hart*, *Fuller* and *De Gaulle*. As early as 1924 he had conducted exercises to explore tank uses, and he became a prime exponent of *blitzkrieg* in *France*, May–June 1940 (Maps 12, 13). In June 1941 Guderian commanded a panzer group in Army Group Centre for the invasion of *Russia*, detached during late July to bolster the slower-moving advance of *Rundstedt*'s Army Group South. Vigorous thrusts by his tanks played a major part in trapping the Russians in the bend of the Dnieper near Kiev. Guderian increasingly opposed *Hitler* on strategic matters, for example on the need for an early drive on Moscow. He was relieved of command in December 1941, after insisting upon a strategic withdrawal rather than a wasteful fight against advancing Russians, and he was employed in rationalizing German tank production. He returned to an influential position on 23 July 1944,

promoted to Chief of Staff of the Army after the purge of officers involved in the 20 July bomb plot against Hitler. He continued to argue over strategic matters and was replaced by General Hans Krebs in March 1945.

Guernica, air raid on, 26 April 1937 *Spanish Civil War* (Map 11). At the time of the attack this north Spanish town was about 10 miles from the main fighting front. Basque and Republican troops were withdrawing from the area. Air raids began on the town, a famous Basque centre, during the late afternoon of this Monday 26 April and continued for about $3\frac{1}{2}$ hours, causing extreme devastation and combined with machine-gunning by the aircraft. The latter totalled 43 machines, including both fighters and Junkers bombers. Pilots were supplied by the German *Condor Legion*. Bombs dropped totalled 100,000 tons of explosives and large numbers of incendiaries. The ostensible target was the bridge crossing the River Oca at the town. But the extent of the raid indicated that the organizer, Colonel Wolfram von Richthofen, Chief of Staff of the Condor Legion, had a wider purpose in mind: incendiaries would be useless against the stone bridge – which in fact remained intact – and comments by the Colonel both before and after the attack revealed that it was intended as a large-scale terror effort to destroy Republican morale. The Germans apparently did not realize the symbolic importance of Guernica as a Basque centre, and failed to anticipate the subsequent outcry by world opinion. The Nationalists attempted to reverse this outcry by claiming that the damage had been caused by retreating Republican forces. It is probable that *Franco* himself was not consulted prior to the attack, but leading Nationalists under him were undoubtedly informed. Nationalist forces took the remains of Guernica on the 29th. The attack later became even more famous through the painting by Pablo Picasso, symbolizing the brutality of war.

Guerrilla warfare Irregular warfare covering terrorism in general, *partisan* warfare, *urban guerrilla* warfare and insurgency or revolutionary warfare. The name originated from the partisan actions of Spanish fighters in the *Peninsular War* acting in conjunction with the regular forces, hence 'guerrilla' meaning 'little war'. Distinctions can be drawn between the various forms listed above, but often the differing types overlap. Partisan fighters normally operate in support of a main, regular army, which is responsible for the final victory in conventional battle; nor are partisans concerned with any aim other than re-establishing a particular state of affairs which existed comparatively recently. In this sense the partisans have a defensive aim. Partisan irregular warfare has long existed, but from it has developed insurgency or revolutionary warfare becoming an increasingly sophisticated form of war in its own right. Revolutionary insurgency warfare is concerned with creating an entirely different state of

affairs than that presently existing. In this sense an insurgency is based on an offensive aim. Moreover, a partisan campaign is usually purely military, seeking a definite military objective. Revolutionary and insurgency campaigns have a political framework upon which the military actions are based: political or doctrinal motivation is well developed before military hostilities commence – partisan warfare either has no such non-military motivation or allows this to develop during the course of fighting. *Clausewitz* writing after the Napoleonic Wars, gave considerable attention to the tactics of fighting guerrilla conflicts, although describing them in purely partisan terms; he related them closely to conventional operations being undertaken simultaneously. Friedrich Engels seemed to sense the development from partisan actions to overall revolutionary or 'People's' War, but he considered primarily a type of sudden, violent mass revolutionary rising rather than gradual and climactic insurgency struggle. Lenin viewed guerrilla warfare in the same light, and even seems to have been unsure of the wisdom of employing partisan methods at all because of their tendency to degenerate into uncontrolled lawlessness. He wrote in 1906: 'Because they are spontaneous and unorganized, these counterattacks may assume inexpedient and evil forms.' A valid concept of revolutionary guerrilla warfare failed to develop out of the events of the *Russian Revolution*, which retained the framework of a conventional civil war even though attempting to establish a revolutionary government: military actions were short and limited and lacked central control. Guerrilla warfare was still seen in basic partisan terms. *Lawrence*, in Chapter 33 of his 'Seven Pillars of Wisdom', described guerrilla tactics in detail, and his study, followed by Liddell *Hart*'s consideration of the 'Indirect Approach', raised guerrilla warfare more to the level of a deliberate strategy. But *Mao Tse-tung* went much farther, with his important theories of revolutionary warfare stemming from his guerrilla experiences in the drawn-out communist struggle in *China*. With Mao came the real division between partisan guerrilla warfare and revolutionary/insurgency guerrilla warfare. The protracted nature of the conflict in China lent itself to irregular unconventional tactics and strategy: the guerrillas were more flexible and resilient than a regular army; moreover the communists lacked training and equipment for a successful conventional army. Both from necessity and doctrine it therefore emerged that a guerrilla movement fighting on its own would be the most suitable weapon. Mao merged revolutionary political aspirations with guerrilla tactics, thereby bringing about revolutionary guerrilla warfare in its modern form. He expounded the ultimate in civil-military relations: the people became the guerrilla army, the army the people, still with strict overall political control. Mao therefore grafted economic and political concepts to the age-old tactics of partisan fighting, and at the same time elevated the latter into a form of fighting independent of conventional armies until the final phase. He used the revolutionary message in the same way as *Moltke* employed the *staff* system: his isolated military units would be given unity and a common denominator through the distribution of a common doctrine; political officers, like Moltke's staff officers, brought about essential coordination. Mao introduced another innovation. Before, both guerrilla warfare experience and doctrine had been based on the need for a regular army that eventually took over from the guerrillas for the final, decisive, battle against the opposing regular army. Mao was the first to see clearly that such an army might be created from the guerrillas themselves: they would wear down the opposing side, and at the same time form into a conventional army for the last stage. Mao's success glorified revolutionary guerrilla warfare and the post-Second World War years witnessed a widespread scattering of such insurgencies. The outbreaks stemmed from a number of causes: the disruption of the Second World War itself; the ending of colonial empires; the spread of weapons; expansion of communications; the East–West ideological split; the attempts by various dissident groups to copy the successful experience of others. There were three main groups of insurgencies, overlapping and intermingled. One type was aimed at overthrowing the existing form of government and establishing a non-communist system: examples, with varying degrees of success, were the Ukraine, *Hungary*, *Cuba* – at least initially non-communist – and the *Yemen*. A second type was anti-colonial, including uprisings in *Indonesia*, *Cyprus*, *Kenya*, *Algeria* and *Angola*. A third type was a pure communist insurgency, although sometimes putting forward other aims in order to broaden support. Examples include China, *Greece*, the *Philippines*, *Malaya*, *Laos* and *Vietnam*. From these wars a number of important theorists have emerged, including *Giap* and *Truong Chinh* in Vietnam, *Nasution* in Indonesia, *Grivas* in Cyprus, and *Guevara* in Latin America. Nasution, and initially Giap and Chinh, agreed with Mao Tse-tung that a guerrilla war should pass through three broad stages: first, the clandestine underground structure should be created, including the cell network; second, these groups should emerge to conduct guerrilla hostilities; third, the guerrillas should shift to regular operations for the final stage. During the first phase the insurgency movement is most vulnerable, but presents a minimal target since it remains hidden; a larger target is offered during the second stage, but by acting in guerrilla fashion the insurgents can be elusive; by the time the third phase is reached the guerrillas should be strong enough to absorb any counter-offensive. The most dangerous period in a guerrilla campaign, calling for the highest degree of skill by the leaders, is the point of transition from one phase to another. Giap, in the *Indochina* war against the French, suffered heavy casualties by moving too early

into the final stage in 1952, but reverted to the guerrilla campaign and later achieved the transition with brilliant success for the final battle of Dienbienphu. Grivas also propounded a three-part system, although with each step being on a lower level than with the large-scale wars in China and Indochina: thus the phases adopted by the EOKA guerrillas in Cyprus were, firstly the underground organization, secondly the move to isolated acts of sabotage, and finally the adoption of widespread guerrilla attacks. Later theorists have modified the lessons taught by Mao, and even Giap apparently changed his ideas in recognition that the counter-insurgency forces can be defeated in one of two ways, either through defeat in battle, or through the inability to stamp out guerrillas leading to demoralization and eventual withdrawal. The latter was apparently the objective in Vietnam and succeeded in persuading the USA to pull out forces. By remaining as guerrillas, the insurgents are even more difficult to defeat although their final victory might take longer to obtain. Difficulties experienced by counter-insurgency forces are immeasurably increased if the insurgents have a secure base from which to operate – as *Castro* and *Guevara* had in the Cuban mountains, Grivas in the Cypriot mountains, and the guerrillas in Malaya in the jungle. This base is even more important if it lies over the border in neighbouring, friendly territory – as with China's help for the Vietnamese in the Indochina War, and North Vietnam's help for the South in the recent struggle. Another important need for insurgents is the acquisition of as wide an appeal as possible in order to gain maximum support from the population: with this, the insurgents have the advantages of being able to promise more than they actually intend to give. Success or failure in an insurgency war therefore largely depends upon the ability to prepare undetected, to establish a base, to create sufficient appeal and to fight long enough in order to persuade the opposition that the political and military cost of continuing would be too great.

Guevara, Ernesto 'Che', 1928–67
Argentine-born guerrilla leader. Doctorate of Medicine, Buenos Aires, 1953; joined Fidel Castro in Mexico prior to revolution in *Cuba*. He landed with Castro on Cuba in 1956 and proved himself a skilled *guerrilla warfare* exponent. After the overthrow of Batista, Castro appointed Guevara President of the Cuban National Bank, and Minister of Industry in 1961. Soon afterwards evidence of disagreement appeared between Castro and Guevara, with the latter apparently anxious to 'export' revolution to other Latin American countries; already, before the Cuban Revolution, he had been involved with militant groups in Bolivia, Peru, Ecuador, Panama and Costa Rica. In 1960 he had published his book 'Guerrilla Warfare', which amounted to a primer for revolt: he put forward the Cuban experiences as a blueprint. Thus Guevara wrote: 'Popular forces can win a war against

an army. One does not necessarily have to wait for a revolutionary situation to arise; it can be created. In the under-developed countries of the Americas, rural areas are the best battlefields for revolution.' Superficially, Guevara's statements seemed to have immense appeal, promising victory to the hard-pressed peasants of South America. 'Guerrilla warfare is a fight of the masses,' he wrote, 'with the guerrilla band as the armed nucleus.' Guevara henceforward disappeared for long periods, training and organizing revolutionary movements elsewhere in Latin and South America. He was killed on 9 October 1967 by government troops in Bolivia. Guevara's attempt to export revolution failed for a number of factors, both personal and wider-ranging. His doctrine contained a number of flaws. Guevara envisaged the struggle mainly taking place in rural areas and warned of the difficulties of attempting uprisings in cities, where he believed the authorities could exert immediate counter-measures; yet without a revolutionary movement in the urban as well as rural sector the guerrilla could never hope to strike direct at the heart of power. In this sense Guevara failed to appreciate the possibilities of the *urban guerrilla war*. In addition, Guevara held the now-oldfashioned view that the guerrilla force must turn into a conventional army before victory could be gained. He wrote: 'It is obvious that guerrilla warfare is a preliminary step, unable to win a war all by itself. What happens is that the guerrilla army swells in size until it becomes a regular army. Only then will it be ready to deliver a knock-out blow.' Guevara therefore failed to appreciate the possibilities of the guerrilla himself achieving success through the gradual wearing down and demoralization of the security forces. Conversely, to build a regular army from guerrillas requires extensive organization which would have been beyond the capability of either Guevara or his fellow-rebels. On a wider scale the revolutionaries had to contend with the inherent lack of cohesion, communications and common cause inside the Latin American countries which resulted in an absence of confidence and initiative leading to mere aimless violence. Above all, Latin America remains inescapably part of the Western world, in outlook and economic dependence, thus blocking Guevara's attempt to shift the countries concerned into the sphere of communist influence.

H

Haig, Sir Douglas, 1st Earl, 1861–1928 British Field-Marshal. Served in the Sudan, 1898, Boer War, 1899–1902, India, 1903–6. In 1914 Haig commanded the 1st Corps of the BEF under *French*, replacing the latter as Commander, 17 December 1915 (Map 10). Supremely self-confident, and with a powerful friend in King George, he believed only vigorous offensives could win the war; inevitable slaughter resulted, especially at the *Somme*, June–November 1916, and *Ypres*, July–November 1917. He failed to establish a good working relationship with *Lloyd George*, who sought offensives elsewhere than the Western Front, and who better trusted the French Commander, *Nivelle*. Bickering continued throughout the war, as did Haig's suspicions of his French ally. From 1919–21 Haig commanded the Home Forces in Britain.

Haldane, Richard Burton, Viscount Haldane, 1856–1928 British politician. Secretary of State for War, 1905–12. Haldane saw his task as modernizing the British Army on a European basis. Officially, the Army's role was still as expressed in the Stanhope Memorandum, 1891: to provide men for India, colonial garrisons and coaling stations, and for home defence. In January 1906 the first Anglo-French military staff talks were held to discuss a common Continental policy, and on the basis of these discussions Haldane pushed forward his Army reforms, aimed at the creation of a British Expeditionary Force (BEF) and the establishment of a Territorial Army (TA) to provide reserves. Owing to Haldane's vigorous implementation of the *Esher* Committee recommendations, important improvements were made at the War Office and with the General *Staff*. Through his measure the BEF of 100,000 men crossed the Channel efficiently and speedily in August 1914. The TA numbered 14 divisions: *Kitchener*, then Secretary of State for War, viewed this 'amateur' force with contempt and declined to use it.

Hart, Sir Basil Henry Liddell, 1895–1970 British Army officer and military theorist. Served during First World War; retired from the Army with rank of Captain, 1927, to concentrate on writing; military correspondent the 'Daily Telegraph', 1925–35; military correspondent and defence adviser 'The Times', 1935–9; personal adviser to War Minister *Hore-Belisha*, 1937–8. His books include 'The Decisive Wars of History', 1929; 'The Future of Infantry', 1933; 'A History of the World War', 1934; 'Europe in Arms', 1937; 'The Defence of Britain', 1939; 'Dynamic Defence', 1940; 'The Current of War', 1941; 'The Strategy of Indirect Approach', 1941; 'This Expanding War', 1942; 'The Tanks', 1959; 'The History of the Second World War', 1973. Like *Fuller*, he believed that *tanks* should be used as more than mere infantry support weapons, but his writings were more specific than Fuller in his advocacy of a step-by-step progress towards mechanization. Unlike Fuller, he believed that infantry still had a vital role to play, but foot soldiers would also have to be mechanized in full armoured divisions. Allied to these innovations should be the strategy of the 'indirect approach': he believed that no general was justified in launching his troops into a direct attack upon an enemy firmly in position. Alternative means could range from encirclement to the 'expanding torrent', a spearhead assault to penetrate the enemy defences which then expanded behind the lines to fan to right and left. Liddell Hart had a strong following among young officers, but more note was taken abroad, especially for the formulation of the *blitzkrieg* technique.

Healey, Denis, 1917– British politician. Secretary of State for Defence in Labour administration, 1964–70, in succession to Peter Thorneycroft and succeeded by Lord Carrington. Healey continued the unification of the three services at the *Defence Ministry*. He also introduced dramatic defence savings, aiming at a cut of £400 million on 1964 prices. Measures included withdrawal of British forces from the Far and Middle East, a severe streamlining of British commitments in general, and drastic reductions in weapons and manpower. Regiments were reduced, the Territorial Army restricted; new projects were cancelled, including the purchase of the F.111 aircraft from the USA and the British TSR2; the fixed wing *aircraft carrier* fleet was phased out. The programme was officially completed in 1969, with British defence policy orientated towards Europe rather than maintaining worldwide '*peacekeeping*' commitments.

Helicopter On 13 November 1907 Paul Cornu made the first free flight in a tandem-rotor device. Igor Sikorsky built two helicopters in Russia in 1909–10, but Juan de la Cierva, in Spain, made the first major breakthrough in the 1920s, with his Autogiro which relied upon the wind to turn the rotor. Yet by the mid-1930s the world helicopter record still only stood at about ⅔ mile and a height of 59 feet. On 26 September 1937 the Brequet-Dorand Gyroplane increased the altitude record to 518 feet; in 1939 the German Focke-Achgelis FW 61 rose to 11,243 feet and covered a straight-line distance of 143 miles. Development was accelerated through the work of Igor Sikorsky, who returned to helicopters with machines such as his VS-300, first flown on 14 September 1939, and his later R-4 version. Although bombing trials from helicopters were made in the USA in 1942, their use was chiefly seen in the transport, rescue and communication roles. The French were the first to use the helicopter as a combat vehicle, in *Indochina* in 1950. *Korea* saw further use, and in *Algeria* French helicopters were fitted with machine-guns, rockets and wire-guided missiles. Development of the gas turbine boosted power. In Borneo during the *Malaysian-Indonesian* hostilities, the use of Wessex and Whirlwind helicopters for troop deployment reduced a 24-hour difficult march to 15 minutes' flying time. In *Vietnam* the Americans developed a sophisticated system of helicopter warfare; this entailed the employment of up to 25 machines in a flight, comprising 9 rocket-firing vehicles and 16 troop carriers; the weapon carriers sprayed the proposed landing zone (LZ) immediately before troop arrival, and reduced ground opposition by releasing up to 48 rockets from each machine. The Americans lost nearly 5,000 helicopters during this war. Helicopters have reduced the paratroop role for *airborne* forces.

Hindenburg Line, final allied offensive against, September–November 1918 *First World War* (Map 10). The Hindenburg defences were completed in April 1917, from Arras, east of Peronne, to the Aisne,

halfway between Soissons and Craonne. The line comprised an outer network held by few men but covered by multiple machine-gun nests, and behind this two heavily fortified systems. The Germans began withdrawing to the line on 23 February 1918, completing the move by early April. From this base were launched the offensives of spring 1918, which began with the heavy fighting at the *Somme* in March. After *Amiens*, *Foch* planned two major assaults on the German defences: a drive by French and US troops along the Meuse valley towards Mézières, and a British thrust east of the Somme; a subsidiary attack would be made farther north between Arras and Ypres. The US–French 4th Army offensive opened on 26 September. The advance slowed in the Argonne forest, and although US troops penetrated the first and second enemy lines in the rough terrain, they were almost blocked before Montfaucon. *Pershing* renewed the offensive on 4 October and by early November his troops were breaking out into the open beyond the Argonne forest, heading for Sedan. The US–French success in the Meuse–Argonne area caused a general German retreat. The British 4th Army shattered German defences on the Selle, 17 October, and the German Army began to disintegrate. Ludendorff resigned, 27 October. Growing disorder broke out in Germany and a socialist government seized power, 9 November. Already, since 7 November, a German delegation had been negotiating with Foch in his railway carriage HQ at Compiègne; talks resulted in agreement at 5 a.m., 11 November. Hostilities ceased at 11 a.m.

Hindenburg, Paul Ludwig von Beneckendorff, 1847–1934 German Marshal and President. Fought in Austro-Prussian and Franco-Prussian Wars; retired 1911; recalled to command forces in East Prussian campaign, August 1914 (Map 9), with *Ludendorff* his Chief of Staff, and won the Battle of *Tannenberg*; appointed C-in-C Austro-German Eastern Front, 1 November, and continued to urge offensive policy in the east and defensive in the west, supported by the Kaiser who overruled *Falkenhayn*; made 300-mile advance in the winter offensive, January–March 1915 (Map 9); replaced Falkenhayn on Western Front, 29 August 1916, again with Ludendorff his Chief of Staff; retired 1919. Hindenburg was President of Germany, 1925–34; he was obliged to appoint *Hitler* as Chancellor, 30 January 1933, and Hitler became President when Hindenburg died, 2 August 1934.

Hiroshima and Nagasaki, dropping of atomic bombs on, August 1945 *Second World War* against *Japan*. On 2 July 1945 *Truman* received a memorandum from Secretary of War *Stimson*. This pointed out that 'the operation for the occupation of Japan following the landing [of invasion troops] may be very long, costly and arduous ... we shall probably have cast the die of last ditch resistance'. Stimson recommended a warning being issued by the USA, Britain, China and Russia, calling upon Japan to surrender or face complete destruction. The latter could be brought about by additional fire raid bombing or through the *atomic bomb*. Truman and his advisers decided upon the latter; Stimson later claimed that the B.29 fire raids would have been more destructive, and the *Combined Chiefs of Staff* planners believed that with conventional land operations the war would probably last until November 1946. An atomic bomb was first successfully tested at Alamagordo, 16 July; the final decision to use the bomb was made on 22 July; *Churchill* was immediately informed and gave his enthusiastic support; *Stalin* was told next day. On 26 July a statement agreed by the USA, Britain and (Nationalist) China was broadcast calling upon the Japanese to surrender unconditionally or face 'prompt and utter destruction'. The Japanese War Council decided that as the declaration had not been formally addressed to the government and as the Russian attitude was unknown, a reply would be delayed. Prime Minister Suzuki prematurely informed newspapers that the government had decided to ignore the declaration. The allies therefore considered the Japanese refused the terms. On 6 August a US Flying-Fortress dropped a 20-kiloton atomic bomb from a height of 7,000 feet above the city of Hiroshima, population 300,000. The bomb was detonated at 1,850 feet. Explosive power was equivalent to 20,000 tons TNT, nearly 40 times as powerful as the heaviest raid in the London *blitz*. Japanese authorities estimate that immediate casualties totalled 100,000 killed and missing, 100,000 injured. A second bomb was detonated over Nagasaki, population 230,000, on 9 August; casualties were less because of the protection of nearby hills, but nearly 40,000 people were killed and about 25,000 injured. Next day Japan offered to surrender.

Hitler, Adolf, 1889–1945 Austrian-born German Führer (leader). Private in Bavarian infantry regiment, October 1914; fought at *Ypres*, November; wounded October 1916, and again from a British gas attack near Ypres, October 1918; he bitterly opposed those who signed the Treaty of *Versailles*, 1919, and joined the extremist German Workers' Party, soon titled the National Socialist German Workers' Party and named 'Nazi' after the abbreviation of the first German word. Hitler failed in an attempt to seize control of Bavaria in the Munich 'putsch', 8 November 1923, and was tried for treason, 26 February 1924. He received only a token sentence and wrote 'Mein Kampf' during his comfortable imprisonment. Nazi Party membership rose from 49,000 in 1926 to 178,000 in 1929. Hitler seized the opportunity offered by the collapse of the German economy after 1929 and the resulting political chaos; he emerged from political manoeuvring as Chancellor, 30 January 1933. He withdrew from the League of Nations in October, and stamped out domestic opposition in the 'Night of the Long Knives', 30

June 1934. He became President in addition to Chancellor on *Hindenburg*'s death, August 1934, and bound the German armed forces – *Reichswehr* – to him through oaths of allegiance. Hitler reoccupied the Rhineland, March 1936, annexed Austria, March 1938, outmanoeuvred British Prime Minister Chamberlain at talks at Godesberg and Munich, September 1938, extended control over the whole of Czechoslovakia, March 1939. Hitler began the *Second World War* after first securing the Eastern Front through a non-aggression treaty with *Stalin*, August 1939. Henceforth he attempted to handle all central direction of the war. Already, as President, he was Supreme Commander of the armed forces, and after the dismissal of *Blomberg*, February 1938, had taken over the functions of War Minister. He constantly overruled his subordinates. *Brauchitsch*, the Army Commander, resigned in late 1941, and Hitler merged this appointment with his own. He became increasingly unstable as war progressed, especially after *Stalingrad*. He refused to listen to those who sought a negotiated peace, and committed suicide in his Berlin bunker, 30 April 1945, having named *Doenitz* his successor.

Ho Chi Minh, 1892–1969 North Vietnamese political leader. Founded Indochinese Communist Party (ICP), January 1930; gained experience fighting with Chinese communists under *Mao Tse-tung*, but was imprisoned by Chinese nationalists under *Chiang Kai-shek*, August 1942 to September

1943. Thereafter he organized the Viet Minh structure, built on the ICP core, for the struggle in *Indochina*, ably assisted by his Defence Minister, *Giap*. After the Geneva Agreement, 1954, his aim was to reunite the two halves of *Vietnam*. The North Vietnamese success in the South in April 1975 led to the renaming of Saigon as Ho Chi Minh City.

Hohenlohe-Ingelfingen, Prince Kraft Karl August zu, 1827–92 Prussian general of *artillery*. Obtained wide experience in the use of artillery in the *Crimean War*, at *Sadowa* in the *Austro-Prussian 'Seven Weeks' War*, and in the *Franco-Prussian War*. During the latter he commanded the Prussian Guards artillery with conspicuous success, putting into use experience so far gained. At Sadowa, for example, 3 July 1866, the Prussian artillery had been late coming into action because it moved at the tail of the column. By contrast, when the French and Prussians clashed at the battle of Gravelotte–St Privat in the Franco-Prussian War, 18 August 1870, Hohenlohe sent his artillery ahead and thus brought the guns into action immediately, breaking up all French attempts to counter-attack. Added to this vigorous deployment of the artillery was Hohenlohe's method of pairing each gun with an ammunition wagon to ensure continuous supply of ammunition. Guns were also fired in a more intelligent fashion. Thus at Sedan, 1 September, Hohenlohe systematically bombarded the whole of the Bois de la Garenne, allocating a

different section of the wood to each of his 10 batteries, with each gun in the battery firing at a different elevation beyond effective rifle range – so reducing French ability to retaliate. The French were completely saturated. Hohenlohe was also responsible for the direction of the bombardment of Paris, commencing 5 January 1871. After the war he wrote several works on military science which had significant influence in staff colleges throughout Europe. These works were translated into English: 'Letters on Strategy', 2 vols, 1897; 'Letters on Artillery', 1888; 'Letters on Infantry', 1889; 'Letters on Cavalry', also in 1889.

Home Guard On 14 May 1940 the British War Secretary Anthony Eden issued a broadcast appealing for male volunteers to enrol in a new organization named the Local Defence Volunteer (LDV) Force. The appeal had been stimulated by the deteriorating situation in the Battle of *France*. Volunteers were to be between the ages of 16 and 65; they would receive no payment although some could claim a meagre subsistence allowance; their task would be to help the main army and the police in the defence of the UK, especially through guarding potential invasion targets such as stretches of coastline, airfields, factories and public utilities and by manning roadblocks. Their role would free the Army for other duties. By 20 May 1940, 6 days after Eden's broadcast, about 250,000 volunteers had been enrolled, and the total reached about 300,000 by the end of the month. Operational control was vested in the C-in-C, Home Forces, then General Ironside; rifles were available for about one-third of the volunteers in those first weeks – the rest had shot-guns, sporting rifles or improvised weapons. Equipment remained short despite the arrival of ·300 rifles from the USA. The LDV changed its name to Home Guard at the end of July 1940, following Prime Minister Chur-chill's suggestion, and gradually the force obtained better training – al-though on an improvised basis. Men also received khaki denim uniforms. Certain selected Home Guard fighters were trained secretly as guerrillas, should the Germans invade. The volunteer aspect was altered slightly by the National Service Act (No. 2) of December 1941, which could compel men to join the Home Guard although only for a maximum of 48 hours' duty per month. From August 1940 Home Guard units were affiliated to the county regiments; recruiting was tem-porarily suspended in October; in February 1941 the rank system was introduced, as in the main army, together with commissions for officers, and the Home Guard therefore moved closer to being a force of part-time regular soldiers. The Home Guard also became a training ground for boys of 17–18 prior to their full call-up. Personnel from the force often en-gaged the regular army in exercises and dress and weapons eventually became virtually identical. By summer 1943 the Home Guard totalled 1¾ million men, organized into 1,100

battalions; average age had dropped to below 30. Disbandment of battalions began at the end of 1944. The British Home Guard was in fact a famous example of many other domestic, part-time organizations aimed at local defence and at bolstering existing authority, such as Prussia's *Landwehr and Landsturm* in Napoleonic times, and France's Garde Nationale, formed originally to preserve order at the start of the French Revolution. Modern examples include the National Guards-men in the USA and Home Guard units in NATO countries such as Norway.

Hood, Lord Samuel, 1724–1816 British Admiral. Commander of Mediterranean Fleet, 1793–5, seizing Toulon, 27 August 1793, but obliged to withdraw in December following land operations in which *Napoleon* participated; seized Corsica, 1794. Hood was recalled in early 1795 due to controversy with the government and never served again. But future mem-bers of the Hood family rendered distinguished service. Lord Samuel's relation Arthur William Acland, 1st Baron Hood, served in the *Crimean War* and was First Lord of the Admiralty, 1835–9, and Lord Samuel's great-great-grandson, Sir Horace, commanded the 3rd Battlecruiser Squadron at *Jutland*, 1916, being killed in the opening bombard-ment.

Hooker, Joseph, 1814–79 Union General, *American Civil War* (Map 3). Fought at *Antietam*, September 1862 gaining nickname 'Fighting Joe'; succeeded *Burnside* as Commander of the Army of the Potomac, 26 January 1863, but outmanoeuvred by *Lee* in *Chancellorsville* campaign April–May, and at his own request was relieved of command, succeeded by *Meade* on 23 June. Hooker continued to serve under *Thomas* and *Sherman*, taking part in Battle of *Chattanooga*, November 1863.

Hore-Belisha, Leslie, 1893–1957 British politician. Secretary of State for War and Army Council President, May 1937 to January 1940. He believed the first priority to be increased manpower: he announced in August 1937 that serving soldiers could extend service after completion of their first term, reservists could rejoin, and the recruiting age was to be raised to 30 years of age. To attract recruits he introduced measures to improve living standards, including relaxation of petty restrictions and more practical uniforms. Hore-Belisha believed the Army hierarchy to be riddled with the 1914–18 mentality and too conservative. He brought about the dismissal of Field-Marshal Sir Cyril Deverell from the post of CIGS; Gort became the new CIGS in 1937. He urged the formation of a Supply Ministry and the introduction of conscription: the creation of the former was announced by Prime Minister Chamberlain on 20 April 1939 and conscription on the 27th. Hore-Belisha was asked to resign in January 1940, owing to friction with Gort, now BEF Commander.

Hotchkiss, Benjamin Berkeley, 1826–85 US arms inventor. Designed the *machine-gun* which bore his name: this appeared shortly after the *Maxim* in 1884. The Hotchkiss, probably inspired by the French *mitrailleuse*, had a slower rate of fire than the Maxim, but could therefore be air- rather than water-cooled, so reducing weight. In 1875 Hotchkiss had already invented a magazine repeating rifle with a bolt action, the patents of which were bought by Winchester. In 1855, Hotchkiss had patented a projectile for rifled artillery which, with later improvements, became widely used in the *American Civil War*.

Hungary, uprising in, 1956 Anti-communist feeling led to increasing disturbances in autumn 1956. Soviet troops fired on protesting civilians, 24–25 October. Also on the 25th the communist government was overthrown and the more moderate Imre Nagy became premier. Soviet troops were requested by the Party Secretary, Erno Gero, and fighting spread until a temporary ceasefire on the 28th. On 1 November about 200,000 Soviet troops and 2,500 tanks and armoured vehicles suddenly surrounded Budapest and moved in to crush all resistance, capturing Nagy and his government on 4 November. About 27,000 Hungarian and 7,000 Soviet casualties resulted.

Hutier, Oskar von, 1857–1934 German General. Commanded 8th Army on the Eastern Front in the *First World War*, seizing Riga, 1 September

1917. His tactics, known as 'Hutier tactics', consisted of masking enemy strongpoints with gas and smoke while infantry and light guns were infiltrated through these positions behind a rolling barrage. This technique discarded the previous practice of a lengthy preliminary bombardment which sacrificed surprise; instead there would be heavier reliance on fast-moving 'shock' troops; the enemy strongpoints would be left for subsequent waves of infantry while the spearheads dislocated the enemy area behind the front line. *Ludendorff* took note of Hutier's operations and incorporated his tactics in the 1918 offensive plans for the Western Front. Hutier himself commanded the 18th Army in the *Somme* offensive, March 1918, which drove a 40-mile salient into the allied line. His tactics can be seen as one of the origins of the *blitzkrieg* concept, while the spearhead shock or *storm troops* came to prominence as the SA – Sturmabteilung.

Hydrogen power and bomb Represented as great an increase in destructive power as the A-bomb from TNT. The H-bomb results from the release of far more of the potential energy of the material employed – Uranium 235 or plutonium and Uranium 238. Russia exploded an H-bomb before the Americans, probably on 12 August 1953. The first US H-bomb was exploded at Bikini Atoll in the Pacific on 1 March 1954, although a thermonuclear (hydrogen) device had been successfully tested at Eniwetok in November 1952. The Bikini bomb equal to 750 atomic bombs of *Hiroshima* size was 15 megatons, with 1 megaton equal to 1 million tons of TNT; H-bombs can be as large as 50 megatons.

I

India–China War, October–November 1962 (Map 19) India signed a non-aggression treaty with Communist China on 29 April 1954. Clashes on the border with Chinese-occupied Tibet nevertheless increased, provoking Indian protests on 28 August 1959 and 10 June 1960. On 20 October 1962 Chinese mountain troops attacked Indian frontier posts in Jammu and in the north-east border region, overwhelming the outnumbered defenders and consolidating a new border line which covered key mountain passes. China declared a unilateral ceasefire on 21 November.

Indian Mutiny, 1857–8 British forces in India comprised a few regular army units and the much larger forces of the East India Company. The latter had developed from the need of the company to guard its goods; the step had soon been taken to employing trained native troops. The ratio of British to native had been fixed at 1 British soldier to every 3 native and never less than 1 to 4. But the Crimean War and local conflicts in Burma, China and Persia drained off British regulars, and by 1857 the ratio had become 1 to 8 – 40,160 European troops as against 311,000 natives. Yet the native sepoys had long been growing increasingly dissatisfied. Rumours abounded, for instance that native religions were to be forcibly suppressed. At this time of deepening tension came the British decision to replace the company's old Brown Bess *muskets* with the new *Enfield*. To load the new rifle the soldier was obliged to tear off a greased patch on the cartridge with his teeth. A rumour, perhaps based on fact, spread that the grease came from the fat of a cow, sacred to the Hindu, or of a pig, considered unclean by the Muslim. The C-in-C India, General Lord George Anson, immediately ordered cartridges to be used ungreased. But mutiny broke out at Meerut, 10 May 1857; next day Europeans at Delhi were massacred, with rebels declaring Bahadur Shah, last of the Moguls, to be their ruler. Anson, who died of cholera on 27 May, was succeeded by Sir John Lawrence, who rushed 3,000 troops to besiege Delhi. His elder brother, Sir Henry, was besieged at Lucknow. The garrison at Cawnpore, under Sir Hugh Wheeler, was surrounded by rebels under Dandu Panth (Nana Sahib); the latter persuaded Wheeler to surrender on 27 June, promising safe passage, but the garrison was immediately massacred. A relief force for Lucknow, led by Sir Henry Havelock, defeated Nana Sahib at Cawnpore on 16 July; during this advance a force under General John Nicholson stormed Delhi, 14–20 September. Havelock entered Lucknow on 25 September, only to be besieged himself: a second relief column under Sir Colin *Campbell* reached the city on 16 November and the garrison escaped to Cawnpore. Campbell marched back to Lucknow in March 1858, defeating rebels on the 16th. Meanwhile a brilliant operation in central India was being undertaken by Sir Hugh *Rose*: his defeat of rebels under Tantia Topi at Gwalior on 19 June 1858 virtually ended the mutiny. Over 2,000 British soldiers were killed in action during the conflict, and a further 9,000 died from disease or sunstroke. The mutiny resulted in a reorganization of the British Indian Army system. The government of India was transferred to the British Crown on 1 September 1858, thus ending the century-long rule of the East India Company; sepoy troops were reduced to about 120,000 by 1864, by which time the European garrison had been increased to about 64,000 men. Another result of the mutiny was the increased use made of Gurkha troops from the independent kingdom of Nepal; many fought alongside the British during the fighting and they would continue to do so in subsequent wars.

India–Pakistan War, May–September 1955 (Map 19) India and Pakistan quarrelled over border lineation from the moment of their independence, 14 August 1947. Relations were also strained over religious issues, India being primarily Hindu and Pakistan Moslem. Independence pains continued, concentrated on Kashmir where the Hindu Raja decided his state should join India and his predominantly Muslim population clamoured to join Pakistan; in January 1957 India annexed Kashmir despite Pakistani protests and UN disapproval. Fighting broke out in April 1965 lasting about 2 weeks in the desolate Rann of Kutch region. Indian forces crossed the ceasefire line in Kashmir on 24 August but halted after UN intervention; Pakistani forces crossed the line on 1 September, and widespread hostilities continued throughout the month. In Kashmir itself, neither side managed to obtain an advantage in wide-ranging tank battles: as soon as one armoured force advanced it found its supply lines endangered by opposing armour and air strikes. Both countries agreed on 27 September to abide by a UN demand for a ceasefire; forces withdrew to lines held on 5 August.

India–Pakistan War, December 1971 (Map 19) Pakistan, divided between East and West on either side of the Indian continent, experienced increasing unrest in the eastern wing of the country. East Pakistan was less obsessed with the Kashmir issue and more willing to seek a settlement with India; West Pakistan practised a policy of repression of Benghalis in the

East. In March 1971 Sheikh Mujibur Rahman of East Pakistan declared this area would become the State of Bangladesh; West Pakistan troops tried to stifle this independence movement, leading to Indian intervention on behalf of Bangladesh. The Indian attack in strength began on 4 December, although some Indian troops had crossed the border into East Pakistan as early as 27 October. The campaign lasted 13 days, with Indian regulars working in conjunction with Indian-trained and armed Bangladesh guerrillas. The Pakistani commander, General Niazi, surrendered at Dacca on 16 December. Fighting had begun in the west with a Pakistani air strike on 3 December, followed by a strong ground offensive mainly directed at points in Jammu and Kashmir which had provided the principal targets in the *India–Pakistan War, 1955*. Pakistani units were unable to sever Indian communications to Kashmir; Indian counter-offensives advanced in Rajasthan and in the Sind Desert. President Yahya Khan of Pakistan agreed to a ceasefire on 17 December. He immediately resigned and was succeeded by Zulfikar Ali Bhutto.

Indochina, war in, 1941–54 (Map 18) This struggle centred on the conflict between French colonial troops and the Viet Minh guerrillas, the latter based on the Indochinese Communist Party formed by *Ho Chi Minh* in 1930 with independence being the immediate aim. Fighting spread over the Indochinese countries of *Laos*, *Cambodia* and Vietnam, but the main operations were undertaken in the area later to become North Vietnam. *Guerrilla warfare* began in 1941, interrupted by the Japanese conquest of the region in the Second World War. Viet Minh groups were reactivated in October 1944 by Ho Chi Minh's principal military commander, *Giap*, aimed at securing control before the French returned in strength. Ho Chi Minh entered Hanoi on 29 August 1945, but left in February 1946 in the face of mounting French pressure. Fighting on a wide scale broke out in December 1946. French pincer movements failed, including operations 'Lea' in October 1947 and 'Ceinture' in November 1947 north-west of Hanoi. *Mao Tse-tung*'s communist victory in *China*, 1949, resulted in a massive boost of supplies to the Viet Minh; Communist China recognized the Viet Minh as the lawful government of Vietnam on 18 January 1950, Russia extended recognition on the 30th, and Poland, Romania, Hungary and North Korea followed suit. Giap now moved into active guerrilla warfare in an offensive which, combined with increased activity by the Pathet Lao insurgents in Laos, forced the French into a fortified line around the Red River Delta. In December 1950 *Lattre de Tassigny* was appointed High Commissioner and commander of the French forces. In early 1951 Giap moved too soon into the final stage of the conflict: full conventional warfare. The Viet Minh fought 3 major battles during the year: at Vinh Yen in January, Mao Khé in March and Day River in May–June, all aimed at penetrating the French defensive lines around the Red River Delta. The Viet Minh therefore reverted to guerrilla warfare and the campaign proved eminently successful Tassigny, seriously ill, left Vietnam on 20 November 1952, returning to France via America where he pleaded for more aid. General Raoul Salan had taken his place as French commander, and a large naval operation in January–February 1953 destroyed the Viet Minh base at Quinhon. But the guerrillas themselves merely melted away. On 8 May 1953 General Henri Navarre replaced Salan. By now the Viet Minh controlled most of the Tonkin area outside the French fortified line, and within these French defences they controlled, partly or wholly, about 5,000 out of the 7,000 villages. The French controlled Saigon and Hué, but the main north–south road – Route Coloniale 1 – was highly vulnerable. Viet Minh strength totalled about 125,000 full-time troops organized in 6 divisions, plus 75,000 regional troops and up to 350,000 village militia. French troops numbered 190,000, of whom about 100,000 were tied to static defences. Navarre attempted to introduce a more mobile policy, for which he needed more men, but the French government opposed the dispatch of additional troops and were anxious over the situation in *Algeria*; NATO nations also opposed more French troops being withdrawn from Europe. Navarre was unable to withstand Viet Minh pressure when Giap again moved into the final, conventional stage in late 1953. This phase

reached its climax with the Battle of *Dienbienphu*, November 1953 to May 1954. The French agreed to the terms of the Geneva Conference, 26 April to 21 July. Vietnam was divided at the 17th parallel; both halves would be independent nations pending unification elections. The USA accepted the Geneva Agreements but reserved the right to take action should they be broken; this led to US involvement in the second *Vietnam* war. French casualties 1945–54 totalled 20,685 Frenchmen, 11,620 légionnaires, 15,229 North Africans and 26,686 local enlisted Indochinese.

Indonesia, War of Independence, 1945-9 The collapse of Japanese occupation of the Netherlands East Indies in 1945 led to a declaration of independence for the Indonesian area, 17 August, issued by Achmed Sukarno. British and Dutch troops arrived on 29 September. The Indonesian People's Army, ably led by Abdul Nasution, undertook extensive *guerrilla warfare* and Sukarno rejected Dutch offers of talks. Dutch troops seized Jogjakarta, 19 December 1948, yet were unable to suppress the guerrillas in the jungle. Fighting ended with the granting of full sovereignty by the Dutch, 2 November 1949; the Republic of Indonesia was proclaimed on 15 August 1950, with Sukarno the President.

Inkerman, Battle of, November 1854 *Crimean War* (Map 4). Eleven days after *Balaklava*, Menshikov's Russian Army of 50,000 men again attempted to strike between the allies and their field support. Only 9 allied regiments, about 15,000 men, stood before the Russian advance, the most that *Raglan* believed could be spared from the Sebastopol siegeworks. The main Russian attack was directed against Inkerman Ridge early on 5 November, while two diversionary attacks were made to block French reinforcements. Fierce fighting continued in the difficult terrain throughout the morning, consisting of fragmented attacks and counter-attacks which revealed extreme courage on the part of the defenders. The arrival of French reinforcements under General Pierre Bosquet tipped the balance. The Russians began to pull back at about 1 p.m. The allies lost about 3,300 men, of whom about 2,500 were British; Russian casualties were as high as 12,000.

Ireland, 1791–1974 The League of United Irishmen was organized in 1791 to fight for Irish independence from the British Government, and France attempted to make use of the struggle during the French Revolutionary and Napoleonic Wars, aiding the Irish insurgents after 1793. In December 1796 Lazare Hoche led an expedition to aid an Irish uprising, but this was prevented from landing by bad weather. A rebellion broke out on 23 May 1798, with French assistance, but the insurgents were defeated at Vinegar Hill, 21 June. In August the French General Humbert landed with about 1,000 troops; he was out-manoeuvred by superior forces under

Lord Cornwallis and the French surrendered on 8 September. The Irish Home Rule question remained a dominating feature of British politics during the nineteenth century. The Young Ireland Party was founded by William O'Brien in 1840, and by 1847 had become the main Irish nationalist organization, gaining increased support through the hardship caused by the potato famines in the 1840s; an unsuccessful insurrection broke out in Tipperary, July 1848. The Fenian Brotherhood, founded 1858, stirred continued unrest despite Irish reforms in Gladstone's administration, 1868–74. Charles Stewart Parnell (1846–91) was elected to Parliament in 1875 and used his political skill to draw attention to the Irish question, becoming leader of the Irish party in Parliament and acting as President of the Irish National Land League. The latter, founded 21 October 1879 by Michael Davitt to gain Irish ownership of tenanted land, was suppressed in 1881 and its leaders arrested. Gladstone, becoming Prime Minister again in April 1880, attempted to make peace with Parnell, who was released from prison on 2 May 1882. Four days later an extremist Irish group known as the Invincibles murdered Lord Frederick Cavendish and Thomas Burke — respectively chief secretary and under-secretary to the Viceroy of Ireland – in Phoenix Park, Dublin. In 1905 the Sinn Fein party was formed by Arthur Griffith, aimed at the establishment of a separate Irish state. On 20 March 1914 the Curragh 'Mutiny' took place, when Brigadier-General Herbert

Gough and other officers at the Curragh barracks in Ireland resigned rather than obey orders to force the loyal population of Ulster to accept Home Rule under the separatists of southern Ireland. Heated Parliamentary debates finally resulted in a Home Rule Bill being signed by King George V on 10 September 1914; this, however, left unsettled whether the northern area of Ulster should be included in the separate southern Irish state, and because of the deteriorating European situation, the Act was postponed. The First World War brought the issue of whether Ireland should fight alongside Britain, as urged by the political leader John Redmond (1856–1918); others believed that the country should remain neutral. Increasing unrest led to the Easter Rising, which broke out on Easter Monday, 24 April 1916, in Dublin and which was immediately condemned by Redmond. Involved in this issue was Sir Roger Casement, a former British consular agent who had joined the Irish nationalists in opposition to a policy of Irish participation in the European war. Casement had travelled to Berlin in 1914 to seek assistance in gaining Irish independence; at the time of the Easter Rising he landed near Tralee but was soon taken into custody. A German vessel carrying munitions was intercepted by British destroyers. The insurgents were suppressed; Casement's subsequent trial as a traitor led to widespread controversy which continued after his execution on 3 August. Sporadic fighting was stirred by the Sinn Fein. On 7 January 1919, 26 of the 73 Irish MPs in the House of Commons at Westminster met in Dublin to establish an independent Irish assembly, the Dáil Eireann; Irish independence was declared on 21 January, and widespread conflict took place between the military wing of the Sinn Fein, known as the Irish Republican Army (IRA), and the Royal Irish Constabulary (RIC). Men of a special constabulary force, known as the 'Black and Tans' from their black belts and khaki tunics, moved into the area with British troops in 1920 to support the RIC. A British promise of dominion status to southern Ireland led to the formal establishment of peace, 6 December 1921. Articles for a treaty recognizing the dominion status of the Irish Free State, covering southern Ireland up to the Ulster border, were signed on 6 December and went into force 20 July 1922. Hostilities continued between the Protestant northern area of Ulster and the Catholic extremists in the south, and relations remained fragile after the official creation of the Irish Free State in January 1923. Southern Ireland withdrew from the British Commonwealth on 21 December 1948, and the Republic of Ireland was proclaimed on 17 April 1949. Terrorist acts in Ulster accumulated during the late 1960s. Sectarian strife between the Protestants and the Catholics, nominally over lack of civil rights for the latter – who represented about 35 per cent of the total population of Northern Ireland – led to 13 deaths during 1969. Also in 1969 the British government dispatched troops to Ulster in an effort to maintain the peace. In December 1969 the IRA split into the 'Officials', less committed to violence, and the highly active minority known as the Provisionals. Twenty people died during 1970, and in 1971 the Provisionals began an all-out offensive, including numerous bomb attacks – the first bomb explosion came on 23 May in a Belfast bar. The British government retaliated with internment of suspects, 9 August 1971. In 1971, 173 people were killed, including 43 British soldiers, and by 1973 Britain found it necessary to withdraw troops temporarily from NATO duties in Germany. Protestant groups such as the Ulster Defence Association (UDA) were formed for self-protection and retaliation. Bombing incidents rose to a monthly average of 81 in 1973, plus 418 shootings per month. These figures dropped slightly in 1974, respectively to 57 and 267, but the year 1974 experienced an increased number of rocket attacks – 16 separate attacks in which 24 rockets were fired; a total of 116 mortar bombs were fired on 16 occasions. By early 1975 British troop strength in Northern Ireland comprised about 14,000 men. The number of civilian and military deaths had risen above 1,000.

Ironclads The *Paixhans* naval shell of the 1830s rendered wooden warships extremely vulnerable and stimulated development of armour plating, encouraged by the Crimean War experience especially at *Sinop(e)*. The French launched the first ironclad ship 'La Gloire', in 1859. Four Gloire-class ships were built, each protected by a 5-inch thick iron belt on the hull. The British followed with HMS 'Warrior', 1860. The battle between the ironclads 'Virginia' ('*Merrimac*') and '*Monitor*', March 1862, revealed that future naval conflicts were likely to consist mainly of hammering barrages. *Tegetthoff*'s victory at Lissa in 1866 seemed to indicate that the ram would be the most effective military weapon. Armour became thicker as the penetrating power of shells steadily increased; vessels became ponderous floating platforms. Then, during the 1880s and 1890s, development in steel manufacture provided armour with strength combined with lightness; mobility returned. By 1900 *battleships* had a speed of 18 knots and yet displaced some 15,000 tons owing to improved propulsion; the *torpedo* resulted in a return to tactics of manoeuvre.

Israel–Arab War, 1948–9 (Map 20) The independent state of Israel was proclaimed on 14 May 1948, following the UN agreement of November 1947 partitioning *Palestine* into separate Jewish and Arab states and the British announcement, January 1948, that the British mandate over the country would be relinquished in May. Israel had only 15,000 mobile troops and lacked artillery, tanks and aircraft; as anticipated, the Arabs attacked in mid-May, utilizing forces from Egypt, Syria, Lebanon, Transjordan and Iraq. Israel threw back Egyptian and Syrian invasion attempts, and held the more formidable British-trained Arab

Legion of Jordan in a bitterly fought battle at Jerusalem. A UN organized truce began on 11 June. A UN *peacekeeping* force arrived on the 20th but was unable to prevent renewed fighting on 8 July. On 12 July Israeli forces drove off an Arab attempt to take Tel Aviv. Another ceasefire, starting 18 July, ended on 15 August, and fighting continued sporadically for the remainder of the year. The Israelis counter-attacked into Egypt, 3–5 January 1949, advancing 35 miles. Peace talks, January–July, finally resulted in armistice agreements in July, but border disputes continued and full war would again erupt in the *Suez–Sinai* campaign, 1956.

Israel–Arab War, 1956 – see Suez–Sinai campaign

Israel–Arab War, June 1967, 'The Six-Day War' (Map 20) On 13 November 1966 Israeli forces launched their largest offensive since the *Suez–Sinai* campaign, attacking a *Fatah* base over the Jordan border; fighting with Syria broke out south-east of the Sea of Galilee on 7 April 1967. On 18 May President *Nasser* demanded that the UN forces in Egypt must withdraw. Egyptian troops then moved into Sharn El-Sheikh, a garrison town over-looking the entrance to the Gulf of Aqaba, through which shipping passed to reach the Israeli oil port of Eilat. On 22 May Egypt announced the blockade of the Gulf. Israeli forces had already begun to mobilize; aircraft struck at Egyptian airfields at 8 a.m., 5 June, and by nightfall the

Israelis claimed to have destroyed the Egyptian air forces: 280 Egyptian aircraft had been eliminated on the ground and 20 in the air; 52 Syrian and 20 Jordanian aircraft had also been destroyed. The Israelis therefore controlled the air, and by the evening of the 5th, forces had crossed the Gaza strip and the Straits of Tiran, together with the west bank of the Jordan, and occupied much of Jerusalem. On 6 June the Israelis consolidated their hold on the Gaza strip and 2 armoured columns crossed the Suez Canal. The Old City in Jerusalem fell to Israeli troops on the 7th; next day the Israelis completed their domination of the Suez Canal, and Egypt accepted ceasefire terms. Syria, after agreeing to a ceasefire on the 8th, began shelling again on the 9th, and the Israelis retaliated by thrusting across the border and dominating the road to Damascus. Fighting died down on the 10th.

Israel–Arab War, October 1973, 'The Yom Kippur War' (Map 20) Egyptian policy under President Sadat, successor to *Nasser* in 1970, was orientated to gaining Israeli withdrawals from territory obtained in the *Israel–Arab War, 1967*. In January 1973 the Arab Defence Council discussed a 'unified plan for military and political action against Israel', and the Arabs received increasing support from the Soviet Union, especially with surface-to-air missiles (SAM) deployed along the Suez Canal. Despite the clear indications of imminent conflict, the Israelis were surprised over the timing of the assault when Syria and Egypt launched an offensive on 6 October. This attack envisaged an Egyptian crossing of the Suez Canal to break through the light Israeli defences at the Bar-Lev line; meanwhile Syrian forces would exert pressure on Israel's north-east border. Israel had to fight an immediate war on two fronts with her forces still mobilizing. The Syrians, launching their main attack against the strategically important Golan Heights, made good progress aided by contingents from Iraq, Morocco, Saudi Arabia and, briefly, from Jordan. By the morning of 7 October Syrian forces had almost reached their pre-1967 War positions along the Golan Heights overlooking the Jordan River. But next day the Israeli counter-offensive began, and by 13 October the Syrians had been pushed back beyond their 6 October starting line; the Israelis began transferring forces from this front to the Suez–Sinai area. Here, the Egyptians had made a copy-book crossing of the Canal, launching mechanized thrusts south of Kantara, just north of Ismailia in the centre, and in the Suez region at the southern end. Egyptian forces from the Ismailia crossing began to sweep south to link with the bridgehead opposite Suez. The next step was to have been a surge eastwards to seize the vital Mitla, Khatmia and Giddi passes in Sinai. But Egypt delayed, hesitant to depart from the SAM air cover. Not until 14 October did Egyptian tanks move in strength outside their air cover, and forces aiming for the Sinai passes were beaten back during the day and next

morning. Late on the 15th Israeli tanks struck through the gap between the Egyptian 2nd and 3rd Armies south of Ismailia, in the battle of Chinese Farm. A small Israeli spearhead crossed the Canal, destroying SAM sites and allowing Israeli aircraft to range farther forward. By the 17th a full army brigade had crossed and was thrusting south to threaten the Egyptian 3rd Army on the east bank opposite Suez. By the time of the final ceasefire early on 24 October the Israelis had surrounded the 3rd Army, and were thus able to use this trapped enemy force as a hostage. Egyptian and Israeli units withdrew to their respective banks of the Canal; in Syria Israeli forces pulled back from within 20 miles of Damascus.

Italy, campaigns in, 1796–7, 1799, 1800 (Map 1) *French Revolutionary* and *Napoleonic Wars. Napoleon* arrived in Nice on 27 March 1796 to begin a brilliant 13-month campaign. His army totalled 41,570 men, mostly ill-trained and ill-equipped; against him were 30,000 Austrians under Jean Pierre Beaulieu and 25,000 Piedmontese under Baron Colli. Napoleon's army stretched along the Riviera Coast. For 3 years French generals had failed in attempts to advance through the passes into Piedmont; Napoleon adopted a new plan. First he feinted for neutral Genoa, drawing the Austrians away from their mountain base at Alessandria. Then, on 11 April, Napoleon swung north to catch the Austrians off-balance at Monenotte, 12 April. He struck the Piedmontese at Millesimo on the 14th, then later in the day turned on the Austrians again at Dredo. Next day the French defeated a further 6,000 Austrians sent to support the Piedmontese. Napoleon rested his army, then swung against the Piedmontese again, inflicting defeat near Vico on 21 April; the Piedmontese sued for peace. Napoleon could now concentrate on the Austrians, deployed across the heavily defended Po River. Napoleon turned from the obvious crossing point at Pavia and hurried downstream to Piecenza; a small French force under *Lannes* secured a foothold on the far bank, and within 48 hours the French Army had crossed. The Austrian Commander fell back to the Adda. Napoleon, feinting north and south, stormed the bridge at Lodi on 10 May, entering Milan on the 15th while the Austrians retreated towards the Tyrol. Napoleon darted into central Italy during June to seize Florence and Leghorn, returning to Milan on 13 July before the Austrians could concentrate behind him. The enemy now numbered over 50,000 men under Count Dagobert Wurmser; the latter sent 18,000 men under General Quasdanovich down the west shore of Lake Garda towards Brescia, while he advanced down the east towards Mantua. Napoleon seized upon the divided Austrian movement, defeating Quasdanovich north of Lonato on 3 August and Wurmser at Castiglione 2 days later. The Austrians again attempted to relieve besieged Mantua, with Wurmser marching down the Brenta valley while General Paul Davodovich

defended the Tyrol. Napoleon defeated the latter at Caliano, 3–5 September, then hurried back to defeat Wurmser at Bassano on the 8th. In a third Austrian relief operation, forces under Baron Josef Alvintzy checked the French at Caldiero on 12 November, but Alvintzy was thrown back at Arcola, 15–17 November. A final Austrian attempt to reach Mantua was defeated at Rivoli, 14 January 1797; Mantua capitulated on 2 February. Napoleon invaded Austria on 10 March, and by 6 April had advanced to Leoben pushing back Austrians under Archduke Charles. The Treaty of Campo Formio followed, 17 October. France's enemies struck back in 1799 while Napoleon was absent in *Egypt*. A Russo-Austrian Army under *Suvorov* expelled French forces after victories at Magnano, 5 April, the Trebbia, 17–19 June, and Novi, 15 August; at the beginning of 1800 the French only held footholds on the Riviera where 40,000 men were deployed under *Masséna*, and in the upper Rhine/Alsace area, where *Moreau* commanded 120,000 troops. Under allied plans General Paul Kray von Krajowa would lead 120,000 men against Moreau, while Baron Michael Melas attacked Masséna with 100,000 Austrians. Masséna's Army was scattered in April, but in mid-May Napoleon crossed the Alps with 36,000 men to defeat Melas at *Marengo*, 14 June, and thus recover Italy.

Italy, 1915–18 *First World War* (Map 9). Italy declared war on Austria on 23 May 1915. Austrian forces were deployed in excellent mountain defences, especially strong in the Isonzo River sector west of Trieste where 100,000 troops were commanded by General Svetozan Borojevic von Bojna. This area would witness the main fighting; numerous clashes took place officially titled Battles of the Isonzo: 4 in 1915, 5 in 1916 and 3 in 1917. The Italians failed to make headway until the 11th Battle of the Isonzo, 18 August to 15 September 1917, when the 2nd Army under General Luigi Capello battered through Austrian defences. German aid arrived in the form of the 14th Austrian Army, comprising mainly German troops under General Otto von Below. The 12th Battle of the Isonzo (Caporetto) began on 24 October 1917, with von Below's regiments using the *Hutier* infiltration method. By 12 November the Austro-German forces had swept the Italians back to the Piave; the offensive was halted through shortage of supplies and through the arrival of 11 British and French divisions under *Plumer*. About 40,000 Italians were killed or wounded in this battle and 275,000 captured; Austro–German losses totalled about 21,000. German forces were transferred to the west for the 1918 offensives, but the Austrians nevertheless opened a new campaign on 15 June 1918, comprising drives at Verona and Padua, checked at the Battle of the Piave, 15 June. The Italian commander, now General Armando Diaz, delayed until July before launching a counter-offensive. This, supported by British and French troops, was halted at Monte Grappo, 23 October, but advanced again to cross the Piave after hard fighting at Vittorio Veneto, 24 October to 4 November.

Italy, 1943–5 *Second World War*

(Map 14). *Mussolini* was overthrown on 24 July 1943; his successor Marshal Pietro Badoglio began negotiations with the allies. *Hitler* started moving reinforcements south; *Kesselring*, German Commander in southern Italy, prepared for the expected allied invasion. This took place on 3 September when *Montgomery*'s 8th Army crossed the channel from *Sicily* to land virtually unopposed in the Reggio Calabria region in the toe of Italy. The Italian armistice was announced on 8 September, a premature move since it alerted the Germans to the *Salerno* landing made by the US 5th Army next day. The struggle for the beachhead at Salerno continued for almost a week, with the US troops commanded by General Mark Clark. Contact was made with Montgomery's 8th Army on 16 September, and the allies advanced north on both coasts – the 8th Army in the east and the 5th in the west. The Americans took Naples on 2 October, but Kesselring deployed forces in excellent defensive positions: these, the 'Winter' or 'Gustav' Line, ran from the estuary of the Garigliano River in the west, along the Rapido, over the mountains, and reached the Adriatic in the east just above the Sangro. Battle continued in the *Cassino* area throughout the winter. Montgomery handed over command of the 8th Army to General Sir Oliver Leese in December, and left Italy to prepare for the *Normandy landings*; allied strength in Italy, under *Alexander*'s overall command, suffered in general from the withdrawal of veteran units. The *Anzio* operation was launched on 22 January 1944, in an attempt to break the Cassino deadlock, but not until mid-May was breakthrough achieved. The allies then advanced on Rome, entered on 4 June, and pushed north. The allied armies were further weakened by the withdrawal of more units for the '*Anvil*' operation against southern France. The Germans blocked the advance at the 'Gothic' Line stretching south of Bologna through Pisa and Florence to Ancona. Fighting continued throughout the winter, with the US 5th Army now commanded by General Lucius Truscott and the British 8th Army by General Richard McCreery. Kesselring was transferred to the German Front, March 1945, being replaced by General Heinrich von Vietinghoff. Not until 9 April was the Gothic Line penetrated, when the 8th Army attacked south-east of Bologna; the US 5th Army broke into the Po Valley on 14 April and Vietinghoff agreed to unconditional surrender on the 29th.

Iwo Jima, Battle of, February– March 1945 *Second World War* against *Japan* (Map 16). Under plans finally agreed by *MacArthur* and *Nimitz*, the next stage after the US reconquest of the *Philippines* was the seizure of the 8-square-mile island of Iwo Jima in the Bonin Group. About 22,000 Japanese army and naval troops were firmly entrenched in concealed gun emplacements, pillboxes and caves. Their commander was Major-General Tadamichi *Kuribayashi*. First US landings were made on 19 February, with the 4th and 5th Marine Divisions battling ashore on the southeast of the island and the 3rd Marine Division landing in the second wave. The commander was Major-General Harry Schmidt. Despite 2,420 casualties the marines managed to sever the island during the first day; they then crept north, taking Mount Suribachi on 23 February. Organized resistance ended on 16 March. Total US casualties were nearly 7,000 killed and over 18,000 injured. Only 212 Japanese surrendered; over 21,000 died. Already, on 14 March, the battle for *Okinawa* had begun.

J

Jackson, Andrew, 1767–1845 US General and 7th President. Defeated Creek Indians at Horseshoe Bend, March 1814, during *American War of 1812*; inflicted devastating defeat on the British at New Orleans, 8 January 1815; returned to Indian fighting, 1818; succeeded John Quincy Adams as US President, 1829, succeeded by Martin Van Buren, 1837.

Jackson, Thomas Jonathan, 'Stonewall', 1824–63 Confederate General, *American Civil War* (Map 3). Served in *American–Mexican War*, 1846–8; resigned from US Army 1852; appointed Confederate Brigadier-General, 17 June 1861, and earned his nickname at the First Battle of *Bull Run*, July. Jackson led Confederate troops in the brilliant *Shenandoah* valley campaign, April–June 1862, and his manoeuvring played a major part in the Confederate victory at the Second Battle of *Bull Run*. His attack on 2 May 1863 at *Chancellorsville* almost shattered the Union right wing, but soon afterwards he fell mortally wounded, fired on in the darkness by his own troops. He died on 10 May.

Japan *Second World War, 1941–5* (Map 16). Japan's onslaught on *Pearl Harbor* and Thailand, December 1941, threw the Western allies on to the defensive. Within a few weeks Malaya had been overrun, *Singapore* taken and the Japanese had conquered *Java* in the Netherlands East Indies, Borneo, the *Philippines, New Guinea* and New Britain, the Solomons and other islands. By May 1942 *Burma* was in Japanese hands. Yet Japan's initial success played against her; over-confident, original plans were enlarged in April–May 1942 to include an offensive over a wider area. This large perimeter, which covered Midway Island, southern New Guinea and the southern Solomons, was too ambitious: the Battle of *Midway*, June 1942, following *Coral Sea*, was one of the most decisive ever fought, helping the allies regain the initiative. The struggle was spread over a number of widely separated areas. In the north, *Chiang Kai-shek* could do no more than hold his own in China. In *Burma*, the allies were unable to make steady progress until mid-1944. The Pacific offered best hope of allied gains. Strategic controversy broke out: both *MacArthur*, Commander of US forces in the Far East, and *King*, Chief of Naval Staff in Washington, agreed there should be an offensive against Rabaul,

New Britain, but whereas MacArthur sought a direct thrust, King urged an island-hopping strategy up the Solomons. The compromise plan worked out by the US *Joint Chiefs of Staff* resulted in both the reconquest of the Solomons, highlighted by the *Guadalcanal* struggle, and also the establishment of US–Australian control in New Guinea and New Britain; both campaigns resulted in the isolation of Rabaul by early 1944. King now sought the main emphasis on a move through the central Pacific, aiming at Formosa via the Marshall, Caroline and Marianas Islands; *Nimitz*, Pacific Fleet Commander, largely supported King. MacArthur urged a reconquest of the Philippines. Again a compromise resulted. The main landings in the *Philippines* began in October 1944. Meanwhile Nimitz had already made his move forward in the central Pacific, and the Marianas Islands were taken in July–August. The last major stepping stones, *Iwo Jima* and *Okinawa*, were taken in early 1945. The war came to its abrupt end with the dropping of *atomic bombs* on *Hiroshima and Nagasaki*, 6–9 August. Ceasefire began on the 15th; the official surrender was signed on 2 September. Japanese dead in the struggle totalled over 1½ million soldiers and 300,000 civilians.

Java, Battles of, February–March 1942 *Second World War* against *Japan*. The campaign for the Netherlands East Indies began on 11 January, with Japanese forces sweeping towards Java. Vastly outnumbered US, British, Dutch, Australian troops and naval units were hastily organized into a combined force under *Wavell* and given the title ABDA Command. The fall of *Singapore*, 15 February, reduced allied chances to a minimum, and in an effort to save all possible manpower from inevitable destruction, the ABDA Command was dissolved on 25 February. On the 27th, surviving allied warships, 5 cruisers and 10 destroyers under Dutch Admiral Karel Doorman, attacked the Japanese Eastern Force approaching Java, escorted by Admiral Takeo Takagi's 4 cruisers and 13 destroyers. This 7-hour naval battle of the Java Sea ended with overwhelming allied losses: Doorman went down with his flagship, and only 3 cruisers and 5 destroyers survived – most sank during the next 48 hours. Java surrendered on 9 March; already the Japanese had invaded the Solomons prior to the establishment of an air base at *Guadalcanal*.

Jellicoe, Sir John Rushworth, 1st Earl, 1859–1935 British Admiral of the Fleet. Appointed by *Churchill* as Second-in-Command of the British Grand Fleet, November 1911; assumed position of Commander, 3 August 1914, replacing Sir George Callaghan; fought Battle of *Jutland*, 1916. His apparent lack of decisiveness aroused intense controversy, but his prime intent was to preserve the British Grand Fleet intact. He was appointed First Sea Lord, 22 November 1916, succeeding Sir Henry Jackson, and was replaced as Commander of the Grand Fleet by his rival *Beatty*. Jellicoe opposed the introduction of convoys in the Battle of the *Atlantic*, and because of this convoy controversy was replaced by Admiral Lord Wester-Wemyss, November 1917.

Jemappes, Battle of, November 1792 *French Revolutionary Wars* (Map 1). A Prussian attempt to invade France, under Carl William, Duke of Brunswick, had been blocked by *Dumouriez* and François Kellermann at Valmy, 20 September, after suffering heavy bombardment from 54 French guns. Dumouriez's Army of the North then raised the siege of Lille, forcing an Austrian army under Archduke Albert to retreat into Belgium (the Austrian Netherlands), where the Austrians went into winter quarters at Jemappes. Dumouriez attacked on 6 November. The Austrians occupied excellent defensive positions in the heights above Jemappes, but had only about 13,000 men against the French strength of 40,000, and were driven from the hills with heavy losses.

Jena, Battle of, 1806 – see Auerstedt

Jervis, Sir John, Earl of St Vincent, 1735–1823 Fought in the Battle of Ushant, 1778; appointed C-in-C Mediterranean Fleet, November 1795, with the young *Nelson* in his command. Jervis blockaded the French Fleet at Toulon in 1796. On 14 February 1797 he defeated the Spanish Fleet at the Battle of *Cape St Vincent*. Lack of

frigates prevented efforts to block the French Fleet carrying *Napoleon* and his army to *Egypt* in June 1798. Jervis relinquished command in June 1799, succeeded by Lord Keith. After service in the Channel, during which he averted mutiny through his foresight and severe discipline, Jervis became First Lord of the Admiralty, 1801–4. He introduced reforms in naval administration, aimed at stamping out corruption.

Jodl, Alfred, 1890–1946 German General. Chief of Staff of Armed Forces Operational Staff during the *Second World War*, next in line of seniority to Chief of Staff of High Command of the Armed Forces (OKW). On 7 May 1945 Jodl signed the documents of unconditional surrender of all German forces. He was executed at Nuremberg, 23 May.

Joffre, Joseph Jacques Césaire, 1852–1931 Marshal of France. Replaced General Augustin Michael as Commander of French Armies in 1914, and through his leadership the French *Plan XVII* was introduced (Map 10). His organization of forces for the Battle of the *Marne* in September showed him to be a capable leader in close touch with his subordinates. His determination not to allow further German advances led to *Verdun*, 1916, during which he counter-attacked at the *Somme*. Failure to achieve decisive results led to his compulsory retirement, 31 December 1916, and his replacement by *Nivelle*;

thereafter he acted as adviser to the General Staff.

Johnson, Lyndon Baines, 1908– 36th US President. Chosen by *Kennedy* as Vice-President, 1960; became President after Kennedy's assassination, 22 November 1963; won overwhelming victory over Republican Barry Goldwater, 1964; sent US Marines to Dominican Republic, 1965. *Vietnam* proved to be Johnson's main preoccupation. He ordered bombing of North Vietnamese naval bases after US warships were attacked in the Gulf of Tonkin, August 1964, and sent increasing numbers of troops to South Vietnam, with the total reaching 23,000 at the start of 1965; these units were now fighting a full combat role. On 31 March 1968 Johnson declared he would not stand in the forthcoming election. He ordered a complete halt to bombing and shelling of North Vietnam on 31 October; on 5 November *Nixon* was elected President.

Joint Chiefs of Staff (US JCS) Set up as a committee of service chiefs, counterpart to the British *Chiefs of Staff Committee*, in the early days of US involvement in the Second World War; acted as the US component in the *Combined Chiefs of Staff*. The JCS has its origins in the Joint Board established in 1903, but this forerunner lacked authority – it only met twice during the First World War. The JCS became a powerful body in its own right during the Second World War, with its members being the Chief of Staff of the Army, the Chief of Staff of the US Army Air Force, Chief of Naval Operations and the Commandant, US Marine Corps. The 1947 National Security Act gave the JCS greater statutory recognition, and the 1949 amendment to this Act officially created the position of Chairman of the JCS: before, the post had been on an 'ad hoc' basis.

Jomini, Baron Henri, 1779–1869 Swiss-born soldier and military theorist. Aide-de-camp to *Ney*, 1803; Ney's Chief of Staff during French campaigns leading to *Austerlitz*, 1805, Jena in the *Auerstedt* campaign, 1806, *Friedland*, 1807, in the *Peninsular War* operations, 1808–11, and in *Russia*, 1812 (Map 1); disappointed by lack of promotion, Jomini crossed to the Russians in August 1813 and served Tsar Alexander as an adviser. He continued to be consulted by the Russians, including during the *Crimean War*. But he never achieved independent command, and his fame rests more on his thoughts on war as expressed in his 'Précis de l'Art de la Guerre', 1838, and to a lesser extent in his 'Histoire ... des Campagnes de la Révolution', 1819–24. Whereas *Clausewitz* concentrated on the nature and essential spirit of war, Jomini devoted himself more to the practicalities of strategy: bringing major forces to bear at a decisive point; manoeuvring to engage one's major forces against only parts of the enemy; engaging these masses not only at a decisive point, but with such speed and co-ordination that offensive efforts are linked. All could be achieved through the choice of the correct line of operations – best obtained through occupying an interior position, with forces closer together and with the enemy having to manoeuvre outside one's own area of operations. Such an interior position enabled forces to be concentrated with greater ease and gave greater scope for offensive action at a number of differing points. Subsequent developments eroded some of Jomini's validity: improved communications, especially through *railways*, eventually undermined the value of an interior position; improved weapon technology, especially the *machine-gun*, gave greater strength to the defensive. Meanwhile the truth of Jomini's teaching was underlined by *Moltke*'s successes in the *Austro-Prussian* and *Franco-Prussian Wars*, and some aspects of his writing continue to be important: the need for intelligence, planning and efficient staff work in the field.

Jutland, Battle of, May–June 1916 *First World War*. The Germans planned to lure the British Grand Fleet to sea, where U-boats could inflict decisive damage on it. Informed by intercepted radio messages of a sortie by the German High Seas Fleet, the British Commander *Jellicoe* did indeed leave his Scapa Flow base, but U-boats failed to attack. The German Fleet under Admiral Rheinhard Scheer cruised north towards the Skagerrak on 30 May, preceded by the *battlecruiser* squadron under Franz von Hipper. Unknown to the Germans, Jellicoe's 24 Dreadnought *battleships* and other warships were approaching, preceded by the battlecruiser fleet under *Beatty*. The latter made contact with Hipper's battlecruisers early in the afternoon of 31 May. Hipper turned south to draw Beatty on to the guns of the High Seas Fleet, while Beatty aimed to block Hipper from his home ports, not knowing the whereabouts of the main enemy force. Both battlecruiser fleets careered south-east, fighting a parallel action at a range of 16,500 yards. German gunnery proved more effective: Beatty's flagship 'Lion', received several hits, the 'Indefatigable' blew up, and 30 minutes later the 'Queen Mary' was destroyed. Soon afterwards Beatty gained first sight of the German High Seas Fleet; he turned north pursued by Hipper. Jellicoe turned south to engage Scheer, hampered by lack of definite information from Beatty. He tried to block the Germans from their home base. Hipper's flagship 'Lutzow' was put out of action; the British lost 2 cruisers and 1 battlecruiser. Many of the British shells failed to explode. Under smokescreen cover Scheer switched course through a brilliantly executed 180-degree turn and headed west, moving out of British range. But Jellicoe still blocked the Germans from their ports; Scheer tried to break through, turning away after receiving heavy British fire: 3 German battlecruisers were severely damaged. After nightfall Scheer managed to crash through the tail of the British line, sinking the battlecruiser 'Black Prince' and making for home. Jellicoe did not pursue. British losses totalled 3 battlecruisers, 3 cruisers, 8 destroyers; German losses were 1 old battleship, 1 battlecruiser, 4 light cruisers and 3 destroyers. Both main fleets remained in being. Jellicoe was criticized for allowing the enemy to escape, with his attackers contrasting Jellicoe's caution with Beatty's aggressiveness. But Jellicoe's supporters stressed the need to keep the Grand Fleet intact, and criticized Beatty's failure to supply Jellicoe with adequate information.

K

Keitel, Wilhelm, 1882–1946 German Marshal. Chief of War Ministry administration, 1935 to February 1938; promoted to office of Chief of Staff of High Command of Armed Forces (OKW) when *Hitler* manipulated the resignation of War Minister *Blomberg*, himself taking over the War Minister's functions. Keitel therefore became Hitler's senior military deputy, with *Jodl* next in line. He signed the formal declaration of surrender, 9 May 1945, and was condemned to death and executed at Nuremberg, 16 October 1946.

Kemal Ataturk, also known as Kemal Pasha, 1881–1938 Turkish General and President. Served in Turkish–Italian War, 1911; showed exceptional ability as divisional commander fighting against the allies in the *Dardanelles*, 1915, afterwards in Caucasus, 1916–17, and Palestine, 1918. In 1919 Kemal organized the Turkish Nationalist Party, and was elected President of a provisional government in 1920 during the *Greek–Turkish War*. He reorganized the Turkish forces, which in general had performed inadequately during the First World War, and defeated Greek forces at the Sakkaria (Sakarya), August–September 1921; thereafter Kemal launched a successful campaign leading to the seizure of Smyrna, September 1822; he advanced on Constantinople and negotiated the Convention of Mudania leading to the Treaty of Lausanne, July 1923. The Turkish Republic was officially established on 29 October with Mustafa Kemal the first President; he was re-elected 1927, 1931, 1935, remaining in power until his death.

Kennedy, John Fitzgerald, 1917–63 35th US President. Became America's youngest-ever President, 20 January 1961, succeeding *Eisenhower*. Deteriorating relations with *Cuba* led to the Bay of Pigs fiasco, April 1961; in July 1961 another crisis arose over Berlin, with Kennedy, backed by Britain and France, refusing Russian demands for allied troop withdrawals; in August the East German government started building the Berlin Wall; in October 1962 came the *Cuba* missile crisis, with Kennedy successfully insisting these offensive weapons must be withdrawn. Kennedy, alarmed at the prospect of a Soviet missile lead, increased the US defence budget threefold, yet this accelerated the arms race. Kennedy's period of office also included the beginnings of the policy of *flexible response*. He made substantial commitments to the defence of *Vietnam*, Thailand and *Laos*. Kennedy was assassinated at Dallas, 22 November 1963, succeeded by Vice-President *Johnson*.

Kenya, Mau Mau uprising, 1952–6 Opposition by white settlers to reforms demanded by Jomo Kenyatta's Kenya African Union led to increasing tension in this British colony, and to the formation of the Mau Mau secret society by the Kikuyu tribe. Riots and murders throughout 1952 resulted in the British declaration of a state of emergency, 20 October. Suspected Mau Mau leaders were imprisoned, including Kenyatta who was sentenced to 7 years on 20 October 1953. A separate East African command, comprising Kenya, Uganda and Tanganyika, was established under General Sir George Erskine. On 15 June 1953 British troops killed 125 Mau Mau terrorists in the Aberdare Forest. The colonial government attempted to remove Mau Mau appeal by undertaking improvements in Nairobi housing conditions; guerrillas were offered amnesty if they could prove they were not guilty of serious crimes. Large-scale operations in the Aberdare and Mount Kenya areas took place from February to June 1955, and the campaign had begun to dwindle by the end of the year. Disparity between Mau Mau casualties and the total of other deaths was wide: between 1952

and 1955 about 10,173 terrorists were killed, compared with 32 Europeans, 24 Asians and 291 non-terrorist Africans. Kenyatta was released on 14 August 1961 and led Kenya to independence, 12 December 1963, as Prime Minister.

Kesselring, Albert, 1887–1960 German Marshal. Appointed Chief of Air Staff, 1936; commanded Air Fleet Two in the invasion of *Poland*, September 1939, and in Battle of *France*, May–June 1940, during which his aircraft attacked *Dunkirk*; one of the 3 air commanders attacking in the Battle of *Britain*; appointed C-in-C Armed Forces South (Mediterranean area), December 1941, and thereafter engaged in operations against allies in North Africa, *Tunisia*, and *Malta*; commander of forces in south *Italy* at the time of the allied invasion, September 1943. On 10 March 1945 Kesselring was transferred from Italy to the defence of west Germany, replacing von *Rundstedt*; in mid-April *Hitler* gave him command of all remaining forces in the south, with *Doenitz* commanding in the north. His units surrendered at the start of May. A British court sentenced him to death, May 1947, but this was commuted to life imprisonment; he was freed in October 1952.

Khrushchev, Nikita Sergeyevich, 1894–1971 Soviet Premier. First Secretary of Communist Party, 1953–64; began process of de-Stalinization after 20th Party Congress, February 1956; replaced Nikolai Bulganin as

Premier, 27 March 1958. During his period of power the Soviet Union began manned space exploration with the flight by Yuri Gagarin, April 1961, thus demonstrating highly skilled Soviet missile technology. Soviet air defence missiles in central Russia shot down a US U-2 'Spy' aircraft, piloted by F. G. Powers, on 1 May 1960, thus precipitating a crisis with the USA; on 9 December 1961 Khruschev boasted that the Soviet Union had nuclear bombs of over 100 megatons. East–West tension was increased by the construction of the Berlin Wall, August 1961, and especially by the *Cuba* missile crisis, October–November 1962. Deposed by Leonid Brezhnev and Aleksei Kosygin, 14–15 October 1964.

King, Ernest Joseph, 1878–1956 US Admiral of the Fleet. Appointed C-in-C US Atlantic Patrol Forces 1940, with these units becoming the Atlantic Fleet in 1941; Chief of Naval Operations from March 1942 to November 1945, representing the US Navy on the US *Joint Chiefs of Staff* and on the Anglo-US *Combined Chiefs of Staff*. King argued vehemently for naval resources for the war against *Japan*, and was engaged in intense debate with *MacArthur* over the use of these resources in the Pacific. He retired in 1945.

Kissinger, Dr Henry Alfred, 1923– German-born US scholar and statesman. Taught at Harvard, 1951–69. He argued against the policy of *massive nuclear retaliation*, declaring that

such a drastic policy would not deter local, more ambiguous communist threats, and contending that massive retaliation could not be the action policy of the USA because its implementation would be suicidal. Kissinger was chosen by President *Nixon* as his special assistant for national security affairs, 1960, with duties including preparation of *National Security Council* meetings, briefing the President and following up presidential decisions. Already, under *Kennedy* and *Johnson*, Kissinger had been frequently consulted on defence matters, and after 1960 he became known as the President's most influential foreign-policy expert. Kissinger was appointed Secretary of State, September 1973, and continued at this post under President Ford. He played a large part in obtaining closer US–Chinese relations, which included the visit to Peking by Nixon in February 1972; he initiated *Vietnam* negotiations which led to the Paris Agreement, January 1973; and a major thread of his career was his work towards 'détente' with Russia, including through the *Strategic Arms Limitation Talks*. Kissinger undertook extensive peacekeeping negotiations between the Arabs and Israelis and between the Greeks and Turks during the 1974 *Cyprus* hostilities.

Kitchener, Lord Horatio Herbert of Khartoum and Broome, 1850–1916 Irish-born British General and War Secretary. Accompanied Wolseley's abortive attempt to relieve *Gordon* at Khartoum in the *Sudan*, 1885; began the reconquest of the Sudan in 1896, becoming a national hero after the final victory at *Omdurman*, September 1898. Kitchener acted as Chief of Staff to *Roberts* in the Boer War, taking over command when Roberts returned to England in December 1900. Subsequent appointments were C-in-C India, 1902–9; Consul-General Egypt, 1911–14; Secretary for War, August 1914 to 1916. During this latter period Kitchener enjoyed far-reaching power, being both minister and virtual army chief. He believed the regular British Army, about 120,000 men in August 1914, to be far too small, yet he despised the Territorial Army which he considered amateurish. On 7 August he made the first of his famous appeals for volunteers, asking for 100,000 men; during the first 18 months of war about 2,476,000 came forward to join 'Kitchener's Army'. He remained a firm advocate of the Western Front despite the slaughter and deadlock, and he failed to provide the *Dardanelles* operation with adequate support. Opposition to Kitchener led to the curtailment of his military authority in December 1915, with the appointment of *Robertson* as CIGS. Kitchener was drowned on 5 June 1916 when HMS 'Hampshire', on which he was travelling to Russia, struck a mine off the Orkneys. *Lloyd George* succeeded him as War Secretary.

Korean War, June 1950 to July 1953 (Map 17) An allied agreement of 15 August 1945 laid down that Japanese forces north of the 38th parallel in Korea would surrender to the Russians, and those in the south to US troops. Thereafter the 38th parallel became a political frontier. The Republic of Korea (ROK) was established, 15 August 1947, following unification failures; the Soviet Union established the Democratic People's Republic of Korea, and as 'adviser' created the North Korean Army (NKA). NKA units comprising 7 infantry divisions and 1 tank brigade invaded the South on 25 June 1950, commanded by Marshal Choe Yong Gun. The surprise offensive made a rapid advance to take Seoul. On the day the invasion began the UN Security Council invited members to assist in obtaining withdrawal of NKA forces; the Soviet Union, boycotting the Council, had no representative present to veto this decision. *Truman* sent orders on 27 June to *MacArthur*, US Far East Commander, to lend US air and naval assistance; on 30 June this order was extended to ground troops. The US 24th Division under General William Dean began moving into Korea on 30 June and fought a delaying withdrawal southeast, 6–21 July, during which the US Commander was captured. On 7 July MacArthur was named C-in-C UN Command. By August the NKA had pushed the US and ROK troops into the Pusan Perimeter; troops in this confined area, commanded by General Walton H. Walker, were in a critical situation. The British 27th Infantry Brigade arrived on 14 September. On 15 September the US 10th Corps under General Edward M. Almond began landing at Inchon, 150 miles north of the Pusan Perimeter, about 20 miles west of Seoul. Troops in the Pusan Perimeter thrust north, and linked with the Inchon landing force on 26 September: on the same day Seoul was liberated; the NKA occupation area had been split in half. UN troops advanced north and by 24 November had occupied two-thirds of North Korea, reaching to Hyesanjin almost on the Yalu River. The latter marked the Korean–Chinese border. The communists launched a massive counter-offensive on 25 November, reinforced by about 180,000 Chinese troops. This attack seized upon the divided nature of the UN advance, which had been split by the rugged terrain into the 8th Army push in the west and the 10th Corps in the east. The 8th Army was forced back to the 38th parallel by the end of the year, while in the east the 10th Corps, totalling 105,000 men, had to be evacuated. MacArthur was bitterly critical over restrictions imposed on him by the UN and Truman; he had not, for example, been allowed to bomb bridges over the Yalu or fly reconnaissance missions over south China, for fear of precipitating full-scale Chinese involvement. The UN situation was rendered even more unsettled by the death of Walker in a car accident, 23 December; he was succeeded by *Ridgway*, given command of all ground operations with MacArthur having supreme authority. A split between MacArthur and Truman, always politically unsympathetic, grew wider. MacArthur insisted that if the

war was to be won there should be a naval blockade of China; China's industrial capacity in Manchuria should be destroyed by bombing; Chinese Nationalist forces from Formosa should be employed; guerrilla operations should be launched in south China. These proposals were refused. Instead, war aims were lowered: the USA, with its UN partners, was now tacitly prepared to end hostilities through negotiation, and despite objections from MacArthur, the objective of uniting the whole country was abandoned. UN forces were pushed back when the communists launched a renewed offensive on 1 January 1951, evacuating Seoul on the 4th. Ridgway began a series of limited counter-operations on the 25th and Seoul was reoccupied on 14 March. The front line again stabilized roughly along the 38th parallel. To Truman this seemed an excellent moment to open negotiations, and MacArthur was informed on 20 March that a presidential announcement was being planned. MacArthur pre-empted this announcement by a statement of his own, 24 March: 'Even under the inhibitions which now restrict the activity of the UN forces . . . Red China . . . has been shown its complete inability to accomplish by force of arms the conquest of Korea.' MacArthur warned that 'a decision of the US to depart from its tolerant effort to contain the war to the area of Korea would doom Red China'. This statement was seen by Truman as belligerent, insubordinate and ruining any hopes of negotiations. MacArthur was relieved of command on 11 April. Ridgway replaced him, with General James van Fleet taking over army command. Fighting entered an ebb and flow pattern which would continue for the rest of the war, with successive communist offensives being repulsed but with UN forces remaining in the vicinity of the 38th parallel. Discussions for an armistice began at Panmunjon on 12 November 1951, and continued in halting fashion until October 1952. *Eisenhower*, becoming President in early 1953, was pledged to end the war. Peace talks were resumed on 20 July and an armistice signed on the 27th. UN casualties totalled 118,515 killed, 264,591 wounded and 92,987 captured. Total communist casualties numbered at least 1,600,000. Apart from the high US proportion, UN forces included men from Britain, Turkey, Canada, Australia, Thailand, France, Greece, New Zealand, Holland, Colombia, Belgium, Ethiopia, Luxembourg and South Africa.

Krupp Works, Essen, Germany Founded in 1810 by Frederick Krupp, 1787–1826, whose son Alfred, 1812–87, began ordnance manufacture in 1847. Thereafter the Krupp Works were famous for arms production, including the 1851 *breech-loading* cannon and the monstrous 'Big Bertha', a 42 cm gun used in the First World War especially during the 1918 *Somme* offensive. Alfred's son Frederick Alfred, 1854–1902, succeeded in the management of the works; control passed to his daughter Bertha,

1886–1957, at his death, and her husband prefixed Krupp to his name, becoming Gustav Krupp von Bohlen und Halbach, 1870–1950. He supported Hitler and acted as President of the Reich Corporation of German Industry. The British took over the Krupp plants in November 1945.

Kurdish War, Iraq, 1961–75 Kurdish tribesmen had long urged local autonomy; repeated denial of their requests led to fighting in northern Iraq, with the insurgents reported to number 2,000 by early 1962. They succeeded in forcing the Iraqi Army to abandon the mountainous countryside; talks in early 1963 broke down, and the Iraqi Army launched a new offensive later in the year, with coordinated air and ground operations. Rebel reports on 30 June 1963 claimed that 167 villages had been bombed or strafed with 634 civilians killed and 1,309 wounded. The fall of the Iraq government, 18 November 1963, resulted in a reduction of military operations: by the end of the year Kurdish forces were said to total about 20,000, rising to 100,000 in 1974 under Mulla Mustafa Barzani. The Kurds received support from fellow-tribesmen in northern Syria, southern Turkey and especially Iran. But a blockage on the flow of equipment and personnel over the Irani border by the Shah of Iran, March 1975, led to a dramatic strangulation of Kurdish insurgent activity.

Kursk, Battle of, July 1943 *Second World War* (Map 15). Known by the

Germans as 'Fall Zitadelle', this battle in *Russia* was intended to regain the initiative following the great Red Army winter offensive which had included *Stalingrad*. German forces under Manstein recaptured Kharkov on 14 March and pushed back the Soviets in the south, but the spring thaw then stopped mass armoured movements. With dry weather, Manstein planned to launch a limited assault against the Red Army salient east of Kursk, in combination with Kluge's Army Group in the centre; he assembled 50 divisions, 16 of which were panzer or motorized, comprising about 900,000 men with about 10,000 guns and nearly 3,000 tanks. About 2,000 aircraft would provide support. Hitler delayed the start; this allowed the Red Army to prepare elaborate defence lines and to plan a counter-offensive. Red Army manpower outnumbered the Germans by about 3 to 2. The 2 Russian commanders in the Kursk salient, General Konstantine Rokossovsky in the north and General Nikolai Vatutin in the south, had a combined total of 2,500 tanks and 10,000 guns, although with fewer aircraft than the *Luftwaffe*. The German offensive began late on 4 July. Kluge's 9th Army attempted to strike into the salient from the north, while Manstein's 4th Panzer Army pushed up from the south. Russian defensive lines prevented deep German penetrations: by 9 July the Russians had only been forced back 10 miles in the north and 30 in the south. On 11 July the Russians counter-attacked. Multiple thrusts were launched towards

Orel, north of the Kursk salient, and towards Kharkov in the south. The Germans were forced to pull back on 13 July with Soviet tanks and anti-tank guns having destroyed 40 per cent of the enemy armour. About 1,000 Germans and 1,400 aircraft were lost, and 70,000 men had been killed or wounded. Alarmed by the allied invasion of *Sicily*, 9 July, Hitler ordered the transfer of panzers from the east; Russian pressure intensified. Manstein abandoned Kharkov on 23 August; Orel had already fallen in the first days of August. The Red Army recaptured Smolensk, 25 September, and Kiev, 6 November.

Kutuzov, Prince Mikhail Ilarionovich, 1745–1813 Russian Marshal. Served in Poland, 1758/9–69; against Turks at frequent intervals in subsequent years, fighting under *Suvorov* at Alushta, 1774, and in the siege of Ismail, 1791. Kutuzov became one of Suvorov's greatest disciples, learning from him many lessons of leadership including the necessity to establish close relations with the ordinary soldier. Kutuzov also obtained invaluable instruction from another of his commanders against the Turks, Peter Alexander Rumyantsev (1725–96), who once declared: 'The objective is not the occupation of a geographical position but the destruction of enemy forces.' Like Rumyantsev, Kutuzov believed that the commander's prime concern was to keep his army in being: as long as forces remained intact, defeat would be impossible; battles should be avoided unless a decisive result could be obtained; rather than fighting a disadvantageous pitched battle, it was better to step back out of reach, rely on manoeuvre, and wait for a more favourable moment – even if this meant abandoning territory. Kutuzov maintained these principles throughout his career with amazing consistency, especially in the 1805 and 1812 campaigns, adhering to them with rigid stubbornness despite highly vocal criticism. Tsar Alexander gave Kutuzov command of the 1st Russian Corps in 1805; he advanced into Austria but found himself exposed after *Napoleon*'s victory at Ulm against the Austrians, and he retreated towards Vienna (Map 1). Kutuzov displayed highly skilled manoeuvring abilities. He made no real attempt to defend Vienna, but led Napoleon northwards towards Russian reinforcements. He then sought to pull Napoleon further away from their supply bases, but was overruled by the Tsar and the Austrian Emperor and despite his warnings the allies attacked at *Austerlitz*, December 1805, with disastrous results. After further cam-

paigning against the Turks, Kutuzov returned to Russia in 1812 to take over from Barclay de Tolly as Commander of the Army in August. By now Napoleon's *Russian campaign of 1812* seemed to be progressing successfully for the invader. Kutuzov wanted to lead the enemy even deeper into Russian territory: after making a stand at *Borodino*, he allowed Napoleon to seize Moscow, then moved south to threaten the enemy communications. The French were bled weaker and finally retreated with Kutuzov hovering on their heels. Thereafter Kutuzov urged full preparations before an allied advance across Prussia, but even though he received the appointment of Commander-in-Chief he found his opinion overruled. He died on 28 April, at the start of the 1813 campaign: the premature Battles of *Bautzen* and *Lützen*, after which the allies were obliged to retreat, vindicated his caution. *Clausewitz*, who served under Kutuzov in 1812, wrote that 'the prudent and wily Kutuzov was his [Napoleon's] most dangerous adversary'.

L

Landwehr and Landsturm The Landwehr was Prussia's reply to the French Revolutionary *Levée en masse*, 1793 – the *conscription* system whereby the nation's manpower could be utilized for war. The Landwehr was based on ideas put forward by *Scharnhorst*, *Gneisenau* and *Clausewitz* after Prussia's disastrous defeats at Jena and *Auerstadt*, 1806. The system originally recruited men aged 18–40, in a proportion of 1 to every 50 citizens; 1 Landwehr battalion, of about 1,000 men, could be used in conjunction with each regular regiment. Older men, 40–60, would be enrolled in another force, the Landsturm, which would act as an irregular army. Frederick William III of Prussia announced the creation of these two bodies on 17 March 1813, at the start of the gigantic *Leipzig* campaign and at first still relying mainly on volunteers; by mid-1813 the Landwehr had risen to 38 infantry and 30 cavalry regiments, totalling 120,000 men. The introduction of the Ladwehr and Landsturm marked a major step towards the Prussian *nation-in-arms*, although the Landsturm was never an effective military force. The work of the Prussian reforms was enshrined in the Defence Law of 3 September 1814 and the Landwehr Law of 21 November 1815, and the Landwehr itself numbered up to 500,000 men by the end of the Napoleonic period. Thereafter this force became a focus point in the constitutional struggle between the old conservative class and the more liberal politicians. The former wanted the civilian Landwehr merged closer to the regular Army, whereas the liberals saw the force as a counter to the old hierarchical system, which relied on rigid professionalism. The struggle continued until *Roon*'s reactionary reforms in the 1860s, which reduced service in the Landwehr and placed this organization under extremely close supervision of the regular Army, thus bringing the civilian Landwehr under greater professional control.

Lannes, Jean, Duc de Montebello, Prince de Sievers, 1769–1809 French Marshal. Discovered by *Napoleon* during campaign in *Italy*, 1796; accompanied Napoleon to *Egypt*, 1798; returned to Europe for campaign in *Italy*, 1800, defeating the Austrians at Montebello, June; his corps provided invaluable service at

Marengo; attacked allied right at *Austerlitz*, December 1805; served in campaign in Prussia, 1806, at Battle of Jena; played a vital role at *Friedland*, June 1807. Lannes was mortally wounded at Aspern-Essling, 21 May 1809, in the opening stages of the *Wagram* campaign (Map 1).

Laos, war in, 1953– (Map 18) As part of French Indochina, the country was affected by the backwash of the Viet Minh struggle in the *Indochina* War, and the communist conflict continued after the proclamation of Laotian independence, 19 July 1949. The Geneva Conference of 1954 recognized Laotian neutrality, but war soon intensified between the Pathet Lao insurgents, supported by Soviet Russia and Communist China, and the Royal Laotian Army supported by the USA. The situation was complicated by the involvement of North Vietnamese forces on behalf of the Pathet Lao, and by a split in anti-communist forces into 'Rightists' and 'Neutral' factions. An uneasy coalition of Neutralists, Pathet Lao and Rightists broke down in April 1963 after the murder of Foreign Minister Quinim Pholsena, who was a Pathet Lao leader. The Rightists and Neutralists managed to merge in 1965, with Prince Souvanna Phouma becoming Premier; his government agreed to US flights over Laos to bomb the 'Ho Chi Minh' trails – supply routes in Laos used by the North Vietnamese in their struggle. Fighting continued in a series of inconclusive clashes centred on the Plaine des Jarres in the north. By December 1973 the North Vietnamese and Pathet Lao forces had managed to seize control of this area. Pathet Lao forces in early 1974 numbered about 40,000 men, integrated with about 60,000 regular North Vietnamese. Royal Laotian forces numbered 74,200, all of whom were in the Army apart from 500 naval personnel and 1,700 in the Air Force: the latter had only about 73 combat aircraft. Pathet Lao/North Vietnamese strategic policy in 1974–5 seemed to be to consolidate their control in the east and north of the country, with these areas being most important in relation to the war in Vietnam.

Lattre de Tassigny, Jean de, 1889–1952 French General. Imprisoned after denouncing German occupation of Vichy France, November 1942, but escaped to England; commanded Free French forces, including in the '*Anvil*' landings in southern France, August 1944; in October the French components in this operation became the 1st French Army under his command; he accepted the unconditional surrender of Germany to France in Berlin, 9 May 1946. Lattre de Tassigny was appointed the first Commander of *NATO* Land Forces, Europe, in 1948; he left this position in December 1950 to become High Commissioner and C-in-C *Indochina*; he immediately introduced an agressive policy, but was unable to subdue the elusive guerrillas. He fell seriously ill and returned to France via the USA in September 1952, where he died soon afterwards.

Lawrence, Thomas Edward, 'Lawrence of Arabia', 1888–1935 Served in First World War in *Middle East* on staffs of General Sir Archibald Murray and, after April 1917, his successor *Allenby*. From January to September 1918 Lawrence operated with a small group of other British officers alongside the Arabs against the Turks. Now a Colonel, Lawrence organized Arab raiding parties attacking the Hejaz Railway running 600 miles from Amman to Medina. The Arabs succeeded in diverting 25,000 Turkish troops and isolated Medina. The Arab Revolt prepared the way for Allenby's successful offensive beginning 18 September 1918. Lawrence and the Arabs entered Damascus at the end of the month. He described his exploits in 'Seven Pillars of Wisdom', 1926, and in abbreviated version in 'Revolt in the Desert', 1927. Despite exaggerations, Lawrence showed himself to be a discerning *guerrilla warfare* theorist. After being an adviser on Arab affairs at the Colonial Office, 1921–2, Lawrence attempted to avoid public attention and later joined the RAF as an aircraftman under the name of Ross. He died in a motorcycle accident, 19 May 1935. During the post-war period he had been befriended by Liddell *Hart*.

Leahy, William Daniel, 1875–1959 US Admiral of the Fleet. Commander, Battle Force, 1936–7; Chief of Naval Operations, 1937–9; Governor of Puerto Rico, 1939–40; US Ambassador to Vichy France, 1940 to May 1942; appointed by *Roosevelt* as his Chief of Staff, July 1942, retaining this position until 1949 (under *Truman* after 1945), acting as direct liaison officer between the President as C-in-C of the US Army and Navy, and the US *Joint Chiefs of Staff*.

Lebel rifle Adopted by the French Army in 1886, this *rifle* derived its popular name from Colonel Nicholas Lebel, 1838–91, a member of a French armaments commission. The Lebel was the first small-bore and *smokeless powder* rifle to be adopted by a major power. The *Gras* had shown that the rate of fire could now only be increased through the introduction of a *magazine*: the Lebel therefore had a tubular magazine holding 8 centre-fire *percussion* cartridges. Improvements in 1893 gave the Lebel an accurate range of about 1,000 yards.

Lee, Robert Edward, 1807–70 Confederate Supreme Commander, *American Civil War* (Map 3). Son of Henry 'Light-Horse Harry' Lee, a brilliant cavalry commander in the American Revolution; served in *American–Mexican War*, 1846–8; commanded detachment which put down uprising at Harper's Ferry at the time of John Brown's raid, 1859. Lee acted as military adviser to *Davis*, 1861–2; his proposal for a Confederate demonstration to divert Union forces, 1862, led to *Jackson*'s *Shenandoah* campaign, May–June. On 1 June Lee replaced J. E. Johnston as Commander of the Army of Northern Virginia; he invaded the north after his victory at the Second Battle of *Bull Run* but was repulsed at *Antietam*, 17 September, by vastly superior numbers. In April 1863 his troops went to battle confident, despite shortages, and skilled manoeuvring led to Lee's great victory at *Chancellorsville*, May. He again invaded the north, but was defeated at *Gettysburg*, July. The year 1864 witnessed brilliant manoeuvring by both Lee and *Grant*, highlighted by the *Wilderness* campaign. At the subsequent siege of *Petersburg* Lee showed himself a master of defensive operations. On 3 February 1865 Davis appointed Lee to supreme command, but he was forced to evacuate Petersburg on 2 April and the final *Appomattox* campaign began; Lee surrendered to Grant on 9 April. His daring, determination and resilience contrasted strongly with Union generals in the war's opening stages. He seemed to intimidate his opponents until Grant emerged. He acted as a Confederate rallying figure: a man of high character. His conception of generalship was to allow his subordinates considerable latitude in carrying out his plans – a method which, although dangerous, encouraged initiative.

Lee, James P., 1831–1904 Scottish-born arms designer in the USA. His military small-arms, produced 1872–95, included the magazine Remington-Lee and the Lee *rifle* introduced into the US Navy. The latter, first manufactured in 1879, incorporated a box magazine located below the action: this device was eventually initiated throughout the world. Lee was also associated with the British Lee-*Enfield*

and Lee-*Metford* magazine-loading systems.

Leigh-Mallory, Sir Trafford, 1892–1944 British Air Marshal. Commander No. 12 Fighter Group during Battle of *Britain*, transferring to No. 11 Group in December 1940; succeeded Sholto Douglas as Chief of Fighter Command, November 1942; appointed C-in-C Allied Air Forces, 1944, prior to the *Normandy* landings, and was responsible for some 9,000 RAF and USAAF aircraft; appointed Air C-in-C South-East Asia, November 1944, but was killed in an air crash on the way to his new post.

Leipzig, campaign and Battle of, August–October 1813 *Napoleonic Wars* (Map 1). Also known as the 'Battle of Nations', this gigantic clash between the Prussian, Russian, Austrian and Swedish allies against Napoleon's armies was the largest and perhaps the most important of the Napoleonic struggle. An armistice, agreed after *Bautzen*, ended on 16 August, with Austria now joining the war against the French. In late August and early September Napoleon's subordinate commanders suffered setbacks at Grossbeeren, the Katzbach, Kulm and Dennewitz. But Napoleon won a brilliant tactical victory at *Dresden*, 26–27 August, and the allies quarrelled over the correct strategy: Frederick William III of Prussia was anxious to protect Berlin; the allied C-in-C, *Schwarzenberg*, was anxious to avoid a premature concentration; *Blücher* urged an early offensive but was overruled. Both sides waited for an opening. Finally, at the end of September, the allies began to move on Leipzig with *Blücher*'s Army of Silesia leading the way; Blücher crossed the Elbe at Elster on 3 October and captured Wartenberg. Leipzig lay 66 kilometres to the south. The French Emperor rushed from Dresden to protect Leipzig. Crown Prince Bernadotte of Sweden crossed the Elbe to support Blücher's right: together their armies totalled 140,000 men. From the south advanced Schwarzenberg's main allied army, totalling 220,000: on 5 October his leading Austrian regiments reached Zwickau, 78 kilometres from Leipzig. Napoleon had less than 200,000 men in the Leipzig area. Schwarzenberg planned to attack through the villages clustered to the south of Leipzig, while Blücher and Bernadotte thrust down the Halle road in the northwest. The gigantic battle began early on 16 October. By the end of this first day Blücher's army had battered a way through to the outskirts of Leipzig, taking the village of Möckern although at great cost to a Prussian corps under *Yorck*. To the south, Schwarzenberg advanced under cover of the largest artillery duel yet experienced – over 2,000 guns – but found progress difficult. By nightfall Napoleon's overall casualties were about 26,000; allied losses were probably over 30,000. Fighting on the second day was delayed by indecision at the allied HQ and lack of co-operation from Bernadotte. Meanwhile Napoleon decided to prepare an escape

route over the Saale and Unstrut. Battle began again on 18 October, with Blücher still hampered by inadequate support from Bernadotte but nevertheless making the most substantial advance: by evening Prussian troops were poised for the final push into the city. Also during the evening, Napoleon issued the order to retreat. Soon after dawn, 19 October, the allies launched their final offensive, comprising 5 major thrusts at various points on the city walls. Blücher broke through first, Napoleon fled back to the Rhine. Allied casualties during the 4 days totalled about 50,000; the French lost twice this number. An average of about 1,500 men were killed or wounded in each hour, day and night.

Lenin, Nikolai, real name Vladimir Ilyich Ulyanov, 1870–1924 Russian revolutionary leader. Exiled to Siberia, 1897, for spreading socialism following his study of works of Karl Marx; while in Siberia he completed his 'The Development of Capitalism in Russia'; he moved to Switzerland, 1900, attempting to stir revolution in Russia during the *Russo-Japanese War*, 1904–5; he remained in Switzerland during the first years of the *First World War*, holding a Socialist Congress, September 1915, which laid the foundations for the Communist International. Lenin was allowed by the Germans to travel to Russia in early 1917 after the outbreak of domestic struggle; he assumed leadership of the revolutionary government from April 1917, overthrowing the moderate provisional government and becoming Premier in January 1918; he accepted the treaty of Brest-Litovsk with Germany, 1918, and led the Bolsheviks during the continuing *Russian Revolution*, 1918–21, with *Trotsky* the War Minister.

Levée en masse The *French Revolutionary War* systems for harnessing the nation's manpower for the struggle, later adopted by the Prussians with their *Landwehr and Landsturm*. A law in February 1793 ordered a levy of 300,000 men to be furnished in contingents by local communities, with this draft excluding politicians, elected officials and even married men. This Act was supplemented on 23 August 1793 by the 'Levée en masse', introduced by *Carnot*: all men between 18 and 25 were liable for call-up. The law declared:

> The young men shall fight; the married men shall forge weapons and transport supplies; the women will make tents and clothes and will serve in the hospitals; the children will make up old linen into lint; the old men will have themselves carried in to the public squares and rouse the courage of the fighting men . . .

By 1813, after the dreadful losses of the 1812 campaign in *Russia*, boys of 15–16 were serving with the colours; they were nicknamed 'Marie Louises' after Napoleon's wife.

Lewis, Isaac Newton, 1858–1931 US soldier and arms developer. Dis-

abled from US Army 1913. In 1911 Lewis invented the machine-gun which bore his name: this gas-operated weapon provided its own cooling air by forcing a fast draught past the barrel. The Lewis gun became the standard light machine-gun in the British Army during the First World War, used also by the French and not surpassed until the introduction of the Bren in 1938. The Lewis gun was the first machine-gun to be fired from an aircraft, in 1912.

Ligny, Battle of, June 1815 *Napoleonic Wars* (Map 1). This major battle of the *Waterloo campaign* took place on 16 June, when 84,000 Prussians under *Blücher* attempted to block *Napoleon*'s main army of 78,000 from splintering the allied front. The clash at Quatre Bras coincided with the battle at Ligny, with French troops under *Ney* attempting to thrust back Anglo-Dutch troops as they hurried from the Belgian capital. Ligny Battle centred on a number of small villages – Wagnelée, St Amand, Ligny itself, Sombreffe, Le Mazy – in an area about 6 miles south of Quatre Bras. The French, enjoying greater artillery strength and better positions, gradually pushed forward during the late afternoon and evening. Blücher, aged 72, insisted upon leading a cavalry charge himself: his horse was shot beneath him and he lay unconscious until rescued by his aide. Command of the Prussian Army fell temporarily to *Gneisenau*. Withdrawal had become inevitable, and Gneisenau almost decided to pull away from the

Anglo-Dutch Army. Blücher recovered in time to order retirement on a line parallel to the British, who were moving back to Waterloo. Prussian casualties at Ligny probably totalled about 16,000, the French about 12,000.

Lincoln, Abraham, 1809–65 16th US President. Succeeded James Buchanan, March 1861; he issued a call for 75,000 volunteers, 15 April, and proclaimed the blockade of southern ports on the 19th (Map 3). Lincoln was also Commander-in-Chief. He showed himself willing to give full power of directing strategy in the civil war to any general who displayed sufficient ability, but not until the emergence of *Grant* did he find such a general. His loyalty to *McClellan* went largely unrewarded, and Lincoln finally dismissed him, November 1862, with the words: 'He has got the slows.' *Burnside* took over as Army Commander, despite this General's reluctance, and doubts of his ability were confirmed by the *Fredericksburg* defeat, December. *Hooker* was next Commander of the Army of the Potomac, but lost at *Chancellorsville*, May 1863. *Meade* assumed command less than a week before *Gettysburg*, but although the battle proved a Union victory, he failed to follow up his success. Finally, in March 1864, Grant was appointed Supreme Commander. The partnership proved unbeatable. Five days after Lee's surrender at *Appomattox*, Lincoln was shot in Ford's Theatre, Washington, by John Wilkes Booth, and he died next day, 15 April.

Andrew Johnson succeeded him as President.

Little Big Horn, Battle of, June 1876 Highlight of the conflict with the Sioux and Northern Cheyennes, 1876–7, during which the Indians were led by *Crazy Horse* of the Oglala Sioux and Sitting Bull of the Prairie Sioux. In June 1876 US forces under Alfred H. Terry converged on Crazy Horse; on the 17th the Indians clashed with soldiers commanded by *Crook* at the Battle of the Rosebud. The Indians withdrew and Crook pulled back to refit. Terry, unaware of the battle, believed his forces and those under Crook could surround Crazy Horse and he sent 600 7th cavalrymen under Colonel George A. Custer to help complete this encirclement. Custer, 1838–76, was a veteran of the Civil War and of previous Indian fighting, especially in the Black Hills, 1874. He followed Crazy Horse's trail, but the Indians moved into defensive positions at Little Big Horn. Without waiting for Terry, Custer attacked. He divided his force into 3 columns and led 1 himself. His column was destroyed – about 212 officers and men including Custer. The other 2 groups scattered, holding out 48 hours until Terry arrived. The Battle of Wolf Mountain, 8 January 1877, led to Crazy Horse's surrender; Sitting Bull was killed on 15 December 1890.

Lloyd George, David, 1st Earl of Dwyfor, 1863–1945 British statesman. Chancellor of the Exchequer, 1908–15, opposing the First World

War until it began and thereafter opposing the emphasis on the Western Front, giving instead strong support for *Italian* operations and the *Dardanelles*. The failure of the latter operation led to political upheaval, with Prime Minister Asquith agreeing to a coalition with the Conservatives, and in this reshuffle Lloyd George became the first Minister of Munitions, 9 June 1915. He immediately revolutionized war production, persuading the trade unionists to accept hard conditions and enlisting female labour; output soared. Lloyd George succeeded *Kitchener* as War Secretary following Kitchener's death, 5 June 1916. Dissension increased between Lloyd George and Prime Minister Asquith, and Lloyd George resigned in late 1916. This led to the fall of Asquith's Coalition, 5 December, and to Asquith's replacement by Lloyd George himself. The new Prime Minister wished to include *Churchill* in his administration, but ex-First Lord of the Admiralty was still politically unacceptable following the Dardanelles failure. Lloyd George proved a dynamic war leader and provided a model for Churchill to follow in the Second World War but his administration was marked by conflict with the military hierarchy, especially with *Robertson*, CIGS, and *Haig*. Lloyd George acquiesced in plans for the *Nivelle offensive*, 1917, but attempted to have Haig brought directly under French command. Despite his preferences for greater effort in Italy, he was unable to prevent Haig's plan for the 'big push' in late summer 1917, leading to the Third Battle of *Ypres*. Lloyd George attempted to reduce the powers of the CIGS, February 1918, whereupon Robertson resigned and was eventually succeeded by General *Wilson*; Haig continued to command the BEF. Lloyd George played a major part in the peace settlement, warning against revenge, but his support for the Greeks in the war between *Greece* and Turkey, 1919–23, threatened a confrontation between British troops stationed at Constantinople and advancing Turkish troops under *Kemal*. Lloyd George was succeeded as Prime Minister by the Conservative leader Bonar Law in November 1922.

Long March, The, 1934–5 Conflict in China had been continuing since the mid-1920s between the nationalist (Kuomintang), communist, and warlord factions, further complicated by Japanese and Russian involvement. By the early 1930s the war was centred on Kuomintang forces under *Chiang Kai-shek* and communists under *Mao Tse-tung*'s political leadership. In October 1934 the communists began a long retreat organized by Mao across south-west China to northern Shensi. The communist 1st Front Army, led by Chu Teh with Mao his Political Commissar, covered 6,000 miles in 13 months, while a shorter route was taken by the 2nd Front Army under Ho Lung. About half the 200,000 communists failed to reach their destination, including those remaining to foment further rebellion.

Long Range Desert Group, LRDG
Formed in early 1940 in North Africa;
conceived by Brigadier Ralph Bagnold
and approved by *Wavell* as a means of
overcoming lack of reconnaissance due
to aircraft shortages. The force eventually grew to 300 New Zealanders,
British, Rhodesian and other nationalities including 12 Americans. The
LRDG carried out over 200 operations, remaining separate from other
raiding groups formed in the *desert
campaign*, including the *Special Air
Services*. The LRDG later undertook
special-force operations in Italy,
Greece, Albania and Yugoslavia; the
unit was disbanded in 1945.

**Long Range Penetration Group –
see Chindits**

Longstreet, James, 1821–1904 Confederate General, *American Civil War*
(Map 3). Commanded rearguard of
Johnston's army, May 1862; Corps
Commander in Second Battle of *Bull
Run*; held Confederate centre at
Antietam, September 1862; engaged
at *Fredericksberg*, December; and at
Gettysburg, July 1863; played an important role at Chickamauga, September 1863, in the *Chattanooga* campaign; seriously wounded in the
Battle of the *Wilderness*, May 1864,
but recovered in time to take part in
the final *Appomattox* campaign.

**Loos, Battle of, September–Oct-
ober 1915** *First World War* (Map 10).
The British Expeditionary Force,
commanded by *French*, lost 65,000
men in this abortive attempt to regain

territory taken by the Germans in the
Battles of the *Frontiers* and the '*Race
to the Sea*'. Over 100,000 French
casualties were suffered at nearby
Vimy Ridge. The British and French
battles, together called the Third
Battle of Artois, finally led to the
realization of the trench deadlock
which had developed. Blamed for the
failure at Loos, French was replaced
by Haig.

Ludendorff, Erich von, 1865–1937
German General. Major-General at
outbreak of *First World War* (Map
10), distinguishing himself in the initial Belgium campaign, August; appointed Quartermaster-General (Chief
of Staff) to *Hindenburg* on Eastern
Front, late August, and this partnership brought victory at *Tannenberg*
(Map 9); he continued to operate successfully in west Poland, urging with
Hindenburg an all-out effort against
Russia at the expense of strength on
the Western Front. The Hindenburg–
Ludendorff team replaced *Falkenhayn*
as Western Front Commander, 29
August 1916; they adopted a defensive strategy, continuing into 1917,
but planned a series of offensives for
1918 starting at the *Somme*. The
attacks failed to bring decisive victory,
and after the allied counter-offensive
at *Amiens*, Ludendorff declared:
'This war must be ended.' He resigned, 27 October, to comply with
Wilson's demand that negotiations for
an armistice would not be opened with
the existing German military dictator-
ship. He thus avoided the stigma
attached to those who signed the

Versailles Treaty. Ludendorff took part in the abortive Munich 'putsch', 1923; the Nazis put him up as candidate in the March 1925 presidential elections, but he won only 211,000 votes out of nearly 27 million. Nazi preference switched to Hindenburg, who won a second election in April; Ludendorff continued to lead crusades against Catholics, Jews and Masons, but without Hitler's support.

Luftwaffe German Air Force developed as a separate service by *Hitler* after 1933 under *Göring* as Cabinet Minister for Air Forces. Thus the Luftwaffe owed its independent development to the Nazis and this inevitably brought allegiance to Hitler. In the 6 years 1933–9 the Luftwaffe rose to a strength of 260,000 men with 21 squadrons. In 1939 the aircraft comprised 1,180 bombers, 366 dive-bombers, 1,179 fighters, 604 reconnaissance, 240 coastal, and 40 ground attack, totalling 3,609. Principal aircraft were the Messerschmitt Me 109 and 110 fighters, respectively with maximum speeds of 357 and 349 mph and ranges of 412 and 565 miles; the Junkers Ju 87 Stuka, with a speed of 199 mph and range of 620 miles; the Junkers Ju 88, serving as a dive-bomber, level-bomber, night-fighter, reconnaissance and torpedo-bombing aircraft, with a speed of 286 mph and range of 1,553 miles; the Heinkel He 111 medium-range bomber, with a speed of 254 mph, range of 1,100 miles; the Dornier Do 17 medium-range bomber, with a speed of 265 mph, maximum range 745 miles. Defects in this list were the absence of a long-range bomber, thus forcing the medium-range types to undertake unsuitable roles, especially during the *Blitz* and Battle of *Britain*. Apart from these two campaigns, the Luftwaffe was envisaged as undertaking the army-support role, especially with the *blitzkrieg* tactic – hence the absence of adequate bombers. In general, aircraft production continued to be excellent despite the allied *strategic bombing* offensive, but from 1943 onwards the Luftwaffe was forced into an increasingly defensive role mainly through acute shortages of fuel. Distribution of the latter was further hampered by lack of firm direction and long-term planning. Nevertheless the Luftwaffe continued to fight with all possible determination, helped by two later additions to the fighter range: the Focke-Wulf Fw 190A, perhaps Germany's most successful fighter with a top speed of over 400 mph and a range of over 500 miles; and the jet-powered Me 262, with a speed of over 600 mph. This jet caused severe problems to the allies advancing into Germany in the final stage of the war, often escaping detection because radar posts were unable to sweep fast enough. Helped by the shorter ranges now being flown, the Luftwaffe fought grimly in the last months of war, attempting to escape the attention of allied bombing strikes against the German airfields by using secondary fields which were well hidden and only occupied for short periods.

Lützen, Battle of, May 1813
Napoleonic Wars (Map 1). Prussia and
Russia signed an offensive-defensive
alliance at Kalisch, 26 February; this
opened the so-called War of Liberation against *Napoleon*, with Prussia
officially declaring war on 13 March.
By this time Napoleon had managed
to gather a new army of 200,000 men,
although many were woefully inexperienced and untrained, and only
two-thirds of this number were available for front-line fighting. The
French were especially weak in cavalry.
Ranged against Napoleon at the opening of the campaign were three
armies. Prince Wittgenstein advanced
from Berlin with about 44,000 men,
mainly Russians but including Prussians under *Yorck* and *Bülow*; south
of Berlin would advance Russians
under the overall commander, *Kutuzov*; while farther south Blücher led
65,000 Prussians from Silesia towards Dresden. Kutuzov died on 28
April and was succeeded by Wittgenstein. By the last day of April his Army
of the Main lay in the vicinity of
Naumberg, while the Army of the
Elbe, under Eugène, Prince of Beauharnais, was drawn up around Merseburg. Napoleon advanced towards
Leipzig, ordering *Ney* to cover this
movement by holding Lützen and the
nearby villages of Klein Görschen,
Gross Görschen, Rahna and Kaja.
About 88,000 Prussian and Russian
troops under Wittgenstein and Blücher
attacked these villages on 2 May;
Napoleon had 100,000 troops in the
vicinity, many of whom were in the
process of moving on Leipzig. He

heard the cannon fire while riding
along the road to Leipzig and immediately ordered corps under *Marmont*
and Henri Bertrand to support Ney.
Blücher urged Wittgenstein to throw
in allied cavalry before these reinforcements arrived, but the Commander-in-Chief refused. Nevertheless, when Napoleon reached the
battlefield the French 3rd Corps was
beginning to give ground; he rallied
the wavering regiments. Late in the
afternoon Wittgenstein at last allowed
the cavalry to attack; the allies took
Kaja and Gross Görschen, but more
French regiments were reaching the
area. Napoleon attacked with the
French Guard supported by 80 guns.
Over 1,000 Frenchmen were killed in
this assault, but the allies were thrown
from the villages. Wittgenstein heard
that Leipzig had fallen, and began to
plan withdrawal. Blücher led a last
cavalry charge which came close to
capturing Napoleon, then the allies
withdrew to *Bautzen*. The French
lost about 18,000 men at Lützen, and
almost as many casualties were suffered during the French advance on
Bautzen. The allies also lost about
18,000 at Lützen, including Blücher's
Chief of Staff *Scharnhorst*.

**Lys-Aisne offensive, April–May
1918** *First World War* (Map 10). After
the *Somme* offensive, March, Luden-
dorff launched a renewed attack on 9
April against the British in Flanders.
Involved in the offensive were the
German 4th Army under General
Sixt von Arnim and the 6th under
General Ferdinand von Quast; de-

fending the area were the British 2nd Army under *Plumer* and the 1st under General Henry Horne. Fighting centred on the town of Armentières. The German advance began after an initial gas and HE bombardment. Once again the Germans used the *Hutier* infiltration tactics, and by 10 April Quast's troops had penetrated 5 miles. On the 11th Arnim thrust 4 divisions against a single British division north of Armentières, and the defenders, denied reserves which had been sent to block Quast's advance, fell back. Also on the 11th the two German armies united and advanced farther west. But on 12 April *Haig* issued his famous 'backs to the wall' order, forbidding withdrawal. The BEF held the advance. Ludendorff had seized a salient, but this was vulnerable to counter-attack, and German casualties totalled 350,000 by 21 April. British losses were 305,000. Ludendorff tried to maintain momentum by striking at the French along the Chemin des Dames in the Aisne region, intended as a diversion before a final thrust against the British. The Germans broke through, 27 May, supported by 4,600 guns, and 36 hours later the advance had reached the Marne at Château-Thierry within 37 miles of Paris. *Pershing* sent the US 3rd and 2nd Divisions, under Generals J. T. Dickman and Omar Bundy, and these rushed into action along the Marne. The US 1st Division, under General Robert Lee Bullard, was engaged at Cantigny, 50 miles northwest, in the first US offensive of the war. For 3 days the Americans blocked the German advance in the Château-Thierry area, then counter-attacked on 4 June. US casualties totalled over 10,000. Ludendorff, after a limited offensive in the Noyon-Montdidier area in mid-June, began his final attempt on 15 July in the Second Battle of the *Marne*.

M

MacArthur, Douglas, 1880–1964
US General. Commanded 42nd US
Division, France, 1918–19; Philippine
Department, 1928; Director of Organization of National Defence for the
Philippine government, 1935 until his
retirement 1937; recalled, July 1941,
as US Commander in the Far East;
forced to evacuate Manila, capital of
the *Philippines*, May 1942. In early
1942 MacArthur was appointed Supreme Commander in the south-west
Pacific. From the start he was involved
in controversy with *King*, Chief of US
Naval Staff in Washington, over the
correct strategy to be followed in this
war against *Japan* (Map 16). Compromise plans resulted in successful
operations against *New Guinea* and
the Solomons, 1943, and in Mac-
Arthur's return to the *Philippines* on
22 October 1944. On 2 September
1945 MacArthur received the official
surrender of Japanese Foreign Minister Shigemetsu. MacArthur, given
the title Supreme Commander for
Allied Powers, acted as Governor of
Japan, 1945–50. On 27 June 1950 he
received orders from *Truman* to direct
air and naval assistance to *Korea*
(Map 17); on 7 July he was named
C-in-C United Nations Command.

He completely reversed the existing
desperate military situation by the
brilliant Inchon landing, 15 September. But controversy reached a climax
over his insistence that restrictions on
operations against Communist China
should be lifted; he was replaced by
Ridgway, 11 April 1951.

McClellan, George Brinton, 1826–
85 US General. Served through *American–Mexican War*; commissioned
Major-General in Union Army, 3
May 1861, operating in Ohio in the
first stage of the *American Civil War*.
McClellan was appointed Union
Commander in the north, 22 July
1861, replacing Irvin McDowell after
the disaster of the First Battle of *Bull
Run* the previous day, and he began
training the force which would soon
become the Army of the Potomac.
Lincoln had to press him to take action,
8 March 1862, and he continued to
hesitate, especially during operations
leading to *Malvern Hill*, July 1862.
He clashed with *Lee* at *Antietam*, 17
September, but allowed the Confederates to retire. He was replaced by
Burnside, 7 November. McClellan stood
against Lincoln in the 1864 presidential
election but was soundly defeated.

Machine-gun, general The first successful machine-gun was the *Gatling*, accepted by the US Army in 1866. Also in 1866 the French produced their *mitrailleuse*, with a greater range than the Gatling – 2,000 yards compared with 1,200 – but it was used inefficiently during the *Franco-Prussian War*. Both these guns, and the *Nordenfelt* version of 1875, suffered from excessive weight. The first truly practical machine-gun was the *Maxim*, patented 1884, adopted by the British in 1889 and later used by every major power. The British *Vickers* was a modified version. Two other machine-guns appeared soon after the first Maxim: the *Browning* and the *Hotchkiss*. Both these had slower rates of fire than the Maxim, giving them a better cooling capacity and consequently decreased weight. Sustained fire did however reveal heating problems, and the *Lewis* was developed in 1911 to overcome this drawback. This became the standard light machine-gun (LMG) of the *First World War* and was only succeeded in 1938 by the Bren ·303, an economical weapon able to fire single shots or short bursts or at a fast rate of 500 rpm. Also prior to the Second World War the Germans developed their recoil-operated, belt-fed MG34, later superseded by the MG42 medium general-purpose machine-gun (GPMG); this had the disadvantage of a very high rate of fire, 1,000 rpm, which could be extremely wasteful. During the war the Russians used the 7·62 mm Degtyarev (DP), drum-fed and gas-operated; this was

improved after 1945 and became the RP-46, still in Soviet service in the early 1970s. The American heavy machine-gun during the war was the Browning air-cooled ·50 inch M-2, firing 100 round belts at 450 rpm. Belgium's Fabrique Nationale FM Type MAG was developed from the modified Browning automatic rifle action, and this gas-operated, belt-fed GPMG was adopted by Sweden in 1958, becoming the standard NATO weapon soon afterwards. Sub-machine-guns have also been developed as one-man infantry weapons for short-range firing. These, using the blowback method of automatic fire, began with an Italian prototype named the Uilla Perosa, 1915, but the first true sub-machine-gun was the Bergmann Musquete MP18 introduced by the Germans in 1918. The Thompson appeared in 1919. A large number of different types were developed from 1925 onwards, including the Bergmann 34, the Schmeisser 28 and the Beretta 38. The later Schmeisser version, the MP38, advanced the design considerably and became the model for most Second World War versions, including the British Sten 9 mm; this had a 32-round magazine, firing at over 500 rpm.

MacMahon, Comte Marie Edmé Patrice Maurice de, 1808–93 French Marshal and President. Established reputation for bravery during *Crimean War*, leading the assault on the Malakoff, 17 June 1855; his reputation was enhanced during French hostilities against Austria, 1859. In the *Franco-Prussian War* MacMahon commanded the 3 corps comprising the main French Army of Alsace. He was unable to prevent Prussian envelopment and fell back to Châlons-sur-Marne, thus opening the road to Paris. He attempted to strike back, 21 August, now commanding French forces in the Army of the Meuse, but was outmanoeuvred by *Moltke* and pushed back towards *Sedan*. During this withdrawal he was wounded at Bazeilles, moments before the Battle of Sedan opened on 1 September. He designated General Ducrot as his successor, not knowing that Wimpffen had already been chosen by Napoleon III, French Emperor. He returned to prominence in 1871 when he organized regular troops to put down a Paris uprising during the 'Reign of Terror'. He was elected second President of the Third Republic, 1873, retiring 1879.

McNamara, Robert Strange, 1916– US statesman. Secretary of Defense, 1961–8, under *Kennedy*, 1961–3, and *Johnson*, 1963–8, succeeded by Clark Clifford. McNamara greatly enlarged and strengthened the power of the US *Defense Department*. He also provided the backing for the increased US involvement in *Vietnam*; this involvement, plus the outbreak of other guerrilla wars and the growth of Soviet nuclear power, led him to propound the policy of *flexible response*, rather than the previous *massive retaliation*.

Maginot Line French fortification system named after André Maginot,

War Minister 1922–4, 1926–9, 1929–30 and 1931. The main work was begun in 1929 after an army committee recommended the construction of a continuous defensive line as urged by *Pétain* – who later changed his mind and supported *Joffre*'s preference for area defence. The Maginot Line eventually stretched 200 miles, starting at the Swiss border and heading north through Alsace to Malmédy. The main sector comprised an elaborate network joined by tunnels with storerooms, engine-rooms and living quarters. Armaments included artillery and machine-guns in rotating concealed emplacements which rose automatically. Considerable debate took place during the 1930s on the desirability of extending the line north, with Weygand among those urging this addition and Pétain violently opposed. No Maginot-type system existed in either Belgium or the Ardennes sector in May 1940 when the Battle for *France* began. German attacks through these areas also exposed the extreme vulnerability of the Maginot Line to pressure from the rear.

Mahan, Alfred Thayer, 1840–1914 US naval officer and author; son of Dennis Hart Mahan, 1802–71, West Point professor and author of textbooks on military engineering and geometry. Mahan graduated from the US Naval Academy, Annapolis, 1859; he was President of the Naval War College, Newport, 1886–9, 1892–3, and US delegate to the first Hague Peace Conference, 1899. Mahan's major books were: 'The Influence of Sea Power upon History, 1660–1783', 1890; 'The Influence of Sea Power upon the French Revolution and Empire, 1793–1812', 1892; 'Types of Naval Officers', 1901; 'Sea Power in its Relation to the War of 1812', 1905; 'Naval Strategy', 1911; and biographies of *Farragut* and *Nelson*. Mahan had two major aims: first, to define the influence of sea power on the destiny of nations; second, to derive principles for naval strategy comparable to *Jomini*'s principles for land warfare. The essence of his strategic doctrine was the value of control of the seas through concentration of force: great fleets should be powerful even at the expense of speed; if inferior, they should be shut away so as to remain a threat – a 'fleet in being'. Mahan's corollary was, 'in time of peace prepare for war' by building up the fleet; linked with this was a second principle: 'War, however defensive in moral character, must be waged aggressively.' Such statements were strongly supported by politicians and admirals who were already embarking on the Anglo-German *naval race* leading to the great *battleship* programmes.

Malaya, operations against communists in, 1948–60, known as the 'Malayan Emergency' Communist terrorism coincided with the announcement of the Federation of Malaya, 1 February 1948, comprising British territory on the Malay Peninsula. A state of emergency was proclaimed on 16 June, and British, Australian and New Zealand troop reinforcements arrived under General Sir Gerald Templar, High Commissioner. Counter-insurgency troop strength eventually totalled 45,000. The overwhelming majority of guerrillas, estimated at 10,000 when the campaign began, were Chinese, and communist efforts to enlist further Malay support never achieved significant success. This enabled the security forces to isolate the enemy and to make use of the traditional dislike between the two ethnic groups. The declared insurgent aim was independence, but this failed to cover the underlying communist purpose of the revolt. Guerrilla war continued for 12 years, with the communist terrorists (CTs) initially achieving some success. This declined after the appointment of Lieutenant-General Sir Harold Briggs as Director of Operations in 1950. His methods included resettlement of the Chinese villagers into areas where they could be more closely watched; the expansion of police and local defence forces; the creation of a unified civilian, police and military system of command. One concept developed during the emergency was the 'hearts and minds' campaigns – the effort to gain allegiance from non-guerrilla elements through the provision of better living conditions. By 1957 the main guerrilla groups had been broken up. The announcement in 1957 of independence for Malaya, as a Federation within the British Commonwealth, effectively removed the ostensible insurgent aim. The emergency was officially lifted on 31 July 1960, although isolated guerrilla pockets remained in the thick jungles on the Thai border – some were still in existence in 1975. Casualty figures during the emergency were 6,705 insurgents killed, 1,286 wounded and 2,696 surrendered; security forces suffered 2,384 killed and 2,400 wounded.

Malaysia–Indonesia hostilities, 1963–6 The Federation of Malaysia was proclaimed on 16 September 1963, adding Singapore Island and the Borneo States of Sabah and Sarawak to the existing mainland Federation of Malaya. The creation of this nation on Indonesia's northern boundary immediately aroused the hostility of Indonesian leader Achmed Sukarno, who announced his intention to 'fight and destroy' the new Federation of Malaysia. Officially, Sukarno declared that this state threatened Indonesia; another reason for his campaign was the need to divert domestic attention from internal political and economic troubles. The campaign involved land and seaborne attempts to infiltrate guerrillas on to Singapore Island and the Malaysian mainland, and infiltration over the 1,000-mile jungle border between Malaysian Borneo (Sarawak and Sabah) and Indonesian Borneo (Kalimantan). Personnel infiltrated on to Singapore and the mainland were untrained or unsympathetic to Sukarno's cause. Land operations in Borneo were nullified by excellent defensive measures adopted by British, Malaysian

and other Commonwealth troops. Sukarno experienced growing domestic difficulties, including an abortive communist coup on 30 September 1965, which was crushed with appalling brutality by Indonesian troops. Sukarno resigned all executive powers to General Suharto, the Army leader, in March 1966; the Indonesian-Malaysian conflict, called 'Confrontation', was officially ended by the Bangkok Agreement, 11 August 1966. British troops numbered over 40,000 at the height of the struggle. Security forces suffered 114 killed and 182 wounded between September 1963 and August 1966. Estimated Indonesian casualties were 602 killed, 886 captured and 222 wounded.

Malta, siege of, 1941–3 *Second World War* (Map 14). Loss of French participation in the Mediterranean, the fall of *France*, 1940, plus the entry of Italy into the war, June 1940, rendered Malta's situation extremely perilous. German air attacks increased early in 1941 with the establishment on Sicily of *Kesselring*'s Air Fleet 10, but the destruction of Germany's élite paratroops during their victory in *Crete*, April–June, meant that a German *airborne* attack on Malta would have to be delayed. In April 1942 Malta's airfields alone received a weight of bombs 27 times as great as that on Coventry in the famous *blitz* raid of October 1940. General Sir William Dobbie, Governor and C-in-C of Military Forces on the island since 1940, successfully sought the award of the newly created George

Cross medal for the population, 15 April 1942. Dobbie, in need of rest, was succeeded by *Gort* on 7 May. Six convoys attempted to reach Malta in 1942, of which two were repulsed and only remnants of the others arrived. About 350 allied fighter aircraft were flown in during the year: at the beginning of the struggle the fighter force numbered 3 ancient Gladiators named Faith, Hope and Charity. Included in the reinforcements were 46 fighters flown in from the US carrier 'Wasp' on 20 May 1942 – within 3 days only 6 remained serviceable. In June 1942 Hitler, elated by *Rommel*'s success which opened the way for the conquest of Egypt, postponed a full-scale attack on Malta. But the *Alamein* victory in the desert and subsequent allied advances enabled forward air bases to be established. These provided cover for convoys; the first major shipment reached the island in November.

Malvern Hill, Battle of, July 1862 *American Civil War* (Map 3). This clash marked the culmination of the 'Seven Days Battles' which followed *Jackson*'s *Shenandoah* campaign. *Lee* ordered Jackson to join him for a Confederate offensive against troops under Major-General Fitzjohn Porter, begining with the Battle of Mechanicsville, 5 miles north of Richmond, on 26 June: the Confederates attacked prematurely before Jackson arrived, and Porter repulsed the assaults before withdrawing to Gaines' Mill. Next day Lee attacked these positions and Porter retired

once more. *McClellan*, overall Union commander, ordered a general withdrawal to the James River; this began on 28 June. Lee pursued, attacking at Peach Orchard, Savage Station, White Oak Swamp and Glendale-Frayser's Farm, 29–30 June. The attacks were rebuffed and Porter moved into excellent defensive positions at Malvern Hill, just above the James. Battle took place on 1 July, with Lee's assaults thrown back. The Confederates lost about 5,000 men in just 2 hours. Despite this victory, McClellan ordered continued withdrawal, conceding the campaign to Lee, who had protected Richmond and now prepared for the second *Bull Run* campaign.

Mannerheim, Baron Carl Gustaf Emil von, 1867–1951 Finnish Field-Marshal and President. Served as a Russian cavalry officer in *Russo-Japanese War*, 1904–5; appointed to organize and command the Finnish Army after the declaration of Finnish Independence from Russian control, 6 December 1917; engaged in hostilities against Bolsheviks, 1918. Mannerheim commanded the Finnish Army against the Russian invasion, November 1939, but was unable to prevent overwhelming enemy forces from penetrating the 'Mannerheim Line', February 1940. He was involved in the German invasion of *Russia*, 1941, with his Finnish Army Group threatening Leningrad. President of Finland, 1944–6.

Mannlicher, Ferdinand Ritter von, 1848–1904 Firearms inventor, born in Germany but moving to Austria at an early age; designed over 150 models of automatic and repeating firearms, many of which were well in advance of his time. His first design was a turning-bolt repeating rifle in 1880, but his first major success came in 1884 with his straight-pull bolt action: this led to the Model 1885 11 mm Austrian service rifle, incorporating his box-type magazine system. The latter improved on the version used with the US *Lee rifle*. Germany adopted a turning-bolt rifle with a Mannlicher magazine in 1888; in 1890 a Mannlicher straight-pull carbine was adopted by Austria. In 1892 he produced his own design of turning-bolt rifle with his magazine system, which was adopted by Holland and Romania.

Mao Tse-tung, 1893–1976 Chinese revolutionary leader. Joined Chinese Communist Party on its formation in Shanghai, 1921; gained increased influence after the failure of communist offensive in central China, July–August 1930, which he had argued against; Political Commissar in Communist First Front Army during *Long March*, October 1934 to November 1935; organized guerrilla warfare against Japanese and Kuomintang Chinese during Second World War; led communist forces against *Chiang Kai-shek* in post-war period, emerging victorious, December 1949, and assuming title of Chairman of Central People's Government; relinquished his position as head of Chinese state, 1959, but retained chairmanship of Communist Party despite the upheaval of the Cultural Revolution, 1966–9.

Marengo, Battle of, June 1800 *Napoleonic Wars* (Map 1). The climax of the 1800 *Italy* campaign. *Napoleon* was attempting to sever communications to the Austrian commander, Baron Michael Melas, at Turin. Melas hurried south-east to prevent this move, concentrating 34,000 men at Alessandria, 30 miles from Turin, on 13 June. Napoleon approached with only 18,000 men, believing Melas to be still to the north, and was engaged at Marengo on the 14th. The outnumbered French right was enveloped; Melas believed the battle to be his, and pulled back prior to moving eastwards. But Napoleon sent for support from Louis Desaix's corps, foraging in the area, and counterattacked in the late afternoon, reforming his broken divisions under cover of Desaix's arrival. The Austrian advance guard was shattered and French cavalry struck the Austrian north flank. Attacks by *Lannes*'s corps and the Imperial Guard wrought further destruction. Austrian losses were over 1,000, French about 4,000 including Desaix. Melas capitulated next day.

Mareth, Battle of, March 1943 *Second World War* (Map 14). *Montgomery*'s British 8th Army crossed into *Tunisia* in early February 1943. *Rommel*, having failed in his Kasserine offensive in mid-February and in his effort to push back the 8th Army at Medenine on 6 March, left North

Africa on 9 March. General von Arnim, his successor, decided on 11 March that his forces would not withdraw from the Mareth Line; this comprised old French defensive positions stretching from the Mediterranean to the Matmata Mountains. To the south-west of these mountains lay the apparently impassable Dahar sand wilderness. But Montgomery was informed of a way through the mountains from Foum Tatahouine; he planned to dispatch a force through this gap, along the edge of the Dahar, and then through the vital Tebaga Pass in the north, which would open a way to the plain of El Hamma and Gabes – behind the enemy. This left hook would consist of the New Zealand corps under Sir Bernard Freyberg, stiffened by additional British armour. Meanwhile the 30th Corps of the 8th Army would deliver the main thrust against the eastern edge of the Mareth Line. Fierce fighting began in the 30th Corps area late on 20 March. After 3 days the 30th Corps had still to make sufficient headway. Montgomery therefore altered his plan: the main blow would be shifted from the British right at the Mareth Line to the left hook at Tebaga, reinforced by 10th Corps armoured units under General Sir Brian Horrocks. These reinforcements arrived late on the 26th and the assault began almost immediately. By midnight the British armour had broken the enemy defences, and with this threat to the rear the Germans were obliged to retreat. The 8th Army advanced for the final stage of the Tunisian campaign.

Marines Whereas most nations with marine forces kept these units on a low manpower level, using them for special duties, the US Marine Corps expanded in the Second World War to become a major field army in its own right. In Britain, by comparison, the Royal Marines were almost completely identified with the highly specialized *commando* role. The US 1st Marine Division were the first American ground forces to take the offensive in the Second World War, landing at *Guadalcanal* and Tulagi on 7 August 1942, and thereafter the marines played a major role in the war against *Japan*. From the US Marine Corps were created the Raider Battalions, formed in 1942 at the urging of *Roosevelt* as a counterpart to the British commandos: the Marine High Command initially disliked this concept and argued against an élite within an élite. The Raider battalions were abandoned later in the war, but the Marine Corps as a whole continued to be an important section of US military strength in the post-war years. Marines were used extensively in *Vietnam*, especially in the northern part of South Vietnam where they clashed with the regular North Vietnamese regiments attempting to cross the so-called de-militarized zone. In 1974, after the withdrawal from Vietnam, the US Marine Corps totalled almost 200,000 men – nearly 25,000 more than the total British Army strength. The Royal Marines have been affected by defence cuts in the early 1970s; in 1975 it was announced that the 4 commando groups would be reduced to 3. Russia developed a marine force during the 1960s: these troops, distinguished by white berets, totalled about 17,000 in 1974.

Marmont, Auguste Frederic Louis de, Duc de Raguse, 1774–1852 French Marshal. Aide to *Napoleon* in campaign in *Italy*, 1796; fought at *Marengo*, 1800, in *Ulm* campaign, 1805, *Austerlitz* campaign, 1805; served in the *Peninsular War*, 1811–12; returned north to take part in the *Leipzig* campaign, 1813; entrusted by Napoleon with the defence of Paris, 1814, but on 5 April he defected with his 6th Corps to the allies.

Marne, Battle of the, September 1914 *First World War* (Map 10). On 4 September *Joffre* issued orders for an allied offensive against the German right wing in the Marne area to throw back the thrust on Paris. Joffre directed the French 6th Army to launch the primary attack eastwards towards Château-Thierry on the Marne, aimed at enveloping the German right commanded by Kluck. Farther south, nearer Paris, the British Expeditionary Force and the French 5th and 9th Armies would move on Montmirail, while farther east the French 4th Army would hold its present position between the Seine and the Meuse; on the eastern end of the allied line the French 3rd would strike north-west towards Verdun and bring about a double envelopment of the enemy. The BEF turned upon the Germans on 5 September; the French 6th, temporarily commanded by

General Joseph Gallieni, Governor of Paris, had already begun its movement eastwards. Kluck believed this movement to be merely a diversionary attack and had continued to press south. Thus, when the BEF and French 5th Army opened a full-scale counter-offensive on 5–6 September, a dangerous 30-mile gap lay between Kluck's 1st Army and General Karl von Bülow's 2nd Germany Army on his left. By 9 September the British were moving into this gap with the French 5th under General Franchet d'Esperey on their right. Bülow decided to retreat, and later in the day Kluck also received orders from the panicked German Command to withdraw: *Moltke* ordered a general retirement to the Noyon-Verdun line. The allies failed to pursue with sufficient vigour, yet Joffre was considered the saviour of France. Moltke was replaced by *Falkenhayn* on 14 September. Each side now attempted to outflank the other in the '*Race to the Sea*'. Casualties for both sides at the Marne were about 250,000 men.

Marne, Second Battle of the, July 1918 *First World War* (Map 10). On 15 July *Ludendorff* launched his fifth and final attempt to overwhelm the allies, with an offensive undertaken by 3 German armies over the Marne on either side of Rheims. The allied commander, *Foch*, was expecting the attack. East of Rheims the German assault was halted within a few hours by General Henri Gourard's French 4th Army. West of Rheims an attack by General von

Boehn's 7th German Army struck an area where allied defences were neither so strong nor so deep, and 14 German divisions penetrated between Rueil and Château-Thierry; they were finally blocked on 15–17 July by General M. A. H. de Mitry's French 9th Army, assisted by US, British and Italian divisions. By the evening of the 17th the allies were counter-attacking, supported by 350 tanks. The French 10th Army drove forward in the main attack, spearheaded by the US 1st and 2nd Divisions; the US 1st alone captured 3,800 prisoners and by 5 August the allies had eliminated the Marne salient. Preparations were made for the *Amiens* offensive.

Marshall, George Catlett, 1880–1959 US General of the Army. Served in France, 1917–18; Aide-de-Camp to *Pershing*, 1919–24. Chief of Staff, US Army, throughout the *Second World War*. Upon taking office in 1939 he embarked on a programme of Army reorganization, preparing the way for eventual US entry into the war. As US Chief of Staff, Marshall sat on the US *Joint Chiefs of Staff* Committee and became 'de facto' Chairman through his close relationship with *Roosevelt*. Marshall also sat on the Anglo-US *Combined Chiefs of Staff*. His name was considered as Supreme Commander for the allied invasion of Europe, but Roosevelt believed him indispensable and the post went to *Eisenhower*. Eisenhower succeeded him as Army Chief of Staff, November 1945, when Marshall retired. He acted as Secretary of State,

1947–9, and of Defense, 1950–1. In June 1947 Marshall proposed that the US should help rebuild the world economy to enable free institutions to flourish after the ravages of the war: this proposal resulted in the Marshall Plan.

Martini-Henry *Breech-loading rifle* introduced into British service in 1871 to replace the stop-gap *Snider*. The new weapon combined the breech mechanism of Hungarian-born Friedrich von Martini and the barrel of Alexander Henry, an Edinburgh gunmaker. The standard Martini-Henry was sighted up to 1,450 yards; it was superseded by the *Lee-Metford* in 1891.

Masséna, André, 1758–1817 French Marshal. Served in *Italy* (Map 1), 1795; fought at Rivoli, January 1797, during the campaign in *Italy* of 1796–7, and in the subsequent invasion of Austria. In 1798 Masséna commanded the Army of the Danube, defeating an allied force under General Aleksander M. Korsakov at Zurich on 25 September. Increasing allied pressure forced him back into Genoa, April 1800, and he capitulated on 4 June after a protracted siege. In 1805 Masséna commanded 50,000 men in north Italy; while *Napoleon* advanced east after the victory at Ulm, October, he struck at Austrians under Archduke Charles, pushing his enemy through the Alps. He fought in the *Wagram* campaign, 1809; in 1810 he was appointed Commander of the French Army of Portugal, fighting against *Wellington* in the *Peninsular*

War; he was repulsed at Bussaco, September, after which Wellington retired to *Torres Vedras*. On 5 May he fought a hard-drawn battle at Fuentes de Oñoro; inconclusive operations continued. Messéna was replaced by August *Marmont*.

Massive retaliation Strategic policy originating from US Secretary of State *Dulles*'s speech to the Council of Foreign Relations, New York, in January 1954, when he declared:

> Local defenses must be reinforced by the further deterrent of massive retaliatory power . . . The basic decision was to depend largely upon a great capacity to retaliate, instantly, by means and places of our choosing.

This speech was made immediately after the *Korean War*; the declaration intended to warn against further communist aggression in the area – if this occurred 'the UN response would not necessarily be confined to Korea'. The announcement inferred a nuclear retaliation, perhaps against the Russian or Chinese homeland, in response to local conventional involvement. The policy was rendered increasingly unrealistic through two main developments. One was the growth of Soviet, and later Chinese, nuclear power, with the consequent erosion of US 'first-strike' advantage – i.e. the ability to attack with nuclear weapons to inflict so much damage that the enemy could not retaliate in kind. The development of Soviet nuclear strength meant that neither nation would avoid colos-

sal nuclear damage in a strategic exchange. Second, the massive retaliation policy failed to deter the spread of *guerrilla warfare* in the 1950s, for which America needed a totally different response. These two factors were instrumental in the formation of the *flexible response* policy in the 1960s, especially by *McNamara*.

Mauser, Peter Paul, 1838–1914 German arms developer. The first successful Mauser *rifle* design was the 11 mm single-shot bolt action weapon adopted by Prussia in 1871. The version developed in 1880 had a tubular magazine, accepted by Prussia in 1884 as the M71/84. Mauser then moved from tubular to box magazines, with the 7·65 mm 1889 version Mauser. The German 7·92 mm M1898 was the most successful Mauser design and most later weapons were modified copies. Mauser also developed a successful recoil-operated military automatic pistol, introduced in 1898.

Maxim, Sir Hiram, 1840–1916 US-born arms inventor. Maxim, who set up a workshop in London, produced the first successful portable *machine-gun* in 1884. Maxim used the gun's recoil to push the breech mechanism forward and chamber the next round, fire and recoil again. The weapon worked more efficiently after the introduction of more powerful *smokeless* propellants in the later 1880s. The gun was adopted by the British Army in 1889, with the design taken over by *Vickers*, remaining in service with several armies for over 70 years.

Meade, George Gordon, 1815–72
Union General, *American Civil War*
(Map 3). Fought as a Divisional Commander under *McClellan* at *Antietam*,
September 1862, and under *Burnside*
at *Fredericksburg*, December; commanded Union Army Corps at *Chancellorsville*, May 1863, under *Hooker*
whom Meade replaced as Commander
of the Army of the Potomac on 28
June – the Union Army's fifth Commander in 10 months. Meade clashed
with *Lee* at *Gettysburg* 3 days later; he
failed dismally to follow up the victory. On 9 March 1864 *Grant* became
Union C-in-C; Meade served him as
Subordinate Commander of the Army
of the Potomac, and was involved in
the siege of *Petersburg*, 1864–5; he
took part in the final *Appomattox*
campaign.

Mercenary Nations have always
hired foreign manpower to help fight
their wars, and these mercenaries have
played a fundamental part in warfare
throughout the centuries, providing a
professional, experienced force to bolster home recruiting material. This
especially applied before the advent of
the *French Revolutionary Wars*: Prussia's army in the time of Frederick the
Great consisted of 50 per cent foreign
troops; Britain relied heavily upon
Hessian troops in the attempt to quell
the American Revolution. Irish mercenaries in the eighteenth century,
named 'The Wild Geese', were found
in many parts of the world, as were
Swiss and Swedish soldiers. Mercenaries brought the benefit of professionalism, and also removed the need

for compulsory enlistment at home:
they helped separate military involvement from domestic affairs, apart from
the intrusion of higher taxes to pay
for their services. But mercenaries
also brought disadvantages: lacking
patriotic motives, they were more
liable to desert. This, in the pre-
French Revolutionary era, affected
tactics: thus the Prussian Army employed rigid linear *close order* formations partly because these tended to
make disciplinary control easier. Mercenaries decreased in importance as
armies were swollen in size during the
French Revolutionary and *Napoleonic
Wars*. Ranks were increasingly filled
through *conscription*, notably the
French *Levée en masse* and the Prussian *Landwehr*. By the middle years of
the Napoleonic struggle the number of
mercenaries in the Prussian Army
had dropped to 30 per cent. Britain,
still with a relatively small Army,
changed less quickly: about 43,000 of
Wellington's troops at *Waterloo*, from
a total of 67,000, were foreigners –
Hanoverians, the King's German
Legion, Nassauers and Dutch-Bel-
gians. After the Napoleonic era, and
with the acceptance of conscription,
the influence of mercenaries dwindled
as far as the major powers were concerned, but small groups of 'soldiers
of fortune' continued to fight especially in the colonial context. Colonial
duties also led to the British use of the
famed Gurkhas, recruited in Nepal
and still amounting to 5 battalions in
1976; similar tasks led to the *French
Foreign Legion*. Mercenaries have
mainly been employed in the peri-

pheral areas since the Napoleonic Wars: for example the 9,600-strong 'Spanish Legion' recruited under special authority of the British Parliament and sent to Spain in the Carlist War, 1834–9; the large numbers of mercenaries fighting in the *Spanish Civil War*, 1936–9, although many from idealistic motives rather than for money; the mercenaries fighting for *Chiang Kai-shek* in 1937; and the mercenary involvement in the post-1945 period, especially in the *Congo*, where the British officer Mike Hoare achieved fame with his 5 Commando, and afterwards on a smaller scale in *Angola*. Guerrilla warfare has in fact opened up fresh mercenary scope, offering employment for professional fighters in these 'small wars'.

'Merrimack' The *American Civil War* duel of this vessel with the Union '*Monitor*', 1862, pointed the way to naval battles of the future. 'Merrimack' was seized by Confederates in spring 1861 after the Union forces abandoned Norfolk naval yard. The vessel, a steam frigate, had been burnt and scuttled; the Confederates raised the hulk, cut down to the berth deck and fixed 4-inch iron plating, with ports for 10 guns. Also added was a 4-foot iron ram. The warship, renamed 'Virginia', was almost awash through the weight of the iron cladding, and took 30 minutes to turn about. But she proved invulnerable to gunfire from Union vessels. The Union answer was the 'Monitor'. The two vessels clashed in the Battle of Hampton Roads off Norfolk, 8 March

1862. The 'Virginia' had more guns than her opponent, 10 to 2, but the 'Monitor's' weapons were more powerful: 11-inch to the 'Virginia's' 7- and 9-inch, and the Union warship had the advantage of a revolving turret. For 4 hours the *ironclads* battered at each other; both were damaged but remained. operational. The 'Virginia's' end only came when the Confederates evacuated Norfolk: her deep draught prevented an escape up the James and she was blown up by retreating Confederates on 10 May.

Mesopotamia, 1914–18 *First World War*. British–Indian troops landed on 23 October 1914 and captured Basra from the Turks on 23 November. British reinforcements in January 1915 brought the strength to 2 infantry divisions plus cavalry and artillery, commanded by General Sir John Nixon. Plans were made for an advance north from Basra to Baghdad. Nixon dispatched General Charles Townshend northwards with a reinforced division; he himself remained at Basra, and was consequently out of touch with the field situation. Townshend defeated Turks under Nur-ud-Din Pasha at Kut-el-Amara, 27–28 September. The British War Office reacted over-optimistically to Nixon's reports, and sent instructions for Townshend's advance to continue. He was blocked by the Turks at Ctesiphon, 22–26 November, and pulled back to Kut. The Turks surrounded this town on 7 December, and British relief attempts were repulsed during January–March 1916; Townshend was forced to surrender his 8,000 British and Indian troops on 29 April. In mid-December 1916 a British–Indian force of 166,000 men under General Sir Frederick Maude began to move north. Maude took Kut, 22–23 February 1917, and Baghdad, 11 March, in an officially executed campaign; he then advanced towards the Mosul oilfields, but died of cholera on 18 November. General Sir William Marshall took command, but a determined offensive was delayed until 23 October 1918, when it seemed a Turkish collapse was imminent and seizure of the Mosul fields was necessary as a 'fait accompli' before hostilities ended. This was accomplished at the beginning of November. The whole Mesopotamia campaign, riddled with indecision and foolhardy orders, cost over 80,000 British and Indian casualties, including nearly 13,000 men who died of disease.

Messines (Mesen), Battle of, June 1917 *First World War* (Map 10). This British battle followed the failure of the French *Nivelle* offensive, April 1917, and formed a preliminary clash to the Third Battle of *Ypres*. At 3.10 a.m. on 7 June, a great chain of mines was exploded on the Messines ridge: the mines, totalling 1 million tons HE, were contained in galleries dug into the rise, two of the galleries being 2,000 yards long. A wide gap was torn in the German defences, into which plunged troops of the British 2nd Army under *Plumer*; the crest was gained, although with 17,000 British casualties. German defenders fell back behind the Ypres Canal, suffering 25,000 casualties.

Metford, William Ellis, 1824–99 British weapons developer. His fame rested on his *rifling* system, aimed at limiting the friction between the bullet and the barrel walls. Metford discovered that rifling grooves of extreme shallowness achieved the best results; his bullet, self-expanding, was so shaped that only the rear portion of the cylinder was actually in contact with the rifling. Metford's discoveries were incorporated into the *Enfield* system of rifling.

Mexico, revolution in, 1910–20 Opposition to the Mexican dictator Porfirio Díaz, President since 1876, resulted in an uprising led by Francisco Madero in October 1910, leading to the overthrow of Díaz on 25 May 1911. Former supporters of Madero were increasingly disillusioned, including Emiliano *Zapata* in the Morelos region south of Mexico City, and the struggle continued despite vicious efforts by General Victoriano Huerta to suppress opposition. Huerta himself turned against Madero, seizing power on 22 February 1913; Madero was murdered. Revolution continued unabated, led mainly by Zapata in the south and Francisco (Pancho) Villa in the north, with the latter under the nominal leadership of Venustiano Carranza. US forces intervened on 21 April 1914, with President Woodrow *Wilson* sending a small force to Vera Cruz; this was withdrawn on 25 November after Cárranza's forces seized Mexico City, 15 August, forcing Huerta to flee abroad. Carranza assumed leadership. Disillusionment was again experienced by his former supporters: Villa and Zapata took Mexico City in late 1914, with Carranza withdrawing to Vera Cruz, but the Villa–Zapata forces came under strong pressure from government troops ably led by Álvaro Óbregón. Carranza, through Óbregón's generalship, established a powerful government, although Zapata remained a threat in the south. In the north, Villa raided across the US border in March 1916 and attacked Columbus, New Mexico, killing 16 people and partly burning the town; this raid resulted in a punitive US expedition into Mexico led by *Pershing*, with an unsuccessful search for Villa continuing until February 1917. Villa's activities died down, and he failed to respond to Zapata's calls for revolt. Sporadic war continued in the south, with Zapata mainly confining his operations to his native state of Morelos. He was killed in April 1919. Opposition to Carranza rose again in early 1920, and now Óbregón turned against the President. His campaign led to the overthrow of Carranza in May, and Óbregón was elected President on 5 September, recognized as such by the US in August 1923. Also in 1923, Villa was assassinated.

Middle East (Egypt, Palestine, Arabia), operations in, 1916–18
First World War. British troops under General Sir Archibald Murray began extending Suez Canal defences eastwards into the Sinai desert in January 1916, with a counter-offensive by 15,000 Turks under German General Kress von Kressenstein being repulsed at Rumani, 3 August. Meanwhile the British and French attempted to encourage revolt among the Arabs in the Turkish-held area, and this resulted in an uprising on 5 June. The Turkish garrison at Medina was attacked, and Turkish troops at Mecca surrendered on 10 June. The Grand Sherif of Mecca, Hussein, proclaimed Arab independence The British cleared the Turks from the Sinai peninsula in early January 1917. On 26 March troops under General Sir Charles Dobell attacked Turkish defences at Gaza, but the attempt failed; another attempt was thrown back on 17–19 April. Murray relieved Dobell yet was himself replaced by General *Allenby*. On 31 October Allenby fought the Third Battle of Gaza, but this time the British demonstrated at Gaza in order to distract attention from the main thrust at nearby Beersheba. Hard fighting led to the capture of the latter, including the seizure of Gaza's water supply, and the Turks pulled back. Allenby entered Jerusalem, 9 December, after overcoming stubborn resistance under *Falkenhayn*, but was prevented from following up his success until autumn 1918 through having to send troops to the Western Front. Meanwhile *Lawrence* and some Arabs under Emir Faisal, son of Hussein, led an Arab revolt against the Turks, attacking the Hejaz Railway running from Amman in Palestine to Medina.

On 18 September Allenby began his offensive against the Turkish line extending from the Mediterranean to the Jordan valley: these positions were held by nearly 40,000 men under General Liman von Sanders. Allenby, with about 57,000 infantry, 12,000 cavalry and 540 guns, burst open a gap on the Mediterranean Coast at the Battle of Megiddo, 19–21 September; he then pressed north, while to the east Lawrence and the Arabs moved in a parallel line. Damascus fell on 1 October and Beirut next day. Turkey signed an armistice on 30 October. British casualties during this campaign totalled 5,350; Turkish losses included 76,000 prisoners.

Midway, Battle of, June 1942 *Second World War* against *Japan* (Map 16). Admiral *Yamamoto* pushed forward plans to seize this island in May 1942, believing that 2 of America's 3 carriers in the Pacific – 'Yorktown' and 'Lexington' – had been sunk at *Coral Sea*, 7–8 May. Immediately *Nimitz* heard of the Japanese plan – the Americans had broken the enemy's codes – he ordered the carriers 'Enterprise' and 'Hornet' to move at full steam to Midway from the south Pacific; 'Yorktown', only damaged at Coral Sea, was repaired in just 48 hours. The US Fleet would therefore comprise 3 carriers, totalling about 250 aircraft; moreover, the battle would be fought within range of 108 US aircraft based on Midway Island itself. Japanese aircraft totalled about 250, on 4 carriers. The main Japanese force sailed east under Ad-

miral Nagumo, with the latter unaware of the powerful US carrier force in the area. He launched half his carrier aircraft against Midway early on 4 June; US aircraft from the island struck at the Japanese Fleet, although without causing significant damage and at great cost. Nagumo retained the initiative by launching his bombers against Midway; he then received reports that a large number of US warships were lying to the north-east, and he changed direction to engage this fleet. This shift in course meant that an initial attack by fighter aircraft from Rear-Admiral Raymond Spruance's 'Enterprise'–'Hornet' carrier force failed to find the target. US torpedo bombers struck soon afterwards but without fighter cover: 35 out of 41 aircraft were lost. The Japanese Fleet sailed on until attacked by dive-bombers from the 'Enterprise', 'Hornet' and Admiral Frank Fletcher's 'Yorktown' in succession. Within an hour 3 Japanese carriers were blazing hulks; the 4th and last, 'Hiryu', steamed north-east and her aircraft managed to damage 'Yorktown'. But US aircraft converged on this enemy vessel, setting it alight during the late afternoon. Japanese losses were 4 carriers, 1 heavy cruiser, 275 aircraft and 3,500 men; US losses were 307 men, 132 aircraft and 2 warships – the 'Yorktown' and an escorting cruiser, sunk by a Japanese submarine when the damaged 'Yorktown' was being towed to Pearl Harbor. Midway was one of the most decisive battles of the war, forcing the Japanese on to the defensive through the destruction of their main carrier fleet.

Minié, Claude-Étienne, 1804–79 French ordnance developer. Invented a new bullet, based on principles worked out by Captain Gustave Delvigne, which permitted faster *rifle* firing. The bullet expanded when detonated, through the explosion of gas in the hollow base, thus forcing the sides out to fit the barrel walls and pushing rings round the base into the *rifling*. This system removed the need for ramming to make the bullet fit tight, and hence reduced loading time. The bullet was adopted in England in the Pattern 1851 rifled musket, known as the Minié rifle; this weapon was superseded by the French *chassepot*, introduced 1866.

MIRV (Multiple Independently Targetable Re-entry Vehicle) This *missile* warhead, designed primarily for a nuclear explosive, is capable of striking a number of pre-programme targets at the same time; US development has been based on the Minuteman and *Poseidon* programmes. Thus by 1974 the USA had deployed over 350 Minuteman III missiles, each with 3 MIRVs; at sea over 320 Poseidon missiles, each with 10–14 MIRVs, had been deployed in some 25 submarines – each submarine having about 16 missiles, and each missile able to strike at up to 14 separate targets. The Soviet Union developed a multiple re-entry vehicle (MRV) but lagged with independently targetable warheads until 1974. By this date the

Soviet MIRVs were probably in an operational stage, designed for the 2 latest Soviet strategic missiles, the SS-17, range about 4,500 miles, and the smaller SS-18. Both these missile types are land based; no Soviet submarine-launched ballistic missile had been tested with MRV by 1976.

Missiles, nuclear Both the USA and the Soviet Union began to concentrate on missile development in the early 1950s, aimed at developing a weapon capable of carrying a nuclear warhead. Initial US progress appeared to lag behind that of the Soviet Union. By 1956–7 US scientists had successfully tested the Jupiter intermediate-range ballistic missile, with a range of over 3,000 miles, but had still to undertake trials with long-range strategic missiles. By comparison, in 1957 the Soviet Union successfully tested 2 long-range missiles, and on 4 October caused apprehension in America by the launching of Sputnik I, proving Soviet pre-eminence in long-range rocketry. US fears of a Soviet missile lead led to a vast increase in expenditure and effort on these weapons during President *Kennedy*'s administration, 1961–3, thus precipitating a nuclear arms race between the two main superpowers. Soviet progress also undermined the US policy of *massive retaliation*; the strategy was replaced by that of *flexible response*. Missiles are classified by range and type. The 3 range categories are: short or tactical (up to 200 miles); Intermediate Range Ballistic Missiles, IRBM (200–1,500 miles);

Inter-Continental Ballistic Missiles, ICBM (1,500 to over 7,000 miles). Type categories are surface-to-surface, surface-to-air (SAM), surface-to-subsurface (anti-submarine), air-to-surface, air-to-air, subsurface-to-surface (SLBM – submarine launched ballistic missiles, such as *Polaris*, *Poseidon* and the Soviet *Sark and Serb*) and subsurface-to-subsurface. The largest missiles in 1977 were 2 Soviet ICBMs code-named by NATO as Scrag and Scarp: about 35 metres long with a range of over 10,000 miles. The primary US land-based ICBM in 1977 was the Minuteman, with a length of up to 18·2 metres; the original Minuteman I became operational in 1963, and the final version, Minuteman III, in 1970: the latter had a range of over 8,000 miles and *MIRV* capability.

Mitchell, William, 1879–1936 US General, pilot and air power theorist. Entered US Army as a private, 1898; served in *American-Spanish War*, 1898, in the *Philippines*, 1899–1902, and in the *First World War*, 1917–18, where he commanded US air forces in France. Mitchell then toured Europe to study the status of air power. He was appointed Assistant Chief of the US Air Service in 1921; his criticism of air policies being pursued by the US Army and Navy Departments culminated in a statement charging the departments with 'incompetence, criminal negligence, and almost treasonable administration of the national defense'. He was court-martialled in late 1925 and sentenced

to a 5-year rank suspension, but he resigned from the Army on 1 February 1926. Mitchell thereafter devoted his time to lecturing, writing and appearing before committees to plead for a US Air Force separate from Army and Navy. His published books include 'Our Air Force', 1921; 'Winged Defense', 1925; and 'Skyways – A Book of Modern Aeronautics', 1930. Mitchell's activities were contemporaneous with those of the Italian air advocate, *Douhet*, and the two men shared many common ideas, although Douhet spoke from an almost scientific point of view, whereas Mitchell argued with extreme patriotism. He wrote:

> The advent of air power, which can go straight to the vital centers and either neutralize or destroy them, has put a completely new complexion on the old system of making war. It is now realized that the hostile main army in the field is a false objective, and the real objectives are the vital centers.

Such statements were passionately supported by later advocates of *strategic bombing*. Mitchell's case for greater recognition of air power in the US military establishment therefore rested on his conviction of the absolute power which aircraft promised, especially as bombers. Civilians would be completely demoralized merely by being driven from their homes through air attack; Mitchell declared: 'A few gas bombs will do that.' He also believed that naval vessels could easily be destroyed by bombing: even if the bomb landed some way off, the under-water explosion would cave in a ship's hull. This latter belief failed to come true, as did Mitchell's gloomy predictions over the extent of civilian demoralization through air raids. On the other hand another of Mitchell's statements, concerning the value of using *airborne* forces behind enemy lines, proved far-sighted.

Mitrailleuse Name used in France to refer to a *machine-gun*, although the original mitrailleuse had a very short life. Invented by Major Fafschamps of the Belgian Army in 1851, the weapon was adopted by the French in 1867. The gun had 25–37 barrels, compared with the *Gatling* which had 6–10, and could put down an extremely heavy fire: 150 rounds per minute over a range of nearly 2,000 yards. The weapon was manufactured in great secrecy prior to the *Franco-Prussian War*, 1870–1, and this 'closed-door' policy prevented adequate training. Consequently, the weapon was incorrectly employed in the war, being matched against artillery rather than infantry, and fired at extreme range. This misuse, combined with mechanical defects and the weapon's unwieldly nature, led to the abandonment of the gun during the latter stages of the conflict.

Moltke, Helmuth von, 'Moltke the Elder', 1800–91 Prussian Chief of Staff. Attended the Berlin War Academy, directed by *Clausewitz*, prior to being assigned to the General Staff, 1828, to which he belonged for over

60 years. In 1857 he became Chief of the General Staff, appointed by William I, Regent of Prussia. William was more interested in the political re-organization of his army than in preparations for military operations, and the powerful figure of Minister of War *Roon* overshadowed the quiet Chief of Staff. Nor had Moltke's office acquired significant prestige. But Moltke used this period of isolation from the political scene, 1857–66, to overhaul military plans and strategic doctrines. He drafted a succession of plans for a war on two fronts, east and west; he improved mobilization schemes to meet threats to Prussia, fully exploiting the benefits of the *railway*. Rail timetables and networks formed the core of his strategic plans, together with the road system being developed in the Industrial Revolution. Moltke studied the possibilities of concentrating an army upon the battlefield itself, rather than before battle. The organization required led to his development of the Prussian *Staff* system. Moltke extended innovations introduced by *Scharnhorst* and Clausewitz, making the General Staff into a nerve system animating the large body of the Army; Staff officers were strictly selected and trained. Moltke's methods, and his own position, came to full prominence in the *Austro-Prussian War*, 1866, especially at the crushing victory of *Sadowa*. By 1870 the Army had been largely formed to his ideas, and all his plans and preparations were fully vindicated in the opening phase of the *Franco-Prussian War*, 1870–1, especi-

ally at *Sedan*. The latter stage of the war was marred by Moltke's clash with *Bismarck*, notably over the proposed bombardment of *Paris* which Moltke originally opposed, and over the need for negotiations after the city capitulated: Moltke believed the war should be prosecuted to the finish. Moltke was succeeded by *Schlieffen* in 1891.

Moltke, Helmuth von, 'Moltke the Younger', 1848–1916 German General, nephew of 'Moltke the Elder'. Succeeded *Schlieffen* as Chief of the General Staff, 1906, and modified his famous plan to be used in hostilities against France and Russia; Moltke's version, with less strength allowed to the German right wing for its offensive against north France, was employed in August 1914. The right wing lacked sufficient power to accomplish the complete encirclement of the French Army. Moltke overestimated the initial success of the German advance in the Battle of the *Frontiers* (Map 10); he moved forces prematurely from the west to the east against Russia, and he interfered with progress being made in the field, especially by Kluck's 1st Army. The allies were able to launch their successful counter-attack at the *Marne*, September, and Moltke was replaced by *Falkenhayn* on the 14th.

'Monitor' The Union Navy's timely answer to the Confederate *ironclad* 'Virginia' ('*Merrimack*') in the *American Civil War*. Responsible for a major part of the design was the inventor

Ericsson. 'Monitor' was a flat raft pointed at stern and bow, and with the deck scarcely above water-level. Her main features were Ericsson's revolving turret containing two 11-inch guns and her heavy armour.

Montgomery, Sir Bernard Law, 1st Viscount Montgomery of Alamein, 1887–1976 British Field-Marshal. Served in the First World War; Commander 8th Division, 1938–9; GOC-in-C South-East Command, 1941–2. Montgomery replaced General N. M. Ritchie as Commander of the 8th Army in the North African *desert campaign*, 13 August 1942 (Map 14); he repulsed Rommel's attack at Alam al Halfa, 31 August to 7 September, then defeated Rommel at El *Alamein*, 23 October to 4 November; he repulsed Rommel's attack at Medenine, 6 March 1943, broke through enemy defences at *Mareth*, 20–26 March, and advanced into *Tunisia*. Montgomery's 8th Army assaulted *Sicily*, July, and invaded *Italy*, 3 September. He was succeeded by General Leese in December, to take command of allied ground forces in the assault on *Normandy*, 6 June 1944 (Map 13); after the breakout in late July he became Commander of the 21st Army Group but retained his overall command of allied ground forces until 3 September, when *Eisenhower* combined this role with his office of Supreme Commander. Friction rose between Eisenhower and Montgomery, with the latter urging a concentrated thrust into Germany rather than an offensive on a wide front as Eisenhower planned. The Supreme Commander did however sanction Montgomery's 'Market Garden' *airborne* operation at *Arnhem*. This, starting 17 September, failed to achieve its objectives and the broad front strategy remained in being. The Germans attempted to make use of allied overstretch in the *Ardennes*, December, and during this counter-offensive Eisenhower transferred command of all US troops north of the bulge to Montgomery except *Patton*'s 3rd Army. On 5 May 1945 Montgomery accepted the surrender of German forces in the north. He served as Commander of the British occupied zone in Germany, 1945–6; he was CIGS, 1948–51, combining this appointment with that of Chairman of the Commanders-in-Chief Committee, Western Union Defence Organization – the forerunner of *NATO*; he served as NATO's Deputy Supreme Allied Commander, Europe, 1951–8. Montgomery's achievements in the Second World War earned him a reputation as a careful, painstaking commander who insisted upon all preparations being completed and all possible strength obtained before he opened an attack. His tactics were straightforward, lacking originality but none the less effective, providing he had sufficient strength to push through his battle plans, as at El Alamein. Montgomery's arrival in the desert coincided with the need to counteract the somewhat glamorous public image enjoyed by Rommel, and the new British commander succeeded through a timely public rela-

tions campaign. He was largely respected and admired by his troops, rather than liked; they responded well to his efforts to bridge the gap between commander and commanded.

Moore, Sir John, 1761–1809 British General. Served in America, 1779–83, in the closing stages of the American Revolution; fought in Corsica, 1794, and thereafter in the West Indies and Ireland. Served as Brigade Commander in Sir Ralph Abercrombie's force which landed in Holland, August 1799; Corps Commander under Sir Ralph in the invasion of *Egypt*, 1801, distinguishing himself in the Aboukir Bay landings, 8 March, and in the main battle with the French outside Alexandria, 20 March. He then commanded troops in south England, introducing valuable innovations in troop training and especially concerning light infantry. After service in Sicily, Moore commanded an expedition to Sweden, May 1808, which proved abortive when negotiations with the Swedish monarch, Gustavus IV, broke down. Moore then proceeded to Portugal, where the *Peninsular War* had just broken out (Map 1). On 6 October Moore received command of all British forces in Portugal, and he was ordered by the War Office to advance into Spain, despite shortage of men, the lateness of the year, inadequate supplies and poor relations with the Spanish allies. The small British force marched to Salamanca, feinted north to draw the French from Madrid, then began an inevitable retreat on 25 December. This led over the mountains to *Corunna*. Moore managed to rally his troops for the Battle of Corunna, 16 January 1809, but fell mortally wounded. He was buried in the ramparts of Corunna.

Moreau, Jean, 1763–1813 French General. Distinguished himself in the *Wattignies* campaign, 1793; commanded Army of Rhine and Moselle, September 1794, advancing from Saar to Mainz (Map 1); drove Austrians back from lower Rhine, April 1797; commanded French forces opposing *Suvorov* in *Italy*, 1799 (Map 1), but was defeated at Cassano, April, and replaced by Barthélemy Joubert, 5 August. Moreau commanded the Army of the Rhine, 1800, and was the first to use the *corps* system. In 1804 Moreau was implicated in the plot by Charles Pichegru and Georges Cadoudal to overthrow Napoleon, and he fled to America. He lived near Trenton, NJ, until 1813, when he returned to Europe and entered Russian service against Napoleon. He was mortally wounded at *Dresden*, August 1813.

Morrison, Herbert Stanley, Baron Morrison of Lambeth, 1888–1965 British Labour leader and politician. Minister of Supply, 1940; Home Secretary and Minister of Home Security, 1940–5; member of *Churchill*'s War Cabinet, 1942–5. As Minister in charge of Home Security, Morrison was responsible for monitoring the effects of the *Blitz*; he provided frequent reports to the War Cabinet on the state of morale, especially in London. The Morrison air-raid shelters, supplementing those named after his predecessor *Anderson*, were intended for indoor use and were introduced during the Blitz: these constructions had a steel plate able to be used as a table in daytime, and wire mesh sides. Over ½ million had been issued free to those of low incomes by November 1941. Morrison acted as Lord President of the Council and Leader of the House of Commons, 1945–51.

Morse, Samuel Finley, 1791–1872 US inventor. Morse, a portrait-painter by profession, interested himself in the possibilities of magnetic *telegraph*; in 1837 he patented the Morse telegraph alphabet or code; the first Morse message was sent over an experimental line from Washington to Baltimore, 24 May 1844.

Mortar Historical origins of this high-trajectory weapon are closely linked to those of the howitzer. Development stemmed from a Dutch gun of 1693, intended to fire heavy projectiles, up to 200 pounds, over a range of up to 2,000 yards. Fire from this weapon would therefore be heavier than a normal cannon bombardment, but lacked distance and accuracy. Frederick the Great of Prussia is believed to have been the first to introduce high-angle howitzer/mortar fire to strike at an enemy positioned behind cover or high ground. Later development, in the nineteenth–twentieth centuries, tended to differentiate the mortar as an infantry weapon and the howitzer as an artillery piece. Trench warfare underlined the value of the mortar: this weapon could be fired into, and from, dead ground, i.e. positions hidden from the opposing troops by the lie of the land. These guns were therefore used extensively during the *First World War*. Mortars were increasingly sophisticated by 1939. The principal German gun of this type was the 'Nebelwerfer', nicknamed by the British 'Moaning Minnie': this had 5–10 barrels and was originally intended for laying down smoke, but was used for HE. There were 3 sizes, the 150 mm, 210 mm and 300 mm, each with a range of over 5,000 yards, and with the largest throwing a projectile of 277 pounds. Howitzers had far greater range: the Russian 122-mm T31/37, for example, had a range of 22,000 yards; the US 105 mm and 155 mm had a range of 16,000 yards and could fire 2 rounds per minute. The British 25-pounder gun could be used as a howitzer for 'drop-shots'. An example of the modern howitzer is the US 115-mm M.114A1, used extensively in *Vietnam* and supplied to NATO countries: this has a maximum range of 14,600 metres and can fire HE, chemical or nuclear shells. It is normally assigned to the US Divisional Artillery units. Modern mortars include the 107-mm and 81-mm guns developed in the USA and supplied to other NATO armies; the 81 mm is assigned to infantry company and platoon levels.

Mountbatten, Louis, 1st Earl Mountbatten of Burma, 1900– British Admiral of the Fleet, great-grandson of Queen Victoria, son of Prince Louis of *Battenberg*. Entered Royal Navy, 1913, serving on *Beatty*'s flagship HMS 'Lion' in 1916. Mountbatten became Adviser, Combined Operations, in October 1941, in succession to Sir Roger Keyes who had the title Director; he remained at this post until October 1943, with his title changed to Chief of Combined Operations in March 1942 with a seat on the *Chiefs of Staff Committee*. He then became Supreme Allied Commander, South-East Asia, a position he held until 1946: his task was to regain *Burma*. Mountbatten's subsequent appointments included Viceroy of India, 1947, Governor-General of India, 1947–8, and Chief of the British Defence Staff, 1959–65.

Mozambique, 1965–75 Guerrilla warfare against Portuguese rule in Mozambique acquired large-scale proportions in early 1965, 4 years after a similar insurgency movement had emerged in Portuguese *Angola*. The main insurgent group was the Mozambique Liberation Front, better known as FRELIMO (Fronte de Libertaçao de Mozambique), organized in September 1962 with headquarters in the Tanzanian capital of Dar es Salaam. Key FRELIMO personnel were trained in *Algeria* and *Cuba*. The Portuguese were unable to exert control despite the eventual dispatch of over 55,000 men. Subsequent events followed those in Angola.

Multi-Lateral Force (MLF) Concept suggested by the US in the early

1960s, comprising a surface fleet of about 25 vessels with men from different NATO nations joined as crew on each warship. The scheme was intended to bring about greater sharing and participation amongst NATO members. The British government made a counter-proposal for a more ambitious multi-lateral Atlantic Nuclear Force (ANF), explained in Denis *Healey*'s 1965 Defence White Paper: the ANF would consist of the British V-bombers (except those required for commitments outside the NATO area); the four British *Polaris* submarines under construction; at least an equal number of US Polaris submarines; and some kind of mixed-manned and jointly armed element or elements in which the existing non-nuclear powers could take part. The idea was too complicated and ANF discussions lapsed. From the original MLF concept did, however, emerge NATO's Standing Naval Force Atlantic, a multi-national non-nuclear force formed in December 1967. This force comprises warships from NATO countries, participating on a rotational basis, although not with crews of mixed nationalities. The strength of the squadron usually amounts to 4 destroyer-type vessels.

Murat, Joachim, 1767?-1815 French Marshal. Took part in campaign in *Italy*, 1796-7 (Map 1); accompanied *Napoleon* to *Egypt*, 1798-9; supported Napoleon in Paris coup, 1799, and married Napoleon's sister the following year; fought in *Italy*, 1800, commanding reserve cavalry at *Marengo*, June; appointed Governor of Paris, 1804; commanded cavalry at *Ulm* and *Austerlitz*, 1805, at Jena in *Auerstedt* campaign, and at *Eylau* and *Friedland*, 1807 (Map 1); became King of Naples, 1808. Murat led a French army into Spain, March 1808, but fell back to the Ebro after Spanish insurrection, May, in the *Peninsular War*. He commanded French cavalry in *Russia*, 1812, taking over command of the remnants of the Grand Army on 8 December after Napoleon's return to Paris. He fought in the *Leipzig* campaign, 1813, but deserted to the allies in February 1814. He rejoined Napoleon's cause in 1815 but was defeated by the Austrians at Tolentino, 2 May. Murat was captured by the allies and executed, 13 October 1815.

Musket Term generally used to describe a smooth-bore military weapon of large calibre fired from the shoulder, with this weapon remaining the standard infantry gun until the widespread introduction of *rifles*. The basic British musket during the *French Revolutionary* and *Napoleonic Wars* was the 'Brown Bess', a name later used to describe all types of British muskets made from 1720 to 1840. In 1794 the British Army was equipped with the cheap Brown Bess produced by the East India Company, known as the India pattern. This had a 39-inch barrel; the last model Brown Bess, known also as the New Land musket, appeared after 1802. All these weapons had a calibre of about ·75 and incorporated a socket bayonet with a triangular 17-inch blade. These muskets were only accurate up to about 90 yards, they had a maximum effective range of about 250 yards, and needed cleaning after about 30 shots. About 15 seconds were needed for loading and firing, half the time required for the earliest rifles – this handicap delayed the general introduction of the weapon until designs improved. French muskets in the Napoleonic era were lighter but not as durable as the British: they threw a lighter ball, and the coarse powder used meant that the barrels had to be scoured even more frequently.

Mussolini, Benito, 1883–1945 Italian dictator. Organized Italian fascism as a political party, 1921; summoned by the Italian King to form a Ministry, 1922. In 1930 Mussolini denounced the *Versailles* Treaty; he overran Ethiopia, 1935–6, withdrew Italy from the League of Nations, 1937, attacked Albania, 1939. Mussolini supported Hitler through the Axis alliance, culminating in the Pact of Steel signed May 1939; he declared war on Britain and France, 10 June 1940. He was overthrown, 24 July 1943, and succeeded by Marshal Badoglio. Mussolini, imprisoned but rescued by the Germans in September, was assassinated by Italian partisans on 28 April 1945.

N

Napalm Incendiary weapon with its name derived from the first syllables of ingredients naphthenate and palmitate; formed from a mixture of petrol and a chemical thickener which produces a tough, sticky gel. Initial experiments used rubber as a thickener, but other means were sought after the Japanese conquest of the Netherlands East Indies cut natural rubber supplies. Much of the research was undertaken by Professor Louis Fieser of Harvard University. Napalm was used by the US in raids on Japan and by the French in *Indochina*: about 25 per cent of Viet Minh casualties between 1952 and 1955 were estimated to have involved napalm burns. Napalm was described by the 'US Armed Forces Chemical Journal' as the 'best all around weapon' in the *Korean War*; it was afterwards used on a large scale in *Vietnam*. The igniting agent, white phosphorus, may penetrate skin tissues and continue smouldering and re-igniting over a considerable time.

Napoleon I (Napoleon Bonaparte), 1769–1821 (Map 1). French Emperor. Born in Ajaccio, Corsica; studied at military school, Brienne, 1779–84, and Paris, 1784–5; served as Artillery Lieutenant, 1785–91; joined French Revolutionary forces in Paris, 1791. Napoleon, now a Colonel, attempted to persuade fellow-Corsicans to support the Revolution in 1792, but was obliged to flee the island for Toulon, June 1793; at Toulon the adoption of a plan he had prepared forced the departure of the blockading British Fleet under *Hood*, December. Napoleon was appointed General of Brigade, 1794, but was arrested later in the year after the downfall of his friend Augustin Robespierre; he was soon released for lack of evidence. In October 1794 he helped put down an uprising by a Paris mob. He was appointed Commander of the Army of the Interior, 1795, and Commander of the French Armies in Italy, 1796. His 1796–7 campaign in *Italy* won him renown. He hurried back from *Egypt*, 1799, upon hearing of the formation of the Second Coalition against France, and sought more power in order to lead French armies against this alliance; he carried out a coup against the Directory, 9 November 1799, and became one of the three Consuls ruling France

His two colleagues resigned after the promulgation of the Constitution of Year VIII (1799), and Napoleon was named First Consul, 24 December. The Treaty of Luneville, 8 February 1801, brought peace between Austria and France following Napoleon's victorious campaign in *Italy*, 1800. Russia had already withdrawn; the Treaty of Amiens, 27 March 1802, resulted in a general European peace; on 2 August 1802 Napoleon was proclaimed Consul for life and he turned to domestic matters. But hostilities were resumed with Britain in May 1803, with Britain imposing a naval blockade of the Continent, and Napoleon prepared to invade across the Channel. On 2 December 1804 he was crowned Emperor. The Third Coalition against France was formed in 1805, with Austria, Russia and Sweden joining Britain. Napoleon's vigorous reaction led to the *Austerlitz* campaign, concluded by the Treaty of Pressburg, 23 December 1805. Napoleon had gained virtual domination over west and central Germany, but Britain remained unsubdued and Prussia took up arms again in 1806 – and suffered devastating defeat in the *Auerstedt* campaign. Napoleon again turned upon the Russians at *Eylau* and *Friedland*, February and June 1807, and the resulting Treaties of Tilsit, July, marked the peak of his power. Only Britain continued to oppose him. The *Peninsular War* began in November 1807 and would continue until 1814, described by Napoleon as his 'Spanish ulcer'. Austria again took up arms –

and was again defeated, at *Wagram*, July 1809. But Napoleon's authority could not be enforced everywhere, and relations with Russia deteriorated: Napoleon's disastrous campaign in *Russia* began in June 1812. His defeat encouraged others to rise against him; in February–March 1813 the massive campaign in Europe began, leading to Napoleon's defeat at *Leipzig*, October. France was invaded in January 1814; Paris fell on 30 March; Napoleon abdicated unconditionally on 11 April and stepped on to Elba on 4 May while the allies installed Louis XVIII as King of France. Napoleon escaped from exile in late April 1815 and landed at Cannes on 1 March to begin 'The Hundred Days'. He again abdicated on 21 June 1815. He died on St Helena on 5 May 1821. Napoleon's success as a commander stemmed from a variety of factors: he demanded strict discipline, but he administered this with fairness and complete impartiality; he took care to reward bravery, and he displayed considerable personal courage; in manoeuvring for battle, and in battle itself, he often employed a strikingly effective combination of feints and flanking movements, coupled with a concentration of force and speed at the decisive point. He manoeuvred the enemy into exposing a vital weakness, then stabbed at this weakness with deadly results. By his concentration of force, usually based on massed *artillery*, Napoleon could make up for deficiencies in manpower strength.

Paradoxically, another of Napoleon's attributes in his earlier campaigns proved a weakness in the later struggles. He insisted upon unity of command; everything stemmed from Napoleon himself. He had an excellent group of marshals, whom he could send with subordinate armies to different areas of the campaign, often widely separated yet retaining an overall pattern through his tight personal control at the centre. But after 1809 war became too much for one man to handle himself, especially when Napoleon suffered increasingly from illness. Cohesion broke down in Russia and in 1813–14 partly through Napoleon's lack of an adequate *Staff* system.

Napoleonic Wars, 1800–15, general (Map 1) Period from the end of the *French Revolutionary Wars*, 1792–1800, marked by the assumption of dictatorial powers by *Napoleon* as First Consul, December 1799, to his final overthrow, 21 June 1815. Warfare in this great upheaval was characterized by the beginnings of the *nation-in-arms* concept. The French Revolution and the subsequent Army reorganization by Lazare *Carnot* had unleashed a monstrous new form of war; Prussia, under *Scharnhorst*'s reforms, followed suit with the *Landwehr* recruitment system, introduced in 1813. Huge armies were being created: the army groups forged by Napoleon for the 1812 campaign in *Russia* numbered 450,000 men; by contrast, Marlborough's army in the Blenheim campaign of 1704 had only numbered 70,000. The allied field force against Napoleon in 1813 totalled over ½ million men, with a further 250,000 in garrisons and in reserve. Such massive manpower had far-reaching effects: on arms production at home, on supply systems, on domestic economies, on command systems – with the *Staff* system being developed – and on the organization and tactics of the armies themselves. The *divisional* and *corps* structure became essential. Tactically, the period witnessed the departure of the rigid, linear lines; instead, light infantrymen assumed increasing importance as skirmishers and flexible troops. The French *tirailleurs* led the way. At sea, a similar flexibility was adopted by *Nelson* with spectacular success. Apart from Napoleon, other great commanders during the period were *Blücher*, *Wellington*, *Kutuzov*, *Moore*, *Schwarzenberg* and a number of Napoleon's own marshals including *Soult* and *Masséna*. From these wars resulted important theoretical writings, especially those of *Clausewitz* and *Jomini*. The period began with the continuation of the War of the Second Coalition, including the campaign in *Italy*, 1800. Operations in *Egypt*, 1800–1 and at sea, including Nelson's victory at *Copenhagen*, April 1801, led to the Treaty of Amiens, March 1802, between France and England. Anglo-French hostilities were resumed in May 1803, resulting in French preparations to invade Britain from Boulogne; Britain gained Austria, Russia and Sweden as allies in 1805, thus beginning the War of the

Third Coalition. Britain was left alone after Napoleon's victories against the Austrians and Russians at *Ulm* and *Austerlitz*, 1805, but gained naval supremacy at *Trafalgar*, October 1805, and Prussia entered the war the following year, only to be defeated in the *Auerstedt* campaign. Remaining Prussian and Russian opposition was suppressed at *Eylau* and *Friedland*, 1807, and Britain was again left alone after the resulting Treaties of Tilsit, July. The *Peninsular War* began in 1807. Austria again took up the struggle in 1809, but was defeated at *Wagram*, July, and signed the Treaty of Schönbrunn in October. *Russia* again rose in opposition to Napoleon; the French Emperor invaded in June 1812. Prussia joined with Russian and Swedish forces for the 1813 campaign, beginning with the Battle of *Lützen* in May; Austria entered the alliance on 12 August; Napoleon suffered defeat at *Leipzig* in October. The allies invaded France in early 1814, with Blücher's Prussians spearheading the attack from Mainz and with the Austrians under *Schwarzenberg* advancing from Langres. Paris fell on 30 March. Napoleon abdicated on 11 April. His return to France on 1 March 1815 began 'The Hundred Days', culminating in the *Waterloo* campaign and Napoleon's final abdication, 21 June.

Nashville, campaign and Battle of, November–December 1864 *American Civil War* (Map 3). General John Hood led his 54,000 Confederates north from *Atlanta* in November,

attempting to destroy *Sherman*'s communications. Sherman refused to withdraw, but sent *Thomas* after the enemy. Thomas attempted to obtain time while he gained recruits, meanwhile sending 34,000 men under General John Schofield against the Confederates. Schofield occupied Franklin, 15 miles south of Nashville, and repulsed an attack by Hood on 30 November, inflicting 6,300 Confederate casualties. Thomas continued to prepare his army until 15 December. He then struck the Confederate left flank at Nashville and threatened to envelop the entire enemy army next day. Hood's Confederates fled in disorder, leaving 5,350 casualties. Union losses were just over 3,000.

Nasser, Gamal Abdal, 1918–70 Egyptian Army officer and President. Acted as principal supporter of General Mohammed Neguib in the military uprising against King Farouk, 22 July 1952, then ousted and replaced Neguib as President, 14 November 1954. Nasser announced the nationalization of the Suez Canal, 26 July 1956, precipitating the *Suez–Sinai* campaign. He proclaimed union with Syria, 1 February 1958, which, with Yemen another partner, created the United Arab Republic. The Egyptian–Syrian partnership broke up, 30 September 1961, but Egypt continued as the UAR. Nasser involved Egyptian troops in the *Yemen*, 1962–5; he led Egypt into the disastrous war with *Israel* in 1967 (the Six-Day War). He was succeeded on his death by Anwar el Sadat.

Nasution, Abdul Haris, 1918– Indonesian General, guerrilla leader and Defence Minister. Educated at the Royal Military Academy, Bandung; commissioned in the Netherlands Indies Army, 1941. During the Japanese occupation of the Netherlands East Indies, 1942–5, Nasution worked in the civil administration and led civil defence forces against Indonesian guerrillas. After the proclamation of independence for Indonesia by Achmed Sukarno in 1946 he was appointed to a minor staff position, but soon rose to prominence amongst the Indonesian nationalists in their fight against the Dutch and their British allies. From 1946 to 1948 he commanded the Siliwangi Division, the crack unit in the Indonesian People's Army; in 1948 he became Chief of the Operational Staff of the Armed Forces. Nasution became Chief of Staff in the Indonesian Army after the Dutch granted the country full sovereignty, November 1949; he fell out of favour in 1952 and was suspended, but was reappointed in 1955. From 1957 to 1959 he acted as Chairman of the Joint Chiefs of Staff; he became Defence Minister in 1959. His doctrine on *guerrilla warfare*, written in 1953, was translated into English as 'Fundamentals of Guerrilla Warfare', 1965, and has a special value in the fact that Nasution was a guerrilla leader who also had practical experience in counter-insurgency op-

erations. Sections of the book dealing with anti-guerrilla methods provide sound advice, such as the need to remove the appeal which the insurgents enjoy amongst the population – 'the guerrilla movement is only the result, not the cause of the problem'. In this way the insurgent can be isolated. He distinguished between *partisans*, whom he calls auxiliary guerrillas assisting the regular forces, and the hard-core insurgents.

National Security Council, US Established in 1947 under the National Security Act to advise the President on national security affairs; presided over by the President or Vice-President. *Truman* only attended sporadically, except during the *Korean War*, and the NSC, meeting about 30 times a year, became more of a forum for debate. *Eisenhower* used the NSC more frequently: in 1953 the Council met 53 times, and Eisenhower added the Secretary of the Treasury and the Chairman of the *Joint Chiefs of Staff* to the membership. *Kennedy* reduced the ancillary staff, believing the body should be an intimate group rather than an elaborate structure. *Johnson* allowed NSC functions to dwindle, but these were revived under *Nixon*, especially through the NSC role played by *Kissinger*: meetings became weekly.

Nation-in-arms Concept based on the total use of a nation's resources in war, expressed by William I of Prussia in 1860: 'The Prussian army will be the Prussian nation in arms.'

The concept covers four separate movements, each of which amounted to a revolution – in manpower, technical changes, managerial innovations and political attitudes. The first, manpower, was symbolized by the Prussian *Landwehr* system and the French *Levée en masse*, which resulted in a massive increase in the size of armies through conscription, in turn helping bridge the gap between soldier and civilian. Managerial improvements had to be introduced to control these forces, leading to the creation of the Prussian War Ministry in 1809 and the development of the General *Staff*, both under *Scharnhorst*. But in the years of peace which followed 1815 the concept of the nation-in-arms slipped partly into obscurity; a gap again appeared between army and people. Armies became smaller and more professional, with the officer class attempting to maintain this conservative situation. Political changes brought the concept to the front once more, especially with the great liberal movements in Europe. Civilians were becoming politically aware, and it was increasingly difficult for the army to stand apart. Technical improvements in weaponry dictated that future wars would involve all sections of society: for manpower in the field, for arms production and for supplying the forces. *Railways* meant that battlefields would spread over the entire country. The *American Civil War*, 1861–5, emphasized that through industrialization modern war was becoming total, and this was con-firmed by the *Franco-Prussian War*, 1870–1. Managerially, *Moltke* introduced dramatic improvements in the General Staff. The nation-in-arms concept came to full fruition in 1914 with the fusion of all four main components – manpower, technical, managerial, political – and in the Second World War no distinction remained between the home and the battle fronts.

NATO (North Atlantic Treaty Organization) Representatives of Britain, France, Belgium, the Netherlands and Luxembourg met in Brussels on 4 March 1948 to consider a treaty of mutual assistance. These countries signed the Brussels Treaty on 17 March, pledging themselves to build up a common defence system. On 30 April the Defence Ministers and Chiefs of Staff of the 5 Brussels Treaty powers began meetings in London to discuss military co-operation. In June the communists began the Berlin blockade, precipitating the *Berlin airlift*; from July, US and Canadian representatives attended the London meetings. In September a military body was created within the Brussels Treaty known as the Western Union Defence Organization; *Montgomery* was appointed Chairman of the Commanders-in-Chief Committee with an HQ at Fontainebleau. The text of a defensive pact treaty for the North Atlantic area was published on 18 March 1949; 3 days before, the original Brussels Treaty signatory powers, plus Canada and the USA, had officially invited Denmark, Iceland, Italy, Norway and Portugal to accede to the Treaty. The North Atlantic Treaty was signed in Washington on 4 April 1949; Greece and Turkey joined in 1952 and West Germany in 1955. Article V of the Treaty provides that an armed attack against one or more of the parties shall be considered an attack against all. In March 1966 the French government under *De Gaulle* announced its intention to withdraw French personnel from the NATO integrated military HQ, to terminate the assignment of French forces to the international command and to request the transfer from French territory of the International Headquarters. The latter moved to Belgium in spring 1967. Allied Command Europe (ACE) has its headquarters, known as SHAPE (Supreme HQ Allied Powers in Europe), at Casteau near Mons, and is responsible for the defence of all NATO territory in Europe, excluding Britain, France, Iceland and Portugal. Allied Command Atlantic (ACLANT) is based at Norfolk, Virginia, and is responsible for the naval defence of the North Atlantic area from the North Pole to the Tropic of Cancer. The third main military command is Allied Command Channel (ACCHAN), based at Northwood, near London. All three come under the control of the Supreme Allied Commander Europe (SACEUR), who has always been a US officer; successive holders of this post have been *Eisenhower*, 1950–2, *Ridgway*, 1952–3, Alfred M. Gruen-

ther, 1953–6, Lauris Norstad, 1956–63, Lyman L. Lemnitzer, 1963–9, Goodpaster, 1969–. The NATO governing body is the North Atlantic Council, comprising ministers of the member countries, which normally meets twice a year under the auspices of the Secretary-General. Advising the Council is the Military Committee, which consists of the chiefs of staff of all member countries except France and Iceland. Other bodies include the Nuclear Defence Affairs Committee (NDAC), which meets at Defence Minister level twice a year, and the Nuclear Planning Group (NPG), subordinate to the NDAC. NATO had about 7,000 tactical nuclear weapons in its European armoury in 1975, compared with a Warsaw Pact total of about 3,500. Ground forces available in Europe numbered about 45 NATO divisions in 1975 compared with 56 *Warsaw Pact* equivalent units. The Warsaw Pact forces had a large superiority in tank totals: about 24,000 compared with under 9,000, and the Warsaw Pact also enjoyed a superiority in tactical aircraft numbers.

Naval race, Anglo-German, 1898–1914 From 1866 to 1882 British naval estimates had remained at just under £11 million; by 1886 the total had risen to £13·5 million. In 1886 Russia announced plans for large increases in her Baltic Fleet; France also declared she was about to increase her cruiser and flotilla forces. An Admiralty Committee under Lord George Hamilton, First

Lord of the Admiralty, declared in 1888 that the British naval establishment must be 'at least equal to the naval strength of any two other countries': this 'Two-Power Standard' became increasingly important as one navy after another sought to avoid being left behind. The focus of the chain-reaction naval race fell upon Britain and Germany. The German Navy, originally merely a subsidiary branch of the Army, achieved greater prominence after 1871 when General von Stosch became Head of the Navy Department, holding this position until 1883; developments introduced by him continued under his successor, Count von Caprivi, and received a greater boost in 1897 when Admiral von *Tirpitz* became Head of the Navy. A seven years' building programme was passed in 1898; in 1900 another naval law was introduced, even more extensive, with Tirpitz declaring that Germany must be prepared for 'a battle in the North Sea against England'. Britain was now spending £27·5 million on the Navy and Germany £7·5 million – in 1886 the German figure had been £2·5 million. Both Tirpitz and *Fisher*, British First Sea Lord, were firm supporters of *Mahan*'s 'big ship' school of thought. In 1904 Britain formed a new Home Fleet at Rosyth, Scotland; in 1905 Germany passed a supplementary naval law. Also in 1905 the keel of the first Dreadnought *battleship* was laid at Portsmouth, completed by October 1906. Three of these ships were laid down in 1907 and 2 in 1908, but in 1908 an amend-ment to the German naval law provided for the construction of 4 similar giant vessels each year until 1911, creating intense panic in Britain. In fact by May 1911 the Germans had only completed 5 Dreadnought-type battleships. By 1914 the British Grand Fleet included 20 battleships and 4 *battlecruisers*; the German High Seas Fleet included 23 battleships but not as powerful as the British versions, plus 4 battlecruisers. The British 2nd Fleet included 15 older battleships. To these the Germans could only answer with 10 inferior battleships, and could find no real opposition to the British 3rd Fleet of 14 old capital vessels.

Nelson, Viscount Horatio, 1758–1805 British Admiral. Served in West Indies, 1780–5; served under *Hood* and *Jervis* in the Mediterranean (Map 1), 1793–7, taking part in the seizure of Corsica, 1794, during which he lost an eye; appointed Commodore, 1796; joined Jervis at the Battle of *Cape St Vincent*, February 1797. Nelson failed in a desperate attempt to seize the well-defended island fortress of Santa Cruz de Tenerife, 24 July 1797 – his first independent command as a flag officer – and was shot through the right elbow, resulting in the amputation of this arm. He rejoined the Mediterranean Fleet under Jervis, now Lord St Vincent, in early 1798, and attempted to block *Napoleon*'s invasion of *Egypt*; Nelson shattered the French Fleet at the Battle of the

Nile, 1 August. He blockaded Malta and Naples during 1799. He was appointed Vice-Admiral, 1801, and served as Second-in-Command to Sir Hyde Parker in a naval operation against Denmark, surprising and defeating the Danish Fleet at *Copenhagen*, April 1801. Nelson was appointed to command the Mediterranean Fleet when hostilities were resumed with France in May 1803, and he blockaded the French Fleet at Toulon for 2 years. In April 1805 Nelson pursued the French to the West Indies and back, inflicting decisive defeat at *Trafalgar*, 21 October 1805. Nelson was struck by a sharpshooter's bullet during the action, with the musket ball breaking his spine; he died in the battle's closing minutes. Nelson's prime characteristics as a naval commander were his instinctive opportunism and his flexibility. The latter enabled him to alter prearranged plans in favour of new moves, often unorthodox, to seize advantage of developing circumstances. He had supreme confidence in himself and in his sailors. Allied to this was a constant search for action aimed at the complete destruction of the enemy's fleet. Often he fought with a kind of inspired blindness: a refusal to take account of the odds against him. Yet this willingness to take risks was backed both by his confidence and by his grasp of the overall situation: Nelson always knew exactly what he was about. In *Mahan's* words:

It is difficult to know which most

to admire – the sagacity which divined the actual, though not the intended, movements of the enemy, the fiery eagerness which gave assurance of a fierce and decisive battle, or the great self-restraint which, in all his fever of impatience, withheld him from precipitating action before every means of information was exhausted.

New Guinea–Solomons campaigns, 1942–4 *Second World War against Japan* (Map 16). Japanese occupation of New Guinea, the Bismarcks and the Solomons was undertaken in January–March 1942, following the initial success of the *Pearl Harbor* offensive. The conquest of the Solomons culminated in airfield construction at *Guadalcanal*, 6 July, which in turn prompted US action against this southern island in the Solomons chain. While the Guadalcanal operation took place, August 1942 to February 1943, the Japanese offensive in the southern New Guinea province of Papua was halted by Australian and US resistance; the allies then counterattacked and inflicted defeat on the Japanese at Buna-Gona, December 1942 to January 1943. Faced with the US success in Papua and Guadalcanal, the Japanese began to reinforce Rabaul, north-east New Guinea and the northern Solomons in early 1943. The allies organized themselves for the attack on the primary objective of Rabaul. The US 3rd Fleet, under Admiral William Halsey, struck north through the Solomons from Guadalcanal, seizing Rendova Island on 30 June. On the same day the other arm of the pincer movement on Rabaul began operations in Papua. This force, the US 6th Army under General Walter Krueger, undertook landings at Salamau in the Huon Gulf, facing New Britain. The campaign continued throughout the summer, with US troops clearing the New Guinea area opposite New Britain, and, in the eastern movement, with the Solomons island-hopping operation proceeding via New Georgia, July–August, Vella Lavella, August–October, and Bougainville, October–December. Not until July 1944 could the last Japanese stronghold in New Guinea be taken, in the Hollandia region. With this accomplished and Rabaul isolated, combat missions for the south Pacific virtually ended. Australian troops continued to contain Rabaul; the campaign shifted northwards to the *Philippines*.

Ney, Michel, Duc d'Elchingen, Prince de la Moskova, 1769–1815 French Marshal. Served on the Rhine, 1799 (Map 1); fought in the Ulm campaign, 1805; guarded Alpine passes during early stages of *Austerlitz* campaign, November; engaged at Jena in *Auerstedt* campaign, 1806; served in *Friedland* campaign, 1807; in *Peninsular War*, 1808–11, leaving Spain to accompany Napoleon to *Russia*, 1812, commanding the French 3rd Corps; fought bravely at *Borodino*, September, and commanded rearguard in retreat from Moscow. Ney

fought at *Lützen*, May 1813, and *Bautzen*, 21 May. He attempted to block *Blücher*'s advance into *Leipzig*, October, and helped defend Paris, March 1814. He was created a peer by Louis XVII during Napoleon's exile on Elba, but rallied to his old leader during 'The Hundred Days'. He attacked the British at Quatre Bras, 16 June 1815, in the early stage of the *Waterloo* campaign (Map 1) and commanded the cavalry at the Battle of Waterloo. He was condemned for treason by the Chamber of Peers, and shot on 7 December 1815.

Nigeria–Biafra, civil war, 1967–70 Intense regional and tribal differences, which dominated Nigerian politics after independence from Britain in 1960, led to increasing violence in the mid-1960s, especially between Ibo tribesmen in the east and the federal government in Lagos. On 15 January 1966 a group of eastern junior officers carried out a coup, in which Prime Minister Balewa and the western politicians Bello and Akintola were assassinated. The revolt was put down by Major-General Johnson Aguiy-Ironsi, Army Commander, who established a military government. On 29 July Ironsi himself was assassinated and replaced by Colonel Jakubu Gowon; the legitimacy of the new régime was stridently challenged by Colonel Odumegwu Ojukwu, Governor of the Eastern Province. On 30 May 1967 the east seceded under Ojukwu as the independent Republic of Biafra. The Federal Navy imposed a blockade of Port

Harcourt, and the Biafrans began a mercenary airlift. Fighting continued throughout 1967; after a battle at Nsukka on 13 July the Federal government claimed to have killed 2,000 Biafrans. The Federal government enlisted aid from both Britain and the Soviet Union, but despite this assistance the Biafrans continued to offer stiff resistance, helped by the fact that many of the Army officers in the rebel force were previously officers in the Federal Army. A new Federal offensive was launched in August 1968, but the Biafrans were now receiving arms of French manufacture through Gabon and the Ivory Coast; on 9 September President *De Gaulle* repeated an earlier French statement expressing sympathy for Biafra. Four African countries – Tanzania, Zambia, Ivory Coast and Gabon – extended diplomatic recognition to Biafra. Port Harcourt was seized in May 1968, but the Biafran HQ shifted to Owerri. This town was also lost in late 1968, but regained in 1969. By now Biafran territory had shrunk to about 1,000 square miles. Federal forces captured Owerri on 11 January; Ojukwu fled, and the Nigerian government accepted formal Biafran surrender on the 15th.

Nightingale, Florence, 'The Lady with the Lamp', 1820–1910 British reformer. Became superintendent of a women's hospital in London, 1853; was asked to go to Scutari early in the *Crimean War*, 1854; organized the barracks hospital, introduced sanitation, and lessened the terrible toll of typhus, cholera and dysentery. She estimated that during the winter of 1854–5, during the siege of Sebastopol, she herself witnessed 2,000 deathbeds at the hospital. Whilst in the Crimea she opened schools and attempted to improve general living quarters. She continued this work after her return to London in 1856. Her 'Notes of Matters Affecting the Health, Efficiency and Hospital Administration of the British Army', completed in 1857, revealed a horrific picture of barracks life, and one sentence in this report became a battle-cry of the reformers: 'Our soldiers enlist to death in the barracks.' The London Borough of Kensington had a civil mortality rate of 3·3 per 1,000; in the Knightsbridge barracks, situated in the borough, the rate was 17·5; yet the soldiers were all young men, selected for their health and strength. She spent the rest of her life fighting for this cause.

Nile, Battle of, August 1798 *French Revolutionary Wars* (Map 1). Reports of *Napoleon*'s plan to invade *Egypt* in late spring 1798 led to the dispatch of a small British Fleet to the eastern Mediterranean under *Nelson*, subordinate to *Jervis*. Lack of frigates prevented the British from gathering sufficient intelligence of Napoleon's route, and the French were able to land, 1 July. Nelson located the French warships on 1 August, situated in Aboukir Bay 15 miles east of Alexandria. The French, under Admiral François Brueys, were confident in the protection of shore batteries and the narrow sandbanks. The French Fleet totalled 16 ships, forming a 2-mile line. Nelson attacked immediately with his 13 ships, dividing his force so that one section sailed between the French line and the shore and the remainder closed from the outer side. The French were caught between two fires. The British displayed superb seamanship amongst the sandbanks; only 2 French vessels escaped.

Nimitz, Chester William, 1885–1966 US Admiral of the Fleet. Commander, 1st US Battleship Division, 1938–9; Chief of Bureau of Navigation, US Navy Department, 1939–41; C-in-C US Pacific Fleet, December 1941 to November 1945, responsible, with *MacArthur*, for prosecuting war against *Japan* in the Pacific area. Nimitz commanded the largest US naval force ever assembled, with his base at Pearl Harbor. Controversy arose between Nimitz and MacArthur over the correct strategy to be followed and whether this should receive Navy or Army emphasis, with Nimitz largely supporting the views of *King*, US Chief of Naval Operations in Washington. In effect, both Army and Navy plans were adopted, with some duplication. Nimitz succeeded King in 1945, remaining Chief of Naval Operations on the US *Joint Chiefs of Staff* until November 1947.

Nivelle offensive, April 1917 *First World War* (Map 10). *Nivelle*, French Commander, believed that the *Verdun* performance could be repeated for a major advance, using surprise and speed. He considered it essential that the British should launch a diversionary attack in the Arras area; *Lloyd George*, British Prime Minister, discussed the plan at an allied conference in January 1917 and agreed to the scheme but, through his dislike of *Haig*, secretly arranged to have the BEF placed under French command. Fierce opposition from *Robertson*, the CIGS, and from Haig, led to a compromise agreement: the BEF would only operate under French orders for the coming offensive and Haig could appeal to London if he thought his army endangered. The British diversion opened on 9 April at *Arras*. The Nivelle offensive began on a 40-mile front east of Soissons on 16 April. The main attack struck towards three steep ridges, slashed by wood-covered ravines. German fortifications were strong, and German aircraft had gained air supremacy. French tanks were destroyed by well-directed artillery fire as they preceded the advance, and the offensive – by the French 6th and 5th Armies – fell into confusion. Infantry managed to take the first German line, but was then blocked. Between 16–20 April the French suffered 120,000 casualties, although the Germans lost equally heavily. Failure brought widespread French demoralization and mutiny, crippling the French war effort for almost 2 months. The British covered this collapse by fixing German attention at *Messines*. A total of 23,385 French soldiers were found guilty of mutiny, but only 55 were shot. Nivelle was replaced by *Pétain*, 15 May.

Nivelle, Robert Georges, 1856–1925

French General. Fought under *Pétain* at *Verdun*, 1916 (Map 10), succeeding him as Commander of the 2nd Army in April, and becoming a national hero through his performance in this battle. Appointed C-in-C of French Armies of the North and North-East following retirement of *Joffre*, 31 December 1916, and immediately planned aggressive Anglo-French offensive. The failure of this *Nivelle offensive*, April 1917, led to his replacement by Pétain, 15 May; he was later exonerated from blame by a Committee of Inquiry.

Nixon, Richard Milhous, 1913–

37th US President. Republican Vice-President under *Eisenhower*, often presiding over *National Security Council* meetings; narrowly defeated by *Kennedy* in 1960 presidential election; succeeded *Johnson* as President, November 1968; resigned 1974 following the 'Watergate' scandal in US domestic politics, and succeeded by Gerald Ford. *Kissinger*, previously his adviser, became Nixon's Secretary of State in September 1973. Nixon started office with the clear determination to end US military involvement in *Vietnam*; the last US troops left the country on 28 March 1973. The Paris Agreement of 27 January 1973, combined with this US withdrawal, allowed the US dissociation from future events in South Vietnam.

Other foreign policy aspects of Nixon's presidency included the restoration of relations with China, including the visit by the President to Peking in February 1972, and closer relations with the Soviet Union aimed at achieving 'détente'; allied to this latter policy was the start of *Strategic Arms Limitation Talks* (*SALT*), leading to two agreements signed by Nixon in Moscow, 26 May 1972.

Nobel, Alfred Bernhard, 1833–96

Swedish-born inventor. In 1850 Nobel, whose father manufactured mines and firearms in Russia, visited the USA and studied under *Ericsson*; he returned to Russia and experimented with nitroglycerine, which he manufactured after 1862. Continued accidental explosions caused him to turn to more stable mixtures: in 1863 he produced dynamite experimentally, and gelatin dynamite followed in 1876. In 1887 and 1888 Nobel patented nitrocellulose, or guncotton, a form of *smokeless* powder from which cordite was later developed. Nobel's researches gave increased understanding of the technique of handling and detonating more powerful explosives – High Explosives (HE) – such as trinitrotoluene (TNT).

Nordenfelt, Thorsten, 1842–1920

Swedish financier and arms producer. The best-known Nordenfelt *machine-gun* was also the earliest, designed in 1872 by Heldge Palmcrantz. This had up to 12 barrels; versions were produced in various sizes from rifle calibre to 1 inch. In the 1890s

Nordenfelt entered a partnership with Hiram *Maxim*, but the joint company had limited success.

Normandy, landings and campaign, June–September 1944 *Second World War* (Map 13). The US *Joint Chiefs of Staff* and President *Roosevelt* had sought such an invasion attempt from an early date, backed by *Stalin*'s desire for a Second Front in Europe. Britain's *Chiefs of Staff* had argued strongly against a premature cross-Channel operation. *Brooke*, CIGS and Chairman of the COS, urged that North Africa must first be cleared, then insisted that *Italy* should be invaded and an advance made northwards. While fully aware of the ultimate need for a cross-Channel invasion, he believed that the Italian campaign would draw German strength from northern Europe, creating conditions necessary for a successful operation in Normandy. The latter was initially code-named Round-up and then Overlord. Vigorous Anglo-US controversy continued throughout 1943, with *Churchill* supporting Brooke, and with the date for the cross-Channel attempt being put back from 1943 to 1944, and finally from May to June 1944. Supreme Commander was *Eisenhower*, with *Montgomery* in command of ground forces, *Leigh-Mallory* commanding tactical air forces and *Ramsay* the naval operations. Over 175,000 allied troops would be engaged in the initial assault, organized into the US 1st Army under *Bradley* and the British 2nd, including a Canadian Corps, under General Sir Miles Dempsey. These troops would be landed on 5 main beaches between the Contentin Peninsula and Le Havre. The US troops would land at beaches code-named Utah and Omaha, while farther to the east the British and Canadians would land at Gold, Juno and Sword. Two *airborne* divisions would be dropped farther inland. *Hitler*'s 'Atlantic Wall' defensive system comprised minefields, strongpoints and road networks. *Rundstedt*, the German Western High Commander, believed primary reliance should be placed on German armoured units placed farther to the rear of these static defences, ready to move forward. *Rommel*, Commander of Army Group B in the invasion area, considered that this would allow the German armour to suffer from massed air attack, and he urged deployment close to the coast. The argument still continued at the beginning of June. Eisenhower, at his Supreme Headquarters Allied Expeditionary Forces (SHAEF), took advantage of a momentary lull in bad weather to launch the invasion on 6 June. The invasion force comprised the largest armada in history: over 4,000 vessels supported by 600 warships. The first troops swept ashore at 6.30 a.m. By the evening of 6 June the British had made lodgments in all their three sectors and had pushed inland up to 6 miles. The US landing at Utah had been successful, but the Omaha attempt had almost encountered disaster: by nightfall this beachhead had still to be extended to 1,000 yards.

Yet the Germans, expecting the invasion in the Pas de Calais area and lulled by the bad weather, had been taken by surprise; the allies joined their beachheads. Attacks on Caen, 13 and 18 June, were repulsed, but Cherbourg fell on 27 June. Montgomery aimed at drawing German armour to the British sector on the allied left, enabling the US troops to break out on the allied right. On 1 August the allied forces were reorganized into the US 12th Army Group, under Bradley, comprising the US 3rd Army under *Patton* and the 1st under General Courtney Hodges; Montgomery commanded the 21st Army Group, comprising the British 2nd Army under Dempsey and the Canadian 1st under General Henry Crerar. Patton struck the main break-out blow on 1 August, stabbing south through Brittany then wheeling east towards Le Mans. To his left the US 1st Army pivoted to threaten the Germans in the Falaise area; this pocket was eliminated by 19 August. Kluge, who had relieved Rundstedt in July, retreated to the Seine; Paris was liberated on 25 August; Kluge was replaced by Model and committed suicide. By 14 September, after faltering through lack of fuel, the allies had reconquered most of France and were pressing against the German border. Allied casualties since 6 June totalled about 230,000 killed, wounded and missing; the German total was about 500,000. Despiet these losses, the Germans prepared to counter-attack in the *Ardennes*.

Norway and Denmark, campaigns in, 1940 *Second World War*. Both Britain and Germany sought to obtain control over Swedish iron ore supplies. These left Sweden either through the Baltic or via Narvik in north Norway: vessels took the ore to German ports by sailing close to the coast, in neutral Norwegian waters. In late November 1939 possible plans to stop the traffic were discussed by the British *War Cabinet*: these plans included violating Norwegian neutrality by landing a force, or by stationing a warship, at Narvik. *Churchill*, First Lord of the Admiralty, suggested mining Norwegian waters to drive the vessels out to the open sea where they could be attacked by the Royal Navy; this method had been employed in the First World War. On 16 February the British destroyer 'Cossack' blocked the German vessel 'Altmark' in a Norwegian fiord, and the Royal Naval Commander boarded the enemy ship to release nearly 300 British prisoners of war. This incident, underlining Norway's tolerant attitude towards Britain's enemy, at last provoked the War Cabinet to take action: Churchill received permission for a minefield in Norwegian waters, and plans were discussed for intervention in Norway combined with a scheme for sending 'volunteers' to aid Finland in the *Finnish–Russian War*. But German plans were nearer completion. On 8 April a series of clashes took place between RN warships escorting mine-layers off the Norwegian coast and German naval forces carrying invasion troops. The German convoys reached their destinations during the next 36 hours, landing troops at the Norwegian ports of Kristiansand, Stavanger, Bergen, Trondheim and Narvik under the command of General Nikolaus von Falkenhurst. German divisions swept into Denmark. Oslo, the Norwegian capital, fell on 10 April. French and British troops were landed at Namsos, Andalsnes and Narvik 14–19 April, but those at Namsos and Andalsnes had to be evacuated on 1–2 May. The landing at Narvik proved more successful, but the allied troops were withdrawn on 8–9 June after the launching of the German onslaught in the Battle for *France*.

O

Office of Strategic Services (OSS)
Second World War. The organization
was built on existing US intelligence
departments in late 1941 and given its
title in June 1942; OSS was responsible
for gathering and evaluating strategic
information, and for planning and
undertaking special services including
espionage, sabotage, guerrilla missions,
propaganda, psychological warfare and
counter-intelligence. Under the en-
ergetic leadership of Major-General
William (Wild Bill) Donovan, the
OSS area of operations covered the
world except for Latin America – the
domain of the Federal Bureau of
Investigation (FBI) – and the Pacific
area where *MacArthur* ran his own
organization. The OSS Detachment
101 operated behind enemy lines in
Burma, and was credited with killing
over 5,500 Japanese and wounding
10,000 more at a cost of 15 OSS lives;
this division also rescued 215 shot-
down pilots. The OSS was also
credited with the rescue of over
5,000 allied airmen shot down in
occupied Europe. A total of 831 OSS
men were decorated for bravery.

**Okinawa, Battle of, March–June
1945** *Second World War* against
Japan (Map 16). The campaign
marked the largest amphibious operation yet launched in the Pacific, involving 180,000 US troops and
marines. These were organized into
the 10th Army, under General Simon
Buckner, comprising the 24th Corps
and the 3rd Marine Amphibious
Corps. Naval operations were undertaken by the US 5th Fleet, commanded by Admiral Spruance; the
naval force was divided between the
amphibious operations and the covering fast carrier group. Joining the
latter was a British carrier force under
Admiral H. B. Rawlings. Japanese
defences on Okinawa consisted of
130,000 men in General Mitsuru
Ushijima's 32nd Army. Preliminary
air operations began on 14 March; the
attacking carriers suffered extensive
kamikaze suicide strikes. Bombardment of Okinawa intensified on
23 March; the first landings took place
on 1 April. These, involving 1,300
vessels, were directed at the south-
west coast. The US Marines turned
north while the 24th Corps struck
south. The Marines made good
progress, reaching halfway up the
island by 4 April, but the 24th Corps
met increasing resistance, especially at
the Machinato defensive line. On
6 April the Japanese Navy launched
a suicidal attempt to destroy the
amphibious force lying off Okinawa.

About 340 kamikaze pilots attacked on 7 April, and two US destroyers and 28 other vessels were sunk, but the carrier Yamato was sunk later in the day. Nearly 400 Japanese aircraft were shot down and nearly 4,000 Japanese sailors killed. More kamikaze attacks were launched on 12–13 April, totalling over 3,000 in all, but the US amphibious force remained in being. By 19 April the marines had cleared the northern two-thirds of Okinawa, but the Japanese had still to be dislodged from their defences in the south, although the Machinato Line was penetrated on 24 April. A fanatical Japanese counter-attack was repulsed on 3–4 May, and Buckner launched an enveloping offensive on the 11th. This continued throughout the remainder of May. Not until 22 June was Japanese resistance finally crushed. The Japanese commander committed harakiri; Japanese dead probably totalled over 130,000; US losses were 13,000 dead and 37,000 wounded.

Omdurman, campaign and Battle of, 1898 Reconquest of the *Sudan* began in 1896 when British and Egyptian troops under *Kitchener* moved up the Nile in a methodical advance: they took Dongola on 21 September and Abu Hamed on 7 August 1897. Kitchener's troops defeated Mahdist dervishes at the Battle of Atbara River, 9 April 1898; the dervish commander, Kalifa Abdullah, began concentrating all remaining strength in strong defensive positions at Omdurman situated just north of Khartoum. The Battle of Omdurman took place on 2 September. The Anglo-Egyptian Army was outnumbered – 26,000 men against 40,000 – but enjoyed the advantage of modern weapons. Machine-guns inflicted heavy casualties on tribesmen attacking the British camp at Egeiga, 4 miles from Omdurman, in the opening phase of the battle. The Kalifa had concealed his 20,000 best troops behind a nearby ridge, planning to ambush the enemy if the initial frontal assault proved successful; with the failure of this direct attack battle activity dwindled. During this lull the 21st Lancers charged a group of enemy concealed in a dry gulch. This charge, in which the young *Churchill* participated, had minimal effect on the battle and caused the loss of 25 per cent of the cavalrymen. Kitchener advanced towards Omdurman. The Kalifa planned to launch two co-ordinated attacks, one commanded by his brother Yakub striking from the west, the other by his son Osman Sheikh-Ed-Din from the hills in the north. The dervishes struck the brigade commanded by Sir Henry Hector MacDonald, but the assaults failed to coincide and MacDonald's troops stood firm. Their discipline and machine-gun fire power enabled the defenders to repulse the enemy, and the dervish forces retreated. Battle casualties showed a wide disproportion, underlining the destructive power of modern weapons: Kitchener's losses totalled less than 500, while the estimated dervish total was 20,000 killed and wounded, plus 5,000 prisoners.

P

Paget, Sir Henry William, Earl of Uxbridge, 1st Marquis of Anglesey, 1768–1854 British General. Fought in Flanders, 1794, Holland, 1799, and under *Moore* in the retreat to *Corunna*, December 1808 to January 1809, commanding the rearguard cavalry with distinction. Paget commanded the British cavalry in the *Waterloo* campaign, June 1815. He arrived too late at Quatre Bras, 16 June, but charged with the Household Cavalry at Waterloo itself, 18 June, and disrupted the French infantry. He was wounded in the battle, losing a leg. His son, Lord George Augustus Frederick Paget, 1818–80, served in the *Crimean War*, commanding the third line in the Light Brigade charge at *Balaklava*, 25 October 1854.

Paixhans, Henri Joseph, 1783–1854 French General and ordnance developer. Paixhans perfected a new shell-gun for naval use during the 1820s and 1830s, adopted by the French in 1837. The Paixhans shell, for use with this weapon, was designed to penetrate the target before exploding, rather than exploding on impact. This projectile improved all previous versions, including *shrapnel*;

before, the sensitivity of shells meant that they could only be tossed by small propelling charges at high angles, to prevent them exploding within the bore. By contrast the Paixhans shell could be fired with a relatively low trajectory, giving greater range and accuracy.

Palestine, guerrilla war in, 1945–8 Jewish grievances, matched by corresponding Arab opinions, had led to serious fighting between 1936 and 1939; included in the Jewish forces were Special Night Squads created and commanded by *Wingate*. Disturbances underwent a temporary lull at the outbreak of the Second World War, but Jewish terrorism recommenced in 1943, with the principal instigators being the so-called Stern Gang and the Irgun Zvei Leumi (IZL), a splinter-group from the more defensive Haganah nationalist organization. Violence against the British intensified after 1946, following the realization that the British Labour government intended to continue strong immigration control, in order to avoid dispute with the Arabs. Terrorism culminated in the blowing-up of the King David Hotel, Jerusalem, causing the death of 91 people. On 29 November 1947 the UN General Assembly agreed to partition Palestine into separate Jewish and Arab states as from 1 October 1948. In January 1948 Britain announced that her mandate over Palestine would be abandoned in May. Both Arabs and Jews prepared for conflict; from the Haganah emerged the Palmach shock force, based on Wingate's Night Squads, and under the able leadership of David Ben-Gurion the Israeli Defence Force was created. The *Israel-Arab War* of 1948-9 began within a few hours of the proclamation of the State of Israel, 14 May.

Paris, siege of, September 1870 to January 1871 *Franco-Prussian War* (Map 6). The Prussian victory at *Sedan*, 1 September, seemed to herald the end of the war, and a popular uprising toppled the Empire on the 4th. But a provisional government was created, with Léon Gambetta the popular leader and General Louis Jules Trochu as President. Gambetta escaped from Paris by balloon to organize nationwide resistance, including the use of *francs-tireurs*. In Paris, Trochu organized defences consisting of 120,000 soldiers, 80,000 'gardes mobiles' – untrained recruits under 30 years of age – and 300,000 'gardes nationales' from among the older population. The siege of Paris began on 19 September. The French refused to submit, despite food shortages and internal dissensions. Major sorties were attempted on 29-30 November and 21 December.

Moltke was persuaded by *Bismarck* to bombard the city, and this began on 5 January 1871: up to 400 shells fell daily in the city, but caused remarkably little damage. The situation inside the capital nevertheless deteriorated. This, combined with French defeats elsewhere, convinced Trochu that further resistance was useless. A final sortie was attempted on 19 January; an armistice was obtained on the 26th, and the Prussians marched in on 1 March.

Partisan warfare Irregular form of fighting which is included in *guerrilla warfare* in general. Unlike modern revolutionary or insurgency guerrilla campaigns, partisan actions are not normally the decisive operation in the war in which they are conducted. Partisans fight in conjunction with regular, conventional forces, and victory or defeat results more from the latter. This applied to the partisan resistance fighters in France during the Second World War, and those under *Grivas* in *Greece*. A further distinction exists between partisan and revolutionary guerrilla warfare: the former has the patriotic aim of re-establishing a particular state of affairs which existed in the comparatively recent past, as in France, while revolutionary warfare is concerned with bringing about an entirely new situation, as in *China*. Again, any political or doctrinal motivation in a partisan war emerges after fighting has started; with revolutionary warfare this concept is well developed before military hostilities commence. The lack of publicized pre-planned revolutionary aims thus distinguished the partisan fighters in Yugoslavia during the Second World War, operating under Tito, from the communist guerrillas in *Indochina*, even though Tito later used the partisan movement as a vehicle for his own political revolution. Partisans have long operated on the fringe of regular armies, attacking communications, supply bases and isolated detachments, and obtaining intelligence information which will help the main army. The Spanish guerrillas in the *Peninsular War* were partisans, rather than revolutionary guerrilla fighters, as were civilians operating in *Russia*, 1812. The *francs-tireurs* in the *Franco-Prussian War* provide a further famous example. Advantages offered to partisans include mobility, ease of dispersal, local knowledge, support from the local population and the vulnerability of modern armies to the severance of supply links.

Patton, George Smith, 1885–1945
US General. Aide-de-Camp to *Pershing* during US raid into Mexico, 1917, and in France, May–November 1917; first officer detailed to US tank corps, November 1917; commanded Western Task Force in '*Torch*' landings, North Africa, November 1942; appointed Commander of US 2nd Corps in *Tunisia*, March 1943, in succession to General Lloyd Fredenhall, linking with *Montgomery*'s 8th army for the final advance on Tunis but replaced by *Bradley* in late April in order to take command of US

forces preparing to invade *Sicily*; led US 7th Army in Sicily, 9 July to 17 August 1943. Patton commanded the US 3rd Army in the *Normandy* invasion, June 1944, spearheading the bridgehead break-out at the beginning of August and linking with the *Anvil* ('Dragoon') force advancing from southern France; he took Metz, 13 December, but then halted his advance and undertook a brilliant right-angled shift of direction to strike into the south flank of the Germans' *Ardennes* counter-offensive, 18 December. He reached Bastogne, 26 December. Patton crossed the Rhine at Oppenheim, 22 March 1945: he had long planned the move in order to be first across; he advanced south of Berlin and reached the Danube by the end of the war in April. Patton suffered fatal injuries in a car crash, December 1945.

Peacekeeping Role adopted by the British Army in the *Indonesian–Malaysian* confrontation, although balanced on the side of the Malaysian security forces, in *Cyprus*, and in Northern *Ireland*. It was hoped that a semi-permanent international force would be created by the *UN* for peacekeeping purposes but the Soviet Union wanted to preserve the principle of exact equality in contributions, while the USA, Britain, France and Nationalist China insisted each country should be able to contribute according to their ability. Differing opinions also existed on the size of the proposed force as a whole. Instead, UN peacekeeping forces have been raised on an 'ad hoc' basis on 5 major occasions. (1) Egypt, 1956–67. The UN Emergency Force, UNEF, amounting to 6,000 men selected from 10 nations, supervised the cessation of the *Suez–Sinai* hostilities of 1956, and was then intended to protect Egypt's borders and separate Israeli and Egyptian forces. But UN forces were not stationed on Israeli soil, and were only allowed in Egypt with *Nasser*'s permission; this permission was withdrawn in June 1967, precipitating the *Israel–Arab War* of that year. (2) UN observers were sent to the Lebanon and Jordan in 1968 to facilitate the withdrawal of US and British troops. (3) UN forces, amounting to 18,000 men and mainly from African countries, were sent to the *Congo* in July 1960; this UN Operation in the Congo, or UNOC, sought to keep the dissidents apart and rescue hostages; the last UN troops left on 30 June 1964, after which the fighting flared up again. (4) West Iran. A security force was established to supervise the transfer of western New Guinea from the Netherlands to Indonesia, September 1963. (5) *Cyprus*. On 4 March 1964 a UN force was sent to the island in an attempt to keep the Greek and Turkish Cypriot communities apart. This force, UNFICYP, remained on the island, with some success, but was unable to prevent the large-scale Turkish invasion in 1974. UN participation in *Korea*, the largest UN military involvement in its history, stands in a separate capacity; although officially intended to protect South Korea from

the North Korean invasion, the UN Army immediately became belligerent and extended the peacekeeping brief by invading North Korea over the 38th parallel. UN peacekeeping restrictions are imposed through the difficulties of defining precise functions; the UN presence is dependent on the agreement of the conflicting parties; difficulties are inherent through the problem of identifying who is responsible for peace having been broken; enforcement of peacekeeping measures is almost impossible. Controversy has arisen over whether member states that have not approved, or participated in, a particular peacekeeping operation are under obligation to help with finance. Such a proposition has been rejected by the Soviet Union and France; the UN force in Cyprus consequently ran at a deficit.

Pearl Harbor, Japanese attack on, December 1941 *Second World War* against *Japan* (Map 16). US–Japanese talks took place in Washington during November 1941, aimed at averting hostilities. The Americans were aware of hostile Japanese intentions, through having broken diplomatic codes, but were ignorant of precise Japanese plans. The latter, drawn up by Admiral *Yamamoto*, Commander of the Japanese Combined Fleet, had been approved by the Chief of Naval Staff, Nagano, on 3 November. The initial offensive would be directed against the *Philippines* and Malaya, followed by the Netherlands East Indies. Pearl Harbor, in the Hawaiian Island of Oahu, base of the US Pacific

Fleet, would be attacked by a carrier strike force. This force would approach on a northern route between the Aleutians and Midway, which, although passing through rough seas making refuelling difficult, would be less liable to discovery. On 17–18 November the warships of the Strike Force sailed from Kure naval base, Japan; after regrouping, this fleet slipped from Tankan Bay in the Kurile Islands under cover of fog. The force, based on 6 aircraft carriers, was commanded by Admiral Chuichi Nagumo. British and US attention was diverted by the departure of a troop convoy from Shanghai, believed to be heading for Indochina but in fact aiming for the Malay peninsula. At Pearl Harbor precautions were still limited to sabotage checks. During 3 December the Japanese Strike Force battled through heavy seas to a point about 2,300 miles north-west of Hawaii; slower escort vessels then turned back. Late on 6 December the Strike Force increased speed to 26 knots; by 6 a.m. 7 December, Hawaii time, the carriers had reached 275 miles north of Pearl Harbor. A few minutes later the first wave of aircraft left for the attack: 40 torpedo bombers, 50 high-level bombers, 50 dive-bombers and 50 fighters. The Pacific Fleet at the US base made an excellent target, with warships berthed alongside each other. The first torpedo landed shortly before 8 a.m. The attack lasted about 2 hours: 5 US battleships were lost, 3 destroyers, 1 mine-layer and almost 200 aircraft. The number of men

killed was above 2,350. Japanese losses were 29 aircraft and 55 men. Yet the Japanese victory was incomplete. The 3 US carriers in the Pacific Fleet – 'Enterprise', 'Lexington' and 'Saratoga' – were absent from Pearl Harbor, and these had been the most important target. Of the Japanese Strike Force, only 1 vessel, a destroyer, would survive the war: 4 of the carriers were sunk at *Midway* in June 1942, the other 2 in 1944 and the 2 battleships at *Guadalcanal*.

Peninsular War, 1807–14 *Napoleonic Wars* (Map 1). In November 1807 a French army under Junot invaded neutral Portugal from Spain, *Napoleon*'s nominal ally, in an attempt to close Portuguese ports to British trade: these ports were the only remaining access points to British trade to the Continent. The conflict would be notable for the cruelty exhibited by both sides, and for the partisan warfare which erupted – so introducing the term *guerrilla* (little war). Portuguese and later Spanish citizens fought alongside the British regular forces, to harass French communications and attack French units, denying the enemy a secure base. Junot captured Lisbon on 1 December and Portugal seemed subdued. Napoleon attempted to extend greater control in Spain; a French army under *Murat* entered the country in March 1808 under the pretext of guarding the coast, but widespread insurrection forced Murat back behind the Ebro. Junot was isolated in Portugal. The British government sent an expeditionary force to Portugal, under the nominal command of Sir Hew Dalrymple; Second-in-Command was Sir Harry Burrard, and third was Sir John *Moore*. The latter was involved with an abortive expedition to Sweden, and leader of the actual troops in the field was Sir Arthur Wellesley (*Wellington*). Meanwhile, Spanish troops under General Castaños defeated French forces under Pierre Dupont at Baylen, 19 July 1808. British troops under Wellesley landed at Mondego Bay, north of Lisbon, on 1 August, and immediately pushed towards Lisbon, inflicting defeat on Junot at Vimeiro on the 21st. Junot capitulated on the 30th. Negotiations led to the Convention of Cintra, dated 1 September, which provided for French evacuation of Portugal. The Convention resulted in loud protests in London and Lisbon; Dalrymple was summoned home and Wellesley left soon afterwards. Command of the British forces was given to Moore, and he received orders to march into Spain – despite shortages of equipment, the lateness of the year, and crumbling resistance by Spanish forces. Invasion began on 11 October, and Moore reached Salamanca in mid-November, to hear that the main Spanish armies had been defeated and that the French were being rapidly reinforced. Napoleon joined his army on 5 November and took over operations in the centre and south, while *Soult* commanded in the north. Prompted by reports that an uprising had taken place in Madrid,

Moore decided to move north towards Soult, hoping to draw the main French strength away from the Spanish capital. The Madrid insurrection soon collapsed, but by 24 December Moore had reached Saldaña, close to Soult's army. Napoleon moved against the small British force, and on 25 December Moore began to retreat over the mountains to *Corunna*. His battered army rallied to fight the Battle of Corunna on 16 January 1809 – during which Moore was fatally wounded – then embarked for England. Napoleon had already returned to France, leaving Soult in command. The British returned in April with the army commanded by Wellesley. He immediately advanced north from Lisbon to attack Soult successfully at Oporto, 12 May. He invaded Spain in June, clashing with the French under *Victor* at Talavera on the 28th; the French pulled back to Madrid. But Wellesley soon found his Spanish allies to be unreliable. The British Commander, now Viscount Wellington, ordered lines to be constructed at *Torres Vedras* north of Lisbon: when the French advanced in July 1810, the British withdrew towards these positions, fighting a defensive battle at Bussaco, 27 September: French forces under *Masséna* suffered nearly 5,000 casualties to the British 1,300. The British reached Torres Vedras on 10 October. The French retired into Spain in November. Both sides struggled for supremacy at the key border fortresses of Ciudad Rodrigo, Badajoz and

Almeida, with operations leading to the Battle of Fuentes de Onoro, half-way between Ciudad Rodrigo and Almeida, on 5 May 1811: this was a drawn battle but with the French suffering heavier casualties. On 16 May operations around Badajoz, farther south, resulted in the Battle of Albuera, when French forces under Soult were defeated by British and Spanish troops under General William Carr Beresford. Inconclusive operations continued throughout the year, then, in January 1812, Wellington took the offensive: Ciudad Rodrigo was stormed on 19 January and Badajoz on 19 April in two savage battles. Wellington advanced into Spain and defeated the French under *Marmont* at Salamanca on 22 July. Madrid fell on 12 August. But the French counter-attacked, repulsing Wellington at Burgos in November and driving the British back to Ciudad Rodrigo. The French suffered increasing problems from the guerrilla warfare: communications from France over the Pyrenees were extremely precarious, and they found it almost impossible to live off the country. In spring 1813 Wellington therefore resumed the offensive, striking deep into Spain while the guerrillas continued their pressure and while a second British force, under Sir John Murray, operated farther east. On 21 June the two sides clashed in the decisive battle of the war, at *Vittorio*. Wellington's victory forced the French back over the Pyrenees, and further successes at Sorauren, 26 July to 1 August, cleared the French from

Spain. Wellington advanced into France early in 1814, defeating Soult at Orthez on 27 February and seizing Bordeaux on 17 March. On 10 April the British stormed the French at Toulouse and although Wellington's army suffered 5,000 casualties, 2,000 more than the French, Soult was driven from the city. Napoleon had already been defeated in the north, with Paris captured by the Prussians and Russians on 31 March.

Percussion system and cartridge

Percussion firearms are those discharged by striking a cap or primer against the cartridge. Before the advent of this system the priming gunpowder was ignited either by being touched with flame, as with the matchlock *musket*, or by striking a flint, as with the flintlock. The Rev. Alexander John Forsyth, 1768–1843, invented the percussion system, although not the percussion cap itself; the system was adopted by the British Army in 1839. Forsyth's invention only applied to muzzle-loaders; percussion developments with *breech-loaders* had to coincide with advancement in cartridges. *Dreyse* incorporated a new cartridge with his needle-gun of 1837, with the needle striking through the paper cartridge to ignite the percussion cap; the latter was, however, placed at the front of the cartridge, rather than at the rear as with modern forms. The cartridge came nearer to the modern version with the device produced by M. Houiller in 1847: this had a percussion cap at the rear although situated at the side. In 1849, M. Flobert patented a cartridge which he used in a rifle named after him: the percussion cap was still at the side of the base but now extended round the flanged rim of the cartridge, with the rim preventing the bullet from slipping down the barrel. G. W. Morse patented designs 1856–8 which covered many of the modern features, but the most significant development was made by Clement Pottet, who patented a cartridge in 1855: this had a base shaped like a metal cup with a rolled edge: the cup had a centre recess to receive a percussion cap. The next major step was the introduction of all-metal walls for the cartridge, as opposed to merely a metallic base as with the Pottet. Colonel Edward Boxer, 1823–98, Superintendent of the Royal Laboratory at Woolwich, invented a coil brass, centre-fire cartridge in 1866, designed for the *Snider* rifle. The modern cartridge finally arrived with the all-brass centre-fire version produced by the armaments manufacturer Kynoch British in the 1880s. The walls of the cartridge were made of metal thin enough to expand upon detonation, thus sealing gas.

Perry, Oliver Hazard, 1785–1819 US naval officer. Hero of the Battle of Lake Erie, 10 September 1813, *American War of 1812* (Map 2). Captain Perry commanded US naval forces on Lake Erie, comprising 2 brigs, 6 schooners and 1 sloop; the British flotilla, under Captain Robert Barclay, consisted of 3 larger vessels,

2 brigs, 1 schooner and 1 sloop. At about noon the British squadron approached the US anchorage in Put-in Bay. Perry sailed his small fleet to meet the enemy, but his brig 'Lawrence' clashed with the British before the rest could close. Perry left his severely damaged vessel and was taken by rowboat to the brig 'Niagara'; he then broke the British line. The 'Niagara' put 3 enemy vessels out of action and by 3 p.m. the British were forced to surrender. Perry died from yellow fever on a voyage on the Orinoco River.

Pershing, John Joseph, 1860–1948 US General. Served in Cuba, 1898, *Philippines*, 1899–1903; Military Attaché, Tokyo, 1905–6, observing operations in *Russo-Japanese War*; Philippines, 1913; commanded force of 10,000 men sent into Mexico in pursuit of Villa, 1916, during the revolution in *Mexico*. In April 1917 Pershing was appointed to command the American Expeditionary Force for US participation in the *First World War*. A divisional organization of about 28,000 men each was used for the AEF, based on his recommendation; 42 divisions were eventually formed, with the first leaving for France in June. The first US operation took place at Cantigny, 28 May 1918, with considerable success, and further success was obtained in the *St Mihiel* offensive, 12–16 September. Pershing joined with the French for the attacks against the *Hindenburg Line*, making steady progress through the difficult

Argonne terrain – although *Foch*, impatient for a more rapid advance, tried to have him removed. Pershing was Chief of Army Staff from 1921 until his retirement in 1924.

Pétain, Henri Philippe, 1856–1951
French Marshal and Premier, hailed as the 'Saviour of France' for his achievements in the *First World War* and condemned for his alleged betrayal of the country in the *Second World War*. Joined the French Army in 1876, attending the military school at St Cyr, and prior to 1914 he spent many years as an infantry officer alternating with periods as an instructor. For the start Pétain was convinced that the increased fire power of modern weapons strongly favoured the defensive, as demonstrated in the siege of Plevna during the *Russo-Turkish War*, 1877–8, and the *Russo-Japanese War*, 1904–5; others in the French Army, notably *Foch*, believed the opposite. Events after 1914 showed Pétain's conviction to be tragically correct. At the outbreak of the First World War Pétain was in fact due for retirement; instead he distinguished himself as Corps Commander in the Artois offensive, 1915 (Map 10); he was sent by *Joffre* to command French troops at *Verdun*, 26 February 1916, and earned fame for his conduct at this defensive battle – his watchword, also attributed to *Nivelle*, was 'They shall not pass'; promoted to Army Group Command in April and succeeded by Nivelle, but on 15 May 1917 replaced Nivelle as Commander of French Armies in

North and North West after the failure of the *Nivelle offensive*. Pétain assumed command at a time when the French Army was completely demoralized and riddled with mutiny; he immediately adopted a policy of firmness and fairness, ably supported by Minister of War Paul Painlevé, 1863–1933. Respected and admired throughout the Army as a man whose defensive views had been proved sound, Pétain was also known for his concern for the lives of his troops – unlike Nivelle. To deal with the mutinies, he demanded that ringleaders should be subjected to summary courts martial and if necessary executed without delay: the government went some way to meet this demand by removing the right of prisoners' appeal. From May to November 1917 there were 412 death sentences in the armies under Pétain's command – a remarkably low number which indicated that he restricted action to the worst offenders. Of this total only 55 were actually shot, including some found guilty of other offences. Pétain's other steps taken to deal with the mutiny included the formation of disciplinary companies for those found guilty of mutiny – these units were given the most dangerous missions – and his policy of establishing better contact between the headquarters and men in the field; conditions of service were eased. Above all, Pétain put into operation his long-held view that the Army must fight a defensive war rather than wasting men in useless, large-scale attacks. He wrote in May 1917 that the enemy must be worn down before a major offensive could be launched; meanwhile great attacks in depth should be avoided. 'The method of wearing down the enemy while suffering a minimum of losses oneself consists of increasing the number of limited attacks, conducted with a great reliance upon artillery; of striking continually against the arch of the German structure until it collapses.' The French Army therefore adopted a limited strategy, for example with small-scale attacks north of Verdun on 20 August and with a larger effort at Malmaison in October. Pétain averted the complete collapse of the French Army, did much to restore morale, and placed his forces in a position to withstand the German offensives in 1918. He successfully defended Paris against the *Somme* onslaught, March 1918, although he was vigorously criticized by the British Commander, *Haig*, for not supporting the BEF sector. He continued to be Army Commander under Foch when the latter was appointed Supreme Commander, 3 April. Pétain, made Marshal of France in 1918, was Vice-President of the Higher French Council of War, 1920–30, during which period he commanded French troops in Morocco, 1925–6. He was appointed War Minister, 1934, arguing in March that it was unnecessary to extend the *Maginot Line*. He became Prime Minister on the resignation of Paul Reynaud, 17 June 1940, at the height of the Battle of *France*; he sued for an armistice and French hostilities ceased on the 25th –

Pétain believed he had taken the only possible action since the French position was hopeless. He continued as French leader during the German occupation, breaking off diplomatic relations with Britain after RN action against French warships, July 1940, and with the USA after the '*Torch*' landings in French North Africa, November 1942, which he urged the French to resist. He fled to Switzerland after the *Normandy* landings; he returned in April 1945 and in August was sentenced to death for aiding the German enemy; this sentence was commuted by *De Gaulle* to life imprisonment.

Petersburg, Battle and siege of, June 1864 to April 1865 *American Civil War* (Map 3). *Grant*'s crossing of the James River, 13–18 June 1864, ending the *Wilderness* campaign, was accompanied by a Union movement against Petersburg 20 miles to the west, led by Grant's subordinate Benjamin Butler. This operation failed, even though Petersburg was weakly defended. Confederate reinforcements blocked a full-scale attack by Grant on 18 June. *Lee* arrived with other troops and the siege began. Lee took full advantage of the defensive qualities of modern weaponry. The Union forces attempted to mine a way through the fortifications, exploding 4 tons of gunpowder on 30 July, but the advantage of surprise was thrown away by gross mismanagement: Union troops under *Burnside* bunched in the crater and suffered nearly 4,000 casualties from Confederate fire.

Grant attempted to divert Confederate forces in mid-August by striking at the Richmond defences 25 miles to the north. Lee's troop movement to meet this threat resulted in the indecisive Battle of Deep Bottom, 14–20 August. Grant switched south again, cutting the Weldon railroad to Petersburg at the Battle of Globe Tavern, 18–21 August, although at great cost. Fierce fighting followed at Ream's station, 25 August, with both sides struggling to control another railroad to Petersburg; the Confederates were thrown back. Further clashes took place during the autumn, at Chaffin's Bluff, 29–30 September, Peeble's Farm, 30 September, and Boydton Farm, 27–28 October. Lee attempted to break the Union grip by a surprise attack on the Union right at Fort Stedman, 25 March 1865, but the Confederates were repulsed with a loss of about 4,000 men, and were thus further weakened. Grant was reinforced by *Sheridan* on 26 March and Union troops, totalling about 120,000 men, outnumbered the Confederates 2 to 1. The Union Army attacked on 29–31 March in the Battles of Dinwiddie Courthouse and White Oak Road; and although Lee managed to check the enemy advance, a further clash at Five Forks on 1 April exposed the Confederate right flank. Lee began withdrawing from the Petersburg–Richmond defences; the *Appomattox* campaign opened.

Philippines, fall of, December 1941 to May 1942 *Second World War*

against *Japan* (Map 16). *MacArthur*'s defensive strength comprised about 120,000 troops, of whom only about 22,000 were US regulars. The Japanese attacking force, under General Masaharu Homma, totalled about 50,000 experienced men. Landings were preceded by heavy bombing attacks: these included a surprise strike at Clark Field, 8 December, which destroyed 18 out of the 35 B-17 bombers and 56 fighters, so reducing air cover. The first Japanese landings were made on Luzon, 10 December, followed by assaults farther south 48 hours later. A stronger amphibious operation against north Luzon took place on 22 December, and additional landings were made in the south on the 24th, threatening to trap the defenders in the centre. MacArthur abandoned Manila on the 26th and withdrew across the island to Bataan peninsula; the Japanese stranglehold on this area tightened during January–February 1942, and on 11 March MacArthur reluctantly left for Australia, handing over command to General Jonathan Wainwright. Not until 3 April could a Japanese breakthrough be achieved, and even then the survivors clung to the small island of Corregidor. Filipino and US troops on this island endured artillery and air bombardments from 10 April to early May. Japanese landings were made on 5 May, and resistance ended next day, although small guerrilla groups continued to operate until the reconquest of the *Philippines* in 1944.

Philippines, Hukbalahap rebellion in, 1946–54 The creation of the Republic of the Philippines, 4 July 1946, was immediately followed by a communist-inspired insurgency, centred on Luzon, under the leadership of Luis Taruc. The 'Huks' had provided the majority of resistance fighters against the Japanese during the Second World War; they were well armed, had intimate knowledge of the wild terrain which offered them an excellent base, and they were incensed by the government's refusal to allow Taruc to occupy the congressional seat he had won in post-war elections. Rebellion intensified in 1948, with the 'Huks' dominating central Luzon. In 1950 Ramon Magsaysay was appointed Defence Minister in charge of anti-communist guerrilla warfare operations. While increasing military action against the 'Huks', he also launched a land reform programme which reduced support for the insurgents. He continued his reforms after being elected President in 1953 and by 1954 the rebellion had dwindled. Isolated guerrilla pockets remained, and occasional outbreaks of violence were still being reported in 1975.

Philippines, rebellions in, 1896–1905 Insurrection against the Spanish rulers broke out in August 1896 under the leadership of Emilio Aguinaldo, but the rebellion faded after Spain promised reforms. Aguinaldo was exiled. The rebellion restarted during the *American–Spanish War*, 1898, with US Commodore George Dewey returning Aguinaldo to Luzon to foment revolt. Under the Treaty of Paris, 10 December, the Philippines were sold to America. The insurgents turned against their new rulers, with Aguinaldo proclaiming Filipino Independence on 20 January 1899. Fighting with US troops began in February 1899 and continued in Luzon until the capture of Aguinaldo in 1902. A humane policy was adopted by the US Commanding General, Arthur MacArthur – father of *MacArthur* of Second World War fame. Sporadic hostilities continued in the southern islands until 1905.

Philippines, reconquest of, July–December 1944 *Second World War* against *Japan* (Map 16). US invasion of the Philippines was preceded by controversy between *MacArthur* and *King* over the correct plans to be adopted in the advance on Japan. The issue was discussed at a Pearl Harbor Conference in July, when it was decided that Mindanao in the southern Philippines should be taken, then Leyte, prior to the conquest of the main island of Luzon. Carrier operations began on 15 September; almost immediately Admiral William Halsey, Commander of the US 3rd Fleet, reported that opposition seemed far less than anticipated, and he suggested an earlier move to the next stage, Leyte. The US *Joint Chiefs of Staff* issued a directive to this effect on 15 September, thus advancing the timetable 2 months. Magnificent staff work overcame the immense problems involved with this change, and the landings at Leyte began on 20 October. MacArthur, commanding the ground forces and the US 7th Fleet, stepped ashore on the 22nd. His return coincided with the naval battle for Leyte Gulf, 22–25 October. This involved 282 warships: 216 US, 64 Japanese and 2 Australian. Preliminary moves included the departure from Japan of the Northern Force under Admiral Jisaburo Ozawa, intended to tempt Halsey's 3rd Fleet from the Leyte area. The Japanese Centre Force, under Admiral Takeo Kurita, steamed north-east from Malaya and the South China Sea. The Southern Force, under Admiral Shoji Nishimura, backed by Admiral Kiyohide Shima's 2nd Attack Force, approached from the south-east. Contact was made with Kurita's fleet on 23 October, and fighting took place south-east of the Philippines for 48 hours; Kurita then headed westwards but returned under cover of darkness on 24 October, aiming to slip through the San Bernardino strait in the Philippine island chain to attack the Leyte landings from the north. The Southern Force, intended to attack the Leyte landings from the south, was thrown back and was thus unable to join Kurita in a pincer movement against the US beachhead. Kurita nevertheless emerged from the San Bernardino strait unopposed at dawn on the 25th, helped by Halsey's decision to move with his 3rd Fleet against Admiral Ozawa's Northern Force which, as intended, lured the Americans from the Leyte area. This only left Admiral Kinkaid's 7th Fleet, acting as escort force for the landings, to block Kurita's attack. Desperate US resistance checked Kurita's advance, and aircraft from Halsey's 3rd Fleet rushed back to give support. Kurita withdrew through the San Bernardino strait. Halsey inflicted heavy damage on Ozawa's decoy fleet – all 4 carriers in this force were sunk, plus other vessels. By evening on 25 October the Japanese Fleets were in full retreat, having lost 4 carriers, 3 battleships, 10 cruisers, 11 destroyers, about 500 aircraft and 10,500 sailors and pilots – included in the latter were the first kamikaze victims. US losses were 3 carriers, 2 destroyers and over 200 aircraft; about 2,800 Americans had died. The victory allowed the landings to continue; Leyte had fallen by the end of December. The island of Mindoro fell on 15 December, confining remaining Japanese resistance to Luzon. The battle for this island began on 2 January 1945, with the Americans having to force through formidable defences manned by Yamshita's 250,000 troops. On 9 January a subsidiary landing was made in Lingayen Gulf in the west, and these troops pushed towards the airfield at Clark Field in the centre; other landings were made in the Manila area between 30 January and 4 February; Manila fell on 4 March. Some of the bitterest fighting took place on the small island of Corregidor, attacked by paratroops and amphibious troops on 16 February: over 4,417 Japanese died fighting this operation alone. Fighting continued in north Luzon until the end of the war. US casualties in the Luzon campaign totalled nearly 8,000 dead and 33,000 wounded; Japanese dead numbered over 192,000; only 9,700 Japanese were captured in combat.

Picq, Ardant du, 1831-70 French officer and military theorist. Served in the *Crimean War*, being taken prisoner in the siege of Sebastopol, 1854; served in Syria and Algeria; killed early in the *Franco-Prussian War*. His 'Études sur le Combat' was not published until 1902; it was probably the most widely read book in the French trenches during the First World War and had considerable influence on French military thinking prior to this conflict, especially on those who supported the belief that the offensive was superior to the defensive. Unfortunately, like *Clausewitz*, du Picq was often tragically misunderstood. His experience in the Crimea convinced him that armies would be more efficient if they were kept small – 'the theory of the big battalions is a despicable theory', he wrote. Quality, not quantity, was most important. He claimed that weapons were only effective in so far as they influenced the enemy's will to resist – morale was all-supreme. He therefore advocated a return to the small, highly professional force. This fostered the spirit of a military nobility in France, epitomized by the victimization of the Jewish officer Alfred Dreyfus, falsely accused of treason in 1894. The French school of the 'offensive à l'outrance' gained inspiration from statements such as 'he will win who has the resolution to advance'. *Foch* matched this by his declaration that 'the infantry are on the move and must arrive'.

Pilsudski, Josef (Jozef), 1867-1935 Polish Marshal and President. Pilsudski, an ardent Polish nationalist, was exiled to Siberia by the Russian overlords, 1887-92; he was arrested again in 1900 but escaped to England; he returned to Poland in 1902 and recruited an underground Polish Army of 10,000 men which fought alongside the Austrians against the Russians, 1914-16. Pilsudski resigned his command in 1916 in protest against German interference in Polish affairs; on 16 November he gained German recognition of Poland's independence, but was imprisoned by the Germans, 1917-18, for refusing to fight. He became the first Marshal of Poland, 1920, fighting against the Bolsheviks. He continued to be active in Polish politics, leading a successful military coup against the government in 1926, after which he became War Minister and Prime Minister, plus Commander of the Army, until his death.

Plan XVII, French, 1914 (Map 10) Introduced by *Joffre* in April 1913, this scheme represented the French strategic plan for the opening offensive in the event of hostilities with Germany. Previously the French had relied upon Plan XVI, introduced in 1911, which provided for an offensive into Alsace-Lorraine to recover these provinces lost to Germany in the

Franco-Prussian War. French forces would therefore concentrate along the south-eastern frontier. This was exactly the French deployment anticipated by the German Chief of Staff, *Schlieffen*, when he prepared his own scheme. Schlieffen's plan was in turn guessed by General Augustin Édouard Michel, French Commander immediately before Joffre, who proposed a concentration on the Belgian border. But Michel's concept was rejected, condemned by War Minister Adolphe Messimy as 'insane', and Michel was soon replaced by Joffre. Thus the latter produced his Plan XVII, a compromise between the original Plan XVI and the Michel concept. The French main effort would be an immediate dual offensive into Alsace-Lorraine, north and south of the Thionville–Metz area, combined with a move by two French armies in the north if the Germans violated Belgian neutrality. Joffre believed that French professionals, though fewer in number, could block the enemy's northern advance.

Plumer, Sir Herbert Charles Onslow, 1st Viscount, 1857–1932 British Field-Marshal. Served in Boer War; commanded 2nd Army at *Messines*, 7 June 1917 (Map 10), and displayed an ability perhaps greater than any other British Commander on the Western Front; commanded 2nd Army at the Third Battle of *Ypres* (Passchendaele), July–October 1917. Plumer was then sent with reinforcements to the front in *Italy*, November 1917; he returned to the Western Front to resume command of the 2nd Army, April 1918, receiving the brunt of the German offensive at Lys during this month. Created Field-Marshal, 1919; Governor of Malta, 1919–25; High Commissioner for Palestine, 1925–8.

Poland, German campaign in, September–October 1939 *Second World War* (Map 13). The Luftwaffe began a bombardment of strategic points inside Poland before dawn on 1 September. Polish defending forces, about 800,000 men, were organized in 6 armies under Marshal Edward Smigly-Rydz. The invaders, commanded by General *Brauchitsch*, totalled over 1,250,000 troops. These were organized in 5 armies in 2 army groups. From the north the 3rd and 4th Armies in General Fedor von Bock's army group attacked from East Prussia and the Baltic Coast towards Warsaw; the 8th, 10th and 14th Armies in *Rundstedt*'s army group attacked in the south. Both thrusts had armoured spearheads, with the Luftwaffe – about 1,600 aircraft – operating in close support. The operation formed a classic *Blitzkrieg* campaign, and this new form of war totally overwhelmed the opposition. By 3 September the Polish Air Force had virtually ceased to exist and Polish armies were splintered into bewildered groups. By 8 September the most heavily armoured German force, General Walther von Reichenau's 10th Army in Rundstedt's army group, was beginning to batter at heavily bombed Warsaw, but was initially repulsed. Soviet troops invaded from the east on 17 September. Warsaw fell on the 27th, Modlin on the 28th; the last Polish resistance was overcome at Kock, south-east of Warsaw, on 5 October. Polish casualties totalled 66,000 dead, over 200,000 wounded and nearly 700,000 captured. German losses were 10,5000 dead, 30,300 wounded and about 3,500 missing. Germany prepared for the Battle for *France*, preceded by the campaign in *Norway*.

Polaris Underwater-launched ballistic missile, which gave the USA a significant lead in strategic missile technology in the 1960s. The *submarine* 'George Washington' became the first such vessel to launch an underwater missile when it fired a Polaris A-1 on 20 July 1960. The Polaris A-1 missile, with a range of 1,200 miles, was superseded by the A-2, 1,500 miles, in 1965. The A-3, range 2,800 miles, became operational with the US Navy in September 1964. In 1975 the US Navy had 21 nuclear-powered submarines, each armed with 16 A-2s or A-3s. The latter were also supplied to Britain: in 1975 the Royal Navy had 4 nuclear submarines, each with 16 such missiles. Successor to the Polaris is the *Poseidon*; Soviet equivalents are the *Sark and Serb missiles*.

Portal, Sir Charles Frederick Algernon, 1st Viscount, 1893–1971 British Air Chief Marshal. C-in-C RAF Bomber Command, March–October 1940; he then succeeded Sir Cyril Newall as Chief of the Air Staff on the *Chiefs of Staff* Committee and on the Anglo-US *Combined Chiefs of Staff*, remaining at this post until the end of the war. Portal was an ardent advocate of the *strategic bombing* policy.

Poseidon Underwater submarine-launched ballistic *missile* developed by the USA in the mid-1960s as a successor to the *Polaris*. The first flight model was successfully tested in August 1968. Poseidon, with an equivalent range to the latest Polaris A-3, about 2,800 miles, has a considerably increased nuclear payload through its multiple independently targetable re-entry vehicle (*MIRV*). In 1976 about 20 US nuclear submarines were deployed with Poseidon missiles, each submarine having 16 missile tubes.

Pound, Sir Dudley Arthur Pickman Rogers, 1877–1943 British Admiral. Commanded battleship 'Colossus' at *Jutland*, 1916; C-in-C Mediteranean, 1936–9; First Sea Lord and Chief of the Naval Staff, 1939–43. During his last appointment he chaired the British *Chiefs of Staff* Committee until *Brooke* took over this function in March 1942, and was a member of the Anglo-US *Combined Chiefs of Staff*. Pound was the only member of the COS Committee responsible both for operational control of his own service and for its actual direction in battle; yet during this period Pound was suffering from a brain tumour; he died on 21 October 1943. He was succeeded by *Cunningham* on the 15th.

R

'Race to the sea', The, September–November 1914 *First World War* (Map 10). Both sides extended operations northwards after the Battle of the *Marne*, 5–10 September, each trying to work round the other's flank. This led to a series of clashes, including Picardy, 22–26 September, and Artois, 27 September to 10 October. The Belgian Army fell back to the coast, surrendering Antwerp at the beginning of October. Farther south the Germans attempted to penetrate at Verdun, where they were repulsed on 25 September, and at St Mihiel, where they carved a salient. To the north the race to the sea continued with the Battle of the Yser, 18 October to 30 November, and the First Battle of *Ypres*, 30 October to 24 November. As the year came to a close the French tried to break through in the First Battle of Champagne, beginning 20 December and continuing into 1915: this made some ground, but the line was re-established by the Germans in March after the French had suffered some 400,000 casualties. Neither side had won the race; both began to dig in. Trenches and fortifications were created almost from the Swiss frontier 350 miles upwards to the coast. In the first 3 months of fighting the British had suffered 85,000 casualties, the French 854,000, the Germans 677,000. The next major attempt to break through would be the Second Battle of *Ypres*, April 1915.

Radar During the 1930s an approach was made to Dr Robert Watson Watt, head of the Radio Department of the National Physical Laboratory, Slough, England, by H. E. Wimpetis, Director of Research at the Air Ministry, to investigate the possibility of a 'death ray'. The Air Ministry sought a method of discharging electro-magnetic radiation sufficiently powerful to damage the engines of an approaching aircraft or 'affect the blood of its pilot'. Watson Watt, discounting such a possibility, instead worked on the principle of radio location. Research on similar lines had already been carried out; a patent had been taken out in 1924, for example, based on the direction-finding capabilities of the cathode-ray tube. But Watson Watt was the first to put theory into practice: on 26 February 1935 he successfully located a test bomber flying across a radio beam. By 1937 the first of the Chain Home (CH) stations, intended to give warning of aircraft approaching the coast at a distance of 40 miles, was in operation. Further stations were working by 1939, playing a vital role in the Battle of *Britain*. Developments during the war included adaptation of radar in naval vessels and in aircraft: the latter included the H2S device producing a crude radar map of the ground, sufficiently clear to show the shape of towns as an aid to *strategic bombing* navigation.

Raeder, Erich, 1876–1960 German Grand Admiral. Chief of Staff under Hipper in the First World War, engaged at *Dogger Bank*, *Jutland* and in British east coast bombardments; C-in-C of the German Navy, 1935–43. Raeder would have preferred to wait until 1944 before opening hostilities in the Second World War, to give time to build up naval strength. He argued for an early effort in the Mediterranean and North Africa, 1940, rather than the preparations for invasion of either Britain or Russia; he showed pessimism over the 'Sealion' plans. Raeder was replaced by *Doenitz*, January 1943, for not stopping British *Arctic convoys* to Russia. He was sentenced to life imprisonment at Nuremberg, 1946, but was released in 1955.

RAF (Royal Air Force) Formed on 1 April 1918 by the amalgamation of the Royal Flying Corps (*RFC*) and the Royal Naval Air Service; by 1918 the RAF had 22,000 aircraft. In 1934 the first steps were taken in rearmament prior to the Second World War; in 1936 the home air force was reconstructed as four commands, Bomber, Fighter, Coastal and Training, followed by the subsidiary Maintenance, Balloon and Reserve Commands. By September 1939 the RAF's strength amounted to 536 bombers (less than half the *Luftwaffe* total), 608 fighters (just over half the Luftwaffe strength) and 96 reconnaissance aircraft (compared to the German total of 604). The RAF had no dive-bombers; the Germans had 366. This gave an overall total of 1,566 aircraft for the RAF including coastal, compared with 3,609 for the Luftwaffe. The RAF had the advantage in terms of quality. Five new aircraft had been developed during the 1930s. The Spitfire first flew in 1936 and the Hurricane in 1936; both aircraft, and especially the Spitfire, had an extreme degree of manoeuvrability. The twin-engined Mosquito, ready for production at the start of the war, did not in fact come into service until early 1941, with a fast performance and with a long-range fighter or bombing role. Two other famous bombers were the Wellington, first flown in 1936, with a range of over 3,000 miles, and the Lancaster, delivered to Bomber Command in early 1942: this could carry a bomb load of 8,000 pounds to Berlin, cruising at 210 mph at about 20,000 feet. On 4 August 1944 the RAF operated its first jet aircraft, a Meteor, against V1s: this type of aircraft put the world's speed record to 606 mph in 1945, increasing this to 616 mph in 1946. Another jet aircraft, the Vampire, was first tested during the war – in September 1943 – although not entering service until after the conflict ended; later versions achieved a top speed of 548 mph. The primary task of the RAF after 1945 was to re-establish itself on a peacetime footing and at the same time to adapt to modern war conditions. Preparation for future hostilities included the need to re-design control and interception systems in view of the fact that aircraft speeds rose by 50 per cent in the decade after 1945. By the mid-1950s this overhaul and modernization of the radar and control system had almost been completed; in 1954 the Hawker Hunter interceptor fighter entered RAF service and proved to be perhaps the most successful post-1945 aircraft, with later versions achieving a top speed of 750 mph at sea level. The Hunter was later joined by the Javelin and by the Lightning: the latter has a maximum level speed of over Mach 2. Bomber Command obtained its first jet aircraft in 1951 with the Canberra: this aircraft had a range of 3,790 miles and a top speed of 580 mph at 30,000 feet. The Canberra became the first jet bomber to cross the Atlantic, in 1951 – RAF Vampires had been the first jet aircraft of any kind to make the crossing, in 1948. The RAF's most powerful aircraft force has been the 'V-bomber' fleet, comprising Valiants, Victors and Vulcans, with the first such aircraft, a Valiant, entering service in January 1955: this force undertook Britain's nuclear role until the introduction of *Polaris*-missile submarines in 1968, the first British

A-bomb being released in tests off Australia, October 1956, from a Valiant. Increasingly, the RAF has assumed a missile-firing role: the first air-to-air guided missile, Firestreak, entered service with Fighter Command Javelin squadrons in October 1958; many Fighter Command and Bomber Command squadrons have since been 'grounded' to undertake surface-to-air missile deployment, especially with the Bloodhound missile which first went into service with the RAF in 1958 as a mobile tactical weapon, and the intermediate range (IRBM) Thor, first obtained by a Bomber Command squadron in 1958. As a recognition of their new roles, Fighter and Bomber Commands were merged on 30 April 1968 to form a new Strike Command, which also includes Signals and Coastal Commands; under their same reorganization Transport Command became Air Support Command. The RAF in 1976 had a strength of about 500 combat aircraft, including Vulcan bombers, Buccaneers, US Phantoms and Lightnings. Other aircraft included the Harrier, formerly Kestrel, which became operational in 1969 as the world's first vertical take-off and landing fighter (VTOL), and the Jaguar, produced jointly with the French.

Raglan, Lord Fitzroy James Henry Somerset, 1788–1855 British Field-Marshal. Served in the *Peninsular War* as Aide to *Wellington*; wounded at *Waterloo*, losing his sword arm. From 1827 to 1852 Raglan was Military Secretary to Wellington, now C-in-C of the British Army. Raglan hoped to succeed to this position but was instead appointed Master-General of the Ordnance. He was given command of the British Army in the *Crimean War*, taking up this post in April 1854. Well-meaning and intelligent, he was nevertheless unsuited for command and for dealing with the incompetence of those around him and in London. He constantly warned that the troops were ill-equipped for the Crimean winter; the Duke of Newcastle, War Secretary, replied that the Crimean climate was 'one of the mildest and finest in the world'. Raglan died 10 days after the failure of the assault on the Malakoff and the Redan, 17–18 June 1855, and was succeeded by General Sir James Simpson.

Railways The advent of the railroad meant that troops could be moved 6 times faster than Napoleon's armies had marched; the fundamental features of *strategy* – time and space – were radically altered. The first railroad was built in the USA in 1828. It was first thought that railways would favour the defensive, a notion shattered in 1859 when *Moltke* rushed Prussian troops south to face the Austrians with unprecedented speed. The role of the rail system became of paramount importance in the *American Civil War*; *Sherman*'s march to *Atlanta*, 1864, would have been impossible without rail transportation: he estimated that he would have needed 36,800 six-mule supply wagons. Moltke's devastating victory in the *Austro-Prussian War* of 1866 was based on his use of the rail system, and he took development even

farther in 1870 at the start of the *Franco-Prussian War*, deploying 400,000 men along a 125-mile front within 16 days. Supplies could come quickly from rear areas. This meant in turn that armies could be bigger, and also that the whole nation was involved in war through the need to provide supplies. This further increased the move towards the *nation-in-arms*. Yet while providing greater mobility, railways could also result in less flexibility: armies tended to be tied to the railway tracks. The system also helped to rob the battlefield of its ability to bring final victory: damage could be more easily repaired in the offensive or defensive lines, and gaps plugged by reinforcements rushing from the rear. Moreover, as developed by Moltke, *Schlieffen* and *Moltke the Younger*, the railway system became an integral part of the mobilization procedure: because mobility had been increased, it became imperative to reach the front before the enemy. Mobilization became part of the operational offensive: troops would be forming and moving forward by railroad, at the same time. This brought immense dangers. Without a breathing space between the call to arms and the opening of hostilities, there would be no time for second thoughts or last-minute diplomatic efforts to avert war: mobilization became a virtual declaration of war. Railway movement to the front was rigid and complicated; once started, the programme could hardly be halted. This helped bring about the holocaust of the *First World War*.

Ramsay, Sir Bertram, 1883–1945 British Admiral. Flag Officer, Dover, in charge of evacuation from *Dunkirk*, May–June 1940; later involved with planning for *'Torch'* landings, French North Africa, November 1942, and invasion of *Sicily*, 1943; Naval C-in-C for *Normandy* landings, June 1944; killed in an air crash, 2 January 1945.

Rangers, US   The first Ranger companies were raised in June 1942 from US troops stationed in Northern Ireland. The idea, based on the British *commandos*, was suggested by Brigadier-General Lucian Truscott, head of the US Mission to Combined Operations. The Rangers first saw action in the *Dieppe* raid, August 1942. They entered North Africa at the end of the year as a full battalion and the force grew to light brigade size in 1943. Two battalions went ashore in the first phase of the *Sicily* invasion, July 1943, and they were engaged at *Salerno*. They lost heavily in the *Anzio* operation, January 1944. One Ranger battalion, the 6th, fought in the *Philippines*, and the 2nd and 5th battalions took part in the *Normandy* invasion, June 1944. The Ranger concept only survived the war on an 'ad hoc' basis with some US divisions forming their own 'Ranger' units; these were used in *Korea*, but were disbanded in the mid-1950s. The Ranger idea was revived slightly during *Vietnam*.

Ratisbon, campaign and Battle of, April 1809 *Napoleonic Wars* (Map 1). Austria resumed hostilities by invading French-held Bavaria on 9 April, with a force under Archduke Charles moving towards Ratisbon (Regensburg). In Italy, another Austrian army under Archduke John repulsed a French force commanded by Eugène de Beauharnais at Sacile, 16 April. Napoleon crossed the Danube to clash with the Austrians at Abensberg, 19–20 April, driving the enemy right wing back towards Ratisbon and the left towards Landeshut. Napoleon pursued the latter but the Austrians escaped from the brief Battle of Landeshut on 21 April, owing to the late arrival of French forces under *Masséna*. Napoleon turned north to join *Davout*, who had been maintaining pressure on the remainder of the Austrian Army, situated south of Ratisbon and totalling about 80,000 men under Archduke Charles – about twice the French strength. Charles attacked on 22 April in the Battle of Eggmühl, but Davout held firm and Napoleon arrived with reinforcements. Charles retreated after a vigorous French counter-attack, losing about 12,000 men; he tried to escape north over the Danube leaving forces at Ratisbon to cover the withdrawal. Napoleon attacked on 23 April; although his troops took Ratisbon they were too exhausted to continue the pursuit. Napoleon entered Vienna on 13 May and prepared to move again against the Austrians: this second campaign would lead to *Wagram*.

Rawlinson, Henry Seymour, 1864–1925 British General. Served with *Roberts* in India, 1887–90; in *Sudan* with *Kitchener*, 1898, and in *Boer War*;

commanded British expedition sent to help defend Antwerp, October 1914, and was almost captured when the city fell; commanded British 4th Army in First Battle of the *Somme*, 1916, and against German Somme offensive, 1918; led his 4th Army forward in *Amiens* counter-offensive, August 1918, and broke through German defences on the Selle, 17 October; commanded allied force sent to North Russia 1918, during *Russian Revolution*; C-in-C India, 1920.

Reichswehr Name given to German Army and Navy after defeat of these armed forces – titled the Wehrmacht – in the First World War, although the old name continued to be used. The new title appeared in the Law on the Formation of a provisional Reichswehr published 6 March 1919. Both the Army and the Navy were severely reduced by the *Versailles Treaty*, June 1919, and the German air forces were banned completely. Nevertheless, Germany contrived to rebuild her armed strength. The Army, cut to 100,000 men by the treaty, was organized by *Seeckt* 1920–5 into an embryonic body capable of rapid expansion; the Navy, forbidden to have new warships larger than 10,000 tons, falsified figures. Hitler formally renounced the clauses of the Versailles Treaty in March 1935; at the same time Germany announced her intention to reintroduce conscription; Germany also officially notified foreign governments that a German Air Force was in existence – the *Luftwaffe* had in fact started development 2 years before.

RFC (Royal Flying Corps) Established 13 April 1912, to comprise a naval wing, an army wing and a central flying school. The idea of a Royal Navy and a British Army wing working in combination failed, and the two split apart into the RFC and the Royal Naval Air Service. In 1914 the respective strengths were 63 operational RFC aircraft and 66 RNAS, including 26 seaplanes. A succession of types, including the FE2B and the DH2, led to the Bristol Scout, the SE5, Sopwith 1½ Strutter and Pup and other aircraft fitted with the ·303 *Vickers* synchronized machine-gun. Output of aircraft rose from 211 in 1914 to 14,168 in 1917; by May 1916 the RFC had established air superiority over the Western Front. By the time of the armistice the British air forces had dropped 8,000 tons of bombs and had fired 12 million rounds of ammunition at ground targets; already, in April 1918, the RFC and RNAS had become the *RAF*.

Ridgway, Matthew Bunker, 1895– US General. Assistant Divisional Commander, 82nd Infantry Division, 1942, becoming Commander later in the year and thereafter leading the division in *Sicily* and *Italy*, 1943, *Normandy*, 1944; commanded 18th Airborne Corps in Germany, 1945, before taking over the Luzon area command. Ridgway succeeded General Walton Walker as Commander of Ground Operations in *Korea*, 23 December 1950; he replaced *MacArthur* as Supreme Commander, 11 April 1951. He was succeeded by

General Mark Clark, May 1952, in order to take over from *Eisenhower* as NATO Supreme Allied Commander Europe (SACEUR); he was US Army Chief of Staff 1953–5.

Rifle, rifling, riflemen A rifle is a firearm with a series of spiral grooves cut into the bore – 'rifling' – which imparts a spinning motion to the projectile; this rotational stabilization gives greater power and accuracy. Probably the earliest military use of the rifle was by Danish troops in about 1611, but the American Revolution, 1775–83, marked the beginning of the successful use of this weapon in war. For many years the rifle continued as a skirmishing weapon rather than for basic infantry tactics: the rifle had a slower rate of fire than the standard smooth-bore *musket* and was hence less suitable for the close-range battles of that time. Riflemen assumed greater importance in the *French Revolutionary Wars*, especially as a result of the example shown by the French *tirailleurs*. Prussian and Austrian equivalents were the Jäger, although not developed to the extent of the French counterpart: the Jäger, who had used rifles in the Seven Years' War, 1756–63, were basically foresters using hunting rifles. As a result of the impact on battle by the swarming tirailleurs, the British also began to develop riflemen to act in conjunction with the line infantry: responsible for early development was the Duke of York, 1763–1827, C-in-C of the British Army from 1798 to 1809, closely aided by *Moore*. Light infantrymen were trained at Moore's Shorncliffe camp as the 95th Foot in the years preceding the *Peninsular War*, and this unit was expanded into the Rifle Brigade in 1816. British riflemen were armed with the Baker rifle, adopted in 1800 and replaced by the Brunswick in 1838. The difficulty in ramming the ball down the rifling resulted in a firing rate of only 1 round per minute, compared with up to 4 per minute for the musket: attempts to improve the firing-rate were closely linked with the development of *percussion* cartridges to replace the rammed ball, and *breech-loading* mechanisms. Minié's bullet, produced in 1849, was adopted in Britain in the muzzle-loading Pattern 1851 rifled musket, known as the Minié rifle. In 1865 the British adopted their first breech-loading rifle, the *Snider*, replaced by the *Martini-Henry* in 1871. Further improvements in rifling resulted from work by *Metford*, whose designs were incorporated in the ·303 introduced into British service in 1888. Meanwhile, simultaneous developments had been taking place on the Continent, with gradual improvement through the French *chassepot* of 1866, the *Dreyse* needle-gun, and the French *Gras* of 1874; the latter incorporated all latest developments such as bolt breech-loading action and a metal centre-fire percussion cartridge. The first practical magazine was the US *Lee* device of 1879, holding up to 10 rounds. Variants of the box-magazine were produced by M. Nagant of Belgium, *Mauser* of Germany and *Mannlicher* of Austria, while the

French developed a tubular magazine used with the *Lebel* rifle of 1886. The next step came with the introduction of *smokeless* propellants, more powerful and giving an accurate maximum range of about 1,000 yards. The *machine-gun* dominated infantry weapons in the First World War, but by 1939 more flexible tactics again gave scope to the individual infantryman armed with his rifle. The latter included the German 7·9 mm KAR-98K with a 5-round magazine; the British Lee-*Enfield* ·303 with a range of 2,000 yards and a 10-round magazine; the Russian M-1930 7·62 mm; and the US P17 ·30-inch which was replaced by the M-1 Garand ·30-inch with an 8-round magazine.

Roberts, Frederick Sleigh, 1st Earl, 1832–1914 British Field-Marshal. Served in *Indian Mutiny*, winning the VC; served in Afghanistan, 1879–80; C-in-C India, 1885–93, Ireland 1895–9. In January 1900 Roberts replaced *Buller* as British Commander in the *Boer War*, with *Kitchener* his Chief of Staff, ending all formal Boer resistance by July; he returned to Britain in December, with Kitchener assuming command. Roberts retired from the Army in 1904 and devoted himself to heading the National Service League: this demanded compulsory military service.

Robertson, Sir William Robert, 1860–1933 British Field-Marshal. Entered Army as a private, 1877; Quartermaster-General of the BEF, 1914, Chief of Staff to BEF, 1915; appointed CIGS December 1915 during the move to restrict *Kitchener*'s authority: he was given direct access to the War Cabinet, took over Kitchener's duty as the government's principal adviser on strategy, and became directly responsible for issuing strategical directives to the generals. He pursued an offensive policy on the Western Front and a defensive policy elsewhere: his first act on becoming CIGS was to insist upon the *Dardanelles* evacuation. He failed to achieve a satisfactory relationship with *Lloyd George*, supporting *Haig*. In February 1918 the Prime Minister attempted to ease him out of the way by offering him the post of Military Representative on the Versailles Committee; Robertson refused to accept and was replaced by Sir Henry Wilson. He commanded British occupation troops in Germany, 1919–20.

Rockets Significant development was not undertaken until *Congreve* introduced his devices in the *Napoleonic Wars*. Thereafter the idea was virtually abandoned for another century. The Germans took up rocket development in the 1920s, in view of the artillery ban imposed by the *Versailles* treaty. Other nations followed, seeking to use rockets as anti-tank, anti-aircraft and *mortar* substitutes – their advantage over the latter lay in their faster delivery. Rockets were, however, inaccurate, and their best use was considered to be in a blanket fire pattern. The Russians were the first to produce a multiple rocket projector, with the Katyusha introduced during winter 1942: this contained a set of 16 rockets each with a 48-pound warhead and a range of 6,500 yards. The Germans followed with the latest version of the Nebelwerfer, having a range of 7,300 yards. Rockets were increasingly used as aircraft armaments, for example with the Typhoon. Strategic rocket development led to the *V-bomb* in Germany (V2). Post-war progress in the West was assisted by a number of German rocket experts, including Dr Wernher von Braun; military development has since been synonymous with the *missile*.

Rommel, Erwin, 1891-1944 German Marshal. Served in First World War. Rommel commanded Hitler's bodyguard in 1938 and during the occupation of Czechoslovakia, March 1939; in August 1939 he was appointed Major-General on Hitler's HQ staff. He received command of the 7th Panzer Division, February 1940, known as the 'Ghost Division'; it formed part of General Hermann Hoth's Panzer Corps, in turn part of *Rundstedt*'s Army Group A for the Battle of *France*, 1940 (Map 13). Rommel advanced on the right of the main thrust through the Ardennes, then wheeled north towards Lille, resulting in the surrender of half the French 1st Army, 30 May; he reached Cherbourg on 19 June. During this campaign Rommel lost 42 tanks and suffered 3,000 casualties, taking 100,000 French and British prisoners and over 300 guns, 450 tanks and 7,000 other vehicles. He arrived in

Tripoli, 12 February 1941, to command German troops – later called the Afrika Korps – supporting the Italians in the *desert campaign* (Map 14), leading to the fight for *Tunisia*, 1943. Rommel left North Africa after the battle of Medenine, 6 March, handing over command to General von Arnim. He was appointed Commander of German troops in north *Italy*, August 1943; in October he became Inspector of the German Atlantic Wall defences in north-west Europe, under Rundstedt; in late December he was appointed Commander of Army Group B, still under Rundstedt. The two men differed over the correct defensive plan: Rundstedt believed the main Allied invasion would be in the Pas de Calais area; Rommel considered it more likely to come between Dunkirk and Cherbourg; Rundstedt believed a central armoured reserve should be collected around Paris; Rommel urged the placing of the armoured divisions along the coast to save the vital panzers from air attack when moving forward. The *Normandy* landings, 6 June, proved Rommel more correct. He was implicated in the 20 July attempt to assassinate Hitler, with the conspirators wishing to place him at the head of the proposed alternative government. On 17 July he was wounded in an allied air attack; he committed suicide, 14 October.

Roon, Count Albrecht Theodor Emil von, 1803-79 Prussian soldier and statesman. Roon claimed that Prussia could only maintain and improve her European position through wide-ranging military reforms, deemed urgent after confusion and inefficiency shown by the mobilization in anticipation of war, 1859. He advocated removing the independence of the civilian *Landwehr*, seen as a breeding ground for liberalism. Roon replaced the more liberal Eduard von Bonin (1792–1865) as War Minister in 1859 and thereafter struggled to have his proposals adopted against parliamentary opposition. By October 1867, stimulated by the Prussian victory at *Sadowa*, Roon considered his efforts to be successfully concluded. His reforms included universal *conscription* without substitution: service with the colours would be for 3 years, beginning at the age of 20, after which conscripts would serve with the reserve for 4 years rather than 2 as previously, before passing into the Landwehr. Service with the latter was cut from 7 to 5 years, under close supervision by the regular Army, so turning this force into a virtual second-line reserve. Prussia was divided into 8 areas, forming an authoritative corps organization. Roon's reforms enabled Prussia to mobilize over 1,100,000 men for the *Franco-Prussian War*, providing a manpower framework for *Moltke*'s plans. Roon was President of the Prussian Cabinet, 1 January to 9 November 1873.

Roosevelt, Franklin Delano, 1882–1945 32nd US President. Distant cousin of President Theodore *Roosevelt*; succeeded Herbert Hoover, March 1933, re-elected 1936 and 1944, the first time a President had re-

mained for three terms. Roosevelt showed himself extremely sympathetic to his friend *Churchill*'s requests for all possible aid, 1940–1. He provided old US destroyers in exchange for US assumption of leases on several British bases in the Western Hemisphere; he promoted the Lend-Lease Act, March 1941, authorizing the provision of war supplies to any nation fighting the Axis. Other spectacular moves by Roosevelt during this period of US neutrality included his offer to buy the French Fleet, June 1940, to prevent these warships falling into German hands – his offer met with no response from the faltering French government – and his attempt to engineer an 'incicent' which would bring the US closer to conflict. Thus Churchill told his War Cabinet in August 1941 that Roosevelt had said 'he would wage war, but not declare it': orders had been given to US destroyers escorting west Atlantic shipping that they were to attack any U-boat 'even if it were 200 or 300 miles away from the convoy . . . Everything was to be done to force an "incident".' Roosevelt acted as C-in-C after the US entry into the war, December 1941, working closely with *Marshall*. He suffered increasingly from ill-health and died on 12 April 1945 of cerebral haemorrhage, succeeded by Vice-President *Truman*.

Roosevelt, Theodore, 1858–1919 26th US President. Distant cousin of Franklin *Roosevelt*; Assistant Secretary of the Navy, 1897–8, resigning at the start of the *American-Spanish War*, April 1898, in order to serve in the field: he organized the first volunteer cavalry regiment, known as 'Roosevelt's Rough Riders', serving in Cuba. Roosevelt was chosen as Vice-President by President William McKinley, 1901, becoming President in September following McKinley's assassination. He was re-elected, 1904. His mediation resulted in the Treaty of Portsmouth to end the *Russo-Japanese War*, September 1905. He declined to stand again for President and was succeeded by his nominee, William Taft, in 1909. Roosevelt unsuccessfully sought military command, 1917–18.

Root, Elihu, 1845–1937 US Secretary of War, 1899–1904. Root came to office at a time when defects in the US services were being revealed by the campaigns in the *American-Spanish War*, 1898, and by fighting in the *Philippines*, 1899–1902. His first annual report, December 1899, sought a *staff* organization to study strategy and war plans; a similar agency for new weapons systems, materials and inventions; an adequate process of selecting officers; improved exercise and training systems; and the establishment of an adequate reserve system. The War College was instituted, November 1901, but the proposal for a general staff was not adopted until the Dick Act of early 1903. This also increased the size of the regular Army to about four times the 1897 strength. A better high command structure was introduced, with large responsibilities being placed on the Chief of Staff. The Militia Act of 1792 was abolished, thus removing remaining vestiges of uni-

versal military obligations. Root was Secretary of State, 1905–9, under Theodore *Roosevelt*.

Rose, Hugh Henry, Baron Strathnairn, 1801–85 British Field-Marshal. Rose operated in central India in the *Indian Mutiny*, undertaking a lightning campaign January–March 1858 with about 3,000 men; he relieved Saugor, 3 February, forced the pass of Madanpur, 3 March, and invested the rebel stronghold at Jhansi, 21 March. He diverted half his small force to defeat a rebel relief force under Tantia Topi, 1 April, then seized Jhansi, 3 April; he defeated rebel forces at Kunch, 1 May, and Kalpi, 22 May; Rose clashed with Tantia Topi again at the Battle of Gwalior, 19 June, and his victory virtually ended the Mutiny. He was C-in-C India, 1860, Ireland, 1865–70.

Rundstedt, Karl Rudolf Gerd von, 1875–1953 German Marshal. Served on General Staff, First World War; commanded Army Group in the invasion of *Poland*, September 1939; commanded Army Group A in the Battle of *France*, May–June 1940; commanded Army Group South in the invasion of *Russia*, June 1941. Rundstedt resigned this command in November 1941, just as Hitler was about to relieve him, and was succeeded by General von Reichenau. He was appointed Commander in the West, 1942, responsible for the organization of the Atlantic Wall defences prior to the *Normandy* landings: he believed the latter would in fact be made in the Pas de Calais area; replaced by Kluge, July 1944, after his failure to block the allied landings, but was recalled in September. Rundstedt commanded German forces in the *Ardennes* offensive, December 1944; he was replaced by *Kesselring*, March 1945, and was captured by US forces the following month.

Russell, Sir William Howard, 1820–1907 Irish War Correspondent, reporting for London 'Times' from 1841. His dispatches from the *Crimean War* in October 1854 revealed the horrors being suffered by British sick and wounded; the subsequent public outcry overthrew Lord Aberdeen's government and prompted the journey of Florence *Nightingale* to Scutari. Similar sufferings had been endured by British soldiers in the past, yet this was the first time that news could reach a large audience at home within a short time of events. Russell's reports provided a foretaste of future news media influence in times of war – an influence which reached a climax in *Vietnam*.

Russia, campaign in, May– December 1812 *Napoleonic Wars* (Map 1). Relations between *Napoleon* and Tsar Alexander I worsened during 1811 over their respective interests in Poland. In early 1812 Napoleon reluctantly turned from domestic French matters and prepared an invasion army. This Grand Army totalled almost 500,000 men, of whom about half were non-French. Napoleon planned to force an early battle, which

would persuade Alexander to negotiate. The right flank of the French invasion was protected by 40,000 Austrians under *Schwarzenberg*; the left was covered by Macdonald's army of similar strength. In the centre would move the Grand Army itself. Facing the French were two main Russian armies, comprising the principal force of 127,000 men under Barclay de Tolly and Pyotr Bagration's 40,000 men farther south between Vilna and the Pripet marshes. Farther south still were 43,000 Russians under General A. P. Tormassov. The Russians were undecided whether to stand or retreat to better defensive positions. Napoleon crossed the Niemen on 24 June and Barclay pulled back, more through indecision than a set policy, managing to join Bagration near Smolensk on 3 August. Here the Russians made a defensive stand, 17 August, but then continued to retreat. Barclay was replaced by *Kutuzov* on the 29th. The new Russian Commander continued the withdrawal, now following a deliberate policy of luring the French deep into Russia. Reluctantly, Kutuzov bowed to pressure from the Tsar and his advisers and fought the defensive Battle of *Borodino*, 7 September. He then pulled away again, withdrawing through Moscow despite the Tsar's strident protests; Napoleon entered Moscow on 14 September, with the capital in flames – the fire had probably been started by retreating Cossacks. He believed Alexander would now seek peace, but repeated overtures for talks failed to find a response. Napoleon delayed as long as possible, but food in the capital grew short, his supply lines back out of Russia were constantly cut by partisans, and the winter approached. Napoleon therefore started to withdraw from Moscow on 19 October, south-west against Kutuzov. The latter moved out of reach after pushing back French probes at Maloyaroslavets, 24 October, and Napoleon was obliged to turn north again to the route used for his advance on Moscow. By the time the main French force reached Smolensk, 12 November, the Army had begun to disintegrate. Napoleon nevertheless managed to rally effective regiments to throw aside Russian troops at Krasnoi, 16–17 November, but *Ney*'s corps of 9,000 men was decimated in a desperate rearguard action. Brilliant leadership by Napoleon enabled the bulk of the surviving fighting units to cross the Berezina, 26–28 November, despite strong Russian pressure, but perhaps as many as 20,000 other soldiers and civilians with the Grand Army were lost at this crossing. And half of those who managed to reach the west bank died in the next stretch of the retreat, on the road to Vilna. Napoleon quit his army and left for Paris on 5 December, to deal with domestic problems and to raise new forces; he handed over to *Murat*. Napoleon's casualties probably amounted to over 300,000 men; Russian losses were at least 250,000. But Napoleon could less easily repair this colossal damage; new recruits would be ill-trained and badly equipped. Losses in guns and cavalry

were extremely difficult to replace. Moreover, Napoleon's defeat encouraged others to turn against him. Prussia joined Russia, and their Armies took the field early in 1813 for a gigantic campaign beginning with *Lützen*, 2 May, and ending with *Leipzig*, October.

Russia, German campaign in, 1941–5 *Second World War* (Map 15). Formal planning for *Hitler*'s invasion, operation Barbarossa, began in December 1940. Hitler believed the Red Army could be defeated within 4 months; this optimism tallied with assessments made by Western leaders and senior officers: *Stimson*, US War Secretary, informed *Roosevelt* that he and the US *Joint Chiefs of Staff* believed Germany 'will be fully occupied in beating Russia for a minimum of one month and a possible maximum of three'. The invasion began at dawn, 22 June 1941. Hitler planned 3 drives. Twenty-nine divisions in General von Leeb's Army Group North would thrust from East Prussia towards Leningrad; 42 divisions in *Rundstedt*'s Army Group South would advance from the Lublin area towards Kiev; 50 divisions in General von Bock's Army Group Centre would advance either side of the Minsk–Smolensk–Moscow line. These gigantic movements totalled 3 million ground troops. Russia's 3 main army groups from north to south, were *Voroshilov*'s North-West Front, 32 divisions, Marshal Semën Timoshenko's 47 divisions in the Western Front, and Marshal Semën Budënny's South-

West Front, 69 divisions. Russian manpower also totalled about 3 million. Tactical surprise was obtained along the whole 2,000-mile front during the initial offensive. The gigantic pincer movements closed round Minsk and Smolensk in mid-July, taking nearly 400,000 prisoners, but to the south Rundstedt found the going more difficult. Despite vigorous protests from his commanders that Moscow was the main target, Hitler insisted on withdrawing strength from the north to bolster Rundstedt; this boost resulted in the capture of Kiev, 19 September, and the surrender of over 660,000 Russians trapped in the wide bend of the Dnieper River. In the north, Leeb's depleted Army Group North invested Leningrad in early October and the Army Group Centre, now commanded by Kluge, reached within 25 miles of Moscow in early December. Hitler again changed this emphasis back to the north, but vital time was lost. The way to Moscow was barred by new Russian armies, created from troops brought from the interior and commanded by *Zhukov*. The German advance bogged down in the appalling winter weather. Hitler dismissed one general after another, including *Brauchitsch* and Leeb, and insisted upon taking personal command himself by radio from Berlin. Then, on 6 December, the Russians counter-attacked, driving forward at Kalini and Tula, north and south of Moscow, and at Izyum in the Ukraine. A German counter-offensive in spring 1942 succeeded in regaining some territory, and Sebastopol fell on

2 July. Encouraged by these successes, Hitler again laid heavy reliance on the thrusts south of Moscow: Bock's Army Group South advanced from Kursk to take Voronezh on 6 July. Hitler reorganized his divisions for the next step; he transformed the original grouping into Army Group B, the northern armies, under General Maximilian von Weichs, and the southern armies into Army Group A under General Siegmund List. Both drove forward in mid-July, with Group B advancing on Stalingrad and Group A moving farther south on the oilfields of the Caucasus. The latter took Rostov on 23 July. The Battle of *Stalingrad* began on 24 August, to end with the disastrous German surrender on 2 February 1943. Meanwhile the Russians launched strong counter-attacks elsewhere: by the end of February 1943, the whole front had been shifted back to a line running from Leningrad just west of Smolensk and Kiev, down to the lower Dnieper; the only German success was an advance by Manstein's Army Group Don which recaptured Kharkov on 14 March. The next offensive began on 5 July with the gigantic and decisive Battle of *Kursk*. Russian victory in this tank battle led to hammer blows along the entire front during the summer and winter: Leningrad was relieved on 19 January 1944, while farther south the relentless Russian pressure resulted in an advance over the Bug and Dniester. Hitler, increasingly demented, relieved Manstein and Kleist, replacing them with Model and Schoerner. German strength had to be depleted by the

Normandy landings, 6 June; 16 days later the Russians launched their summer offensive under Zhukov. The Russian 3rd, 2nd and 1st Front struck north of the Pripet marshes, aiming at Minsk and Warsaw; Minsk fell on 3 July; the premature *Warsaw rising* began on 1 August. Hitler's satellite countries collapsed: Romania capitulated on 23 August; Bulgaria defected on 8 September; Russian troops swept into Yugoslavia in October. The final invasion of *Germany* would now begin.

Russian Revolution, 1917–22 Unrest in Russia, which had broken out in December 1905, continued throughout the First World War. Misery suffered under the wartime conditions fed the communist-inspired revolt which erupted in March 1917, and which led to the overthrow of Tsar Nicolas II on the 15th. The new régime, under Alexander Kerensky, attempted to continue the war against Germany, but the Russian communists, or Bolsheviks, overthrew the Kerensky régime on 6 November, 1917. *Lenin* and *Trotsky* then negotiated the armistice of Brest Litovsk with Germany, signed on 15 December. The Bolshevik struggle for dominance in internal politics soon spread into Poland, Finland, the Baltic States, Siberia and the Ukraine. The latter area, and South Russia, proved to be the decisive regions. By January 1919, after a year of insurrection and confused skirmishing, Bolshevik forces were growing into the Red Army, with Trotsky merging together differing factions; against them were the Whites,

led in name at least by General Anton Deniken in the Kiev region, by Admiral Alexander Kolchak in Siberia, by General Nikolai Yudenich in the Baltic provinces and by General Peter Wrangel in the Caucasus area. Also opposing the Reds were Japanese forces which seized Vladivostok on 30 December 1917, and a small British–French–US expedition which seized Murmansk in June 1918 and Archangel in August. In May 1919 the main campaign opened with Trotsky taking the offensive in the east against Kolchak's army in Siberia, while Red forces went on to the defensive in the south and north. Trotsky's force, with General Tukhachevski in command, pushed back Kolchak and in the autumn forced back Wrangel's army, which had taken Kiev on 2 September. White opposition crumbled, with only a small force under Wrangel managing to hold out in the Crimea. Wrangel attempted to advance during 1920 but was driven back into the Crimea and evacuated by British vessels in November. The puny allied attempts to intervene came to nothing, including a US expedition of 2 regiments under General William S. Graves at Vladivostok, August 1918.

Russo-Japanese War, 1904–5 (Map 8) The conflict had immense importance as an indicator of modern fire power. Focus of the war was Port Arthur. Japan, dependent upon command of the sea, first sought to destroy this enemy base, after which it was intended to launch an offensive in Manchuria and Korea. The Russians were handicapped by the need to bring men and supplies over the 5,500-mile single-track railway from Moscow, with this railroad having a 100-mile gap at Lake Baikal. Japan struck suddenly at Port Arthur on 8 February 1904; the port was immediately subjected to close blockade. The Japanese landed in the Liaotung Peninsula in early May, and the siege of Port Arthur began with the Battle of Nanshan on the 25th. Japanese troops in the 2nd Army, under General Yasukata Otu, took this Port Arthur outpost but with nearly 5,000 Japanese casualties compared with the Russian total of 1,500. The loss of Nanshan Hill uncovered the port of Dalny (Dairen), which became a Japanese base and the HQ of General Maresuke Nogi, Commander of the 3rd Army. Reinforcements to this army brought the total of Japanese besieging troops to 80,000 by August, plus 474 field- and siege-guns – twice the manpower strength of the Russian defenders. The latter were, however, protected by 3 main defensive lines. The Japanese managed to prise the Russians from hills to the east of the port on 7–8 August, although at heavy cost. The Russian Fleet in the harbour moved out 2 days later, commanded by Vilgelm Vitgeft; the blockading Japanese Battle Fleet under Heihachiro Togo moved to intercept and the two fleets engaged in long-range bombardment. This Battle of the Yellow Sea ended with the Russians retreating back into harbour after the death of Vitgeft. Meanwhile, Russian troops under General Stakelberg, intended to relieve Port Arthur, had been blocked by the Japanese 2nd Army under General Yasukata Oku at the Battle of Telissu, 14–15 June, and these and other Russian forces under General Count Keller pulled back during August into positions around Liao-Yang, 150 miles north of Port Arthur. At the port, the Japanese launched another offensive, 19–25 August; this made little progress and resulted in 15,000 Japanese casualties, compared with 3,000 Russians. Repeated assaults during September through to November caused terrible Japanese losses. In the north, the Japanese advanced against the Russians in late August, resulting in the Battle of Liao-Yang which continued until 3 September. Casualties for both sides were heavy. The Russians, under Kuropatkin, withdrew north, turning on the following Japanese at Sha-Ho, 5–17 October, after which the exhausted armies dug in. At last, in November, the end came at Port Arthur. The Japanese attackers under Nogi concentrated on positions overlooking the harbour, with a vicious offensive beginning 27 November. The Russian outposts were overrun on 5 December, after about 11,000 Japanese had been slaughtered. The Japanese could now fire on the Russian Fleet in the harbour and could work forward into the Port Arthur defences; this grim operation continued throughout December, despite appalling weather, and the last Russian position fell on 1 January. Next day the Russian Commander, General Anatoli Stësel, surrendered his 11,000 survivors. About 31,000 Russians were lost during the siege; but Japanese casualties probably totalled 60,000 killed and wounded. In the north Kuropatkin was reinforced to 300,000 men in early 1905, and attacked the Japanese under Iwao Oyama on the 26th; the Japanese managed to cling to their positions. Soon afterwards Oyama also received reinforcements. On 21 February began the Battle of Mukden, with Oyama ordering Nogi's 3rd Army to push forward against the Russian right. This movement almost succeeded, but Kuropatkin rushed forward reserves to prevent a complete encirclement. Hard fighting continued for 2 weeks. Oyama reinforced Nogi's army at the beginning of March, and by the 7th the Russian right flank had been pushed back even farther. Kuropatkin feared his communications might soon be severed and disengaged, so conceding victory. Russian casualties totalled about 100,000 men, the Japanese about two-thirds of this number. Main activity now took place at sea. On 15 October 1904 the Russian Baltic Fleet had begun the long voyage via the Indian Ocean to the Far East. The Fleet, comprising 8 battleships, 8 cruisers, 9 destroyers and other smaller vessels, was commanded by Admiral Zonvy Rozhdestvenski; facing this force was the better-armed Japanese Fleet under Togo, totalling 4 battleships, 8 cruisers, 21 destroyers and 60 torpedo boats. The Russians entered Tsushima Strait on 27 May 1905. Both fleets approached each other in line-ahead formation, but then the Japanese turned north, hoping to cross the Russian line to deliver a continuous broadside. The Russians also turned, first north-east then east, and the action opened at a 6,400-yard range. The Japanese benefited from a 15-knot top speed compared with the Russian 9-knot, and Togo skilfully manoeuvred his warships to envelop the enemy. After about 120 minutes 2 Russian battleships and 1 cruiser had been sunk and the Russian Commander was wounded. Admiral Nebogatov assumed command. Retreat took place during the night, harried by Japanese cruisers, destroyers and torpedo boats; only 5 Russian destroyers and 1 cruiser managed to escape. Japanese losses totalled just 3 torpedo boats. This Japanese victory at the Battle of Tsushima, combined with the earlier victory at Mukden and the fall of Port Arthur, persuaded the Russians to seek peace. The Treaty of Portsmouth, 6 September, ended the war. Japan gained Korea; Russia surrendered Port Arthur and evacuated Manchuria. Japan's success tended to obscure the hard fact that victory against defenders armed with modern weapons could only be achieved at colossal cost.

Russo-Turkish War, 1877–8 Continuing unsatisfactory Russo-Turkish relations, which had broken into conflict in 1828–9 and in 1853–6 during the *Crimean War*, led to further hostilities in April 1877. The situation was aggravated by Russian desires to move south to gain a warm-water port. Russia declared war on 24 April and immediately invaded Romania and Turkey's Caucasian provinces: invasion forces in Romania totalled over 100,000 men, and those in the Caucasian region about 70,000, all under the command of Grand Duke Nicholas. Turkish forces numbered about 135,000 men under Abdul Kerim. Both sides displayed considerable ineptitude. The Russian advance in Romania made easy progress after that country's declaration of independence from Turkey, and an advance guard under General Ossip V. Gourko crossed the Danube in late June, seizing the vital Shipka (Schipka) Pass on 19 July. This opened the way for a powerful Russian thrust into the Balkans, but the Russians halted in order to take the fortress of Plevna. The Turks were allowed to throw up defences to block a further Russian advance and the siege of Plevna dragged on. The Russians attempted to break through the enemy positions on 3 major occasions: 20 and 30 July and 11–12 September. The Turks tried to force a way out on 10 December, led by Osman Pasha, but were pushed back and Plevna capitulated immediately afterwards. The siege cost the Turks 5,000 men, and Russian casualties numbered about 2,000. Finally, after suffering defeat at the Battle of Senova south of the Shipka Pass, 8–9 January 1878, Turkey sought an armistice, signed on 31 January. Hostilities ended with the Treaty of San Stefano, 3 March; Turkey conceded the independence of Montenegro, Serbia and Romania; Bulgaria came under Russian control. The war was notable for the use of latest fire power developments which clearly aided the defence – a lesson overlooked in subsequent years despite the further example shown by the *Russo-Japanese War*.

S

Sadowa, Battle of, July 1866 *Austro-Prussian War* (Map 5). *Moltke* aimed at a classic encirclement of the enemy. He was in direct telegraphic touch with his armies, supervising operations from Berlin until travelling to the front in late June. His Austrian opponent, General von Benedek, attempted to concentrate along the upper Elbe, north of Königrätz. The Prussian 1st Army approached from the north-west, while the 2nd advanced from the east; Benedek lost his chance to strike at one before the other arrived – the Austrians took 3 days to prepare for battle, in direct contrast to Moltke's aim of concentrating on the battlefield itself. Moltke intended the 1st Army to strike from the west, while the 2nd drove south down the Elbe valley to seal retreat; the circle round the enemy would be closed by the left wing of the 2nd and the right wing of the 1st operating against the Austrian flanks and rear. The two sides were about equal in manpower: 220,000 Prussians against 190,000 Austrians and 25,000 Saxons. Austrian cavalry and artillery was superior to the Prussian, but the latter had far stronger infantry, both in terms of tactics and arms, which included the breech-loading *Dreyse* needle-gun. The Prussian 1st Army, under Prince Frederick Karl, attacked at dawn on 3 July in driving rain, but the corresponding assault by Crown Prince Frederick William's 2nd Army was delayed through a telegraph failure, and Austrian artillery checked the initial Prussian attack. Benedek failed to take advantage, and the Prussian ring grew tighter. The 2nd Army moved to attack the Austrian northern wing at 2.30 p.m., while the Prussian Guard reserve artillery battered the Austrian centre. Moltke's infantry made full use of their superior fire power and inflicted heavy casualties on the trapped Austrian regiments until Benedek ordered retreat, covered by his artillery. Moltke's plan had partly failed, but Sadowa was still a brilliant victory: Austrian casualties totalled 45,000, including 20,000 prisoners, compared with 10,000 Prussians.

St Mihiel, Battle of, September 1918 *First World War* (Map 10). German occupation of the St Mihiel salient had constituted a threat to allied movements in Champagne since 1914. In 1918 the removal of this salient formed an important preliminary to the final offensive against the *Hindenburg Line*. *Foch*, Supreme Commander, entrusted the US 1st Army under *Pershing* for this task, and the attack was launched against the two sides of the salient on 12 September, combined with an assault against the centre by French troops. The offensive was immediately successful, with troops from either side of the salient converging by nightfall on the first day. The Germans were cleared from the area by the 16th.

Salerno, allied landings at, September 1943 *Second World War* (Map 14). The assault on mainland *Italy* had begun with *Montgomery*'s successful 8th Army landings at Calabria, 3 September, on the toe of Italy. While these British troops made their way north, the main allied landings were launched at Salerno, below Naples, on the 9th. German defenders under *Kesselring* were on the alert, and the premature announcement of an Italian armistice, 8 September, allowed the Germans to disarm their former allies. Defensive positions were covered by well-sited machine-gun posts and by mobile artillery batteries; tanks from the 16th Panzer Division had been moved up to the coast. The landings, undertaken by the US 5th Army commanded by General Mark Clark and comprising the US 6th Corps and British 10th, therefore met stiff opposition: by nightfall the allies only held 4 beachheads, none of which had penetrated more than 3 miles inland. Reinforcements were rushed in. Kesselring

launched a major counter-attack on the 13th, using over 600 tanks, but the offensive was halted by a heavy naval bombardment. On the 16th the allies broke out from Salerno and joined with Montgomery's 8th Army. Allied losses at Salerno were over 15,000 men killed and wounded, German about 8,000.

SALT (Strategic Arms Limitation Talks) On 26 May 1972 President Nixon and the Soviet leaders signed two agreements to limit strategic weapons. These resulted from talks between representatives of the two countries during the preceding 4 years, largely at the instigation of *Kissinger*. The 1972 agreements, termed SALT I, were however restricted in scope. One consisted of a treaty to limit *antiballistic missile defences* (ABM), the other amounting to an interim arrangement limiting offensive strategic missiles prior to resumed negotiations (SALT II). This second agreement did not mention mobile strategic delivery systems, such as submarines and aircraft.

Sandys, Duncan Edwin, 1908– British politician. Prior to 1939 Sandys belonged to *Churchill*'s small group urging rearmament, giving full support to Churchill – his father-in-law – in warnings over likely German aggression; served with British forces in *Norway*, 1940; disabled on active service, 1941; Finance Member of Army Council, 1941–3; Under-Secretary of Supply Ministry, 1943–4. Sandys was selected by Prime Minister Churchill to chair the *War Cabinet*

Committee examining the possibilities of German secret weapons code-named 'Crossbow' – the eventual *V1 and V2*. He reported on 29 May 1943, revealing the likely existence of long-range rocket development, and he continued to insist on the danger despite doubts expressed by others, notably Churchill's scientific adviser Professor Lindeman (Lord Cherwell). Sandys acted as Minister of Works, 1944–5, and as Minister of Defence from January 1957 to October 1959. During this latter period he announced, in 1957, the decision to supplement the nuclear V-bombers force with ballistic rockets, initially through the establishment of the US Thor missile in British bases and later including the development of Britain's own missile, Blue Streak. The latter was cancelled in 1960 and eventually, after other abortive projects, Britain acquired the US *Polaris* missile. In 1957 Sandys also announced the plan to end Britain's *conscription*, National Service.

Sark and Serb missiles The former is the Soviet submarine-launched ballistic missile which first appeared in 1962; it was believed by NATO experts to be equivalent to the US *Polaris*, although with a range of only about 350 miles. By 1975 about 36 such missiles were probably deployed. Serb, first displayed in November 1967, was intended as the Sark successor: this missile, equivalent to the US Polaris A-2, probably has a range of about 750 miles. Up to 16 Serb missiles can be deployed on 1 submarine; about 60 missiles were distributed in 1975. Unlike the US *Poseidon*, neither the Sark nor the Serb has *MIRV* capability.

Scharnhorst, Gerhard Johann David von, 1755–1813 Prussian General and military reformer. Born near Hanover, and served in the Anglo-Hanoverian Army in the Netherlands, 1793; entered Prussian service, 1801; taught at military school, Berlin, becoming Director in 1804; Chief of Staff to Brunswick in 1806 campaign, fighting at *Auerstedt*, 14 October, and acting as *Blücher*'s Chief of Staff during the retreat to Lübeck; commanded Prussian Corps at *Eylau*, February 1807 (Map 1). After the Treaties of Tilsit, July 1807, Scharnhorst became Chairman of the Military Reorganization Commission, working with *Gneisenau*, *Yorck* and other generals, and helped by *Clausewitz*. His commission advocated a wider recruiting base, the admission of non-nobles into the officer corps, relaxation of harsh discipline, and the introduction of more flexible tactics. Scharnhorst was largely responsible for the implementation of these measures. He became 'de facto' War Minister, March 1809, in addition to being Chief of the General Staff; he urged hostilities against the French during Austria's abortive *Wagram* campaign, 1809. Scharnhorst was removed from the War Ministry in June 1810, following pressure from Napoleon for his dismissal, but he remained a powerful influence. He acted as chairman of a commission on tactical reforms in 1811, which introduced far more flexible tactics and drill, and he further developed the Prussian *Staff* system. Scharnhorst was engaged in diplomatic activities during Napoleon's campaign in *Russia*, 1812. He helped implement the *Landwehr* system in 1813 and acted as Blücher's Chief of Staff at the opening of the campaign against the French; he was fatally wounded at *Lützen*, 2 May, and died on 28 June. Gneisenau replaced him on Blücher's Staff.

Schlieffen, Alfred von, 1833–1913
German Marshal and Chief of General Staff. Attended War Academy, Berlin, 1858–61; staff officer during the *Austro-Prussian War*, 1866; thereafter he alternated between posts on the General Staff, headed by *Moltke* the Elder, and staff work in the field, including during the *Franco-Prussian War*. In 1891 Schlieffen became Moltke's successor. He attempted to find an answer to Germany's basic strategic problem: how to deal with war against Russia in the east and France in the west. In 1893 the Franco-Russian alliance magnified this dilemma. Moltke's recommended answer had been for Germany to conduct a defensive war in the west and an offensive campaign in the east. Schlieffen reversed this plan. A stalemate against France and protracted war against Russia, where vast plains allowed evasive tactics, would enable Britain to intervene; France must therefore be overrun in minimum time, through the encirclement of her armies, making full use of railways. Finally, in 1905, there emerged the so-

called Schlieffen Plan which was basically an embodiment of schemes drawn up by him between 1897 and 1905: Germany would only deploy one-ninth of her forces in the east against Russia; this army would attempt a limited encircling offensive when the Russian forces separated to filter round the Masurian Lakes, and then would fall back behind the Vistula fortresses. By temporarily ignoring the Russian threat, Schlieffen hoped to be able to assemble sufficient strength for the decisive offensive against the French. Rather than attempting to push through the more difficult terrain to the south, the German armies would stab against France from the north, even though this would violate Belgian neutrality and would hence probably precipitate British intervention. In his 1905 memorandum Schlieffen therefore advocated the ratio of strength between right (north) and left (south) wings being about 7 to 1, leaving south Alsace virtually unprotected. The offensive would revolve around Metz, sweeping from a line running Verdun–Dunkirk, and then swinging round Paris to throw the French against their own fortresses and the Swiss frontier. The French could attempt an offensive of their own against the weakly defended Alsace-Lorraine area, which Schlieffen considered would be indecisive and would draw further French strength from the vital area in the north. Alternatively, the French could concentrate in the north: this was indeed advocated by General Michel in 1911 but was rejected.

Instead the French *Plan XVII* was adopted, for an advance in Alsace-Lorraine. However, Schlieffen's plan was changed in the years following his retirement in 1906. His successor, *Moltke the Younger*, rightly considered that the situation had altered: Russia had gained greater strength; a French attack in Alsace-Lorraine might be more successful than Schlieffen had believed likely. Moltke still based his plans on Schlieffen's idea of a stronger German deployment against France than Russia, although he adjusted the proportion to give greater strength in the east than Schlieffen had envisaged. More drastically, Schlieffen's plan for a wheeling right wing in the west, striking via Belgium, was radically reduced. Instead of a 7 to 1 ratio, Moltke decided upon a 3 to 1 ratio between north and south, in order to block a French offensive in Alsace-Lorraine. So, in 1914, the German right wing in the north lacked strength for a complete encircling movement; the French lacked strength to overcome German opposition in the south; stalemate resulted after the Battles of the *Frontiers*. In the east, Schlieffen's concept was vindicated with the success at *Tannenberg*, August 1914.

Schwarzenberg, Prince Karl Philipp von, 1771–1820 Austrian General. Fought under Archduke John against *Napoleon* at Hohenlinden, 2 December 1800, and in *Wagram* campaign, 1809 (Map 1); commanded 40,000-man Austrian Army allied to the French in campaign in *Russia*, 1812; commanded Bohemian Army after Austria's declaration of war against France, 12 August 1813, replacing Barclay de Tolly as allied C-in-C on 17 August; defeated by Napoleon at *Dresden*, 26–27 August, but combined with other armies for Battle of *Leipzig*, 16–19 October; crossed into Switzerland, January 1814, to start advance on Paris; pushed back by *Napoleon* at Montereau, 18 February, but defeated Macdonald at Bar-sur-Aube, 27 February, and repulsed Napoleon at Arcis-sur-Aube, 20–21 March; defeated *Marmont* and Mortier at La Fère-Champenoise, 25 March; Paris surrendered, 31 March. Schwarzenberg deployed his Austrian Army along the southern Rhine during the *Waterloo* campaign, 1815.

Scorched earth Method of war whereby one combatant attempts to hinder as far as possible the movement and sustenance of the opposing force through the destruction of all available communication and supply facilities, and through the creation of maximum havoc. The policy can be employed either by a retreating force attempting to delay the invader, as a defensive tactic, or by an invading army to prevent counter-attack and to persuade the enemy from further hostilities. In the latter case the destruction serves as a demoralizing weapon threatening further devastation: the policy forms a terror tactic for deterrent purposes against both military and civilian opposition. The technique has always existed: examples from history include Saladin's attempt to delay Richard I's advance in the Third Crusade, 1192, and the devastation by the Persians of their own country in the face of Selim I's Ottoman invasion, 1515. An army living off the land, perhaps far from its bases, was especially vulnerable to such a defensive method. *Napoleon*'s Grand Army accordingly suffered acutely from the enemy's scorched earth tactics in the campaign of Russia, 1812. *Sherman* employed this means of warfare in offensive fashion during his celebrated advance through Georgia on Confederate *Atlanta*, 1864, when he received instructions from his Federal Commander, *Grant*, to 'clean the country where you go of railroad tracks and supplies. I would also move every wagon, horse, mule and hoof of stock as well as Negroes.' Sherman himself commented: 'The utter destruction of the roads, houses and people will cripple their military resources ... I can make Georgia howl.' Modern armies, whilst not living off the land to the same extent as in previous eras, are vulnerable in other ways: mechanized forces are tied to roads and railways, and such armies require a constant supply of fuel and ammunition. If this supply can be severed by retreating forces through a scorched earth policy, then the advance of the opposing army will be critically hindered. Recent examples include the Russian defensive methods used against the invading Germans in 1941. *Strategic bombing* can be seen as a form of scorched earth policy waged offensively in an attempt to deny the enemy basic resources – and also to terrorize the enemy into submission.

Scott, Winfield, 1786–1866 US General. Fought in *American War of 1812*, commanding troops which took Fort George at the mouth of the Niagara, 27 May 1813; appointed Brigadier-General and responsible for reorganization of US forces on Niagara Front, April–July 1814. Scott served on the Canadian border, 1838–9. He commanded the US Army in the *American-Mexican War*, 1846–8. After political bickering over plans for the campaign, he left Washington on 24 November 1846 and established his HQ at Tampico for an invasion of central Mexico. He took Mexico City on 13 September after a brilliant campaign. Scott was General in Chief of the US Army at the outbreak of the *American Civil War*; he advocated a harsh policy against the breakaway south, including a vigorous blockade and an invasion by 300,000 men. This scheme, the Anaconda Plan, was rejected except for the blockade. Scott retired from the Army and was succeeded by *McClellan*, 1 November 1861.

'Sealion', invasion of Britain operation, 1940–1 *Second World War* (Map 13). On 2 July, immediately after the fall of *France*, *Hitler* announced that 'a landing in England is possible, providing that air superiority can be attained and certain other necessary operations fulfilled'. No date was set; preparations would begin immediately. Opposition came from *Raeder*, head of the Navy, who urged the defeat of Britain through 'submarine warfare, air attacks on convoys and heavy air attacks on her main centres'. Yet Hitler, in Directive No. 16 issued on 16 July just after the opening of the Battle of *Britain*, declared: 'I have decided to prepare a landing operation ... and, if necessary, to carry it out.' Heading a list of essential preliminary steps was the condition that 'the English Air Force must be so reduced morally and physically that it is unable to deliver any significant attack'. Despite *Göring*'s optimism, the Luftwaffe failed to gain supremacy; the German Navy chiefs continued to argue against 'Sealion', issuing a memorandum on 29 July advising against the operation in 1940. Raeder said the weather was unpredictable and a calm sea essential; Army requirements for a broad landing front, from the Dover Straits to Lyme Bay would be impossible for the Navy to meet. Hitler decided on 31 July that preparations would still go forward, with 15 September the target date. The Germans massed an armada of vessels, including nearly 2,000 barges, in German, Belgian and French harbours. Invasion scares reached a climax on 7 September, when the British *Chiefs of Staff* announced Alert No. 1 – 'invasion imminent and probably within 12 hours'. This coincided with the beginning of the *blitz*. The new bombing campaign marked Hitler's tacit admission of defeat in the Battle of Britain, and this failure to win air supremacy meant the virtual abandonment of 'Sealion'. On 17 September Hitler postponed the operation indefinitely.

Second World War, general, 1 September 1939 to 2 September 1945 (Maps 12–16) *Aircraft* dominated warfare during this period, including *aircraft carriers* at the expense of *battleships*. Working in conjunction with the other main development, the *tank*, and with mobile infantry, aircraft provided *blitzkrieg*; working on their own, aircraft resulted in *strategic bombing*. Air superiority became essential over the battlefield; hence the importance of the Battle of *Britain* in preventing the cross-Channel invasion, '*Sealion*'. Aircraft and tanks obviated the fears of those who believed there might be a return to trench warfare: such fears nevertheless lay behind the British desire to delay the *Normandy landings* until all possible conditions had been met. Warfare had become mobile again, from the vast tank battle of *Kursk* to the sweeping *desert campaigns*, down to the tactical operations of the newly formed *commandos*, *airborne* forces, and offshoots like *Wingate*'s *Chindits*. Other developments foreshadowed the end of tank and aircraft domination: *rockets*, leading to the *V-bombs*, pointed the way to modern missiles; *atomic* warfare was introduced at *Hiroshima and Nagasaki*. Forty-four nations participated in the German war; eleven in the *Japan* war. Such a vast outpouring of manpower called forth new means of total war production and new means of control, both in the central direction of the war and in the actual combat areas. At the decision-making centres were the US *Joint Chiefs of Staff*, the British *Chiefs of Staff* and, when joined in allied discussions, the *Combined Chiefs of Staff*. The absolute commitment to war in civil and economic as well as military fields, placed a heavier responsibility than ever before on such bodies as the British *War Cabinet* and *Defence Committee*. The most senior military officers needed to be superb administrators as well as strategists – men like America's *Marshall*, *King* and *Arnold*, Britain's *Brooke*, *Dill*, *Pound* and *Portal*. This administrative requirement spread into the field: *Eisenhower* proved the prototype of the modern managerial type of Supreme Commander. Hitler's brutal daring and blitzkrieg tactics, combined with allied unpreparedness, gave him the initiative for the first $2\frac{1}{2}$ years of war: *Poland* (September 1939), *Norway* and Denmark (April 1940), *France* (June 1940). The *desert campaign* opened in North Africa, but Britain's victories against the Italians were reversed through the need for troops in *Greece* and by the simultaneous arrival in the desert of German troops under *Rommel*. The fall of Greece was followed by *Crete* in May 1941. In North Africa the war would swing to and fro until El *Alamein*, autumn 1942. This battle coincided with the turning-point of the war: in Churchill's perceptive phrase, 'the end of the beginning'. *Russia*, invaded in June 1941, was now sweeping back contrary to all expectations. The Americans had at last entered the ground war in the West with the allied '*Torch*' landings in French North Africa, November 1942. *Malta*'s siege was ending; the battle

for *Tunisia* ended in May 1943; *Sicily* fell in August; the campaign in *Italy* began at *Salerno* in September. As the allies battered at *Cassino* in early 1944 and attempted to leap forward at *Anzio*, final plans were being made for the invasion of north-west Europe. The battle for *Normandy* began on 6 June; in August a subsidiary invasion was thrown at the south of France, operation '*Anvil*'/'Dragoon'. Germany made her last attempt to break the stranglehold in the *Ardennes*: failure meant increased exhaustion; in January 1945 the final *invasion of Germany* began. Meanwhile the lonely war in the *Atlantic* and *Arctic* had been painfully won. Germany was always considered the primary enemy, a decision which made victory over *Japan* no less essential and increased the difficulties through shortage of resources. Over 15 million servicemen died in the war, including perhaps 9 million Russians, 3 million Germans, 390,000 from the British Empire, 290,000 Americans, 80,000 Italians. About 65,000 British civilians were killed, compared with 1,500 in the First World War; about 108,000 French civilians died in the fighting, 300,000 Japanese, 600,000 Germans. The total of Russian civilian dead may have reached 13 million.

Sedan, Battle of, September 1870
Franco-Prussian War (Map 6). Nearly 200,000 Prussians advanced upon the French from south, west and north. *Moltke* again attempted a battle of encirclement as he had tried against the Austrians at *Sadowa* in 1866. He

placed his massed artillery, 426 guns, in a semicircle on the heights above Sedan, where the 120,000 French under *MacMahon* had been man-oeuvred into a bend of the Meuse. The Prussian guns opened fire on 1 September. French cavalry attempted a breakout in the north-west, but this failed in the face of withering fire from the Prussian infantry's *breech-loading Dreyse* weapons. MacMahon, wounded in the opening stages of the battle, handed over command to Auguste Ducrot, who tried to organize a thrust through the Prussian lines in the south during the afternoon, but this was also beaten back. The Prussian encirclement grew tighter. Ducrot believed the position to be hopeless; he was superseded by General Em-manuel de Wimpffen, who refused to concede defeat. Prussian artillery con-tinued to inflict heavy casualties; the French Emperor Napoleon III rode out to surrender, and shortly after-wards the French forces laid down their arms. French losses during the battle amounted to about 14,000 killed and wounded, plus 21,000 prisoners: to the latter were now added a further 83,000, plus 419 guns. Prussian casualties during the battle totalled about 9,000. Now Moltke advanced on *Paris*.

Seeckt, Hans von, 1866–1936 Ger-man General. Senior Staff Officer, 1914–18; War Ministry representative on the Versailles Conference delega-tion. Seeckt became Chief of the Army Command, March 1920, in effect Chief of the General Staff. He em-barked on a policy of building a highly trained and efficient nucleus for a new German Army, capable of rapid ex-pansion once the *Versailles* treaty re-strictions had been swept aside. Due to the Versailles limitations on the size of the Army, only the best were chosen and vigorous selection proce-dures were adopted. Seeckt's stiff training programme emphasized tech-nical and weapons training, co-ordina-tion of arms, communications and mobility. The Great General Staff, abolished by the Versailles terms, re-emerged as a section of the War Ministry known as the 'Truppenamt'. Seeckt was forced to resign in October 1926 through a combination of domestic rivalry and French pressure; from 1932–5 he assisted in training Chinese nationalists in their fight against communists.

Shenandoah valley campaigns, May–June 1862; July 1864 to March 1865 *American Civil War* (Map 3). In April 1862 *Lee*, then military ad-viser to Confederate President *Davis*, urged that a demonstration should take place in the valley to draw the Union troops under *McClellan* and McDowell from their threat on Richmond. Responsible for this diversion was 'Stonewall' *Jackson*, who moved into the Alleghenies on 1 May with about 18,000 Confederates; he threw back Union troops under John Frémont on 8 March, then hurried north down the valley, threatening the rear of Mc-Dowell's 40,000-strong army con-centrating at Fredericksburg. Jackson turned on Nathaniel Banks in the last week of May, driving him back to Winchester and then across the Potomac via Harper's Ferry, 25 May. *Lincoln* ordered McDowell north from Fredericksburg. Jackson was outnumbered and withdrew south, repulsing Frémont at Cross Keys on 8 June and Union forces under James Shields at Port Republic on the 9th; he then moved over to join Lee for the 'Seven Days' Battles' leading to *Malvern Hill*, 1 July. The valley again became a major campaigning ground in July 1864, when Confederate troops under Jubal Early struck north towards Washington. Union forces under Lew Wallace were brushed aside at the Battle of Monocacy River, 9 July, and Early reached the outskirts of Washington before withdrawing. He invaded again on 23 July, defeating *Crook*'s forces at Kernstown and Winchester, and reaching as far as Chambersburg. *Grant* raised the Army of the Shenandoah to deal with this threat, placing *Sheridan* in command with orders to 'eat out Virginia clean and clear . . . so that crows flying over it for the balance of the season will have to carry their own provender'. After a hesitant start, Sheridan threw back Early at the Battle of Opequon Creek (Third Battle of Winchester) on 19 September, and again at Fisher's Hill on the 22nd. For the next 6 weeks Sheridan turned the rich valley into a desolate wilderness. Then, on 19 October, Early caught the Union Army offguard – Sheridan was absent at the time – attacking before dawn at Cedar Creek. By noon it seemed the Union Army was defeated. Sheridan

reached the battlefield after a dramatic 25-mile ride, rallied his regiments and regrouped them on the battlefield; the Union counter-attack drove the Confederates back down the valley. Both Early and Sheridan joined their respective commanders for the final stage of the siege of *Petersburg*.

Sheridan, Philip Henry, 1831–88 Union General, *American Civil War* (Map 3). Cavalry Colonel at Missionary Ridge, November 1863, during *Chattanooga* fighting; appointed by *Grant* as Union Cavalry Commander, spring 1864, raiding in the Richmond area during the *Wilderness* campaign, May; commanded Army of the Shenandoah during the *Shenandoah* valley campaign, August 1864 to March 1865; joined Grant at *Petersburg* and played a major part in the final assault. Sheridan reached *Appomattox* on 8 April to forestall *Lee*'s attempted withdrawal south. He succeeded *Sherman* as US Army Commander in 1884.

Sherman, William Tecumseh, 1820–91 Union General, *American Civil War* (Map 3). Fought at First Battle of *Bull Run*, 21 July 1861; served under *Grant* at *Shiloh* and Corinth, 6 April, 3 October 1862; sent by Grant with 40,000 men in an amphibious operation on *Vicksburg*, December 1862, but defeated at Chicksaw Bluffs, 25–29 December; acted as mobile force preventing any Confederate attempts to relieve Vicksburg, June–July 1863; fought at Lookout Mountain and Missionary

Ridge, 24–25 November, in the *Chattanooga* campaign, then relieved Knoxville. On 5 May 1864 Sherman began his celebrated march to the sea via *Atlanta*, reaching Savannah on 21 December. He moved north through the Carolinas in early 1865, reaching Goldsboro on 23 March. He succeeded Grant as US Army Commander, 1869, handing over to Sheridan on his retirement, 1884.

Shiloh, campaign and Battle of, January–April 1862 *American Civil War* (Map 3). The Confederate Commander Albert Sidney Johnston established a defensive line across Kentucky in late 1861, to block river movements on the Mississippi, Tennessee and Cumberland. In February 1862 the Union Brigadier in this area, *Grant*, launched a bold operation to split the Confederate defence. He sent gunboats up the Tennessee; these overwhelmed Fort Henry on 6 February then sailed back downstream and up the parallel Cumberland, while Grant moved overland to attack Fort Donelson held by 15,000 Confederates under Major-General John B. Floyd. A Union gunboat attack was beaten off, 14 February, and next day a Confederate infantry push almost broke through the encircling Union lines, but Grant immediately counterattacked and took the fort. Casualties were 2,832 Union troops and 16,623 Confederates. Grant pushed southeast to Nashville, supported by troops from the Army of the Ohio under Major-General Don Carlos Buell, and this town fell on 25 February.

Johnston concentrated his 40,000 troops around Corinth, about 100 miles south-west of Nashville. Grant rallied his men after a surprise Confederate attack near Shiloh on 6 April, and the exhausted Confederates were driven back by artillery and gunboat fire. Johnston was killed and succeeded by General Pierre Beauregard. During the night, 6–7 April, Buell's army reached Grant's force from Nashville, and began to be ferried across the Tennessee. Grant attacked soon after dawn on the 7th, defeating the Confederates by noon. Beauregard retreated to Corinth. On 11 July Grant was appointed to command the Army of the Tennessee; errors by his subordinate, William Rosecrans Sr, enabled the Confederates to escape at Corinth, 3–4 October. Grant then turned towards *Vicksburg*.

Shrapnell, Henry, 1761–1842 British artillery officer and ordnance developer. In 1784 he developed the artillery ammunition officially known as spherical case until it acquired his name, generally spelt without the final letter. Shrapnel consisted of a tubular canister packed with musket balls, which was detonated in the air by several consecutive fuses, thus spraying the contents over the enemy. The idea would eventually have deep influence, enabling artillery to seek out and destroy men behind defences in a way which direct fire could not accomplish. Shrapnel was first used in action by the British in the seizure of Surinam, South America, in 1804.

Sicily, allied conquest of, July–August 1943 *Second World War* (Map 14). Code-named 'Husky', this operation was preceded by the capture of the nearby island of Pantelleria, 11 June, and by a month-long bombardment of enemy air bases. On 9 July *airborne* forces were landed on Sicily, prior to an amphibious assault by *Montgomery*'s 8th Army including Canadian troops, landing in the Pozallo, Noto and Syracuse region in the south-east, and by *Patton*'s US 7th Army at Licata and Gela farther west. Beachheads were secured during the first day, and the defenders pulled back to positions in the critical Catania and Messina area in the north-east. Patton's forces thrust along the west coast and also towards the centre of the island, taking Caltanissette in the centre on 18 July and cutting off the western corner to seize Palermo on the 22nd: the US forces then split, one section moving back to take Marsala in the western tip, seized on 23 July, the other advancing in the opposite direction towards Messina, capturing Defalu on the 27th. Montgomery's 8th Army had meanwhile pushed up the east coast towards Catania. Progress in this sector slowed in the rugged region around Mount Etna; British and Canadian troops also suffered increasing casualties from malaria. Opposition was now directed by General Hans Hube. Fighting intensified as both the British and US wings tried to push forward for Messina; finally, on 11 August, the enemy began to withdraw. Evacuation was completed on 17 August with 100,000 German and Italian troops escaping to the mainland, plus 10,000 vehicles. Also on 17 August the US 3rd Division entered Messina. The allies prepared for the campaign in *Italy*.

Singapore, fall of, February 1942 *Second World War* against *Japan* (Map 16). Contingency plans for the defence of Singapore and the Malay peninsula had been discussed by the British *War Cabinet* and *Chiefs of Staff* throughout 1941: these plans included a proposed operation to move troops over the Malaya–Thai border to occupy Thai ports in the Kra Isthmus, operation 'Matador', a step which the British were reluctant to take in view of resulting violations of Thais overeignty. Instead the Japanese made surprise landings at the Kra Isthmus ports, 7 December, at the same time as the assault on *Pearl Harbor*, and began to sweep south. By 9 December the Japanese were able to operate over 150 aircraft from newly acquired Thai bases; the first air attacks on Singapore had been made the previous day, and alarming gaps in the air defences were soon revealed. By 9 December the RAF had lost 60 of the 110 aircraft for the defence of Malaya, and the Japanese acquired decisive air superiority. The RAF, despite warnings by local air commanders, had remained under-strength during previous months, with the main excuse for the failure to send more aircraft being the arrival of other valuable weapons, supposedly to make good RAF deficiencies: these alternative weapons were the capital ships 'Prince of Wales' and 'Repulse'. Both were sunk on 10 December. British troops in Malaya, mainly the 11th Division under General A. E. Percival, were steadily forced back. On 16 December the newly appointed Commander in the Far East, *Wavell*, sent a report on the defences of Singapore island, to which the British troops under Percival would soon have to withdraw: this report pointed out that existing defences had been laid down to protect the island from a naval offensive, on the assumption that mainland Malaya would still be in British hands and the RAF would still be providing air cover. Prolonged defence of the island from a land attack would be virtually impossible. Withdrawal from the mainland was completed on 31 January. Reinforcements arrived, but these would have to be pushed direct into action after weeks of dulling sea voyage and with inappropriate training. On 8 February the Japanese invasion began; within 24 hours the enemy had penetrated about 5 miles inland. By 13 February the Japanese were within 5,000 yards of the seafront and had captured the vital water supply. Next day *Churchill* wired permission for surrender; Percival did so later on the 14th. British losses were about 90,000 men captured and 35,000 killed or wounded during the campaign; Japanese casualties numbered about 10,000.

Sinop(e), Battle of, November 1853
Crimean War (Map 4). While British and French warships converged on Constantinople in an attempt to en-courage the Turks, the Russian Admiral Paul S. Nakimov moved against Turkish naval forces in the Black Sea, catching the enemy at the Turkish naval base of Sinop on 30 November. The Russian Fleet, comprising 6 ships of the line, 3 frigates and other smaller craft, immediately attacked the enemy flotilla in the harbour; this included 7 frigates, 3 corvettes and 2 small steamers, commanded by Admiral Hussein Pasha. A 6-hour engagement followed, in which the Russians used shell guns based on the *Paixhans* design; the battle underlined the transformation in naval warfare brought about by this type of ordnance: the Turkish flotilla was totally destroyed.

Skirmishing Battlefield tactics in the eighteenth century included only a minor role for skirmishing troops. Rather than flexible fire power through light infantrymen, the European armies relied upon massive controlled volleys fired from troops in rigid *close order* formation. The American Revolution, 1775–83, indicated that skirmishers should be given a more important role, but the effectiveness of the American *riflemen* was largely ignored by most European nations. The French *tirailleurs* of the Revolutionary Wars marked an abrupt change from the prevailing tactics: these skirmishers acted independently ahead of the main French *columns* to disrupt the enemy and to make use of flexible, enveloping methods. Implications spread beyond the battlefield: skirmishers, being allowed to use their own initiative, contrasted sharply with the restrictions imposed on infantrymen moving in close order – the latter were expected to behave almost like robots. Conservatives argued that it might be disastrous to permit greater freedom of thought to troops of the line: they might become insubordinate, not only in the army but in society as a whole. Liberals argued in exactly the opposite fashion. Thus the Prussian Dietrich Adam von Bülow declared that the old linear tactics were the 'tactics of serfs'; he argued for 'human' against 'clockwork' methods. Prussia largely resisted change until after the catastrophic defeats of the *Auerstedt* campaign which underlined the extreme vulnerability of close order troops in the face of latest fire power; Prussia therefore began to make greater use of light infantrymen, called Jäger and Schützen, until by 1813 nearly one-third of the 46 Prussian infantry battalions under arms comprised these troops. The development of skirmishing progressed parallel to that of *riflemen*. During the *Peninsular War*, *Wellington* introduced an extra company of riflemen to each of his brigades, to reinforce the 3 light companies which had become standard in the British brigade. The separate Rifle Brigade came into existence in 1816. Tactics continued to grow more flexible during the nineteenth century, although still retaining a linear basis until the advent of mechanized warfare in the twentieth century.

Skoda, Emil von, 1839–1900 Czech engineer and armaments manufac-turer; founded Skoda Works in Pilsen, 1866, which he developed into a famous factory for development and manufacture of military equipment. The Skoda Works specialized in large artillery pieces. Emil's son Karl (1879–1929) was Director of the company from 1909.

Slim, Sir William Joseph, 1st Viscount, 1891–1970 British Field-Marshal. Served in First World War; served in Sudan and Syria at outbreak of Second World War before moving to *Burma* (Map 16); assumed command of Burma Corps, March 1942, during early Japanese advance and, under *Alexander*, extricated his troops in a brilliant withdrawal during May; commanded 14th Indian Division during 1943, under *Wavell*, attacking into Arakan. In October 1943 all allied ground forces operating against the Japanese in Burma from India were grouped into the 14th Army under Slim, himself under *Mountbatten* as Supreme Allied Commander South-East Asia; Slim was therefore responsible for the ground direction of the reconquest of Burma. This was highlighted by the victory at Imphal in late 1944, by Slim's skilled crossing of the Irrawaddy in February 1945, and by the capture of Mandalay in March. Slim was CIGS, 1948–52, thereafter being Governor-General and C-in-C Australia until 1960.

Smokeless powder Battlefields in the *Napoleonic Wars* were swathed in thick smoke from the guns, caused by the explosive mixture used. The effect was often to reduce visibility to a few yards, hampering the commander's control over his men and his handling of the battle. The smoke also obscured the artillery targets, thus cutting down the effective range. This situation remained until the advent of smokeless powders in the 1890s. These powders were developed from nitrocellulose, or guncotton, and nitroglycerine, both discovered in 1846. The latter was manufactured by *Nobel* from 1862 and from 1867 was absorbed in porous material as dynamite, but was still unsuitable for use in firearms since these high explosives (HE) were extremely liable to shatter the guns. Development therefore continued using nitrocellulose alone, as manufactured by *Vieille* in 1886 and by Nobel in 1887–8. The French Army was the first to adopt a smokeless powder, using Vieille's Poudre B which gave an accurate rifle range of up to 1,000 yards. Further research by Nobel led to cordite, easier to handle and more powerful than Poudre B.

Smuts, Jan Christiaan, 1870–1950 South African General and statesman. Smuts conducted negotiations with the British during early 1899, aimed at obtaining time for the South African Republic to prepare for war against Britain: and the *Boer War* began in October 1899 with a well-planned Boer offensive. He thereafter served as a local commander, leading Boer forces in the Cape area, 1901–2. After the war Smuts played a large part in the establishment of the Union of South Africa. He helped Prime

Minister Louis Botha to suppress an extremist uprising led by Christiaan De Wet against the Union, 1914–15; in 1916 he was appointed to command British troops fighting Germans in British East Africa. He acted as South African representative in the Imperial War Cabinet, 1917–18, and he attended the Paris Peace Conference with Botha. Smuts was Prime Minister of the Union of South Africa, 1919–24, Minister of Justice, 1933–9, Prime Minister 1939–48.

Snider, Jacob, ?–1866 US firearms inventor. His Snider rifle was adopted in 1865 as the first general-issue *breech-loading rifle* for the British Army. The standard muzzle-loading *Enfield* was converted to the Snider breech mechanism; the weapon became even more effective with the introduction of Colonel Boxer's centre-fire *percussion* cartridge, 1867. The Snider remained the basic British breech-loader until the introduction of the *Martini-Henry*, 1871.

Somerville, Sir James Fownes, 1882–1949 British Admiral. Served in First World War. Retired in 1939 through ill-health, but returned to active service in early 1940 as Commander of the Mediterranean Fleet based at Gibraltar. He was obliged to attack the French Fleet at Oran, July 1940, when the French refused to allow these vessels to come over to the allies or sail beyond German reach. Somerville was responsible for the continued attempts to take supplies to *Malta*. He played an important part in the sinking of the 'Bismarck', May 1941, by moving his warships north from the Mediterranean to intercept. He was appointed Commander of the Eastern Fleet in April 1942, taking part in the capture of Vichy-French Madagascar, September–November, aimed at forestalling the establishment of Japanese bases. Somerville was appointed head of the British naval delegation to Washington, August 1944.

Somme, First Battle of, June–November 1916 *First World War* (Map 10). The battle began on 24 June with a 7-day bombardment, after plans had been delayed by the German offensive at *Verdun*. *Joffre*'s aim was for *Rawlinson*'s 4th British Army to push north of the Somme, with *Allenby*'s 3rd Army to his left; south of the Somme, *Foch*'s Army Group of the North would undertake a holding attack. The advance began on 1 July; by nightfall the British had lost about 60,000 men, 19,000 of them dead – the greatest 1-day loss in the history of the British Army. The attack continued, and a night offensive on 13 July cracked the German line. Cavalry charged into the gap, pushing back troops under General Fritz von Below, but reserves were slow to arrive and the cavalrymen were slaughtered: this was the last large-scale use of cavalry in western Europe. On 15 September *Haig*, BEF Commander, launched another major offensive south-west of Baupaume in the centre of the line, spearheaded by tanks – the first time this weapon had been used in signifi-

cant numbers. Out of 47 tanks brought to the front, only 11 were engaged, and these proved underpowered. They nevertheless helped push the line forward: at its deepest this had now advanced about 5 miles from the 1 July starting point. The battle came to an end on 18 November. British casualties totalled 420,000, French 195,000, yet the Germans suffered even worse – about 650,000.

Somme, Second Battle of, March 1918 *First World War* (Map 10). The Somme was chosen by the *Hindenburg–Ludendorff* partnership as the area for the first of the German offensives in 1918, launched to gain a decisive victory before US entry reached crippling proportions. The German High Command hoped to drive a wedge between the allied armies: the French, under *Pétain*, would be concerned with the defence of Paris, while the British under *Haig* would be primarily concerned with covering their communications to the Channel ports. Ludendorff also intended to use the *Hutier* infiltration tactics: spearheading the attack would be special *stormtroopers*. The offensive began on 21 March under cover of heavy fog; the attack spread over a 60-mile front, with the German 17th, 2nd and 18th Armies striking against the British. Hutier himself commanded the 18th Army, and his tactics proved successful against the thinly-spread British 5th Army under General Sir Matthew Gough, but the British 3rd under General J. H. G. Byng managed to hold the German 17th and

2nd after a limited withdrawal. Haig appealed to the French for help, without receiving adequate response. Hutier forced across the Somme, and on 23 March the Germans began a long-range bombardment of Paris from a distance of about 65 miles. For this barrage the Germans used the so-called Paris Gun, eventually 7 in number. These are often confused with the famous Big Berthas, notorious in the history of *artillery*, and they were in fact probably designed by the same man, Professor Rausenberger of Krupp's. The Paris Gun was a 38-cm naval gun given a 21-cm calibre through the addition of an inner tube: the latter projected beyond the parent weapon and was extended by a 6-metre smooth-bore tube, providing a 130-foot barrel in all which was heavily braced. The shell weighed 264 pounds, containing a 400-pound powder charge: it was estimated that one gun would only be able to fire 60 rounds before the barrel became too worn. The bombardment of Paris lasted until 9 August: 183 shells landed on the city and 120 outside, killing 256 people and wounding 620. Civilians adapted well to the barrage, retaining excellent morale and in fact becoming even more determined. On 26 March *Foch* was appointed co-ordinator for the Western Front, and was further elevated to the status of Supreme Commander on 3 April. The German drive lost momentum: shortages of supplies stopped a further advance, combined with a lack of mobile units to exploit the breakthrough. The British suffered over 160,000 casualties during the

offensive: Gough was relieved and the remains of the 3rd Army incorporated into *Rawlinson*'s 4th. French casualties numbered about 77,000, German about 200,000. Hindenburg and Ludendorff nevertheless had already begun the next offensive, in the *Lys-Aisne* sector of Flanders on 9 April.

Soult, Nicolas Jean de Dieu, Duke of Dalmatia, 1769-1851 French Marshal. Soult established his reputation during the Swiss campaign of 1799, serving under *Masséna*, under whom he also served during the defence of Genoa in the 1800 campaign in *Italy*. He fought at *Austerlitz* (Map 1), 1804, as a Corps Commander, at Jena in the *Auerstedt* campaign, 1806, at Pultusk, December 1806, *Eylau*, February 1807, and in the remainder of the *Friedland* campaign (Map 1). He commanded French forces in north Spain, 1808, during the *Peninsular War*, pursuing the British under Moore to *Corunna* (Map 1). He remained in the Peninsula until final defeat in 1814. Soult acted as War Minister under Louis XVIII, December 1814 to March 1815, but transferred his allegiance back to *Napoleon*, acting as his Senior Staff Officer in the *Waterloo* campaign. He lived in exile, 1815-19, but returned to France in 1820; he was War Minister 1830-4, 1840-4.

Spaatz, Carl, 1891– US General and Air Commander. Joined Army, 1914, transferring to Army Air Section, 1915; Commanding General US Army Air Forces, European Theatre,

1942–3, based in East Anglia; in February 1943 he was appointed Commander of the North-West African Air Force in *Tunisia*, remaining Mediterranean Commander for the subsequent *Sicily* and *Italy* operations. In January 1944 Spaatz became C-in-C of the US Strategic (Bombing) Air Forces, North-West Europe, supervising the massive *strategic bombing* raids; in March 1945 he became Commander of US Strategic Air Forces in the Pacific. Spaatz was Chief of Staff, *US Air Force*, 1947–8.

Spanish Civil War, 1936–9 (Map 11) The resignation of dictator Primo de Rivera (1870–1930) in January 1930, who had assumed authority in 1923 after a bloodless revolution, was followed by a series of disturbances in Spain combined with changes in leadership. The upheaval resulted in the election of a leftist coalition on 16 February 1936, under Manuel Azaña; unrest and tension continued. On 18 July the garrisons in 12 cities in Spain and 5 in Spanish Morocco revolted simultaneously, and *Franco* flew from the Canary Islands to take command of the mutineers. In late July he advanced north towards Madrid, moving via Badajoz with 30,000 regular troops, among them men of his Spanish *Foreign Legion*; other rebel troops, about 15,000 men under General Emilio Mola, moved south on the capital from Burgos. Involvement by outside nations began, with the Russians sending aid to the communist 'Loyalists' (republicans) and with Germany and Italy assisting the

Nationalists under Franco. German assistance, eventually numbering about 6,000 servicemen and just over 60,000 non-combatants, soon received the title of the *Condor Legion*. Italian participation included infantry and light tanks. Russian aid covered air force personnel, artillery, tanks and general military advisers. Other participants included 'volunteer brigades' formed internationally to help the Loyalists: 12 such groups were eventually created. Both sides attempted to unify their scattered elements during early autumn 1936. On 4 September a Loyalist government was formed at Madrid under Francisco Largo Caballero; in October Franco was officially appointed leader of the Nationalists. His forces steadily converged on Madrid, laying siege to the city on 6 November – this would last for 2 years, 4 months. The Loyalist government established new headquarters at Valencia, leaving the defences of Madrid under General José Miaja. Russian assistance played an important part in the continuing survival of the Loyalists in the city, including dive-bomber support in the defeat of an Italian attack launched March 1937. This offensive, aimed at Guadalajara north-east of Madrid in an attempt to isolate the city, failed dismally. But a Loyalist offensive from Madrid, attempted July 1937, was thrown back. Elsewhere Franco's Nationalists gradually gained control of the countryside and major cities, investing Bilbao on 1 April 1937 and taking this northern centre on 18 June. The Loyalists, under Juan Negrín after the fall of Caballero on 17

May, came under increasing pressure. Outside powers tried to limit the conflict: a non-intervention committee was established in London, and 29 nations, including Italy and Germany, attempted to patrol the Spanish Coast to prevent outside supplies. The Loyalists received increased sympathy and support after the bombing of the Basque town of *Guernica*, 26 April. Three days later Franco's troops swept into the rubble of this town and also occupied nearby Durango. The danger was always present of a full-scale intervention by foreign powers: a Loyalist air strike against the German battleship 'Deutschland' at Ibiza, May 1937, resulted in a Luftwaffe attack on Almería, 31 May; submarine attacks off Oran on the German cruiser 'Leipzig', 15 and 18 June, allegedly by Loyalists, led to Germany and Italy refusing to continue their participation in the international naval patrol. The French President, Léon Blum, made a renewed call for non-intervention on 1 August. After a series of submarine attacks, probably launched by the Italians, against ships carrying supplies to the Loyalists, a conference at Nyon in September resulted in the establishment of an Anglo-French naval patrol: this was authorized to attack any submarine, surface vessel or warship illegally attacking a non-Spanish vessel. Meanwhile, the fighting in Spain approached stalemate after Loyalists failed to swing the war in their favour despite offensives in early 1938. Franco's troops now held most of Spain, but Madrid continued to be undefeated. Finally, in December 1938 the Nationalists began a widespread campaign; Barcelona fell to Franco on 26 January 1939; the Loyalist cause seemed hopeless. France and Britain at last recognized Franco, 27 February. Madrid surrendered on 28 March. The war, which cost over 115,000 lives in battle, executions and air raids, revealed the full potential of latest weapons, especially aircraft. The message was, however, often misinterpreted. Publicity given to the air raid horrors of Guernica and Madrid apparently confirmed the writing of air theorists like *Douhet* and *Mitchell*, reinforcing the belief that future wars could be won by massive air bombardment. Yet supporters of air power overlooked the fact that Madrid had survived for 28 months, despite the almost total lack of Loyalist means of retaliation.

Special Air Service (SAS) Formed in North Africa, 1942, by Major David Stirling, Scots Guards, and intended for deep-penetration raids and sabotage behind enemy lines; the name was a cover for this purpose. Groups were small and highly mobile, equipped with Jeep vehicles and Vickers, Browning, Thompson and Bren guns. They proved successful in destroying German and Italian aircraft on the ground. Stirling himself was captured in *Tunisia*, 1943. An SAS airborne brigade was formed in 1944 for working behind the lines in Europe, comprising 1 Belgian, 2 British and 2 French battalions. The SAS green beret was adopted by the US *Special Forces*. Both the Belgian and British

Armies retained the SAS force after the war. The British SAS Regiment, split into three or four groups, remained highly active in missions to various parts of the world. Volunteers are selected from the regular army regiments for short-term SAS service, after which they return to their units; operations have been undertaken in Borneo, during the *Malaysian–Indonesian* hostilities, in *Cyprus*, *Aden*, *Ireland*, and in the Persian Gulf. In 1974-5 SAS personnel were acting as 'advisers' in Dhofar, the south-west province of Oman.

Special Forces, US, known as the Green Berets Élite force based on the British Special Air Service, SAS, trained for special penetration, raiding and counter-insurgency operations; selected from closely-vetted volunteers. The Green Berets operated extensively in *Vietnam*, where they were based in special camps notably in the central highland area. Part of their mission was to train local tribesmen in guerrilla tactics; they also carried out intelligence missions, closely coordinated with the Central Intelligence Agency (CIA). In 1969 the US Army announced that charges of murder and conspiracy to murder were being made against Green Beret officers in Vietnam, including the Commander, Colonel Robert Rheault, following the alleged murder of a Vietnamese; the charges were later dropped on the grounds that the CIA was refusing 'in the interests of national security' to make witnesses available.

Special Operations Executive (SOE) *Second World War*. Established after a meeting on 1 July 1940, chaired by *Churchill*, to overcome duplication between various government departments aimed at 'undermining the enemy' through propaganda and sabotage. The SOE was formed under Hugh Dalton, head of the Ministry of Economic Warfare. Dalton worked closely with the *Chiefs of Staff*, who agreed that the SOE should be responsible for offensive subversive activities which did not involve the use of officers or men wearing uniform. The main area of SOE activities was in the occupied European countries: Poland, Belgium, Holland – where the espionage network was infiltrated by the Germans, France – where a famous SOE agent was Odette Sansom – and in the Balkans.

Square Basic infantry formation on the battlefield until the tremendous increase in fire power during the nineteenth century rendered such positions too vulnerable. The sides of each infantry battalion square were three or more ranks deep, with the artillery usually placed at each corner and with the cavalry sheltering in the centre. The outer rank of infantrymen knelt with bayonets angled upwards: these bayonets, combined with the massed volleys from infantrymen behind, offered excellent defence against enemy *cavalry* charges; a well-disciplined, intact square could be virtually impregnable against such attacks. But the compact square offered an easy target for artillery; nor could an infantry volley be as great as with the line formation when all men faced the front. The essence of infantry drill therefore consisted of being able to move rapidly from line to square formation and vice versa.

Staff system Development progressed on two related levels: staff officers working with the regiments in the field, and a central organization on the General Staff level. As armies increased in size the commanding general could no longer deal directly with all the principal administration. Staff officers therefore became essential, handling the problems of supply organization, transmission of orders, manpower returns and general administration. On a higher level, staff officers could help prepare operational plans and could join with the commander in decision-making: the office of Chief of Staff became increasingly important. *Scharnhorst* reorganized the Institution for the Young Officers, Berlin, a military school founded in 1763 by Frederick the Great; this establishment was reopened in May 1810 as the 'Allgemeine Kriegschule' (General War School). *Clausewitz* was one of the lecturers. With common instruction, doctrines and outlook, the staff officers could be dispersed throughout the Army to provide continuity of policy. Thus the period 1813–15 saw a number of effective partnerships in the Prussian Army between chiefs of staff and their respective commanders: *Blücher* was ably assisted by Scharn-

horst and then *Gneisenau*; the military reformer Hermann von Boyen worked with General Frederick von *Bülow*; Clausewitz acted as Chief of Staff to General Walmoden and then General Thielmann. Napoleon also had a Chief of Staff, with this position filled by Louis Alexandre *Berthier* 1808–14 and by *Soult* in 1815, but the French leader used this officer more as a secretary than a partner. *Wellington* also took insufficient advantage of the opportunities offered: his staff work was shared amongst a Military Secretary, the Adjutant-General and the Quartermaster-General. The Prussians continued to lead development: Helmuth von *Moltke* (Moltke the Elder) was responsible for increasing the prestige of the Chief of General Staff after he assumed this office in 1857. He trained staff officers in his own image, selecting twelve special pupils a year from the Berlin War Academy and supervising their instruction with ruthless efficiency. After training, they were dispatched to various parts of the Army; the resulting cohesion played a major part in Moltke's success in the *Franco-Prussian War*. Britain and America still hesitated to follow Prussia's example. Improvements were, however, introduced on the lower regimental or army corps level. In England, the Staff College was established at Camberley in 1858, based on the Royal Military College which had existed at Farnham since the beginning of the century. The Russian equivalent was the Nicholas General Staff Academy, St Petersburg; France's St Cyr college, founded in

1648, was gradually modernized. Developments in America followed the reorganization by *Root*: the War College was formally instituted in 1901 and the General Staff was created by the Dick Act of 1903. The creation of a high-level British General Staff came after the recommendations of the *Esher* Committee, January 1904. The post of Chief of the General Staff – Chief of the Imperial General Staff (CIGS) after 1907 – was established; at the same time the old post of Commander-in-Chief of the Army, traditionally closely linked to the monarch, was abolished, the last incumbent being *Roberts*. The Second World War saw the dramatic growth in importance of the British *Chiefs of Staff* Committee and the US *Joint Chiefs of Staff*.

Stalin, Joseph, real name Joseph Djugashvili, 1879–1953 Soviet dictator. Joined the Bolsheviks, 1903; imprisoned 1913–17, freed with the start of the *Russian Revolution* and became a close assistant to *Lenin*; member of the revolutionary military council, 1921–3. Between 1925 and 1928 Stalin was engaged in a bitter leadership struggle with *Trotsky*, amongst others, from which he emerged as virtual dictator. He embarked on an ambitious programme of rapid industrialization and collectivization of agriculture, during which he sought stability in foreign affairs, signing non-aggression pacts with Poland and France, 1932, and Italy, 1933. At the same time Stalin sought to maintain the support of the Soviet Army by reducing political interference. The reaction came in Stalin's purges of the Army, begun in mid-1937: an estimated 3 out of the 5 marshals, 13 out of 15 army commanders, 57 out of 85 corps commanders, 110 out of 195 divisional commanders and 220 out of 406 brigade commanders were removed from office, many being executed. This had a severe debilitating effect on the Army, shown by the inadequate performance in the *Russo-Finnish War*, 1940, and lack of military preparedness had already prompted Stalin's effort to avert or delay hostilities with Germany through the non-aggression pact of August 1939. The Red Army had still to recover from the purge when Hitler's campaign in Russia began in June 1941. Stalin remained in tight control during the subsequent struggle, as C-in-C, Commissar for Defence and Chairman of the Council of People's Commissars. As soon as possible he subdued military heroes who might otherwise have become rivals: the removal of *Zhukov* from the Berlin Command, 1946, marked his policy of pushing the Army into the background.

Stalingrad, Battle and siege of, August 1942 to February 1943 *Second World War* (Map 15). Hitler's invasion of *Russia* reached its climax in the summer of 1942. German forces, pushed back from Moscow, were concentrated on Stalingrad further south. Troops from the German 6th Army, under General Frederick von Paulus, thrust into the city during September. Then, on 19 November, the Red Armies launched a sudden counter-attack; this comprised the Stalingrad Front in the south and the Voronezh, South-West and Don Fronts in the north. Trapped inside the pincer was Paulus's 6th Army; the rest of the German Army Group B reeled back. Hitler ordered Paulus to stand fast; a relief force under Manstein pushed to within 35 miles and was then beaten back. Paulus stayed; an escape-bid would probably have failed anyway – fuel for the 6th Army was now extremely limited. The Luftwaffe could only drop 70 tons of supplies a day, at the most; this help dwindled as the main German front line was gradually forced west. Paulus surrendered on 2 February 1943: 93,000 Germans went into captivity. But the stand at Stalingrad had helped the remainder of the Army Group B to withdraw.

Stark, Harold Raynsford, 1880–1972 US Admiral. Chief of Naval Operations, 1939 to March 1942. As holder of the latter post Stark was a member of the US *Joint Chiefs of Staff* and the Anglo-US *Combined Chiefs of Staff*. His views found ready acceptance with British planners. His memorandum on US National Defense Policy, known as Plan D and submitted in November 1941, recommended that if America entered the war there should be an offensive war in the west against Germany and a defensive war in the Far East against Japan. Stark supported the British policy of full-scale operations in North Africa, even at the risk of delaying a cross-Channel invasion into Europe. Stark was succeeded by *King* in March

1942 and thereafter commanded US naval forces in the European Theatre of Operations.

Steam power, naval The earliest steamboat was probably constructed in America by James Rumsey in 1775: this used a form of water-jet propulsion rather than making use of the paddle wheel. The latter means of propulsion was utilized in subsequent steamboats, for example in the first steam-propelled armoured ship, the 'Fulton', built in 1813 by Robert Fulton in America. The Royal Navy at first condemned such vessels as 'tea kettles' and continued to discuss the idea even after John *Ericsson*'s screw propeller, introduced in 1836, made possible a much more efficient system than the paddle-wheel. Even by 1840 there were only 29 steamers out of 239 vessels in Royal Naval commission. Yet naval machine propulsion provided new vigour and speed, reduced reliance on the weather, and injected far more flexibility into naval operations. At the same time the necessity of keeping fleets supplied with fuel acted as a tether: the battle fleets became more dependent upon bases, thus tending to introduce a more defensive-minded strategy. The Royal Navy solved the problem of fuel supply by establishing coaling points in a chain around the world, as for example Aden, yet these stations had also to be defended and the search for secure bases was liable to precipitate conflict.

Stilwell, Joseph, 1883–1946 US General. Served in France, 1917–18;

spent many of the inter-war years in China acquiring wide knowledge of the struggle between nationalists under *Chiang Kai-shek* and communists under *Mao Tse-tung*. From March 1942 Stilwell acted as Chief of Staff to Chiang. The China–Burma–India Command was created in July 1942, under Stilwell's command, making him responsible for the flow of aid to China and also for US and Chinese troop operations in India and Burma, although with the latter he operated under British control (Map 16). This meant that Stilwell had to obey directives from the US *Joint Chiefs of Staff*, from Chiang, and from the British Commander in India. The complicated system ran into difficulties, partly through the unrealistic division of responsibilities and partly through 'Vinegar Joe' Stilwell's own character. His relations with Chiang deteriorated, with the Chinese leader supporting *Chennault*'s demand that his supplies for the air struggle in China should have priority over the other air-lifted resources. Stilwell's position was further confused in October 1943, when *Mountbatten* was appointed Supreme Commander South-East Asia: Stilwell became Deputy Supreme Commander and thus senior to *Slim* in this respect – but Slim was senior to Stilwell as Commander of the Ground Forces. Japanese pressure against the Chinese during 1944 finally broke relations between Chiang and Stilwell: Chiang refused to accept his advice and demanded his recall. Roosevelt reluctantly replaced Stilwell with General Albert [Wedemeyer, 18 October 1944.

Stimson, Henry Lewis, 1867–1950 US statesman. Secretary of War, 1911–13; served in France, 1917–18; Governor-General Philippines, 1927–9; US Secretary of State, 1929–33. Stimson returned to the office of War Secretary in 1940, under *Roosevelt*, remaining in this position until 1945. He argued strongly for an early cross-Channel invasion attempt and condemned Mediterranean operations as a 'dispersion debauch'. In 1945 Stimson presented the case to *Truman* for using the *atomic* bomb against Japan.

Stormtroopers In 1918 the Germans employed specially trained groups of men as part of the *Hutier* infiltration tactics. The groups were known as stormtroops – 'Sturmabteilung' (SA) – ordered to bypass enemy strong points in the trench defensives and sweep behind the opposing lines. The spirit of the SA continued in the 1920s as an élite force semi-independent of the main German Army, the Reichswehr. By the mid-1930s a deep rivalry had grown up between the Army and the SA; *Hitler*, to eradicate the growing power of the SA and also to commit the Reichswehr close to his nazi cause, turned against the Sturmabteilung in the 'Night of the Long Knives'. After this purge, 30 July 1934, the SA sank into relative insignificance. Another body took over the élite stormtrooper role: the 'Schutzstaffen' (SS). This organization had begun in April 1925 as a small bodyguard to protect Hitler; it was greatly expanded as a reward for the part played in the 30 July purge and also to keep the Army under surveillance and control. In 1940 SS units received the title Waffen – armed – and eventually numbered 38 divisions, totalling 600,000 men under Heinrich Himmler. Members acquired a reputation for brutality and extreme nazism similar to that of the Gestapo, the Prussian Secret State Police formed under Göring.

Strategic Air Command (SAC) First-line US strategic bomber force created in 1946 under General George Kenney. SAC grew rapidly in importance and size under General Curtis LeMay, who succeeded Kenney in 1948: the manpower total of 45,000 rose to 200,000 by the close of the 1950s. SAC was the prime US instrument of nuclear deterrence, and became especially prominent after the '*massive retaliation*' speech by *Dulles*, 1954. The main SAC aircraft in the early and mid-1950s were the giant B-36 six-engined propeller bomber, followed by the B-47 Stratojet which flew for the first time in December 1947, the B-58 Hustler – which took SAC over the speed of sound in the late 1950s – and the Boeing B-52 Stratofortress. The first B-52 flew in October 1952 and numerous versions followed for both strategic bombing and reconnaissance roles. The B-52 was used extensively in *Vietnam* and remains the backbone of SAC aircraft strength: in 1976 SAC had 463 bombers, all of which were B-52s

except for 66 FB-111s. In 1976 SAC also had a *missile* armoury of 1,054 ICBMs, mainly Minuteman 2 and 3 missiles plus a small number of Titan 2s. In 1962 the claim was made that SAC managed 85 per cent of the free world's megatonnage, and this figure is probably still valid. Operating from Colorado, Nebraska, SAC is the principal instrument in the Western strategic nuclear deterrent despite restrictions imposed by *SALT* – Strategic Arms Limitation Talks.

Strategic bombing, offensive against Germany *Second World War* (Map 13). *Douhet* and *Mitchell* believed bombers would play the dominating role in the next conflict. Such convictions, fully supported by Britain's *Trenchard* and apparently backed by the experiences of the *Spanish Civil War*, led to the belief that no defence existed against the bomber: it was assumed that each ton of HE dropped on a city would cause 50 casualties, and that massive areas would be devastated. During the greater part of the Second World War the bomber was the only weapon which could strike direct against Germany; this bolstered the argument of those who believed that these precious aircraft should be used against the German homeland, opposed by those who thought they would be better employed against German forces in the field: the argument was further crystallized between 'area' bombing advocates, i.e. a blanket 'blitz' to saturate cities, or 'strategic' bombing against specific targets linked to the enemy war effort. Further contro-versy, between the British and US lines of thought, centred on whether daylight or night raids should be carried out; the latter, as urged by the British, offered more protection for the bombers, but implied area rather than pinpoint bombing of specific targets through the navigational re-strictions involved. *Portal* presented a paper on bombing policy to the *Defence Committee* in January 1941, urging a major effort to destroy Germany's oil resources by striking at the synthetic oil plants. Eden, the Foreign Secretary, opposed the plan because the German people would be largely unaffected; *Churchill* also believed population centres should be attacked. In the event Portal's plan was adopted and remained the bomb-ing policy during early 1941, but bad weather plus high aircraft losses meant results were well below expecta-tions. In May 1941, Churchill received a powerful paper from Trenchard, urging a massive onslaught on German morale by bombing population centres. Acting on this paper and on new ad-vice from economic experts that the German transportation system should be attacked, the COS submitted fresh recommendations to the Defence Committee on 25 June: Britain should have separate short- and long-term policies, directing bombers against the transportation system in the short term and, when sufficient force became available, undertaking 'the direct attack on the morale of the German people'. These recommendations were embodied in a directive dated 9 July.

Some 10,000 sorties were flown during the period July–September, but al-though up to 12,000 tons of bombs were dropped the effect was un-spectacular. In February 1942, Sir Arthur 'Bomber' Harris became Chief of RAF Bomber Command. His ad-vocacy of full-scale bombing of Ger-man population centres received powerful support from Churchill's scientific adviser, Lord Cherwell – formerly Professor Lindeman. He addressed a memorandum to Churchill in March, declaring:

> Over 22 million Germans live in 58 towns of over 100,000 inhabi-tants . . . Our forecast output of heavy bombers, including Wellingtons, between now and the middle of 1943 is about 10,000. If even half the total load of 10,000 bombers were dropped on the built-up areas of these 58 German towns the great majority of the inhabitants . . . would be turned out of house and home.

The RAF began a full-scale offensive against German cities with a raid on Cologne, 30 May 1942, striking Essen 2 nights later with equal force. But by the autumn of 1942 Bomber Command losses had climbed to the unacceptable rate of 5·3 per cent, mainly through efficient German night-fighters. The number of raids was reduced, but air-craft strength in each operation was increased: the highly skilled Pathfinder Force was used in a 'follow-my-leader' technique to locate and mark the target. Meanwhile the US 8th Air Force began operating from British airfields in early summer 1942. Contrary to the British policy of area bombing by night, the Americans entered the European war with the firm view that specific industries and services were the most promising targets, and that if these were to be hit accurately, the attacks had to be made in daylight. Under the management of the US Chief of Air Staff, *Arnold*, this policy included the use of heavily armed B-17 Flying Fortresses, which, if flown in sufficient strength, were believed to carry sufficient protection of their own without the need for fighter protection – the targets being outside fighter range from Britain. By August 1943 the US 8th Air Force was ready to begin large-scale operations. Chosen for attack were the ballbearing factories at Schweinfurt and Regensburg: a series of raids began on 17 August and lasted until October. Production at the factories was seriously hindered, with output dropping to 35 per cent of the pre-war level, but the Germans had already begun to establish new factories elsewhere. Moreover, the US attempt to fly daylight raids without fighter protection proved extremely costly: in a raid on 14 October 62 aircraft were lost and 138 damaged, out of 228. Daylight penetration raids of this kind were sharply reduced for the remainder of 1943; moreover, production at the target factories soon rose again. Nor had the RAF raids achieved decisive success. Numbered among the British targets were German aircraft plants: in response to the RAF raids the Germans began a more vigorous programme of subdividing

and dispersing the aircraft industry. RAF attacks continued, with 3,636 tons of bombs dropped in the last week of February 1944, yet during 1944 the German Air Force is estimated to have accepted a total of 29,807 aircraft of all types, compared with 8,295 in 1939 and 15,596 in 1942. In addition to these raids, Bomber Command had begun to concentrate on Berlin, starting with a major raid on 18 November 1943. US aircraft joined in, largely abandoning pinpoint bombing, and raids increased after the arrival of the P51 Mustang, which gave excellent high-speed long-range fighter protection. Between 18 November 1943 and 31 March 1944 over 20,200 sorties were flown against the German capital. Yet area bombing failed to lead to the submission of the German people. The Luftwaffe was driven from the skies not by strategic bombing, but mainly by the air battle fought with allied fighter pilots: enemy losses spiralled after the arrival of the US P51s and P47s. Allied area bombing was abandoned in spring 1944 as all available forces were switched to the preparation of the *Normandy* landings. After the invasion the primary targets were oil dumps and oil plants: at last the strategic bombing offensive had significant effect. German oil plants were producing an average of 316,000 tons per month when the attacks began; production fell to 107,000 tons in June, and 17,000 tons in September 1944. Consumption far exceeded production from May 1944 onwards, crippling the *Ardennes* counter-offensive in December. During the war about 130 major towns in Germany received heavy air attacks, including 30 on Berlin, 21 on Brunswick, 40 on the Mannheim/Ludwigshafen complex, 18 on Cologne, 16 each on Munich and Hamburg. The raids on Dresden, 13–16 February 1945, although amongst the most infamous and causing a firestorm which resulted in casualties of between 80,000 and 110,000 killed and injured, formed part of a pattern which also included raids on Leipzig and Chemnitz to ease the Russian advance. Probably over 600,000 Germans were killed in the strategic bombing offensive, including perhaps 80,000 in Berlin; by comparison, the *blitz* on Britain caused 60,000 deaths.

Strategy The conduct of war, as distinct from *tactics* which cover the conduct of fighting. Thus strategy involves the distribution and application of all military means, including both armed forces and supplies, to fulfil the objectives dictated by national policy; tactics involve the distribution and application of forces and techniques on or near the battlefield itself. *Napoleon*'s skill as a strategist was fully revealed in the *Austerlitz* campaign; wherever possible he attempted to win a campaign before the first battle was fought, by combining rapid marching and deception to pass round the enemy's flanks and sever communications. The development of *railways* in the following decades had immense impact on Napoleon's strategic concepts of manoeuvre, with troops and supplies able to be moved in far

greater numbers and at six times the speed. *Moltke* the Elder demonstrated the advantages to be gained: his victory in the *Franco-Prussian War* was a brilliant strategical accomplishment. So too was *Grant*'s pincer movement in 1864–5. *Schlieffen* attempted to use Moltke's concepts in his plan for the German offensive against France and Russia, but by 1914 both sides had similar opportunities to use railway networks, and the stalemate of trench warfare resulted. Weapon power through *machine-guns* greatly inhibited tactical movement in the field, to such an extent that the overall deadlock bogged down strategic attempts to manoeuvre. In turn the strategic stalemate encouraged supports of an indirect strategic approach, for example the *Dardanelles* operation. *Tanks* and *aircraft* brought a return to the basic strategic principle of manoeuvre in the Second World War, and, because this conflict became worldwide and multi-national, 'grand' strategy had to be introduced to describe the higher level of application of total resources. The nuclear missile age brought new considerations: for the first time in history, the war could be decided with the initial bombardment. Yet it soon became clear that neither side would win, and this realization brought a change from the existing strategic policy of *massive retaliation* to one of *flexible response*. Moreover, because both sides would be reluctant to initiate a self-destructive nuclear war, or to risk the danger of such a war starting, the old idea of the indirect strategic approach re-emerged: placed in its modern context, this indirect approach could be seen as the attempt to achieve political objectives without resorting to maximum, i.e. nuclear, violence. *Guerrilla warfare* therefore became increasingly common.

Stuart, James Ewell Brown, 'JEB', 1833–64 Confederate General, *American Civil War* (Map 3). Resigned from US Army to join Confederate service, 1861. Stuart took a cavalry division on a spectacular encircling movement round the Union forces, June 1862, destroying stores near *McClellan*'s HQ and acquiring valuable information which *Lee* used for the subsequent operations leading to *Malvern Hill*, 1 July. He screened Lee's army during the Second Battle of *Bull Run* and the *Antietam* campaign, 1862; commanded the Confederate right at *Fredericksburg*, December 1862; screened Lee during the *Chancellorsville* campaign; and succeeded *Jackson* as Corps Commander after the Battle of Chancellorsville, May 1863. Stuart fought at Brandy Station, 9 June, the largest purely cavalry action of the war, at the start of the *Gettysburg* campaign; he commanded the cavalry force at Gettysburg itself, 1–4 July. Stuart was mortally wounded at Yellow Tavern, 11 May 1864, after the Battle of the *Wilderness*, and died the following day.

Submarine The American inventor David Bushnell, 1742?–1824, experimented with a crude submarine during the latter years of the eighteenth century: his 'Bushnell's Turtle', egg-shaped and hand-propelled, could sail beneath an enemy ship and fasten a 150-pound explosive charge actuated by a clockwork time-fuse to the keel. Further attempts at submarine warfare were made in the *American Civil War* using semi-submersibles. On 5 October 1863, for example, the Confederate craft 'David' – a cigar-shaped, steam-driven vessel – caused extensive damage to the USS 'New Ironsides' by exploding a 60-pound copper-cased *torpedo*, manipulated on a long spar, against her hull. But significant submarine development had to await the simultaneous development of the petrol engine and the electrical storage battery. The first Royal Navy submarine was launched in 1902, developed by John P. Holland, a British emigrant to America. France led all other powers in submarine building in the first years of the twentieth century. Germany lagged behind; *Tirpitz* even declared that this vessel was essentially a defensive weapon. The German attitude changed after 1905, when the firm of *Krupp* proved with the Karp class that a diving boat with real fighting value was possible. In 1913 the Germans produced a diesel-powered Unterseeboot (U-boat), as opposed to petrol-powered. By 1914 the German submarine fleet included 10 of these diesel warships, with 17 more being built; the Germans also had about 30 petrol-powered vessels. The British submarine fleet totalled 55 vessels, the French 77 – most of them very small – and the Americans owned 38. On 8 August 1914 the German U-15 fired a torpedo at the battleship HMS

'Monarch', without success, but nevertheless marking the first occasion when an automotive torpedo had been fired against an enemy from a submarine. The submarine war on commerce began on 20 October 1914, opening the Battle of the *Atlantic*. All major nations continued to develop submarines after 1918; by September 1939 the British had 70 of these vessels, France 72, Germany 98 and Italy 115. Asdic, or Sonar, had been developed by the British in the 1930s: this underwater sound echo ranging device was however in its infancy in 1939; its use required skill and persistence, and two or three escorts were generally necessary to locate a submarine accurately. In 1940 the Battle of the *Atlantic* reached crisis proportion. The major submarine development after 1945 was the introduction of nuclear power. The US submarine 'Nautilus' was the first nuclear-powered vessel of this type, and also the first of any kind to use this revolutionary propulsion system. 'Nautilus' was commissioned on 30 September 1954; she had a range of 2,500 miles submerged, and a diving depth of 700 feet. Her sister ship, 'Seawolf', established an underwater record in 1958 by cruising for 60 days – 15,700 miles – beneath the surface. In 1959 the 'George Washington' appeared, the first nuclear-powered submarine armed with a nuclear missile, the *Polaris*. HMS 'Dreadnought' was the prototype British nuclear-powered submarine, completed in 1963.

Sudan, campaign in, 1883–5 In late 1883 Mahdi Mohammed Ahmed of Dongola declared himself a prophet and led his dervish tribesmen against the Egyptian and British rulers. A force of about 10,000 Egyptian troops under General William Hicks was defeated at El Obeid, 3 November. Dervish fighters under Osman Digna struck against Egypt's Red Sea ports, defeating another force at El Teb on 4 February 1884. Britain decided to evacuate the Sudan, and on 18 January *Gordon* arrived at Khartoum to supervise this withdrawal. The city was invested by Mahdist fighters; the siege lasted for almost a year. Khartoum was overrun on 26 January 1885, with Gordon killed in the fighting: 2 days later a relief force under *Wolseley* finally reached the city, only to withdraw again. The Mahdi died on 21 June 1885, but his successor, the Kalifa Abdullah, completed the acquisition of control over the Sudan. Britain allowed this situation to remain until 1898, when the campaign began leading to the Battle of *Omdurman*, 2 September 1898.

Suez–Sinai campaign, October–December 1956 (Map 20). *Nasser* assumed power in November 1954; also in 1954 British troops were withdrawn from the Suez Canal zone, and by June 1956 Britain had completed the withdrawal from Egypt as a whole, ending 74 years of military occupation. Nasser began negotiations with Russia in June to obtain a loan needed for the building of the Aswan dam. In July the US Secretary of State *Dulles* withdrew a US loan offer, made in October

1955; 1 week later, 26 July, Nasser announced the nationalization of the Suez Canal, until then owned by the predominantly British Suez Canal Corporation. Britain and France, who considered this nationalization a threat to world peace, joined with America to discuss the possibility of organizing the Canal user states into an association: this would impose its own terms of passage. The communist countries, on the other hand, supported the Egyptian action. Thwarted in their attempt to achieve international control, Britain and France began preparations to repossess the Canal by force; France also felt a need to offset Nasser's support for the rebels in *Algeria*; the Israelis prepared to drive into the Egyptian Sinai desert from the east – this would provide the Anglo-French pretext for their own military intervention. The 3 countries co-ordinated their plans, although it is doubtful if the British Cabinet under Prime Minister Eden communicated its foreknowledge of the Israeli invasion scheme to the senior British Military Command. On 29 October Israeli forces under General Moshe *Dayan* crossed the frontier and thrust into the Sinai, with Israel claiming she merely sought to destroy guerrilla strongholds. Four Egyptian divisions were routed at a cost of 180 Israeli dead. On 30 October, acting under their pre-arranged plan, France and Britain issued Israel and Egypt with a 12-hour 'ultimatum' to end hostilities. Israel accepted, subject to similar Egyptian agreement; Egypt rejected the ultimatum, and Anglo-French air strikes

on Egyptian air bases began on the 31st. The allied ground operation was not however begun until 5 November; the delay, caused by faulty planning, allowed world opinion time to react, and both Russia and the USA issued stern protests during the next few days. On 5 November British paratroops, flown by helicopter from Cyprus, landed at Port Said, while British and French warships bombarded the harbour and landed troops. By 6 November Port Said was under Anglo-French control, and the advance continued along the Canal. A UN demand for a ceasefire was reluctantly obeyed by France and Britain on 7 November; to the east, Israeli forces were within 30 miles of the Canal. Allied losses were 33 dead and 129 wounded; total Egyptian losses are unknown, but Israel claimed to have taken 7,000 prisoners and reported 3,000 Egyptian dead. Anglo-French forces were withdrawn from Egyptian territory by 22 December. The Suez Canal was reopened by UN salvage crews on 7 March 1957. Israel withdrew inside her own territory, guaranteed by UN supervision of the Straits of Tiran and the Sinai border. Nasser's demand that these UN *peace-keeping* forces should be removed, made on 18 May 1967, heralded the beginning of the next *Israel–Arab War*.

Summerall, Charles Pelot, 1867–1955 US General. Fought in Boxer Rebellion, *China*, as a Lieutenant: during the Battle of Peking in this conflict he calmly walked under fire to the wall of the Imperial City and chalked an aiming mark for his gunners; served with AEF in Flanders, 1917–18, commanding the US 1st Division, July–October 1918; Chief of Staff, US Army, 1926–30. His *artillery* technique used in the closing stage of the First World War was later elaborated by the US Field Artillery School: this involved the application of massed fire, centring from a single Fire Direction Centre which could manipulate and control a number of batteries to achieve maximum effect.

Suvorov, Count Alexander Vasilievich (incorrectly Suvarov), 1729–1800 Russian Marshal. Served in Seven Years' War, 1756–63, and against the Turks, 1773–4, 1788–90. In 1798, aged 70, Suvorov was given command of a Russo-Austrian Army charged with expelling the French from *Italy* (Map 1); he drove the French in front of him, entering Milan in triumph on 28 April; although outnumbered by French in the area, he defeated Macdonald at the Battle of Trebbia, 17–19 June, then defeated Joubert at Novi on 15 August. But later in the year he suffered defeat at the hands of *Masséna* in the battle of Zurich. He was appointed to command the Russian Armies in 1800, but died soon afterwards.

T

Tactics The term refers to the conduct of fighting on or near the battlefield itself; *strategy* refers to the conduct of the war as a whole. The development of mobility and fire power had a fundamental effect on the development of tactics during the period 1792–1970. During the *French Revolutionary* and *Napoleonic Wars* infantry tactics received greater flexibility through the greater use of skirmishers, for example with the French *tirailleurs*, as opposed to the previous rigid linear formations. The French *column*, together with the *division* and *corps* structure, allowed commanders a greater choice of formation; armies were deployed in less stereotyped and more mobile fashion. Developments in fire power during the nineteenth century eventually had immense impact on tactical mobility, favouring the static defence and leading to the sterile tactical situation in the First World War. Tactics employed during this war relied upon mass assault combined with artillery barrages. Then, towards the end of the conflict, two developments pointed the way ahead. The first was the *Hutier* tactical technique of infiltrating enemy lines, with special *stormtroopers* providing the spearhead; the second was the introduction of the *tank*. These, together with the growth of tactical air power and the introduction of mechanization in general, restored tactical mobility in the Second World War, especially with *blitzkrieg*. Mobility increased after 1945 with the even greater mechanization of infantry in the European Theatre and with the introduction of the *helicopter*. *Guerrilla warfare* brought its own tactical systems, dependent upon small-sized units both for insurgency and counter-insurgency operations. Naval tactics underwent a similar progression during the period. *Nelson* fought in a far more flexible fashion than his predecessors, pushing aside formal methods. After the Napoleonic Wars mobility was reduced through the introduction of greater fire power, notably with the *Paixhans* shell, and with the consequent adoption of armour in the *ironclads*. The introduction of *steam power*, while providing flexibility in battle through reduced reliance on wind, also tied fleets to coaling bases, and was hence similar to the railway system on land. Naval battles became massive artillery duels; the ram, as used by the Austrian Commander

Tegetthoff in the Battle of Lissa, 20 July 1866, seemed the ultimate weapon. But tactics again became flexible with the advent of lighter armour, more powerful propulsion, and through the *torpedo*, *submarine*, fast destroyers – and with air power leading to the decline of the *battleship*, replaced by the *aircraft carrier*.

Tank warfare, development of, 1900–39 The caterpillar track was invented by Richard Edgeworth as early as 1770; during the Crimean War a small number of steam tractors proved successful in muddy terrain. But tank development remained dormant until the arrival of the internal combustion engine, patented by Gottlieb Daimler in 1885. In 1899 Frederick Simms produced a design in Britain for a 'motor-war car', using a 16 hp Daimler engine: the vehicle had a bullet-proof shell and was armed with 2 *Maxim* guns in revolving turrets. The British War Office rejected the idea and showed similar lack of interest in subsequent schemes. In September 1914 *Kitchener* asked *Churchill* if the Royal Navy would assume responsibility for the air defence of Britain: Churchill decided that aerial control should be maintained over an area inland from Dunkirk and patrols undertaken on the ground, declaring: 'We must support the aeroplane with sufficient armed motor cars.' The Germans retaliated by digging small trenches across the roads; Churchill therefore requested studies to be made of 'cars carrying the means of bridging small cuts in

the road'. Soon afterwards he inspected work being undertaken by Admiral R. H. S. Bacon, General Manager of the Coventry Ordnance Works, for a tractor designed to haul artillery. Simultaneously with these moves, Colonel E. D. Swinton began to consider the possibilities of a vehicle that could cross broken battlefield ground; amongst his ideas was an adaptation of the US Holt tractor. Discussions accelerated, and a project machine was tested in February 1916, condemned by Kitchener as 'a pretty mechanical toy'. Nevertheless *Haig* sought to use these machines – code named 'tanks' – in France as early as possible. They were first employed in significant numbers at the *Somme*, 15 September 1916, but thrown forward in unco-ordinated fashion. The machines continued to be used in driblets until *Cambrai*, November 1917, when 378 tanks went forward 'en masse' with dramatic results. An even more impressive performance was achieved at *Amiens*, August 1918. Development stagnated after 1918. Germany was virtually disarmed under the terms of the *Versailles Treaty*; the US Tank Corps was abolished by the 1920 Defense Act; production halted in France. Intense controversy arose over the part to be played by tanks in future wars, with this argument not only raging over relative merits of tanks versus cavalry, but even as to whether the tank might replace infantry. The tank advocate *Fuller* seemed to argue the latter. His extreme support for the tank created stronger opposition to the new concept of armoured warfarea nd delayed progress; other tank theorists such as Liddell *Hart* saw an important future role for the infantry in armoured divisions. Opponents of the tank pointed to the limitations of this machine, as revealed in 1916–18: readily bogged in soft ground; track grip often insufficient for climbing slippery slopes; defeated by water obstacles; limited circuit of action and consumed large quantities of fuel; mud easily jammed track chambers; speed limited to about 5 mph; defective vision for the crew; vulnerable to artillery fire and other modern weapons such as armour-piercing bullets; expensive when compared with defensive arms such as mines; difficult to control when moving in mass. In 1922 the number of British tank battalions was restricted to 6, compared with 126 infantry battalions. The Tank Corps, based at Bovington, nevertheless struggled to gain greater recognition, not only of the basic tank idea, but also for the concept of tanks operating in close co-operation with mechanized infantry as armoured divisions. The latter idea was attempted in the Experimental Mechanized Force, created in 1927: this carried out impressive demonstrations in 1928. Yet by the end of 1928 there were only 4 regular Royal Tank Corps battalions, plus 2 units in India under the title of Armoured Car Groups. Powerful support for further tank development came in an assessment of the 1927–8 experiments, contained in an official booklet 'Mechanized and Armoured Formations' by Brigadier Charles

Broad – known as the 'Purple Primer'. Other experiments did take place, despite severe financial restraints: in 1931 the 1st Brigade, Royal Tank Corps, was created for trials on Salisbury Plain, but this force did not reassemble until 1934. Also in 1934 came a tentative agreement that the old Cavalry Division should be replaced by a Mobile Division, aimed at mechanized infantry and tank co-operation, but this remained undeveloped in September 1939. By contrast the Germans had pressed ahead with similar formations: in 1935 3 Panzer Divisions were formed, comprising all-arms groups, and following *Guderian*'s ideas. In France, despite theories propounded by *De Gaulle*, tanks were seen as playing an essentially cavalry role of reconnaissance and screening, not as a decisive element in their own right. In Russia, despite close liaison with the Germans, no attempt had been made to adopt a policy of offensive manoeuvre: instead, the policy aimed either at sustained, i.e. positional, defence, or mobile defence envisaging strategic withdrawal. German progress was superior in two vital aspects: the total number of tanks, and the use to which these tanks would be put, with the latter based on the shattering *blitzkrieg* concept.

Tannenberg, campaign and Battle of, August–September 1914 *First World War* (Map 9). Under the final German war plan, as modified by *Moltke* the Younger, German strength was increased in the east: the German 8th Army, under General Max von

Prittwitz, was deployed in East Prussia, based on Königsberg for a delaying operation in the event of a Russian advance. On 17 August 1914 the Russian North-West Army Group, under General Yakov Jilinsky, crossed the border into East Prussia, comprising the 1st Army commanded by General Pavel Rennenkampf and the 2nd under General Alexander Samsonov. Rennenkampf's 1st Army was checked by the German 1st Corps under General Hermann von François at Stallupönen on the 17th. Yet this success complicated Prittwitz's own plans: he aimed to defeat the 1st Army then turn upon the 2nd, but the check on the 1st had stopped short of a decisive victory and might now lead to a disastrous delay. Prittwitz hurriedly pulled back his 1st Corps and attacked the Russian 1st Army at Gumbinnen on 20 August, but again failed to inflict decisive defeat, and meanwhile the Russian 2nd was moving round the southern German flank. Prittwitz, stricken by panic, telephoned Moltke to seek permission to withdraw: Moltke immediately replaced Prittwitz with *Hindenburg*. *Ludendorff*, Hindenburg's Chief of Staff, ordered plans prepared for a move against the Russian 2nd while delaying actions were undertaken against the 1st. This decision was approved by Hindenburg on the 22nd: they found a similar scheme had already been adopted by Colonel Max Hoffman, Prittwitz's Chief of Staff. This similarity of views has been used as an example of the common thinking as encouraged by the German *Staff* system. Thus a division and a corps were already moving from the front facing the Russian 1st Army in order to bolster forces against the Russian 2nd. Samsonov, 2nd Army Commander, became overconfident: he announced over his radio that 25 August would be a day of rest for his troops, and he added to his incompetence by transmitting uncoded messages, so giving the Germans exact locations of Russian troops. The Germans made final preparations on the 25th and attacked on the 26th to begin the Battle of Tannenberg. The right flank of the Russian 2nd Army was pushed back, the left enveloped; encirclement continued on the 27th, and only then did the Russian Army Group Commander, Jilinsky, realize the predicament of Samsonov's 2nd Army: he ordered the 1st to advance, but Rennenkampf delayed. By nightfall on the 29th the envelopment of the 2nd Army was complete. Russian captives totalled 125,000 men; the unknown number of dead included Samsonov, who may have committed suicide. Hindenburg and Ludendorff pushed north-east against the 1st Army, attacking on 9 September in the First Battle of the Masurian Lakes. Rennenkampf, outnumbered and with his forces split, retreated on the 14th having lost 145,000 casualties. German casualties in the 2 main battles were under 25,000; Russia never fully recovered.

Taranto, naval air attack on, November 1940 *Second World War* (Map 14). Twenty-two Fleet Air

Arm aircraft were released from Admiral *Cunningham*'s carrier 'Illustrious' shortly after dark, 11 November, from a point about 170 miles off the Italian naval base of Taranto. Despite heavy defences at the port, 3 Italian battleships were left in a sinking condition, including the new 'Littorio', 2 cruisers were badly damaged and 2 other vessels sunk. Only 2 British aircraft were lost. This stroke altered the balance of naval power in the Mediterranean: half the Italian Battle Fleet was disabled for at least 6 months. Without this victory the situation at *Malta* would have been intolerable.

Taylor, Maxwell Davenport, 1901– US General and diplomat. Commander, US 101st Airborne Division, 1944, serving in *Normandy*, *Ardennes* and central Europe; Chief of Staff, European Command, 1949; first US Commander Berlin, 1949; Commander US 8th Army, *Korea*, 1953; C-in-C Far East Command and UN Command, 1955; Chief of Staff US Army, 1955–9, opposing force reductions as proposed by *Eisenhower*; *Kennedy*'s military representative, 1961–2, being sent by him in late 1961 to assess the situation in South *Vietnam* – following which, on 16 November, Kennedy announced an increase of US advisers in the country; Chairman, *Joint Chiefs of Staff*, October 1962 to July 1964; Ambassador to South Vietnam, 1964–5.

Taylor, Zachary, 1784–1850 US General and 12th President. Fought against Indians, including in the Black Hawk War, 1832, and against Seminole's in 1837, winning Battle of Lake Okeechobee, 25 December; Commander of the Army of Texas, 1845, and rose to prominence during the *American–Mexican War*; elected President 1849.

Tedder, Sir Arthur William, 1st Baron Tedder, 1890–1967 British Marshal of the RAF. Served in First World War, transferring to RFC, 1916; AOC Far East, 1936–8; Director-General of Research and Development, Air Ministry, 1938–40; Deputy AOC-in-C RAF Middle East, 1940–1; AOC-in-C Middle East from June 1941, succeeding Sir Arthur Longmore, to January 1943, succeeded by Sir W. Sholto Douglas. During this period Tedder was responsible for gaining RAF air supremacy in the *desert campaign*; Air C-in-C Mediterranean, 1943, at the time of *Tunisia* and *Sicily*; Deputy Supreme Commander under *Eisenhower*, 1943–5; Chief of Air Staff, 1946–50.

Tegetthoff, Count William von, 1827–71 Austrian Admiral. Commanded squadron of 7 *ironclads* and 1 wooden vessel which attacked an Italian squadron of 10 ironclads and 22 wooden vessels, under Admiral Carlo I di Persano, in the battle of Lissa (Vis), 20 July 1866. Tegetthoff struck in wedge-shaped formation, ramming the Italians despite superior gunfire and sinking 3 ironclads. This battle led naval experts to believe that the ram was the superior naval weapon.

Telegraph First demonstrated by K. A. Steinheil and immediately taken up by *Morse*. Land telegraph systems were rapidly developed in the 1840s; the Crimean War was the first full-scale conflict in which this form of communication was used. In America, development was stimulated by the growth of the railroads prior to the Civil War. *Moltke* the Elder relied upon the system to implement his war plans for the Austro-Prussian War, 1866, and the Franco-Prussian War, 1870; the speed and ease of telegraph communication helped armies to concentrate on the battlefield itself.

Texan War of Independence, 1835–6 Famous for the siege of the Alamo, 23 February to 6 March 1836, which followed armed uprising by American settlers against the Mexican government. The Alamo, San Antonio, was held by 188 Texans including the frontiersman Davy Crockett; opposing them were 3,000 Mexican regulars under General Antonio López de Santa Anna, Mexican President. The defenders threw back several attacks before being massacred; Mexican casualties numbered over 1,500. On 2 March, 4 days before the Alamo fell, the Texan Declaration of Independence was proclaimed and an army raised under Sam Houston. Santa Anna marched to meet this force and the two sides clashed on 21 April at San Jacinto. Houston, with only 740 men, took the enemy by surprise and routed the Mexican Army. Santa Anna was captured. The USA recognized the new republic on 4 July, with Sam Houston elected Texan President. Texas eventually sought and obtained annexation to the USA. Ill-feeling between the USA and Mexico over the Texas question formed a major factor in the outbreak of the *American–Mexican War*, 1846–8.

Thomas, George Henry, 1816–70 Union General, *American Civil War* (Map 3). Won renown in the *Chattanooga* campaign, August–November 1863, with his determined stand as Commander of the Union left wing at Chickamauga, 19–20 September, earning the name 'Rock of Chickamauga'; chosen by *Grant* to replace Rosecrans as Commander of the Army of the Cumberland, October, playing a major role in the victory at Chattanooga, 25 November; took his army into Georgia, 5 May 1864, in *Sherman*'s march on *Atlanta*; dispatched with his army to *Nashville*, where he decisively defeated forces under *Hood*, December; commanded Military Division of the Pacific, 1869–70.

Tirailleurs French light infantrymen, developed during the French Revolution. These skirmishers formed part of each battalion, acting as a screen for the unit when manoeuvring between battles; in battle itself they advanced ahead of the *column* to probe enemy lines. Their tactics were flexible, making full use of cover and literally swarming over the battlefield to disrupt the enemy. *Wellington* countered this French tactic by sending out a skirmishing line of his own and also by deploying his troops on the slope of a hill away from the enemy.

Tirpitz, Alfred von, 1849-1930 German High Admiral. State Secretary of the Navy and Prussian Minister of State, 1898-1916, responsible for a massive increase in German naval production in the Anglo-German *naval race* prior to the First World War; he declared that Germany must be prepared for 'a battle in the North Sea against England'. Tirpitz hoped that the acquisition of greater German naval power in the North Sea would oblige Britain to move warships to this area from the Mediterranean and the Far East, thus undermining British control of these waters; in fact, Britain relied on French assistance, and the two countries were therefore brought closer together. At the outbreak of war Tirpitz protested at the 'muzzling policy' which restricted the German High Seas Fleet to its bases in order to avoid possible loss, during which time British strength gradually increased. He urged the introduction of unrestricted submarine warfare against Britain in the Battle of the *Atlantic*; failure to open this unlimited offensive led to Tirpitz's resignation on 17 March 1916. He took refuge in Switzerland after Germany's defeat, but later returned and was a member of the Reichstag, 1924-8.

Tito, Josip, real name Broz or Brozovich, 1892– Yugoslav Marshal and President. Tito, a former metal-worker and labour leader, emerged as the most prominent Yugoslav resistance leader after the occupation of the country by the Germans in April 1941. His guerrilla bands displayed far more activity and loyalty than rival guerrilla groups such as the Chetniks; as a result the British War Cabinet extended virtual recognition to Tito despite his pro-Soviet leanings. A meeting between *Churchill* and Tito took place at Naples in August 1944; Tito visited Stalin in September. Thereafter the question of Yugoslavia's post-war position became prominent; British troops from *Italy* advanced to Trieste in late April 1945, but Tito had already established a powerful position. He acted as Prime Minister, 1945-54, and President thereafter. His communistic policies have proved relatively moderate, and included criticism of the Soviet intervention in Czechoslovakia, 1968.

Tobruk, fighting at, 1941-2 *Second World War* (Map 14). Tobruk, about 50 miles from the Egyptian border in Libya, was a valuable supply base. Initially held by the Italians, the port was isolated by the British 7th Armoured Division – the famous Desert Rats – in early January 1941 during *Wavell*'s first major offensive, and the Italian garrison was overcome on 22 January. *Rommmel*'s offensive in late March swept the British back to the Egyptian border, but failed to take Tobruk; the port was left as a British-held position behind the German–Italian advance. Besieged on 10 April, the garrison held out against heavy attacks until 28 November. The defenders became famous, especially the 9th Australian Division under General L. Morshead. Rommel had to bring his supplies over 475 miles from Tripoli, and therefore concentrated his efforts on taking Tobruk during the summer of 1941, throwing back *Wavell*'s counter-offensive in June – after which Wavell was replaced by *Auchinleck*. Rommel's attention remained fixed on Tobruk when Auchinleck launched his offensive in November, enabling the British Commander to obtain the initial advantage. The Tobruk garrison broke out on the 23rd, during the battle, and attacked the Germans from the rear: Rommel's withdrawal in December enabled the British to advance beyond the port to El Agheila. Rommel again advanced in January 1942; checked at Gazala, he thrust forward once more, 28 May, and Tobruk was taken on 21 June, remaining in German possession until after El *Alamein*, October–November.

Tojo, Eiki (Hideli after 1941), 1885–1945 Japanese General and Prime Minister. Military Attaché in Germany, 1919, and thereafter head of Japanese secret police; Minister of War, 1940–1, replacing the more moderate Konoye as Prime Minister, October 1941; he still kept his powerful position as War Minister. In November Tojo approved the final plans for the Japanese offensive, including the attack on *Pearl Harbor*. He resigned in July 1944, following US successes in the south Pacific. Tojo attempted suicide; he stood trial and was hanged as a war criminal on 22 December 1945.

'Torch', operation against French North Africa, November–December 1942 *Second World War* (Map 14). The allied invasion of north-west Africa marked the introduction of US troops in the ground war against Germany. The operation stemmed from the British policy that for the moment the main allied emphasis should be in the Mediterranean area. Supreme Commander of 'Torch' was *Eisenhower*; the British Admiral *Cunningham* commanded the allied naval operations. Preliminary movements began at the same time as *Montgomery*'s 8th Army clashed with the German–Italian forces under *Rommel* at El Alamein. The enemy in North Africa would now therefore be attacked from the east by the 8th Army and by 'Torch' troops thrusting from the west. The 'Torch' landing areas had been the subject of considerable allied controversy: the British *Chiefs of Staff* wanted these assault points to be as far into the Mediterranean as possible, to achieve the earliest advance on Tunisia before Rommel could be reinforced; the US *Joint Chiefs of Staff* believed the landings should be made farther west, on the Atlantic Coast, thus easing naval supplies difficulties and reducing the danger of Spanish intervention in the narrow Straits of Gibraltar. The British warned that the Atlantic Coast suffered from heavy swell. A compromise was eventually reached; three main landings would be attempted. Two of these would be inside the Mediterranean: the Eastern Task Force, comprising 33,000 British and US troops under US General Charles Ryder, spearheaded by the British 1st Army under General K. A. N. Anderson, would sail direct from Britain to attack Algiers; the Centre Task Force, 39,000 US troops under General Lloyd Fredendall, also sailing direct from Britain, would attack Oran. The third assault would be launched direct from America, and would strike at the Atlantic port of Casablanca: this, the Western Task Force, amounted to 35,000 US troops under *Patton*. A further problem existed over the likely reception from the French – the landings would be attempted in French Algeria (Oran and Algiers itself) and in French Morocco (Casablanca). The landings were made after nightfall on 7 November. French resistance at Algiers was overcome by the evening of 8 November; Oran fell on the 10th; at Casablanca, where landings had been hampered by the swell, the French were overcome by the 11th. Already, on 10 November, a French ceasefire in North Africa had been proclaimed by Admiral Darlan, C-in-C of French forces who had been in Algiers at the time of the invasion. Despite Darlan's assassination by an extremist in December, the French now co-operated. About 1,000 German reinforcements were arriving in Tunisia each day. British parachutists dropped at Bône on 12 November and others were dropped at Soul el Arba, 20 miles over the Tunisian border, on the 17th. Anderson's British 1st Army advanced through Bône and over the border to Tabarka, and the ring around Tunis and Bizerta seemed to be tightening. The British Commander attempted a push against Tunis on 25 November, but was repulsed. Farther south British and US troops succeeded in thrusting to Djedeida airfield, 10 miles from Tunis, but allied casualties rapidly increased against determined German opposition. By 3 December the attackers were having to fall back, and the advent of the rainy season hindered the flow of supplies from Algeria. The attack bogged down; not until February 1943 would the final battle for *Tunisia* begin.

Torpedo The name originates from the torpedo fish, a ray with an electric apparatus for killing its prey. The US inventor Captain David Bushnell first applied the word to the device which he produced in 1775: this 'torpedo' comprised an explosive charge fixed to an enemy hull and actuated by a clockwork fuse. Early torpedoes fell into two categories: stationary devices which exploded against vessels brushing them, later classified as mines, and moving devices which depended on the close proximity of a control ship. The latter were named 'spar torpedoes': an explosive charge was fixed to the end of a long rod, in turn attached to the bows of a small launch which manoeuvred to explode the device against the opposing hull. Spar torpedoes were first used during the *American Civil War*. Another torpedo contraption was a towed explosive charge, invented by Captain John Harvey, RN, and his brother Commander Frederick Harvey, RN; this, appearing in the 1860s, enabled the control vessel to be about 150 yards from the enemy. The first automotive torpedo was produced in 1868 by the British naval engineer Robert Whitehead, then working at Fiume in Austrian Italy. This device was self-propelled through compressed air; the Austrians bought Whitehead torpedoes in 1868, followed by the British in 1871, and by 1881 Whitehead's customers included Germany, with 203, France, 218, Italy, 70, Russia, 250, Argentina, 40, Belgium, 40, Denmark, 83, Greece, 70, and Portugal, 50. By this date Britain had 254. The first successful Whitehead torpedo attack took place on 25 January 1878 during hostilities between Russia and Turkey when, according to the Russians, 2 converted merchantmen sunk a Turkish revenue steamer. By the latter years of the nineteenth century a torpedo shortage had arisen, and other versions beside the Whitehead model were obtained by various navies: these included the torpedo developed by Captain J. A. Howell in America from 1870, which relied upon a fly-wheel for propulsion, and which was bought by the US Navy until 1892. Torpedo tubes were first built into submarines in 1885 by Thortsen *Nordenfelt*, the Swedish armaments developer. The first use of an auto-motive torpedo fired by a *submarine* against an enemy vessel took place on 8 August 1914, when the German

U-15 attacked – unsuccessfully – the British battleship 'Monarch'. Torpedoes were first dropped from an aircraft during tests on 28 July 1914, using a Short seaplane flown by Lieutenant Arthur Longmore, RN. The first torpedo-boat had been built in London docks as early as 1873. By 1914 torpedoes had grown in size to the British 21-inch design, with a range of 7,000 yards at 41 knots. Modern development has led to the acoustic torpedo, self-guided on to the target, and to the semi-torpedo weapon known as Subroc: this follows an underwater path before surfacing as a missile: a nuclear charge is released over the target area which lands in the water to sink and explode at a pre-determined depth.

Torres Vedras, defences at, 1810
Napoleonic Wars : Peninsular War (Map 1). During summer 1810 *Wellington* ordered defensive lines to be prepared along a 26-mile front between the mouth of the Zizandre on the Atlantic to Alhandra on the Tagus, enclosing the Portuguese capital of Lisbon. The British Army, pursued by the French under *Masséna*, moved into the lines in October. The system comprised linked hill forts and numerous redoubts; maximum use was made of contours; arcs of fire were carefully measured, and semaphore messages could be flagged from one end of the line to the other in minimum time. The network was defended by 25,000 Portuguese militia, 8,000 Spanish troops and 2,500 British artillerymen and marines. Principal

British and Portuguese regular units could rest and prepare for a resumption of the offensive. French attempts to break through failed, and Masséna's troops suffered heavily from disease and starvation.

Trafalgar, Battle of, October 1805 *Napoleonic Wars* (Map 1). French Admiral Pierre Villeneuve sailed from Cadiz on 20 October, ordered to unite his Franco-Spanish Fleet of 33 vessels with other French ships moving on south Italy. *Nelson*, commanding the British Fleet of 27 vessels lying off Cadiz, pursued the French southeast towards the Straits of Gibraltar. Manoeuvring continued throughout the 20th. Soon after dawn on the 21st the French Admiral deployed his fleet into line of battle; Nelson did likewise, and the two fleets converged. At 11.35 a.m. Nelson hoisted his famous battle signal on his 104-gun flagship 'Victory': 'England expects that every man will do his duty.' Nelson attacked in two lines, with the 'Victory' leading the northern thrust and Admiral Collingwood's 'Royal Sovereign' heading the southern. They approached the enemy fleet, which was strung out in irregular fashion, at right angles. At 12.45 the 'Victory' cut into the French line, almost ramming the enemy vessels; farther south Collingwood's squadron was already mauling the French. The French Fleet was broken into scattered segments, suffering repeated close broadsides. At 1.25 p.m. Nelson fell mortally wounded by sniper fire at a range of 40 feet. At this time the 'Victory'

was closely engaged with the French 'Redoubtable'. Nelson's flagship herself suffered serious damage during the battle: her wheel was shot away shortly after the start, and the ship had to be steered by ropes attached to the tiller. But the twin stab of the British lines proved disastrous for the French. After 5 hours 18 enemy ships had been taken, and the remainder fled, of whom only 11 reached Cadiz. Nelson died during the early evening. The British lost 1,587 killed and wounded, although no ships. French and Spanish casualties numbered about 14,000. Britain acquired a control of the seas which she would retain throughout most of the nineteenth century.

Trenchard, Sir Hugh Montague, 1st Viscount, 1873–1956 British General and Marshal of the RAF. Entered Army 1893, rising to rank of Major-General, transferring to the *RFC* in 1914; became GOC RFC, 1915, and Chief of the Air Staff in the first Air Council, formed January 1918. Trenchard resigned in April, 1 week after the official formation of the *RAF*, following quarrels with Lord Rothermere, Air Secretary. By now Trenchard had become a fervent believer in the potential of the bomber, and in June 1918 he established his Independent Air Force. This, the first *strategic bombing* force to be created, was intended to bomb rail and industrial centres behind the German front; it had an average strength of 75 day-bombers, 49 heavy night-bombers and 16 fighters. In

October Trenchard began to organize an Inter-allied Independent Air Force to comprise contingents from all allied air forces, aimed at supporting the projected 1919 ground offensive by air strikes deep into Germany. In February 1919 *Churchill* invited Trenchard to return as Chief of the Air Staff; he remained until 1929, responsible for the establishment and growth of the Air Ministry. Both then and later Trenchard was committed to the idea of the bomber force; he retained his conviction during the Second World War, expressed in a powerful memorandum on the *strategic bombing* offensive dated May 1941.

Trotsky or Trotski, Leon, real name Leib or Lev Davydovich Bronstein, 1879–1940 Russian revolutionary and minister. Became a revolutionary in the 1890s, escaping to England in 1902 after a period in exile; joined *Lenin*, then returned to Russia, 1905, and was rearrested; escaped to Austria. Trotsky argued against participation in the First World War; he returned to Russia after the outbreak of the *Russian Revolution*, March 1917, and became Lenin's principal colleague. Trotsky, as commissar for foreign affairs, led the Bolshevik delegation at peace negotiations with Germany. He was transferred to the Commissariat of War and organized the 5 main Red Armies opposing the Whites in the continued revolutionary struggle. He displayed superb administrative capabilities, forging these armies from rough non-military material. He re-

cruited former Tsarist officers, named 'military advisers' or 'specialists', who proved extremely valuable in the struggle. Central direction of the war stemmed from the Revolutionary Military Council, led by Trotsky. After the victory Trotsky turned to economic administration. Subsequent to Lenin's death, 1924, Trotsky was defeated in the power struggle by *Stalin*, who became Russian leader in 1926. Trotsky was banished, January 1929; he settled in Mexico, 1937, where he was murdered in August 1940.

Truman, Harry, 1884–1972 33rd US President. Chairman of special Senate Committee investigating the National Defense Programme during the Second World War, aimed at revealing waste and inefficiency in war production; elected Vice-President, November 1944; became President on the death of *Roosevelt*, 12 April 1945. In July he attended the Potsdam Conference with Stalin and Churchill – the latter being replaced by Attlee during this summit: the conference had been called to discuss post-war European matters and the continuing war against Japan. Regarding the latter, Truman agreed with a memorandum put forward by US War Secretary *Stimson* on 2 July, which suggested the use of the *atomic bomb* against Japan. Truman had been unaware of the existence of the atomic bomb until informed by Stimson on the day of Roosevelt's death. His administration was marked by the growing deterioration in East–West relations; he put forward his 'Truman Doctrine' offering US aid to nations resisting either direct or indirect communist aggression. Truman also fully supported the creation of *NATO*, which coincided with the *Berlin Airlift*, 1948–9. In 1950 he authorized US development of the *H-bomb*. Also in 1950 Truman responded rapidly to the outbreak of the *Korean War*. During this conflict he became engaged in acute controversy with *MacArthur*. Truman was succeeded by *Eisenhower* in 1953.

Truong Chinh, 1909– North Vietnamese politician and revolutionary warfare theorist. Joined Revolutionary Youth League, 1928, which was created by *Ho Chi Minh* in 1925, and the Indochinese Communist Party (ICP) in 1930; arrested by French in Hanoi, November 1930, and imprisoned until 1936. In 1941 Truong Chinh became Secretary-General of the ICP under Ho Chi Minh, and thereafter he played a leading part in the struggle against the French in the *Indochina War*; he fell out of favour after the victory over the French in 1954, mainly through his ideas on collectivization of agriculture, but was named a Vice-Premier of North Vietnam in 1958 and has continued to be influential. Documents written by him have been translated into English, notably 'The August Revolution', 1946, and 'The Resistance Will Win', 1947: these reveal his theories on revolutionary *guerrilla warfare*, closely allied to those of *Mao Tse-tung;* his doctrines continued to

be relevant during the *Vietnam* war, and he linked the struggles in Vietnam to similar conflicts elsewhere.

Tunisia, campaign in, February–May 1943 *Second World War* (Map 14). In the east, along the old French fortified zone at Mareth, lay *Montgomery*'s British 8th Army, which took Tripoli on 23 January and thus ended the 3-year *desert campaign*. To the west, bogged down by the winter rains, were the allied forces which had landed in French North Africa in the '*Torch*' operation: these units were under the tactical control of British General Kenneth Anderson, comprising the British 1st Army in the north and General Lloyd Fredendall's US 2nd Corps in the south; overall commander was *Eisenhower*. Opposing the allies were General von Arnim's 5th Panzer Army in northeast Tunisia and *Rommel*'s Afrika Korps in the centre. At the beginning of February Rommel prepared his Kasserine offensive. He planned to strike through the central mountains against the inexperienced US 2nd Corps, aiming at the Tebessa area where the allied forces were assembling for a resumption of the offensive; meanwhile Arnim would advance against the British 1st Army in the north. But Rommel was handicapped by lack of supplies and by a lukewarm reaction to his plan from Arnim and from *Kesselring*, overall commander of the Axis forces in the Mediterranean area. The offensive nevertheless began with Arnim striking through the Faid pass on 14 February; next day Rommel advanced to Gafsa. His panzers battered through the vital Kasserine pass on 20 February, but co-operation between Rommel and Arnim broke down and by now the allied troops were beginning to recover. On 21 February Rommel's panzers were moving towards Thala, virtually the last obstacle before Tebessa; his advance was blocked by a thin defensive line thrown up by the British 26th Armoured Brigade, reinforced by an artillery column from the 9th US Division. On 22 February Rommel had to withdraw, his ammunition and fuel almost exhausted. Arnim's threat remained in the area farther north, with his troops pinning down the British 5th Corps at the coastal end of the 1st Army line; Rommel therefore shifted his forces eastwards to strike at the 8th Army. This assault took place at Medenine on 6 March but was repulsed by strong British artillery fire from excellent defensive positions and by the RAF's air superiority. Rommel left North Africa on 9 March; Arnim took over. He decided on 11 March that he would attempt to maintain the defensive position at Mareth in the east: his hopes were destroyed by Montgomery's successful offensive at *Mareth*, 20–26 March; the Germans and Italians pulled back into the Tunisian mountains, and US forces from the west, now commanded by *Patton* in succession to Fredendall, made contact with 8th Army units for the final drive north to Tunis. Eisenhower became Supreme Commander of all forces in North Africa, with *Alexander* – previously Montgomery's commander in the east – as his deputy. On 28 April troops from the 8th Army were transferred to the offensive now launched by the 1st Army in the west against Tunis; the US 2nd Corps advanced against Bizerte. Leading armoured cars of the British 7th Armoured Division – among the original units in the famous Desert Rats – reached the centre of Tunis on 7 May; the US 34th Division entered Bizerte at about the same time. The Germans surrendered on the 12th. Over 238,000 prisoners were taken in the final campaign for Tunisia.

U

Undersea Long-range Missile System (ULMS) Suggested successor to *Polaris* and *Poseidon*. The system involves a new strategic nuclear missile equipped with *MIRV* capabilities, plus a new class of nuclear submarines. Each submarine might carry up to 20 missiles. The extended range, perhaps over 6,000 nautical miles, would allow the ULMS fleet to operate from 55 million square miles of ocean, compared to the $3\frac{1}{2}$ million of the Poseidon force.

Urban Guerrilla Warfare A modern form of terrorism and *guerrilla warfare* in general which seizes upon advantages offered by aspects of urban existence. These include high-density population, difficulties of detection, anonymity, ease of supply, and the vulnerability of modern communications to isolated attack and interference – together with the disproportionate amount of chaos caused by one relatively small incident. The guerrilla uses the environment as a place in which to hide and work, in the same manner as a rural guerrilla might use wild, inhospitable terrain. Hijacking, seizure of hostages, assassination, scattered bombing – all are

undertaken beneath the cover of daily urban life. The maxim by *Mao Tse-tung* that the guerrilla should be like the fish in the sea, indistinguishable from others and hence hard to identify, assumes even greater relevance since the urban sea is far more teeming. Like all guerrillas, the urban terrorist relies more upon subtlety of initiative than upon his weapon armoury: this initiative strives towards the basic aim of persuading the opposing force that it is unprofitable – in terms of human life, political popularity and social stability – to continue the denial of guerrilla demands. The urban guerrilla seeks political rather than military victory. His chief danger, apart from the increasingly sophisticated detection devices used by the security forces, is that terrorism might alienate the local population to such an extent that the guerrilla becomes extremely vulnerable and denied support. Such isolation of the guerrilla from his environment is far more likely after attacks have become indiscriminate. On the other hand the security methods themselves might alienate the uncommitted section of the population, especially if these methods also became indiscriminate through frustration experienced by the anti-guerrilla body. In their efforts to combat the terrorist, the security forces are likely to infringe personal liberties of innocent sectors of the population, leading to opposition from this sector which again adds to the unprofitable nature of the denial of guerrilla demands. This situation was in danger of reaching acute form through the internment system adopted in Northern Ireland. Both guerrilla and anti-guerrilla have therefore to attempt a fine balance, but generally the terrorist has the further advantage of time being on his side. Urban guerrilla warfare is the latest form of guerrilla conflict: as recently as 1960 the insurgent leader *Guevara* advised in his 'Guerrilla Warfare' against urban campaigns, on the grounds that the security forces enjoyed too much strength through the centralized control of the cities. In the decade 1965–75 many terrorist groups ignored such a warning, including the IRA and the Palestinian fighters, although often the urban guerrilla has been characterized by an apparent effort to restrict demands to a specific, relatively small objective, i.e. the release of certain prisoners. By such limited demands the urban guerrilla creates a situation whereby the unprofitability level for continuance of anti-guerrilla operations is reached sooner.

USAF (United States Air Force)
Military aviation in America was a responsibility of the Signal Corps from 1907 until 1918, when the US Army Air Service was organized. In general the state of US aviation was deplorably low when the country became involved in the First World War; pilots had to be trained abroad. In 1917–18 funds for army aviation were raised from $300,000 to $700 million, but the end of the war arrived before significant progress could be made. This state of affairs came under vigorous attack from *Mitchell*, who argued strongly for the creation of an Air Force separate from the Army and Navy. Mitchell's efforts failed. Yet although the US Army Air Force was still officially under the control of the Army during the Second World War, the USAAF was far from being merely an Army support force. Its *strategic bombing* offensive, against both Germany and Japan, provided a role virtually independent of the Army, and gave the USAAF a powerful argument for a post-war life as a separate service. Major US fighter aircraft during the war included the Curtis P40 'Tomahawk' and 'Kittyhawk', the first mass-produced US fighters, with maximum speeds of 357 mph and a range of 1,400 miles; the P38 Lightning, an excellent long-range escort with a speed of 414 mph; the P47 Thunderbolt, faster than the Lightning and able to act as a bomber; the P51 Mustang, probably the war's best long-range escort fighter, with a maximum drop-tank range of 2,700 miles. Bombers included the Douglas SB Dauntless, range 874 miles; the B24 Liberator, range 2,100 miles; the B17 'Flying Fortress', which acted

as the principal bomber over Europe, heavily armed and with a range of 2,100 miles; and the B29 Super-fortress, used against Japan. The latter aircraft dropped the atomic bombs on *Hiroshima and Nagasaki*, August 1945. Atomic weapons, which gave the USAAF a vitally important post-war role, rendered a continued linkage with the Army completely unfeasible; the independent US Air Force came into being in September 1947 as a result of the National Security Act. General *Spaatz*, known as the 'Father of the USAF', was the first Chief of Air Staff. The *Strategic Air Command*, SAC, became the world's most powerful strategic force. The USAF retained the strategic nuclear role after the bomber had become out-dated by the *missile*: the USAF Ballistic Missile Division was established in 1954 and SAC gradually took more missiles into its armoury. *Vietnam* saw a return to the active bomber role, with SAC B52s employed against the enemy; ironically, it was also discovered in Vietnam that fast modern tactical aircraft are difficult to employ in close support ground operations, the speed being too high to enable the pilot to identify small targets: propeller-driven aircraft were therefore resurrected in the US and sent to Vietnam. In 1976 the USAF – apart from SAC – had about 5,000 combat aircraft. Aircraft included the swing-wing F-111 tactical fighter, the highly successful Phantom multi-role fighter, the Super Sabre interceptor and fighter-bomber, and the F-105 Thunderchief and F-84 Thunderstreak fighter-bombers.

V

V-bombs (V1; V2) German development of *rocket* delivery systems began in the late 1920s, accelerating after the start of the Second World War. In May 1943 a special committee was formed by the British War Cabinet to study implications of the German programme, code-named 'Crossbow'. Photographs were studied of the main German development sites at Peenemünde on the Baltic Coast, and reports from agents were closely sifted. Some experts, notably Churchill's scientific adviser Professor Lindeman (Lord Cherwell), discounted rockets as being scientifically impossible in view of the fuel-to-weight ratio. At the same time estimates were made by Herbert Morrison, Minister of Home Security, that up to '4,000 casualties, killed and injured, and very heavy damage, might be caused by the explosion in London of one such rocket'. Peenemünde was bombed by the RAF on 17 August 1943, causing sufficient damage to delay the launching of the V1s. The first of these 'pilotless aircraft' landed on London and surrounding counties on the night of 13 June 1944; 3 days later a sustained offensive opened, continuing for 2 weeks at a rate of about 100 a day. By the end of August, when *Montgomery*'s advance in Europe overran the major launching sites, about 6,275 had been fired against England, plus others against the Normandy invasion force; nearly 3,500 had been destroyed over England by fighters, guns or balloons; nearly 5,500 people had been killed and 16,000 injured. The Germans, denied the V1 bases within range of Britain, still fired them at the advancing allied forces in France, and also began launching V1s from HE 111 bombers. Final preparations were made to the rocket known by the British as the V2. This, referred to by the Germans as the A4, had started development before the V1, classified the FZG 76 by the Germans: it had first been flown in June 1942, but needed a more elaborate firing site and difficulties had been encountered with the control mechanisms. On 8 September 1944 the first V2s were fired against London. These rockets were 45 feet long and weighed 14 tons; no warning could be given of their arrival. The V2 bombardment continued until 27 March 1945, with the last V1 being launched 2 days later. A total of 1,100 V2s were sighted over Britain, of which 518 reached London; they killed 2,724 people and badly injured 6,000.

Verdun, Battle of, February–December 1916 *First World War* (Map 10). This major German offensive against the French 2nd Army began on 21 February; *Falkenhayn* aimed to eliminate the 2nd Army salient and shatter French morale by inflicting the maximum number of casualties. The assault by the German 5th Army under Crown Prince William struck along an 8-mile front, and made an initial advance into this hilly, wooded region. *Joffre* prohibited further retreat and sent *Pétain* to assume command of French forces in this sector. The German advance was halted on 26 February, but the offensive was resumed on 6 March against the western flank of the salient. A series of attacks and counter-attacks continued throughout March, with Pétain ably assisted by Generals *Nivelle* and Charles Mangin. By the end of March virtually the only French supply route still open was a narrow secondary road called 'The Sacred Road' by the defenders; yet Pétain's watchword – also attributed to Nivelle – remained effective: 'They shall not pass.' A third German offensive was started on 9 April, maintained until 29 May. Pétain was promoted to Army Group Commander and succeeded by Nivelle, who proved equally stubborn. The Germans managed to take Fort Vaux and Thiaumont Farm in the east of the battlefield at the beginning of June,

and pressure in late June almost broke the French line. Phosgene gas was used, for the first time. French artillery cover remained magnificent, and the German offensive finally closed on 11 July: 15 German divisions had to be transferred to reinforce the east, where the Russians had opened their *Brusilov* offensive; Falkenhayn was replaced by *Hindenburg* and *Ludendorff*, 29 August, and they moved on to the defensive. On 24 October and 15 December Nivelle thrust troops forward and regained large areas, capturing 115 guns. French casualties totalled 500,000 dead and wounded; German losses were almost 440,000. Meanwhile on 24 June another bloody offensive had begun, launched by British troops in the First Battle of the *Somme*.

Versailles, Treaty of, 1919 Signed 28 June between the allies and associated powers and Germany. Clauses dealing with Germany's defeated armed forces reduced the size of the Army to 100,000 men, for internal law and order and frontier duties; conscription was abolished; fortifications dismantled; severe restrictions placed on armaments; naval strength was limited to 6 battleships and 30 smaller vessels, with no new warship to be built larger than 10,000 tons; the General *Staff* was reduced from 34,000 to 4,000 men; all military and naval aircraft were prohibited.

Vickers British armaments firm founded by Edward Vickers in 1828 as a steel-manufacturing company;

developed by Albert Vickers as an armaments works in 1888, becoming Vickers *Maxim* in 1896 with the purchase of the Maxim *machine-gun* design: the resulting Vickers machine-gun remained in service with several armies for over 70 years, with only limited modifications. Chairman cf Vickers Maxim in the 1890s was Sir Basil Zaharoff (1850–1936), who was said also to be associated with the *Krupp* and *Skoda* interests. The firm of Vickers was merged in 1927 with the Elswick Engineering Company founded by *Armstrong*, so forming Vickers Armstrong. The names Vickers and Vickers Armstrong have been associated with a wide variety of weapons, including the Royal Navy's nuclear *submarine* fleet beginning with 'Dreadnought', laid down in 1959, and the Chieftain main British battle *tanks*.

Vicksburg, campaign of, April–July 1863 *American Civil War* (Map 3). Amongst *Lincoln*'s primary plans for defeating the Confederacy was a thrust to slice the south in two by gaining control of the Mississippi; in early 1863 preliminary operations began to accomplish this aim through the seizure of Vicksburg. Defending Vicksburg were 50,000 Confederates under General John C. Pemberton, mainly deployed on the eastern, or Vicksburg bank of the river along a 40-mile front. Farther south at Port Hudson was another Confederate garrison of 15,000 men. The Union Commander, *Grant*, had about 50,000 men on the west bank. His intention

was to cross the river south of Vicksburg, while *Sherman* diverted Confederate attention with a feint north. Grant would also make use of Union gunboats on the Mississippi, commanded by *Farragut* and Nathaniel Banks. On 17 April Grant rushed his army, less Sherman's corps, overland to Hard Times at the southern end of the Fredericksburg defensive line, and vessels commanded by Admiral David Porter supplied the new base in a series of daring night runs. Grant swept across the Mississippi on 31 April, while Sherman began diversionary operations and cavalry under Colonel Benjamin Grierson attacked Baton Rouge. A Confederate blocking force was repulsed at Port Gibson, 1 May, and Grant marched east after waiting for Sherman. His immediate objective was Jackson, about 50 miles from Vicksburg, where a force of about 9,000 Confederates had been assembled under General Joseph Johnston. Grant, with 41,000 men, pushed the Confederates from Jackson on 14 May and, leaving Sherman, he stabbed west for Vicksburg. Pemberton had brought the Confederate Army out to bar this advance, occupying strong positions at Champion Hill. Grant rushed into the attack, taking personal command; Pemberton fell back to the Bug Black River. The new Confederate position was stormed on the 15th, and Pemberton retreated into Vicksburg itself. Siege began on 23 May after Grant had twice failed to penetrate the defences. Pemberton surrendered his starving troops on 4 July. Grant's Vicksburg campaign rates among the most brilliant of the war.

Victor, Claude, Duc de Bellune, christened Claude Victor Perrin, 1766–1841 French Marshal. Corps Commander under Napoleon in campaigns in *Italy*, 1796–7, 1800; served in *Friedland* campaign, 1807; in *Peninsular War*, 1808–9; rejoined Napoleon's forces for the campaign in *Russia*, 1812; served in Germany and France 1813–14, but transferred allegiance to monarchy during Napoleon's exile, and remained opposed to him during the *Waterloo* campaign. Victor later presided over the trial of officers accused of treason – among those sentenced to death was his old colleague, *Ney*; Minister of War, 1821–3.

Vieille, Paul Marie Eugène, 1854–1934 French engineer. Invented a smokeless powder, 'Poudre B', in 1886, which comprised gelatinized nitrocellulose mixed with ether and alcohol, rolled into thin sheets. This new propellant was more powerful than gunpowder, giving an accurate rifle range of up to 1,000 yards.

Vietnam, war in, 1954–75 (Map 18). The Geneva Convention, 1954, officially ended the *Indochina* war between Vietnamese nationalists and the French. Vietnam was divided into two separate nations by the 17th parallel; French troops were withdrawn. The terms of the Convention stipulated that free elections would be held in 1956 throughout North and South Vietnam in order to reunite the country. But Ngo Dinh Diem, appointed Premier of South Vietnam in June 1954, declared in July 1956 that preliminary discussions for the election would not be held with the North Vietnamese: Diem claimed the people of the North would not be able to express their will freely. He also accused the North of attempting to start terrorism in the South. The US administration, under *Eisenhower*, placed great faith in Diem as a unifying factor in the muddled South Vietnamese political situation. Meanwhile the insurgents gradually built up strength in the South, passing through the first phase of *guerrilla warfare*, i.e. the creation of a clandestine cell structure prior to moving into the second stage of overt guerrilla conflict. Rather than reacting to this threat the South Vietnamese forces, with US advice, were organized on conventional as opposed to counter-insurgency lines, based on the belief that the primary use of these forces would be to block an attempted conventional invasion from the North. Instead came a steady rise of insurgency operations within the South as the insurgents moved into open guerrilla warfare. According to US figures a total of 452 village chiefs were assassinated, kidnapped or defected in 1957–8; by January 1960 the rate of loss had risen to 15 per week. In 1958 the regular guerrilla force was estimated at about 3,000 men: this figure rose to 7,000 by 1960. On 20 December 1960 the National Front for the Liberation of South Vietnam was officially formed, called the Viet Cong by its opponents. On 18 October 1961, President Diem proclaimed a state of emergency. In November *Kennedy* announced an increase in aid, although troops would remain in a non-combat role; this announcement followed a visit to the country by General Maxwell *Taylor*. By February 1962 the total of US military personnel in South Vietnam was about 4,000, under General Paul Harkins; NLF main force and part-time strength was about 50,000. South Vietnam fell into increasing political confusion, climaxing on 1 November 1963 with the assassination of President Diem. From there on the political leadership of the country changed hands frequently – General Duong Van Minh, General Nguyen Khanh, Tran Van Huong, General Nguyen Ky and, from September 1967 to April 1975, Nguyen Van Thieu. Meanwhile the US 'advisers', commanded after April 1964 by General William Westmoreland, faced a virtually impossible task, and in mid-1964 the military term 'escalation' became increasingly used. On 2 August 1964 2 US destroyers were attacked by North Vietnamese patrol boats in the Gulf of Tonkin. President *Johnson* ordered air action against 'gunboats and certain supporting facilities in North Vietnam' as a reprisal following the violation of US passage in 'international' waters. By 1 January 1965 US military strength in South Vietnam had risen to about 23,000 men; a limited bombing offensive against North Vietnam was begun in February; in March the US troops' role in South Vietnam switched from advisory to combat, officially announced in June by which time US strength was over 70,000: the total reached 215,000 by March 1966. In April 1966 B52 strategic bombers from Guam struck North Vietnam for the first time. US officials in Saigon estimated infiltration of North Vietnamese regular troops into South Vietnam was running at the rate of 5,500 per month. In May 1967 an attempt was made to hinder this infiltration by moving US Marines into the 'De-Militarized Zone' (DMZ) separating north and south along the 17th parallel; by June US troop strength had risen to about 465,000. Bombing of the north intensified, with a record 197 missions flown on 4 August. Johnson announced in August that he had authorized raising the US troop level to 525,000; the South Vietnamese leader, now Thieu, following his victory over Ky in the September elections, aimed to raise South Vietnamese strength to 685,000; the US Command in Saigon estimated enemy strength to be between 223,000 and 248,000 men, plus up to 85,000 political cadres. So far the fighting itself had been divided into three main categories: a virtual conventional war in the northern area of South Vietnam, mainly between US Marines and regular North Vietnamese troops; repeated hard-core guerrilla attempts to seize the central highlands around Pleiku, thus splitting South Vietnam in half; and lower-level guerrilla actions elsewhere in the country, especially in the highly fertile Mekong Delta district. The NLF and North Vietnamese troops made ground during the annual wet season, April–October, when bad visibility reduced US air cover; the Americans and South Vietnamese regained ground during the dry season. A lull fell over the fighting in late 1967. Then, on 30 January 1968, the NLF launched their 'Tet' offensive, with simultaneous attacks on more than half South Vietnam's provincial capitals and 25 airfields. Fighting was especially fierce at the old imperial capital of Hué. Despite heavy NLF casualties, and despite the failure of the supposed aim to bring about a general insurrection, pacification plans in South Vietnam were set back an estimated decade. President Johnson began to search for an escape from the war and the US bombing policy against North Vietnam was used as a potential bargaining instrument in negotiations. On 10 May 1968 US and North Vietnamese delegates met in Paris; in October the bombing of the North was temporarily halted. *Nixon* was elected President on 5 November on the understanding he would seek an ending to US involvement, and in May 1969 he suggested that US troops might be withdrawn; in June, after a meeting with Thieu on Midway Island, he declared that 25,000 combat troops would leave South Vietnam in July–August. The movement proceeded steadily despite continued NLF activity. The last US ground combat units were pulled out on 11

August 1972. On 27 January 1973 the USA, South and North Vietnamese and the Provisional Revolutionary Government of South Vietnam (PRG, basically the NLF) signed the Paris Agreement after prolonged negotiations instigated by *Kissinger*. This provided for a ceasefire, an International Commission for Control and Supervision (ICCS), withdrawal of foreign troops, repatriation of prisoners, and eventual reunification of Vietnam. The war cost 56,226 US dead and 303,601 wounded. Up to the time of the 'ceasefire' over 180,000 South Vietnamese had been killed and 485,000 wounded since 1961. North Vietnamese and NLF over the same period rose to about 900,000 dead. Since 1965 the USA and South Vietnamese had expended some 15 million tons of ammunition. The Americans lost nearly 3,700 aircraft and about 4,900 helicopters. The Paris Agreement achieved nothing. It left the North Vietnamese and NLF in possession of strategic areas in the South, notably in the central highland region, and the communist offensive intensified in late 1974 and early 1975; in March 1975 the northernmost provinces of South Vietnam were abandoned by the Thieu government; this precipitated a collapse of morale among South Vietnamese forces. The latter totalled about 460,000 troops at the beginning of 1975, and over 300 combat aircraft; North Vietnamese regular troops in South Vietnam were over 150,000, mainly in the north and north-west. The offensive quickened in March–April, with the fall of Da

Nang and Hué to the North Vietnamese and with a tightening NLF grip on the Mekong Delta region. In early April the central highlands were at last under firm communist control; non-communist territory amounted to a shrinking enclave around Saigon. President Thieu announced his resignation on 21 April, and North Vietnamese forces concentrated for the final push on the capital. The US Senate refused the dispatch of further aid, despite appeals from President Ford for financial assistance. Communist spearheads advanced on Saigon from the west and down Highway One from the north, and finally entered the city on 30 April with minimum resistance from remaining South Vietnamese forces; the name of the southern capital was changed to Ho Chi Minh City.

Vitoria, Battle of, June 1813 *Napoleonic Wars* (Map 1). The battle marked the decisive engagement between British and French forces in the *Peninsular War*, with respective armies commanded by *Wellington* and King Joseph Bonaparte, *Napoleon*'s brother. Joseph entered the Zadorra River valley intending to join with regiments moving from Pamplona under Clausel. Wellington attacked on 21 June before this junction could be achieved. French forces were deployed facing an expected assault from the west, but Wellington planned that, in addition to this attack, thrusts would be made from the hills in the south and north. Difficult terrain in the north delayed the British offensive from this direction, but the multiple thrusts nevertheless shattered French defence and by mid-afternoon Joseph was in full retreat. The French lost 7,000 men and 143 guns. Allied casualties were high, about 5,000, but many of them were merely missing as they scrambled for loot.

Voroshilov, Kliment Efremovich, 1881–1969 Russian Marshal and President. President of Revolutionary Military Council and People's Commissar for Defence, 1925–40, under *Stalin*, surviving the 1937 purges and introducing a number of innovations into the Red Army, including mechanization, an Air Force, and a defensive system based on strategic withdrawal. During Hitler's campaign in *Russia*, Voroshilov commanded the North-West Front in the Baltic countries; with *Zhukov* he directed operations to relieve Leningrad, January 1944; President of USSR, 1953–60.

W

Wagram, campaign and Battle of, May–July 1809 *Napoleonic Wars* (Map 1). Napoleon's victory at *Ratisbon* resulted in his capture of Vienna, 13 May. The Austrians now reorganized themselves; Archduke Charles concentrated about 100,000 men on the north bank of the Danube. Napoleon still hoped to cross near Vienna via the island of Lobau, which the Austrians had neglected to fortify in strength, and *Masséna*'s corps used this stepping-stone to force a bridgehead on the 20th. The French were able to occupy the villages of Aspern and Essling on the north bank, and the Battle of Aspern-Essling continued throughout the 20th. The villages were constantly taken and retaken, and hard fighting was resumed on the morning of the 21st. The situation suddenly changed with the collapse of a bridge over the main stream of the Danube, destroyed under pressure of Austrian boats loaded with stones, and isolating French troops on the northern bank. Archduke Charles committed his reserves, and after intense struggle Napoleon was obliged to order retreat. Each side suffered about 20,000 casualties; included in the French casualties was Marshal *Lannes*. Austria failed to concentrate all available troops, and by June Napoleon had gathered about 170,000 men in the Vienna–Lobau region, outnumbering opposing forces under Archduke Charles. Archduke John was ordered to bring more Austrians from Hungary, but was repulsed at Raab by a French corps under Eugène on 14 June. Eugène marched north to join Napoleon at Vienna. On the night of 4 July Napoleon feinted east of Aspern and Essling, then struck hard at these strongly defended villages. The Austrians were forced back into a second defensive line, and on 5 July the main Battle of Wagram began. To prevent a junction between Archduke Charles's force and Archduke John's 50,000 troops, Napoleon attacked the Austrian left, closest to Archduke John's approaching army. Archduke Charles countered by thrusting between Napoleon's left and the Danube. Stalemate ensued during the 5th. Next day Napoleon massed most of his 480 guns to bombard the Austrian centre: probably the greatest artillery concentration so far experienced in war. Combined with this barrage was a strong infantry assault, while troops under *Davout* began to encircle the Austrian left. The Austrian flank was thrown back and the centre penetrated. The Austrians withdrew; the French, exhausted and apprehensive over the imminent arrival of Archduke John, were unable to take full advantage of the victory. Both sides had suffered heavily: about 30,000 Austrian casualties, 32,000 French. Archduke Charles resigned after an internal dispute, and was soon followed by Archduke John. Prince Klemens Metternich became Austrian Foreign Minister, urging a policy of peace, and the Treaty of Schönbrunn resulted on 14 October.

War Cabinet *First* and *Second World Wars. Lloyd George* created a First World War model which was followed by Chamberlain and *Churchill* in the Second World War: a small War Cabinet with a minimum of members having direct ministerial responsibilities, so leaving them free to devote most of their efforts to the War Cabinet. Thus Lloyd George's War Cabinet had only 5 members, of whom only the Chancellor of the Exchequer had departmental responsibilities. Chamberlain tried to adopt a similar system in September 1939, but the inclusion of Churchill, First Lord of the Admiralty, meant the addition of the other 2 service ministers. Total membership came to 9. Churchill, becoming Prime Minister in May 1940, further streamlined the system to 5 members with only 1, the Foreign Secretary, having a ministerial post. Service ministers were excluded. Churchill's War Cabinet also obtained Labour representation through the presence of Attlee. By August 1943 the number of War Cabinet ministers had grown to 8, with 5 having departmental posts, but by now there had been a shift in function. The War Cabinet was no longer so concerned with the daily running of the war: meetings, which were almost once a day in spring 1940, dropped to 174 in 1942. A heavier proportion of Cabinet business was devoted to economic, social and general affairs, rather than strategic matters. The latter had become the concern of Churchill and the *Defence Committee.*

Warsaw Pact Military alliance formed by the 'treaty of friendship, mutual assistance and co-operation', signed at Warsaw, 14 May 1955, by the Soviet Union, Albania, Bulgaria, Czechoslovakia, East Germany, Hungary, Poland and Romania. This treaty was the communist reply to *NATO* and the re-militarization of West Germany. Yugoslavia refused to join; Albania left in September 1968. The Pact comprises a Political Consultative Committee and the Joint High Command. The first is attended by the First Secretaries of the Communist Party, heads of government and foreign and defence ministers. The Joint High Command consists of a C-in-C and a Military Council; in the event of war the forces of the other pact countries would be operationally subordinate to the Soviet High Command.

Warsaw rising, August–September 1944 *Second World War*. Soviet tanks reached the vicinity of Warsaw on 29 July, advancing towards Germany. On the same day Moscow Radio issued an appeal from the Polish communists in Moscow, addressed to Warsaw citizens: 'By direct active struggle in the streets . . . of Warsaw the movement of final liberation will be hastened.' Two days later Russian tanks were rumoured to have pierced German defences east of the city. At 5 p.m. next day, 1 August, the Warsaw Rising erupted, between underground forces under General Tadeusz Bor-Komorowski and German occupation troops. But the Russian thrust towards the city faltered; on 4 August the Germans counter-attacked. Bor-Komorowski appealed for help from the Polish government-in-exile, based in London. Flights by British aircraft from Italy, mostly piloted by Poles, dropped supplies on 4 August, but of this flight of 15 aircraft 6 were lost and only 2 succeeded in reaching the city. Churchill informed Stalin of the Polish request for aid, but the Soviet leader replied on 5 August that the Poles in Warsaw were fighting an impossible battle. By the end of the first week in August the Germans had split the city into sectors, each of which was ruthlessly combed. Appeals for help were discussed by the British *Chiefs of Staff* on 7 August; *Portal*, Chief of the Air Staff, claimed the Polish underground had begun their campaign prematurely and that flights to the city were impracticable. But on 8 August these suicidal attempts to reach Warsaw from Italy – the only allied controlled area with return range – were resumed. The British COS apparently did not share Polish suspicions that the Russians were deliberately delaying their offensive, in order to allow the eradication of non-communist Polish fighters by the Germans, but the British nevertheless issued strong appeals to Stalin that ground facilities might be offered on Russian-held territory for flights to Warsaw, thus reducing the distance and enabling more flights. Churchill and *Roosevelt* issued a joint appeal on 20 August; Stalin sent his refusal on the 23rd and branded the Polish Underground Army as a 'group of criminals'. Aircraft from the Polish wing in Italy continued to attempt to drop supplies: in operations between 17 and 27 August a total of 46 sorties were successful, but by 28 August only 3 aircraft remained available. The *War Cabinet* agreed on 4 September that Churchill should attempt to persuade Roosevelt to allow US aircraft – the only ones available – to drop supplies in Warsaw, 'if necessary gatecrashing on Russian airfields'. But Roosevelt replied next day that US intelligence sources believed the Germans had recovered full control in Warsaw. Roosevelt was misinformed: Polish fighters continued to struggle in the ruins and desperate appeals for help continued to reach London. The War Cabinet was informed on 5 September that 182 sorties had been flown from Italy in the past 3 weeks; of these 35 aircraft were missing and 88 had made successful or semi-suc -

cessful drops. Stalin at last began to show signs of willingness to co-operate: he informed Churchill on 9 September that airfield facilities would be offered. Weather conditions ruled out an allied flight until 18 September; meanwhile the Russians opened a limited offensive on the 11th and dropped supplies over the city – few of the parachutes opened. On 18 September 110 heavy bombers of the 8th USAAF flew from East Anglia and dropped 30 per cent of their supplies for the loss of 9 aircraft. A planned US repeat mission was not launched in time. Polish resistance had virtually ceased by 2 October. An estimated 200,000 Polish men, women and children were killed or wounded in the Rising; German casualties were 10,000 killed, 7,000 missing and 9,000 wounded. Russian troops entered the city a few weeks later.

Waterloo, campaign and Battle of, May–June 1815 *Napoleonic Wars* (Map 1). *Napoleon* landed in France on 1 March 1815 and so began 'The Hundred Days'. By early May the respective war plans were nearing completion. Facing Napoleon in Belgium was *Wellington*'s Anglo-Dutch Army of 95,000, based on Brussels, and the 120,000-strong Prussian Army under *Blücher*, who had his HQ at Namur on Wellington's left. Wellington drew his supplies from Ostend and Antwerp, while the Prussian line of communications stretched in the opposite direction to Coblenz; in the event of disaster to either or both armies, their lines of retreat might carry them

farther apart. Napoleon therefore fixed his attention on the vulnerable hinge between them. The French Commander would only be able to take 124,000 men to battle, despite a display of incredible energy since his return. He therefore intended to drive a wedge between the two allied armies, aiming at Charleroi and Brussels, destroying each in turn before further forces – Austrian and Russian – could strike against him. Wellington was hampered by his delicate relations with the Dutch, and both he and Blücher were hindered by lack of an intelligence system. The two Commanders agreed that if the French advanced on Charleroi, Blücher would move forward to positions in front of Sombreffe and Wellington would concentrate at Quatre Bras, 8 miles northwards. Napoleon left Paris on 12 June; by nightfall on the 14th he had moved his headquarters to Beaumont. General Count von Zieten, commanding Blücher's 1st Corps at Charleroi, sent warnings to Blücher and Wellington. The Prussians began to advance to their forward position during the morning of the 14th. Wellington preferred to wait before moving to Quatre Bras, believing Napoleon might be attempting to sweep round the northern Anglo-Dutch Army to cut British communications to the sea: a premature advance to Quatre Bras would expose the Anglo-Dutch Army to such an outflanking movement. Zieten's troops attempted to block the enemy, but were pressed back on the road to Fleurus during the early hours of the

15th. Blücher left Namur at 1 p.m. on the 15th, heading for the front; his other corps were moving forward as fast as possible to aid Zieten, with the exception of Bülow's 4th Corps which delayed in the rear due to a staff misunderstanding. Wellington believed that Napoleon might still be attempting to strike north-west to sever British communications; early in the evening he ordered his regiments to take up positions between Grammont and Nivelle – even though this would incline his army away from the Prussians. Zieten's Prussian troops retreated through Fleurus and took up defensive positions on the road to Sombreffe. Late in the evening Wellington at last appreciated that Napoleon was heading towards the hinge between the Anglo-Dutch and Prussian Armies, and he issued orders for a concentration between Nivelle and Quatre Bras, bringing his regiments closer to the Prussians. Wellington then went to the Duchess of Richmond's famous ball. There he received more news: the French were thrusting towards Quatre Bras long before the Anglo-Dutch forces could concentrate in that area. The Prussian positions spread along Ligny broke, and there, in the early afternoon of 16 June, Napoleon threw his main forces forward while Ney's corps attacked the Anglo-Dutch forces at Quatre Bras. The battle between the main French thrust and the Prussians at *Ligny* lasted into the night, and Blücher himself narrowly escaped death. His army was forced to withdraw while Blücher was still incapacitated. *Gnei-*

senau assumed command during his absence, and the danger existed that his dislike for Wellington might tempt him to select a retreat route leading away from the Anglo-Dutch. This dislike had been increased by the events of the day. Wellington had ridden over to discuss affairs with Blücher at the mill of Bussy before the fighting; he had promised support to the Prussians – if he was not attacked himself. Gneisenau overlooked this proviso. The Anglo-Dutch regiments which had reached Quatre Bras had been fiercely engaged by Ney after 3 p.m., and Wellington's slow concentration had ruled out support being available for the hard-pressed Prussians at Ligny: battle at Quatre Bras began with only 8,000 Anglo-Dutch troops under Count Perponcher-Sedlnitzky confronting 21,000 French. Not until evening could Wellington's strength be raised to 30,000, and the Anglo-Dutch then counterattacked to drive the enemy from positions taken during the afternoon. Both sides suffered about 4,000 casualties. In the early hours of the 17th Blücher recovered sufficiently to make the decision to move in a parallel line to the Anglo-Dutch Army. The British pulled back to a position near the village of Waterloo, level with Wavre which was reached by the Prussians during the afternoon of the 17th after a fumbling French pursuit. At 11 p.m. Blücher received a message from Wellington, requesting at least 1 Prussian corps to be sent to aid the Anglo-Dutch in the expected attack by Napoleon. Blücher agreed to bring

3 corps; the move from Wavre to Waterloo began early on the 18th. The Battle of Waterloo opened soon after 11 p.m. During the initial phase the fighting centred upon Chateau Hougoumont, on the right of the Anglo-Dutch line which spread along the hillside behind La Haye Sainte and Papelotte, south of Waterloo village itself. At about 1.30 the main fighting shifted towards the Anglo-Dutch centre. Four French divisions, led by Jean Baptiste d'Erlon, thrust forward for La Haye Sainte and Papelotte; Wellington's infantry stood from their cover on the reverse slopes of the hillside, and threw back the attacks. Wellington ordered his cavalry, commanded by Paget, to support the infantry, and the French reeled back. A lull fell over the battlefield. At about 2.30, without instructions from Napoleon, Ney ordered the French cavalry to charge: over 5,000 horsemen pounded the British squares. Wellington received repeated reports that his regiments were suffering heavy casualties; some squares had collapsed, and the French pressure in the centre remained intense. But at about 4.20 p.m. the first Prussian guns roared from the fringe of the woods to the east. Already Napoleon had been obliged to divert reinforcements from Ney to face this new threat, but the Prussian 4th Corps under Bülow, first to arrive, struck at the French right flank. Ney's pressure in the Anglo-Dutch centre nevertheless succeeded in pushing back Wellington's troops from La Haye Sainte, and capture of this strongpoint exposed the Anglo-Dutch centre to close-range French musket volleys. At the same time Ney brought up a battery of horse artillery and this, at 300-yards range, smashed into the remaining British squares. But Zieten's corps arrived to bolster the Anglo-Dutch left flank. Napoleon had delayed too long in launching his last and most powerful weapon at the allied centre – the Imperial Guard. Now these élite troops had to attack without cavalry support. The British threw them back, and counter-attacked. The French Army collapsed. Napoleon managed to escape, but pursuit of the French – undertaken by the Prussians – continued throughout the following days. Napoleon abdicated on 21 June. The French lost about 30,000 men at Waterloo, one-third captured; Anglo-Dutch casualties were about 15,000, Prussian 7,000.

Wattignies, Battle of, October 1793 *French Revolutionary Wars* (Map 1). In August 1793 France neared collapse, following internal disruption and external pressure from Austrian, Prussian and British forces. On 23 August the French Committee of Public Safety decreed the *levée en masse*; *Carnot* hurried his reorganization of the French forces; recruits were rushed to the front. The Army of the North, 42,000 men under Jean Nicolas Houchard, was thrown against the Duke of York's British and Hanoverian troops at Hondschoote, east of Dunkirk, on 6 September. York's troops only numbered 13,000, but were trained professionals; they nevertheless fell back through weight of numbers. Houchard followed up this success by routing the Prince of Orange's Dutch forces at Menin, 13 September. Yet his failure to man-oeuvre the Austrians out of eastern France led to his recall and replace-ment by *Jourdan*; Houchard was guillotined. Carnot ordered Jourdan to advance on Maubeuge, invested by 30,000 Austrians under Frederick Josias, Prince of Saxe-Coburg, and this movement led to the Battle of Wattignies, 15–16 October. The French, 50,000-strong, were blocked on the first day, but Jourdan pushed forward on the 16th to drive back the Austrian right flank, and Saxe-Coburg retreated eastwards. French successes would continue in the *Fleurus* cam-paign, 1794.

Wavell, Sir Archibald Percival, 1st Earl, 1883–1950 British Field-Mar-shal. Served in South Africa and India prior to the First World War, fought mainly in the Middle East; C-in-C Middle East, 1939–41. During this latter period Wavell fought with severely depleted troop strengths in a number of scattered areas, including *Greece*, *Crete*, Abyssinia, Kenya, Syria, Iraq, and most of all in the North African *desert campaign*. Never achieving good relations with *Chur-chill*, Wavell was replaced by *Auchin-leck* on 1 July 1941, and took over Auchinleck's previous post as Commander in India. His command area was hurriedly extended in January 1942 to include the Malaya peninsula and *Singapore*, plus the

Dutch East Indies; defence of the latter was known as ABDA – American, British, Dutch, Australian – Command, but this under-strength joint force was unable to prevent the overwhelming Japanese conquest of the area, and Wavell reverted back to his prime responsibility, India, for the struggle over *Burma*. He became Viceroy of India in 1943, and retained this appointment until *Mountbatten* succeeded him in 1947. Wavell was also a fine military writer; his books included 'The Palestine Campaigns', 1928; 'Allenby', 1940; 'Generals and Generalship', 1941; and 'Allenby in Egypt', 1943.

Wellington, 1st Duke of; Sir Arthur Wellesley until 1809, known as 'The Iron Duke', 1769–1852 British General and Prime Minister. Entered Army in 1787, and thereafter served extensively in India, establish-ing his reputation during the Second Maratha War, 1803–5. In July 1808 Wellesley, then the youngest Lieu-tenant-General in the Army, received instructions to take a force to Portu-gal; a number of officers were senior to him on this expedition, but he arrived on 1 August and immediately marched against the French to begin British participation in the *Peninsular War* (Map 1). His victory over Junot at Vimeiro on 21 August led to the Convention of Cintra, under which French forces left Portugal. Wellesley returned home, with Army Command reverting to *Moore*. He returned to Portugal in June, and thereafter fought the Peninsular War to its victorious conclusion in 1814. Wellington acted as British Ambassador to France, 1814, and British representative at the Congress of Vienna, 1814–15, prior to the *Waterloo* campaign (Map 1). He commanded the Army of Occupation in France, 1815–18, and was Master-General of Ordnance with a seat in the Cabinet, 1818–27; he was C-in-C of the British Army, 1827–8, then became Prime Minister until November 1830; he served as Foreign Secretary under Peel, 1834–5, and became C-in-C of the Army again in 1842 until his death. He exerted a powerful influence over British military affairs, and his outdated shadow continued to be cast over his successor Hardinge and over his protégé *Raglan*, British Commander in the *Crimean War*. Wellington never lost a major battle, although he only faced *Napoleon* once, at Waterloo, by which time the French Emperor was ill and suffering acutely from lack of resources. Strategically, Wellington was a master at choosing the correct defensive or offensive policies to fit circumstances, able to transfer from one to the other at the most opportune moment – as, for example, with the *Torres Vedras* operation. Tactically, he overcame the French *column* and *tirailleurs* by avoiding exposure of his own line and by protecting this line against skirmishers through *riflemen* of his own. He placed his infantry on reverse slopes wherever possible, as at Vimeiro and Waterloo, and he secured his flanks through use of natural terrain and through his *cavalry*, which he used for screening rather than

charges. Rather than firing *artillery* 'en masse', in Napoleon's manner, Wellington employed his guns in a selective fashion at the critical moment. Wellington's primary weapon was therefore the infantry, usually deployed in a 2-deep line so that every man could fire his weapon. He has been criticized for describing his soldiers as 'the scum of the earth', in a letter written during the Peninsular War; on the other hand he could have been referring to the recruiting material from which the troops came, not the finished product; in 1831 he added a significant sentence: 'It is only wonderful that we should be able to make so much of them afterwards.' As a commander, Wellington was not an innovator. Instead he insisted upon the qualities of permanence and system: the former allowed the benefits of experience to be brought forward and the second – through excellent organization – allowed these benefits to be put into practice. Both were reflected in Wellington's elaboration of the *divison* structure, which had been introduced into the British Army in 1807 following the French example. Wellington used the experience gained by others with divisional units, especially the system of control which they provided within an army, but he then allowed his division to become virtually self-sufficient under his overall command in order to increase the Army's flexibility. In the last months of fighting he seemed to be tending towards a *corps* organization, probably to secure some further degree of delegation. The same attitude of system combined with flexibility and initiative was displayed in Wellington's attitude towards the *Staff* structure. Unlike the Prussians he never allowed himself to be partnered by a strong Chief of Staff: to him, command was indivisible. Instead, Wellington relied upon close collaboration with General Sir George Murray (1772–1846), Quartermaster-General from April 1809 to May 1812, and again after March 1813. For a short time in late 1812 General Sir James Willoughby Gordon acted as Wellington's Chief of Staff, but the appointment proved a failure. In all, Wellington's prime characteristic was his ability to dominate: he exerted strong influence, and acted as a unifying factor, yet at the same time allowed delegation and initiative under his shadowing authority.

Whitney, Eli, 1765–1826 US inventor and arms producer. Whitney competed for a contract offered by the US Congress, 1798, for the manufacture of muskets on a large scale: he proceeded to design machinery for making identical parts in quantities to gauges, thus pioneering mass arms production. These interchangeable parts also reduced costs: his musket cost $13.40. His initial output of 10,000 muskets was followed by other Federal contracts for 33,000 muskets between 1812–24 and production continued at his Whitney Armoury after his death; the factory made 15,001 rifle-muskets and 11,214 revolvers during the American Civil War. The armoury ceased operations in 1888.

Wilderness, campaign and Battle of the, March–June 1864 *American Civil War* (Map 3). *Grant*, appointed Union General-in-Chief on 9 March after his *Chattanooga* victory the previous autumn, now sought to destroy the Confederate Army of North Virginia under *Lee*. The Confederates, about 60,000-strong, were positioned south of the Rappahannock, west of Fredericksburg. To reach the enemy, Grant would have to advance into the difficult Wilderness terrain, covered with dense thickets, which extended from Richmond to the Rapidan–Rappahannock Rivers. While Grant launched this offensive with the 105,000-man Army of the Potomac, *Sherman* would undertake the second part of the Union pincer movement by advancing into Georgia via *Atlanta*. Grant crossed the Rapidan on 4 May. Lee immediately concentrated against the Union troops as they struggled through the Wilderness thickets. A major attack by Grant on the evening of the 6th was blocked, during which *Longstreet* was seriously wounded. Grant moved south next day, seeking to cut Lee's communications, but the Confederate Commander had already deployed a defensive force to check this attempt, and for the next 10 days the armies fought the costly, indecisive Battle of Spotsylvania. A subsidiary action took place at Yellow Tavern, 11 May, when *Sheridan*'s raiding cavalry met Confederates under *Stuart*: the latter was mortally wounded. Grant again tried to encircle Lee's right, but this attempt was blocked by Lee's skilful withdrawal to positions on the North Anna River, 22 May. Fighting again took place during the next 10 days at the Battle of North Anna and Haw's Shop, with both armies gradually shifting south towards Richmond. Grant launched a renewed assault on 3 June to begin the Battle of Cold Harbour, which lasted until the 12th, this time endeavouring to split Lee's army. Repeated Union attacks were beaten off. While Sheridan's cavalry raided westwards, clashing with Confederates under Wade Hampton at Trevilian Station on 11 June, and while other Union forces demonstrated before Richmond, the bulk of Grant's army slipped across the James River, 13–18 June, after brilliant engineering work to erect a pontoon bridge. Grant threw his available forces at *Petersburg*, 8 miles away. But the initial attack failed, resulting in the siege of Petersburg, June 1864 to April 1865.

Wilson, Sir Henry Hughes, 1864–1922 British Field-Marshal. Appointed Director of Military Operations, the War Office, in 1910, and immediately intensified the Anglo-French discussions on co-operation in a Continental war – these had been held in desultory fashion since 1905; by 1911 Wilson had in effect agreed with the French General Staff that in the event of war with Germany the whole of the British Expeditionary Force would be deployed on the exposed left flank of the French Line. Wilson replaced *Robertson* as Chief of the General Staff, February 1918, retaining this position until 1922. Elected MP for

North Down, *Ireland*, in 1922, Wilson advocated drastic measures against Sinn Fein members, and was murdered later in the year.

Wilson, Sir Henry Maitland, 1st Baron, 1881–1964 British Field-Marshal. Served in Boer War and First World War; Commander British Army of the Nile, 1939–40; GOC-in-C Cyrenaica, March 1941, and appointed Commander of forces in *Greece* in the same month, under *Wavell* as Middle East Commander; Commander, allied forces in Syria and Transjordan, summer 1941; Commander in Persia-Iraq from December 1941; appointed Middle East Commander, February 1943, in succession to *Alexander*, being succeeded by General Sir Bernard Paget, December 1943; became Supreme Allied Commander Mediterranean, until November 1944, when he was succeeded by Alexander; he succeeded *Dill* as Head of the Joint Staff Mission to Washington, January 1945–7.

Wilson, Thomas Woodrow, 1856–1924 28th US President. Succeeded President William Howard Taft, March 1913; he intervened in the *Mexican Revolution*, ordering the landing of US forces at Vera Cruz, April 1914, and the dispatch of forces under *Pershing* in March 1916 to seek Pancho Villa after the latter's raid into New Mexico. Wilson was re-elected in 1916 after his Democrat Party had promoted the slogan: 'He kept us out of the war.' Wilson himself had refused to use neutrality as a campaign promise, and the introduction of unrestricted submarine warfare by Germany in the Battle of the *Atlantic* brought US participation in the struggle, April 1917. On 8 January 1918 he outlined to Congress his Fourteen Points on the basis of which a peace might be obtained. In October 1918 the Germans notified Wilson of their acceptance of an armistice based on these Points, and the armistice was signed on 11 November. Wilson attending the Versailles Peace Conference overestimated his support at home: strong opposition existed in the Senate over the peace terms based on the League of Nations, especially from isolationists led by Henry Cabot Lodge. Wilson began a speaking tour in early September 1919, but suffered a stroke on the 25th. He continued his fight from the sickbed, without success; he was succeeded by Warren Harding in 1921, and the USA moved further into an isolationist position.

Wingate, Orde Charles, 1903-44 British General. Creator and Commander of Special Night Squads used by Jewish forces during the Arab revolt in Palestine, 1936-9, with these groups being the forerunner of the *Israeli* Palmach. Wingate created and led a guerrilla organization in Ethiopia, which undertook operations against the Italians, 1940. He then conceived, trained and led the *Long Range Penetration Group*, known as the *Chindits*, which fought against the Japanese in *Burma*, 1943-4. Wingate died in an air crash in Burma, March 1944.

Wireless The first wireless transmission was made in 1892 by Sir William Preece, 1834-1913, over ¼ mile. In 1895 Guglielmo Marconi, 1874-1937, sent a message over 1 mile near Bologna, and in 1900 he dispatched and received signals over the Atlantic, 3,000 miles. By 1914 this means of communication had developed sufficiently to play a part in warfare, vastly improving the existing *telegraph* line network.

Wolseley, Garnet Joseph, 1st Viscount, 1833-1913 British Field-Marshal. Fought as Captain in *Crimean War*, wounded and losing an eye during an assault on Sebastopol, 18 June 1855; served in *Indian Mutiny* operations, taking part in the relief of Delhi, September 1857; in China, 1860; and in Canada, 1861-70; commanded Ashanti expedition, 1873-4, destroying the Ashanti capital of Kumasi, February 1874; Commander in Natal, 1875, Cyprus, 1878, southeast Africa, 1879-80; in campaigns in *Egypt*, 1882, Wolseley commanded the expedition to relieve *Gordon* at Khartoum in the *Sudan*, 1884, arriving 28 January, too late to save the British Commander. Wolseley was Commander-in-Chief of the British Army 1895-9, and proved a vigorous reformer; he headed the so-called Wolseley Ring, a group of influential senior officers in the 1880s and 1890s; he put into effect *Cardwell*'s short-service system and abolished the purchase of commissions.

Wounded Knee Creek, 'Battle' of, December 1890 This so-called battle ended the short-lived Sioux War in South Dakota, 1890–1, the last major Indian conflict. Leadership of the Sioux had passed to Chief Big Foot following the death of *Sitting Bull*, 15 December 1890. Big Foot tried to evade the US troops but fell ill with pneumonia; en route to seek safety he was surrounded by US cavalry, to whom he surrendered his 120 men and 239 women and children. The Indians were escorted to a camp at Wounded Knee Creek, close to the encampment of the US 7th Cavalry, Custer's old regiment which had been defeated at *Little Big Horn* in 1876 and which was now commanded by Colonel James Forsyth. Firing broke out on 20 December during the hand-over of the few weapons which the Indians possessed, and the Indians were slaughtered by the US carbines and by Hotchkiss machine-guns: about 300 of the total of 350 Indians were estimated killed, including Big Foot.

Wright, Wilbur, 1867–1912 and Orville, 1871–1948   US aircraft pioneers. The two brothers became interested in the possibilities of aviation in the early 1890s and experimented with kites and gliders. On 17 December 1903 they made the first successful flight in a motor-powered machine, when their airplane stayed in the air for 59 seconds and travelled 852 feet at Kitty Hawk, North Carolina. On 5 October 1905 their aircraft made a successful circular flight of $24\frac{1}{4}$ miles, staying aloft for 38 minutes; on 31 December 1908 they flew 124 kilometres in France. They manufactured an airplane for the US War Department, 1908, but this crashed during tests on 17 September; the machine was repaired and successfully tested in June 1909. Wilbur died on 30 May 1912; Orville sold his interest in the Wright Company in 1915, but later became Director of the Wright Aeronautical Laboratory, Dayton, Ohio.

Y

Yamamoto, Isoroku, 1884–1943 Japanese Admiral. Served in Russo-Japanese War; appointed Vice-Minister of the Navy, 1936, and Chief of the Aviation Department of the Navy, 1938; he became C-in-C of the Japanese 1st Combined Fleet in 1939. Yamamoto drafted Operation Order No. 1 dealing with the initial offensive in the Second World War. On 2 December Yamamoto issued the pre-arranged code to the Strike Force proceeding towards *Pearl Harbor*, indicating that the attack should be made on the 7th. Despite the initial success, Yamamoto warned that Japan lacked resources to survive a long war. His subsequent orders led to the Battle of the *Coral Sea*, May 1942, and *Midway* in the same month; operating from his HQ at Truk, he gave close personal supervision for the defensive measures in the south and south-west Pacific; he was shot down and killed by US aircraft, 18 April 1943.

Yemen, civil war in, 1961–5 Sporadic fighting had already been taking place along Yemen's southern border with the British *Aden* Protectorate, with Yemen supplying arms to rebels fighting against the British in the Rad-fan mountain area. In 1961 an insurgency started within Yemen itself against the ruler, Immam Ahmed. The rebels were supported by *Nasser*'s United Arab Republic. Fighting intensified after the death of Immam Ahmed and the assumption of the crown by Prince Saif as-Islam Mohemmed a Badr, 19 September 1962. Insurgents proclaimed the 'Free Yemen Republic' on 27 September and the rebel government was recognized by communist nations on the 29th. Colonel Abdullah al-Sallal, the insurgent leader, was proclaimed President on 31 October. Egyptian troops entered the country to support Sallal, rising to 35,000 men by 1965, and the UAR initiated *chemical* warfare in the country in 1966, using mustard-gas and phosgene. The Royal forces, aided by Saudi Arabia, succeeded in investing the Republic capital of San'aa at the end of 1967; President Sallal was overthrown by a coup during the year and the Republican leadership split. But the Royalists proved unable to inflict a decisive defeat, with forces suffering heavily from air attack whenever they attempted to concentrate: Republican aircraft were reported to include 24

MiG-19s sent by Russia. The invest-ment of San'aa was broken in March 1968; the capture of Sa'dah, the last Royalist stronghold, was claimed in September. Isolated pockets con-tinued to resist until 1971.

Yorck, Count Hans David Ludwig von Wartenburg, 1759–1830 Prus-sian Marshal. Fought in Poland, 1794, and against the French during the *Auerstedt* campaign, 1806, com-manding the Prussian light infantry, 'Jäger', and joining with *Blücher* in the retreat to Lübeck where he was captured, 6 November. Yorck parti-cipated in the reorganization of the Prussian Army undertaken by *Scharn-horst* and *Gneisenau*, advocating con-scription. He commanded a Prussian corps in the French Army after Prus-sia allied herself with Napoleon in 1812, remaining in the Riga region during the subsequent French cam-paign in *Russia*. He was persuaded to sign the Convention of Tauroggen, 30 December, which neutralized the troops under his command, and which led to Prussia's break from France. He fought at *Lützen*, May 1813, and was appointed a Corps Commander under Blücher in August, fighting with dis-tinction at the Katzbach, 26 August, Wartenburg, 3 October, and in the Battle of *Leipzig*, 16–20 October. He continued as a Corps Commander under Blücher in the 1814 campaign, but retired prior to the *Waterloo* cam-paign in 1815.

Ypres, First Battle of, October–November 1914 *First World War*

(Map 10). Fighting at Ypres, one of the final battles in the '*Race to the Sea*', began in mid-October with an attempt by the BEF to prevent a Ger-man drive on the Channel ports. The Ypres Front was only held by thin lines, but the defenders managed to repulse the initial German attacks; on the left, the Belgians opened sluice gates to halt the Germans, and an area 2 miles wide was flooded to a depth of 4 feet. The German attacks dwindled on 19 October following the arrival of reinforcements. A counter-offen-sive continued until 28 October with very heavy casualties. On 29 October the German Commander, *Falkenhayn*, ordered a resumption of the attack, which continued until heavy rains and snow brought the battle to an end on 11 November. By now about 80 per cent of the original BEF had been destroyed – about 58,000 British casualties. French casualties were 50,000, German 130,000. The allies were left in an unfavourable salient 6 miles deep, overlooked by German lines on the surrounding hills.

Ypres, Second Battle of, April–May 1915 *First World War* (Map 10). At 5 p.m. on 22 April the German Commander, *Falkenhayn*, launched a heavy assault aimed at throwing the BEF from the Ypres salient. Included in the initial bombardment was the emission of chlorine gas from about 5,000 cylinders, used for the first time. The main attack fell on the British 2nd Army under General Sir Horace Smith-Dorrien; heavy casualties were inflicted on Canadian troops rushed forward to bolster the line, but the German advance was halted. On 27 April Smith-Dorrien decided a limited withdrawal should be made; he was instantly relieved of command by *French* and replaced by *Plumer* – who issued the same withdrawal order. The battle ended after a last German attack, 24–25 May. Allied losses, mainly British, totalled 60,000 men killed and wounded, German about 35,000.

Ypres, Third Battle of (Passchendaele), July–November 1917 *First World War* (Map 10). Preceded by the seizure of *Messines ridge*, June. On 31 July the British Commander, *Haig*, began the offensive with a twin thrust towards the village of Passchen-daele: British forces were separated into the 5th Army, under General Hubert Gough, initially with the main role, and the 2nd Army under *Plumer*. The weather broke during the evening of the 31st, and Haig added further delay by deciding to reverse the roles of Gough and Plumer. The latter pushed forward over shell-holes brimming with water and through thick mud, against German mustard-gas attacks – used here for the first time. The British managed to seize the village of Passchendaele, 6 November – about 5 miles from their July starting line. These miles cost 240,000 British casualties; German losses were about equal. The British launched one more offensive before the year ended: at *Cambrai*, 20 November.

Z

Zapata, Emiliano, 1879?–1919
Mexican revolutionary leader. Zapata
played a constant role during the upheavals of the *Mexican Revolution*,
1910–19, fighting a succession of Presi-
dents – Madero, Huerta, Carranza –
whom he deemed to be corrupt.
Idealistic and yet an excellent *guerrilla
warfare* commander, Zapata cam-
paigned mainly in his native state of
Morelos, south of Mexico City; he
refused to take the leadership of the
revolutionary campaign as a whole,
and displayed no inclination to assume
any kind of power in Mexico City itself. His importance lies in his instinctive grasp of the techniques of revolutionary guerrilla warfare, which in
some respects predated the doctrines
propounded by *Mao Tse-tung*: he
insisted that the military struggle must
always be linked to political aims;
battles should be avoided unless abso-
lutely necessary; the support of the
people was the prime weapon to be used
against counter-revolutionary forces.
Zapata's main preoccupation was the
introduction of agrarian reforms for
the Morelos peasants. He was lured
into a trap and murdered, April 1919.

Zeebrugge and Ostend, British
raids on, May–June 1917; April

1918 *First World War* (Map 10).
Royal Naval vessels bombarded the
German destroyer and submarine
bases at these two ports in early summer 1917, causing some damage but
failing to disrupt enemy U-boat operations in the battle of the *Atlantic*.
More drastic attempts were made on
23 April 1918. Admiral Keyes, commander of the RN Dover Patrol,
organized an attack by about 75 warships; one, the cruiser 'Vindictive'
commanded by Captain A. F. B. Car-
penter, steamed into Zeebrugge with
a destroyer and submarine escort, and
disembarked demolition parties. A
submarine packed with explosives was
blown up against the submarine pen
gates. An attack against Ostend on the
same day failed to achieve significant
results.

Zhukov, Georgi Konstantinovich,
1895–1970 Soviet Marshal. Entered
Army 1915; served in Bolshevik forces
during the *Russian Revolution*; commanded forces against the Japanese
in Mongolia, 1938–9. Zhukov was
appointed Commander of the Red
Army Central Front, October 1941,
responsible for the defence of Moscow and launching his counter-attack
in December. He began a renewed

offensive in November 1942, now commanding all four Soviet Fronts, which led to the collapse of the German Line and the isolation of *Stalingrad*; he took personal command of the 1st Ukrainian Front, January 1944, and continued to drive west, pressing into Poland in July. Zhukov commanded the main Russian Army Group – 1st White Russian – for the final invasion of *Germany*, then assumed control of the Combined Army Groups for the Battle of Berlin; he eliminated all resistance by 2 May. Zhukov was Deputy Minister of Defence, 1953–5, and Minister, 1955–7.

Zulu War, 1879 Britain's annexation of the Transvaal, April 1877, eventually led to fighting with the Boer settlers, 1880–1, and the *Boer War* of 1899–1902. Meanwhile, conflict arose between the British and native Zulu tribesmen led by Cetewayo. About 5,000 British troops and 8,200 native soldiers invaded the area on 11 January 1879. The Commander was General F. A. Thesiger, Viscount Chelmsford, an experienced officer who had fought in the Crimean War, the Indian Mutiny and in the Abyssi-

nian campaign of 1868. He had just completed service in the Kaffir War, 1878. Chelmsford advanced in 3 main columns. The centre force was surprised by Zulus at Isandhlwana, 22 January, and destroyed; Chelmsford was absent at the time. On 22–23 January Cetewayo struck the second column, attacking its base camp at Rorke's Drift; the Zulus withdrew in the face of superior fire power. British troops under Colonel C. K. Pearson were besieged at Eshowe, January–April, but were finally relieved by Chelmsford. On 29 March a British force under Sir Evelyn Wood beat off a Zulu attack at Zambula. Soon afterwards Chelmsford received reinforcements, and in early summer he launched a major offensive towards Cetewayo's camp at Ulundi. The Battle of Ulundi, 4 July, decided the war. The British, about 5,000-strong, were outnumbered 2 to 1 by the Zulus, but fire power and disciplined drill achieved an overwhelming British victory. The Zulus lost about 1,500 killed, compared with a British casualty total of 100 dead and wounded. Cetewayo was captured on 28 August, and later imprisoned in England; he died in 1884.

MAPS

Legend:
- Italian Campaign 1796-7
- Italian Campaign 1799
- Italian Campaign 1800
- Campaign against the Third Coalition 1805
- Campaign against Prussia and Russia 1806-7
- Austrian War 1809
- Campaign of the Peninsular War 1808-13
- Russian Campaign 1812-13
- 1815 Campaign
- 1814 Campaign

Lübeck
Dunkirk · Hondschoote
Ostend · Antwerp
Boulogne · Tournai · Brussels
· Jemappes · Waterloo
Coblenz
Merseberg
Halle · Leipzig
Kösen
Auerstedt · Jena
Naumberg
Menin · Mainz · Würzburg · Amberg
Lille · Beaumont · Kaiserslautern
Paris · Valmy · Saarbrücken
Montereau · Strasbourg · Ratisbon
· Bar-sur-Aube · Abensberg · Eggmu
Ulm · Landshut
Stockach
FRANCE · Zurich · AUSTRIA · Salzb
· Freiberg · Innsbruck
EMP
Lyon
Bordeaux · Milan · Brescia · Rivoli
Corunna · Lugo · Turin · Lodi · Arcola
Astorga · Bilbao · Sorauren · Orthez · Gap · Magnano · Pavia · Castiglione · Mantua
Vittorio · Digne · Nice · Marengo · Bologna
Ôporto · Saldaña · Burgos · Toulouse · Marseilles · Cannes · Genoa · Florence · Anc
Bussaco · Almeida · Salamanca · Toulon · Leghorn
Mondego Bay · Ciudad Rodrigo · Tudela · ITALY
Torres Vedras · Sarragossa
Lisbon · Alhandra · Talavera · Gerona · Rome
Badajoz · PORTUGAL · SPAIN · Barcelona
Albuera · Ciudad Real · Tarragona · Volturno
· Baylen · Tortosa · Naples

Cadiz · Malaga
Gibraltar

Calatafimi · Aspre
Marsala · Palermo

1 French Revolutionary and Napoleonic Wars

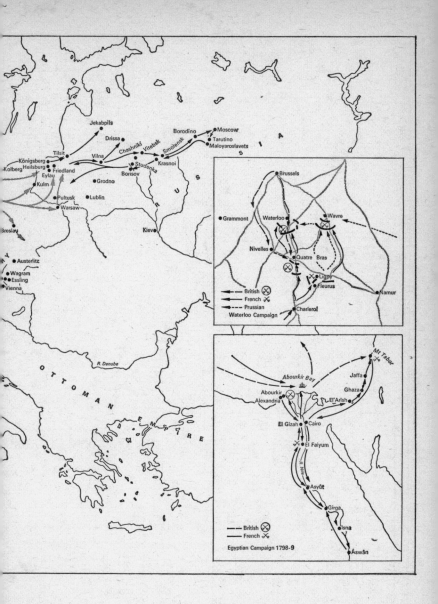

Jekabpils

Drissa

Königsberg
Kolberg Heilsburg
Eylau
Kulm
Pultusk
Warsaw
Breslau

Tilsit
Vilna
Chashniki Vitebsk
Grodno
Lublin

Borodino Moscow
Smolensk Tarutino
Krasnoi Maloyaroslavets

Studenka
Borisov

Kiev

Austerlitz
Wagram
Essling
Vienna

R. Danube

OTTOMAN EMPIRE

R U S S I A

Brussels

Grammont   Waterloo   Wavre

Nivelles   Quatre Bras

Ligny
Fleurus

Namur

Charleroi

British
French
Prussian

Waterloo Campaign

Abourkir Bay

Mt Tabor

Jaffa

Abourkir
Alexandria

Ghaza
El'Arish

El Gizah Cairo

El Faiyum

R. Nile

Asyût

Girga

Isna

Âswân

British
French

Egyptian Campaign 1798-9

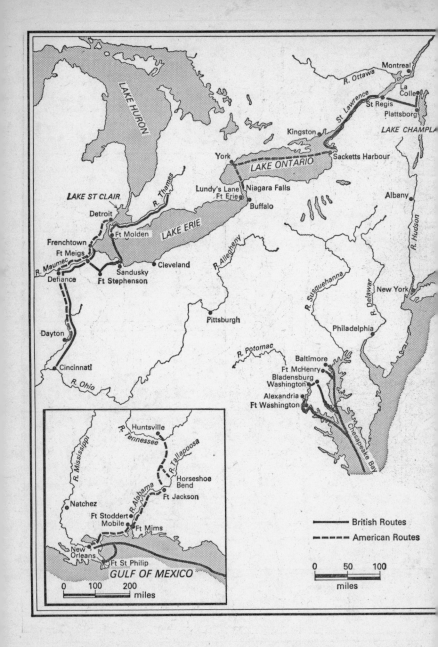

Lake Huron

Lake St Clair

R. Thames

Detroit

Ft Molden

Lake Erie

Frenchtown

Ft Meigs

R. Maumee

Defiance

Sandusky

Ft Stephenson

Cleveland

R. Allegheny

Dayton

Cincinnati

R. Ohio

Pittsburgh

York

Lake Ontario

Lundy's Lane
Ft Erie

Niagara Falls

Buffalo

Kingston

R. Ottawa

Montreal

La Colle

St Regis

Plattsborg

St Lawrence

Sacketts Harbour

Lake Champlain

Albany

R. Hudson

R. Susquehanna

R. Delaware

New York

Philadelphia

R. Potomac

Baltimore

Ft McHenry

Bladensburg

Washington

Alexandria

Ft Washington

Chesapeake Bay

R. Mississippi

Huntsville

R. Tennessee

R. Tallapoosa

Horseshoe
Bend

Ft Jackson

R. Alabama

Natchez

Ft Stoddert

Mobile

Ft Mims

New
Orleans

Ft St Philip

GULF OF MEXICO

0   100   200
miles

—— British Routes

------ American Routes

0   50   100

miles

2 American War of 1812

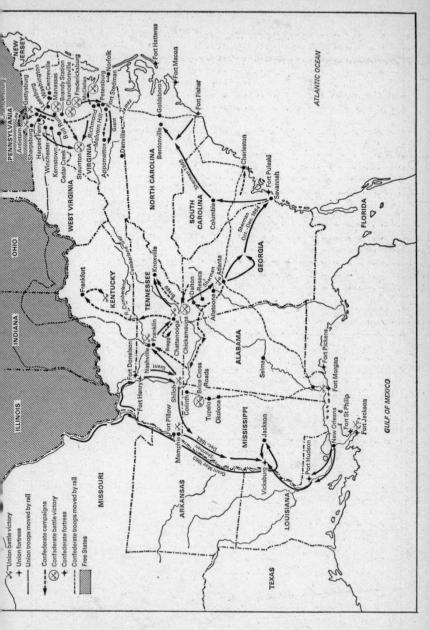

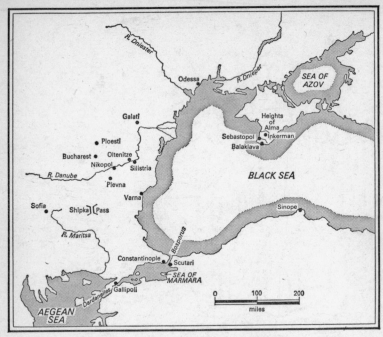

4   Crimean War 1853–6 (incorporating Russo-Turkish War, 1877)

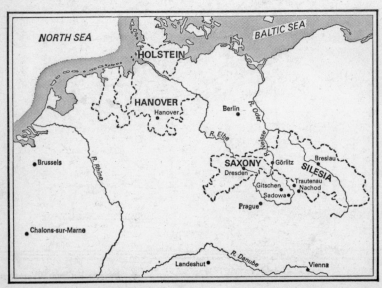

5   Austro-Prussian War 1866

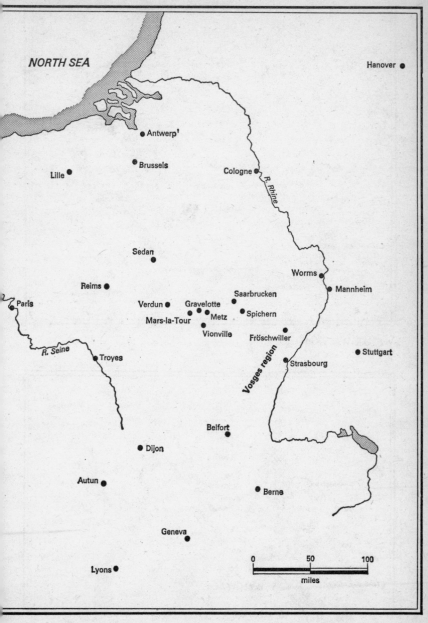

NORTH SEA

Hanover ●

● Antwerp¹

● Brussels

Lille ●

Cologne ● *R. Rhine*

Sedan ●

Reims ●

Worms ●

Paris ●

Verdun ● Saarbrucken ● Mannheim

Gravelotte ● Spichern ●

Mars-la-Tour ● Metz

Vionville ● Fröschwiller ●

R. Seine

Troyes ● Stuttgart ●

Strasbourg ●

Vosges region

Belfort ●

Dijon ●

Autun ●

Berne ●

Geneva ●

0   50   100

Lyons ●

miles

6 Franco-Prussian War 1870–1

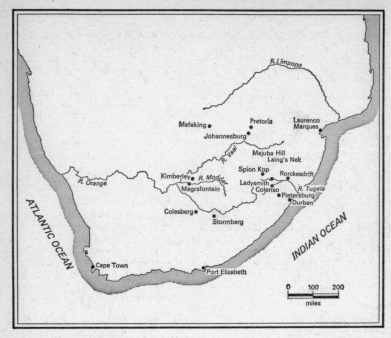

7   Boer War 1899–1902

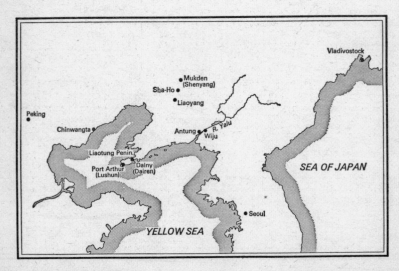

8   Russo-Japanese War 1904–5

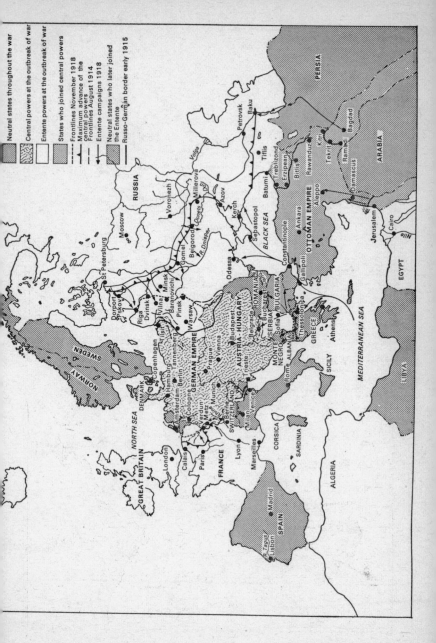

Neutral states throughout the war

Central powers at the outbreak of war

Entente powers at the outbreak of war

States who joined central powers

Frontlines November 1918
Maximum advance of the
central powers
Frontlines August 1914

Entente campaigns 1918

Neutral states who later joined
the Entente

Russo-German border early 1915

PERSIA

Baku

Petrovsk

Tiflis

Trebizond

Batumi

Erzerum

Rawanduz

Bagdad

ARABIA

Kitri

Tekrit

Ramadi

Damascus

Bitlis

Ankara

OTTOMAN EMPIRE

Aleppo

Jerusalem

Cairo

Nile

EGYPT

Constantinople

Gallipoli

BLACK SEA

Odessa

Sebastopol

Kerch

Azov

RUSSIA

Volga

Voronezh

Moscow

Millerova

Byigorod

Gomel

R Dnieper

R. Don

Minsk

St Petersburg

Dorpon

PSKOV

Riga

Dvinsk

Vilna

Baranovichi

Pinsk

Warsaw

MEDITERRANEAN SEA

LIBYA

ALGERIA

ROMANIA

BUCHEST

BULGARIA

Sofia

SERBIA

Belgrade

MONTE
NEGRO

ALBANIA

GREECE

Thessalonica

Athens

Budapest

AUSTRIA-HUNGARY

Vienna

Prague

Trieste

Venice

Milan

Rome

SICILY

SARDINIA

CORSICA

SPAIN

Madrid

R Tagus

Lisbon

FRANCE

Paris

Calais

London

GREAT BRITAIN

NORTH SEA

DENMARK

Copenhagen

GERMAN EMPIRE

Berlin

Hamburg

Hannenberg

Amsterdam

Cologne

Verdun

Metz

Munich

SWITZERLAND

Berne

Lyon

Marseilles

SWEDEN

NORWAY

9 First World War 1914–18

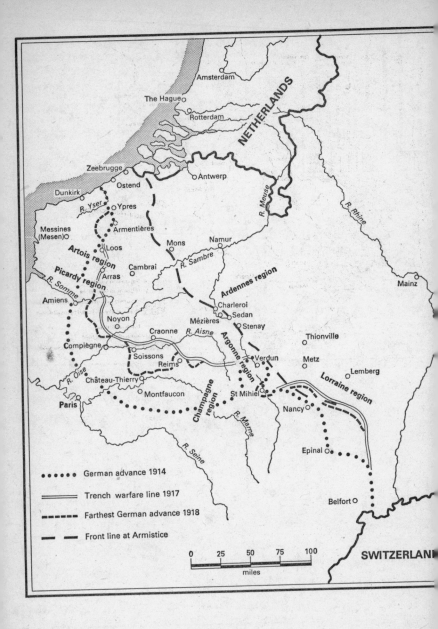

German advance 1914
Trench warfare line 1917
Farthest German advance 1918
Front line at Armistice

10 First World War: Western Front 1914–18

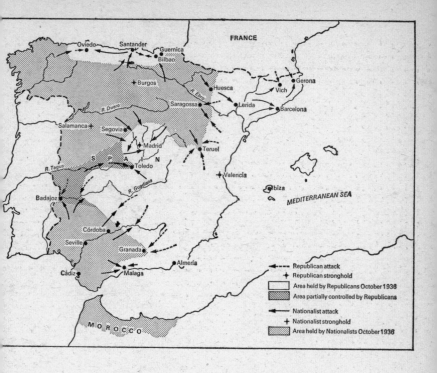

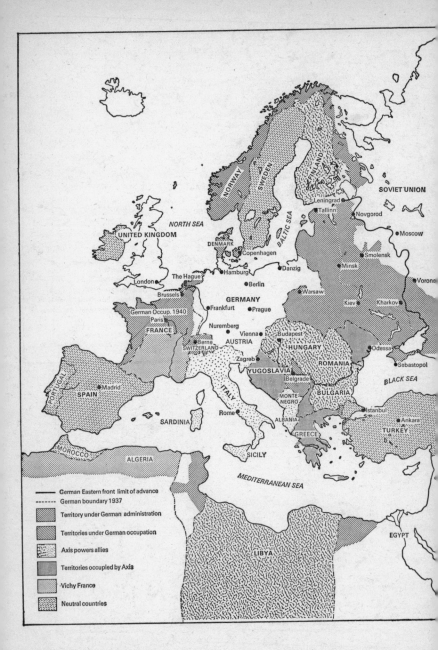

ICELAND

NORTH SEA

UNITED KINGDOM

London

Brussels

German Occup. 1940

Paris

FRANCE

PORTUGAL

SPAIN   •Madrid

MOROCCO

ALGERIA

NORWAY

SWEDEN

FINLAND

BALTIC SEA

SOVIET UNION

Leningrad
•Tallinn   Novgorod
                        •Moscow
DENMARK
Copenhagen   •Smolensk
Hamburg Danzig   •Minsk
The Hague Berlin
                •Warsaw   •Vorone
GERMANY   Kiev   •Kharkov
Frankfurt •Prague
Nuremberg Vienna Budapest   •Odessa
Berne AUSTRIA HUNGARY ROMANIA   •Sebastopol
SWITZERLAND Zagreb YUGOSLAVIA
                Belgrade BULGARIA BLACK SEA
ITALY   MONTE
          NEGRO •Istanbul
Rome•   ALBANIA   •Ankara
SARDINIA   GREECE   TURKEY

SICILY

MEDITERRANEAN SEA

LIBYA   EGYPT

--- German Eastern front limit of advance
----- German boundary 1937
Territory under German administration
Territories under German occupation
Axis powers allies
Territories occupied by Axis
Vichy France
Neutral countries

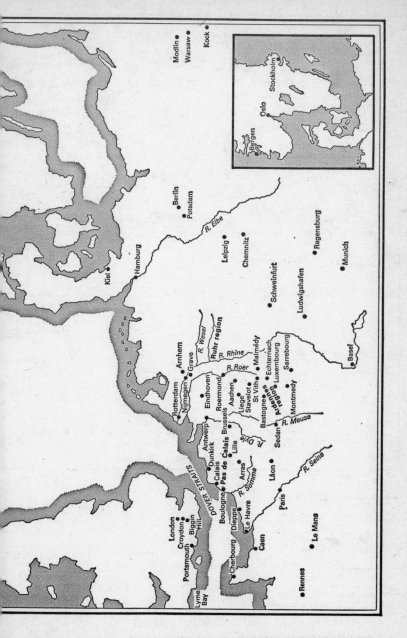

13 Second World War: Europe 1939-45

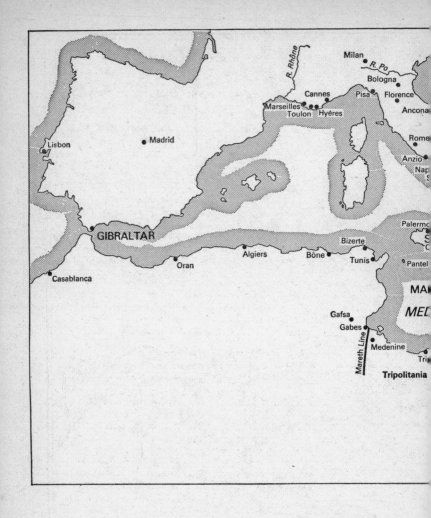

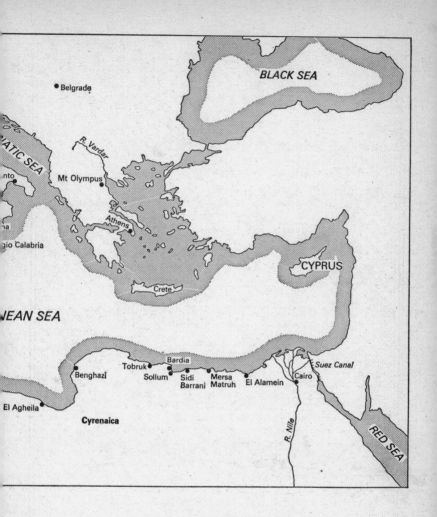

15 Second World War: Russian Front 1941–5

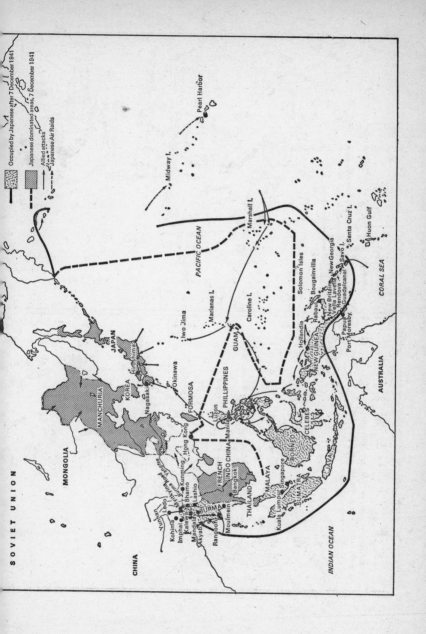

16 Second World War: The Far East and the Pacific Theatre 1941-5

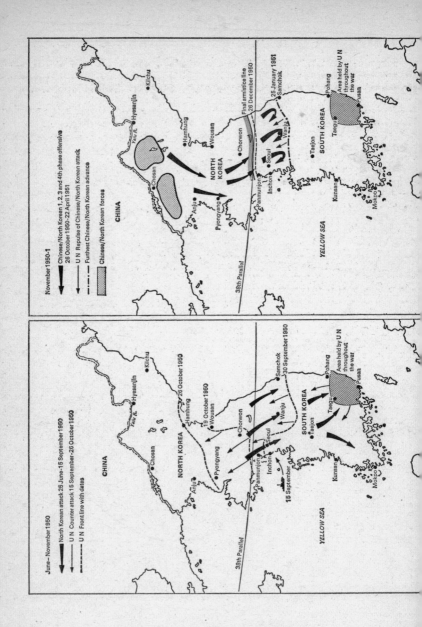

November 1950-1

→ Chinese/North Korean 1, 2, 3 and 4th phase offensive
26 October 1950–22 April 1951

→ U N Repulse of Chinese/North Korean attack

Furthest Chinese/North Korean advance

▨ Chinese/North Korean forces

Final armistice line 26 December 1950

25 January 1951

Samchok

Area held by U N throughout the war

Pusan

Chorwon

NORTH KOREA

Hamhung

Wousan

Hysenjin

Kilchu

Yalu R.

Chosan

Anju

Pyongyang

CHINA

38th Parallel

Panmunjon

Inchon

Seoul

Wanju

Taejon

SOUTH KOREA

Taegu

Pohang

Kunsang

Mokpo

YELLOW SEA

June – November 1950

→ North Korean attack 25 June–15 September 1950

→ U N Counter attack 15 September–26 October 1950

U N Front line with dates

26 October 1950

19 October 1950

Samchok
30 September 1950

Area held by U N throughout the war

Pusan

Chorwon

15 September

Hamhung

Wousan

Hysenjin

Kilchu

Yalu R.

Chosan

Anju

Pyongyang

NORTH KOREA

CHINA

38th Parallel

Panmunjon

Inchon

Seoul

Wanju

Taejon

SOUTH KOREA

Taegu

Pohang

Kunsang

Mokpo

YELLOW SEA

17 Korean War 1950–3

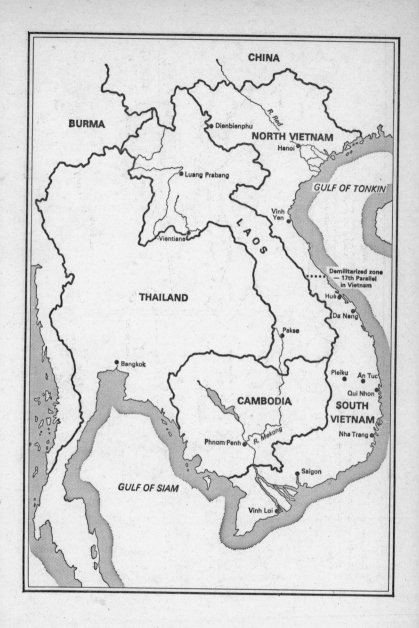

CHINA

BURMA

Dienbienphu

R. Red

NORTH VIETNAM

Hanoi

GULF OF TONKIN

Luang Prabang

Vinh Yen

LAOS

Vientiane

Demilitarized zone
— 17th Parallel
in Vietnam

THAILAND

Huê

Da Nang

Pakse

Bangkok

Pleiku   An Tuc

Qui Nhon

CAMBODIA

SOUTH VIETNAM

Phnom-Penh   R. Mekong

Nha Trang

Saigon

GULF OF SIAM

Vinh Loi

18   Indo-China

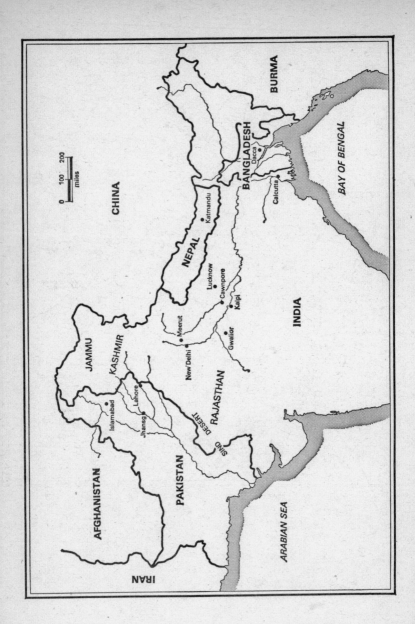

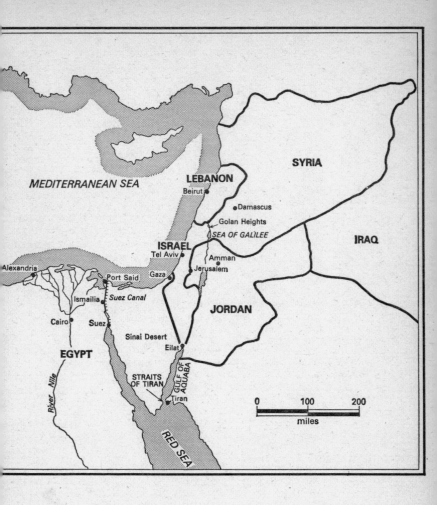

MEDITERRANEAN SEA

SYRIA

LEBANON
Beirut •

• Damascus

Golan Heights

SEA OF GALILEE

IRAQ

ISRAEL
Tel Aviv •

• Amman

• Alexandria

Port Said

Gaza •

• Jerusalem

Ismailia

Suez Canal

JORDAN

Cairo •

Suez •

Sinai Desert

EGYPT

Eilat •

River Nile

STRAITS
OF TIRAN

GULF OF AQABA

Tiran

0   100   200

miles

RED SEA

20   Middle East, post 1945

Index

Note Page numbers printed in bold refer to entries in the text devoted to that particular subject.

Basra, 213
Bassano, 172
Bastogne, 35–6, 246
Bataan peninsula, 254
Batista, Culgencio, 104, 156
Battenberg, Prince Louis Alexander of, 52; *see also* Mountbatten
Battlecruiser, general, 52–3, 56, 114
'Battle of Nations', *see* Leipzig
Battleships, general, 14, 53–4, 100, 125, 169, 204, 233, 284, 311
Bautzen, battle of, 54–5, 60, 87, 141, 188, 192, 199
Baylen, battle of, 249
Bay of Pigs, 105
Bayonet, general, 55–6, 224
Bazooka, 31
Beatty, Admiral Sir David, 43, 52, 56, 14, 176–7, 179–80, 223
Beaulieu, General Jean Pierre, 171
Beauregard, General Pierre, 68, 288
Beaverbrook, Lord William, 56, 67
Becquerel, Antoine Henry, 44
Belfort, battle of, 131, 138
Belgium, campaign in, Second World War, 12, 129–30
Below, General Fritz von, 293
Below, General Otto von, 173
Ben Bella, Ahmed, 20
Benedek, General von, 278
Benghazi, 112
Ben Gurion, David, 245
Bennigsen, Count Levin, 120–1, 133
Beresford, General William Carr, 250
Beretta sub-machine gun, 202
Berezina, 272
Berlin, allied bombing of, Second World War, 305
Berlin, battle of, 1945, 139
Berlin, Treaty of, 1850, 57
Berlin Airlift, 56–7, 231, 322
Berlin Wall, 181, 183
Bermann sub-machine guns, 202
Bernadotte, Crown Prince of Sweden, 193
Berthier, Marshal Louis, 57, 298
Bertrand, General Henri, 46, 199
Bhutto, President Zulfikar Ali, 164–5
Biafra–Nigeria war, 235–6
'Big Bertha', 39, 186, 294
Bikini Atoll, 162
Bilbao, 295

Billottee, General Gaston, 129
Biological Warfare, *see* Chemical and Bacteriological Warfare
Bir Hacheim, 112, 128
'Bismarck', 44, 53, 54, 293
Bismarck, Prince Otto von, 48, 57–9, 220, 245
Bittenfeld, General Karl, 48
'Black and Tans', the, 168
Bleriot, Louis, 13
Blitz, the, 28, 59, 142, 198, 222, 284, 305
Blitzkrieg, concept of, 14, 38, 59, 125, 130, 135, 148, 155, 162, 198, 258, 284, 308, 312
Bloch, Jean de, 59
Bloodhound missile, 29
'Bloody Ridge', battle of, 147
Blomberg, General Werner von, 59–60, 135, 158, 181
Blücher, Marshal Gebhard von, 60, 70, 141, 192–3, 194, 199, 281, 298, 337–9
'Blue Water' principle, 100
Blum, President Leon, 296
Bock, General Fedor von, 129, 258, 272
Boehn, General von, 209–10
Boer War, general, 50, 60–2, 63, 69, 76, 79, 90, 93, 104, 132, 294, 350
Bofors, 28, 31
Bojna, General Svetozan von, 173
'Bolt from Blue' principle, 100
Bonar Law, Andrew, 196
Bonin, Eduard von, 269
Booth, John Wilkes, 195
Bordeaux, 250
Borgne, Lake, 25
Bor-Komorowski, General Tadeusz, 336
Borny, battle of, 131
Borodino, battle of, 62–3, 188, 271
Bosquet, General Pierre, 167
Botha, Louis, 63, 90, 292
Bougainville, 235
Boumedienne, Colonel Houari, 20
Bourbaki, General D., 138
Bourne, General A. G. B., 92
Bovington, 312
Boxer, Colonel Edward, 251, 292
Boxer Rebellion, 308
Boydton Farm, 254
Boyen, General Hermann von, 298
Boys anti-tank rifle, 31
Bozzaris, Marco, 144

To H.G.P. with appreciation and gratitude

Contents

Maps

Preface

This is the first single encyclopedia to bind together the main threads involved in the development of war, 1793–1975. Previous military reference books have concentrated on battles or weapons or personalities; this has been compiled in an attempt to cover all three, plus other aspects equally essential to an understanding of modern war, including conceptual topics such as strategy, tactics and various theories and principles. The aim has been to produce a book providing a reference framework to the factors involved in the convulsion of warfare during this period; one aspect relates to another to give a more comprehensive coverage.

Vigorous selection has obviously been required to keep the book within a reasonable length. As many items have been rejected as chosen, and those included have been subjected to ruthless restraint. It is nevertheless hoped that all major topics are dealt with, both for an overall outline and as a means for further exploration.

I express my gratitude to all those who helped with the compilation of the entry list, especially Brian Bond, King's College, London, Michael Elliot-Bateman, Manchester University, and Gwynne Dyer, Sandhurst. I only regret that many of their exhaustive suggestions could only be included as part of other items; responsibility for the selection, of course, rests entirely upon myself. I needed more help from my wife Betty with this book than with any other: as always, her response proved greater than all possible expectation.

Words in italics refer to other relevant entries where more information can be obtained. The following abbreviations have been used: AEF (American Expeditionary Force), ANZAC (Australian and New Zealand Army Corps), AOC (Air Officer Commanding), BAOR (British Army of the Rhine), BEF (British Expeditionary Force), C-in-C (Commander-in-Chief), GPMG (General Purpose Machine-gun), GOC (General Officer Commanding), ICBM (Inter-Continental Ballistic Missile), IRBM (Intermediate Range Ballistic Missile), LMG (Light Machine-gun), NATO (North Atlantic Treaty Organization), OKH (Oberkommando des Heeres, German Army High Command), OKW (Oberkommando der Wehrmacht, German High Command of all three services), OSS (Office of Strategic Services), SA (Sturmabteilung, German stormtroopers), SACEUR (Supreme Allied Commander, Europe), SHAPE (Supreme Headquarters, Allied Powers in Europe), SOE (Special Operations Executive), SS (Schutzstaffel), STOL (Short Take-off and Landing), RFC (Royal Flying Corps), VTOL (Vertical Take-off and Landing).

A

Absolute war Concept marking an extension of total war. The latter is a conflict harnessing all national resources – economic, financial, technological – to the furtherance of military aims, but with these aims nevertheless politically motivated. Absolute war is one in which political aims are smothered; when military power becomes overriding at the expense of political control. On a lower level total war represents the involvement of civilians in war, as opposed to campaigns merely being waged against other armies with civilians largely unaffected. *Sherman*'s march to *Atlanta* in 1864 was total war; indeed *Grant*'s whole campaigning policy can be considered total, but it stopped short of being absolute: Grant remained subordinate to the President, *Lincoln*. War approached absolute form in the *First World War*: the generals achieved supremacy, especially the *Hindenburg–Ludendorff* partnership in Germany. *Clausewitz* warned against such military dominance and in doing so defined absolute as opposed to total war:

> Policy . . . is interwoven with the whole action of War and must exercise a continuous influence upon it . . . War can never be separated from political intercourse, and if this is done in any way . . . we have before us a senseless thing without an object.

Nuclear warfare, with no possible achievable political aim for either side, would be absolute.

Aden Area of last fighting involvement of British troops during the withdrawal from 'East of Suez', a policy undertaken from 1964 in the abandonment of former Empire territory. The last British servicemen left Aden on 29 November 1967, after 128 years of British rule. Hostilities by insurgents had begun in 1963, aided by groups in the *Yemen*, and reached a peak in the final year with 2,600 incidents. From December 1963 to November 1967, 135 British servicemen were killed. British rule ended with the granting of independence to South Arabia, later the South Yemen Republic.

Airborne forces Paratroop operations first came near to reality in early 1918, when the US Army Air Service officer *Mitchell* gained *Pershing*'s ap-

proval for dropping men of the 1st US Infantry Division behind German lines, but this operation was superseded by the ending of war. *Chennault* in the USA demonstrated the use of paratroops in 1925 and 1928 but failed to receive official backing. In 1927 the Russians became the first to drop airborne troops in combat, operating against tribesmen in Asia. Russian developments were further stimulated by Tukhachevsky in the early 1930s and an independent Russian parachute division was created; *Wavell* watched a Russian exercise in 1936, but his report attracted insignificant attention in the British War Office. Tukhachevsky was executed in 1937 during *Stalin*'s purges and the Russian airborne programme lapsed. Meanwhile the Germans had formed an experimental airborne staff in 1935 under General Kurt Student; an airborne division, the 7th, appeared in 1939. German paratroops were first used during the invasion of *Norway* and Denmark in April 1940. On 10 May 1940 airborne troops were employed extensively in the invasion of Belgium, dropped from 450 aircraft, and German plans for the invasion of Britain, operation *Sealion*, envisaged up to 8,000 paratroops in the first wave. About 11,000 airborne soldiers from Student's 11th Air Corps were thrown into the battle for *Crete*, May 1941, but the heavy casualties suffered in the seizure of the island turned *Hitler* against the airborne concept. In June 1940 *Churchill* had urged the raising of 4,000 British airborne troops, and General Sir Frederick Browning was instructed in October 1940 to raise an airborne division. The first British airborne operation took place on 10 February 1941, when 38 parachutists blew up the Tragino Aqueduct, Italy. The USA formed the 501st Parachute Battalion in September 1940, and a Provisional Parachute Group was created in 1941. Three airborne divisions were employed in the *Normandy* landings, attempting to improve on methods already used in the invasion of *Sicily* in the previous year. In September 1944 the US 82nd and 101st Divisions joined with the British 1st for the unsuccessful operation against *Arnhem*. By 1945, 5 US airborne divisions and several independent airborne regiments had been created. The French sent 17 parachute battalions to *Indochina* – 11 of which were captured at *Dienbienphu*; between 1948 and 1954 the French carried out over 200 airborne drops. French paratroops were also used in *Algeria* where their élite status caused friction with the ordinary conscripts and helped play a part in the subsequent mutiny. In general, however, the paratrooper has reverted more to the role of ground infantryman: rather than parachute drops, forces are moved by *helicopter*, with this machine assuming increasing importance as an air transport vehicle – especially shown by the US operations in *Vietnam*. By contrast, during the US involvement in Vietnam only one tactical parachute operation was conducted. Parallel with the use of airborne forces has been the development of air portable equipment, de-

signed with minimum weight, easily transferable parts and able to be dismantled as far as possible. Such equipment ranges from medical items to special aluminium vehicles and *artillery*: the largest Russian helicopter, the Mi-12, set an official record by lifting loads of nearly 40 tons. Artillery designed for an airborne role includes the US 105 mm howitzer M.102, transportable in the Caribou fixed-wing aircraft or in the Chinook helicopter.

Aircraft At the end of the eighteenth century the British inventor Sir George Cayley produced designs for model heavier-than-air craft, and he constructed a 5-foot model glider in 1804. In doing so Cayley laid down the basic principles which lay behind the earliest aircraft, including the method whereby a sturdy wing structure could be obtained by adopting a wire-braced biplane or triplane layout, and the use of dihedral angles between the wing pairs to improve aerodynamic stability. The French naval officer Felix du Temple designed and tested a monoplane in 1857 which had a propeller and was first equipped with a clockwork motor, later adapted to steam: this was probably the first heavier-than-air craft to take off and fly under its own power. The *Wright* brothers made the first successful flight in a motor-powered machine in December 1903. By 1914 all major participants in the *First World War* had developed rudimentary air power: Germany was credited with 12 aircraft 'factories'. France had 8 aircraft

manufacturing establishments, with French development spurred on by the engineer and pioneer pilot Louis Blériot, 1872–1936, who made the first Channel flight in a heavier-than-air machine in July 1909. Britain's *RFC* was formed in April 1912 although with less than a dozen pilots. Machines possessed by all belligerent nations combined came to less than 2,000 in 1914, and these aircraft were nondescript types. Various specific categories soon emerged: single and dual seater fighters, observation aircraft and, by 1917, larger aircraft designed for bombing. Fighters included the French Nieuport and Spad; these had a top speed of 91 mph and 119 mph respectively; the British BE2C, with a top speed of about 90 mph; the German Fokker, which by 1917 had won control in the air with the introduction of a synchronized system enabling the *machine-gun* to fire through the whirling propeller. Later aircraft included the British Sopwith Camel: this had a top speed of about 120 mph and carried 25-pound bombs. Bombers included the British Handley Page, the Italian Caproni and the German Gotha. Fighter squadrons were usually equipped with about 18 aircraft, observation and bombing squadrons with 12. Life expectancy for pilots was extremely short: the British had 1,300 aircraft operating in support of their armies at the beginning of the Second Battle of the *Somme*, 1918, but when fighting ended a few weeks later only 200 remained. Nevertheless, by 1918 the allies had about 8,000 aircraft against the enemy's 3,300. Naval air

power was also being developed: the age of the *aircraft carrier* had opened, and the British Fleet Air Arm came into being in 1924. Post-war developments covered the establishment of organizations specifically concerned with air power – the *RAF* was created from the RFC in the last months of the war and the *Luftwaffe* emerged after 1933 – or the establishment of organizations still linked with the Army, as for example the *US Army Air Force*. Yet apart from Germany, the major powers failed to develop air power to a sufficient degree prior to 1939, despite the pleadings of theorists such as *Douhet* and *Mitchell*. The Second World War saw the emergence of air power through *strategic bombing* already advocated by men such as Britain's *Trenchard*, through the great fighter conflicts such as the *Battle of Britain*, and through close ground support as epitomized by *blitzkrieg*. The British designer Frank Whittle had studied the concept of jet propulsion during the 1930s and the Gloster–Whittle E28/39 flew for the first time in May 1941. The first flight of a jet aircraft had already been made by the Germans, with the Heinkel He 178 in August 1939, which led to the Messerschmitt Me 262. From the British development emerged the Gloster Meteor, in service with the RAF in 1944. Aircraft entered the supersonic age in October 1947 when Captain Charles Yeager of the USAF flew a specially built Bell X-1 rocket aircraft beyond the speed of sound – the so-called Mach 1. The term Mach 1 represents 760 mph at sea level, fall-ing to about 660 mph at 36,000 feet and above. Latest developments have been to increase maximum speeds to the region of Mach 8, and to introduce greater versatility through STOL (short take-off and landing) and VTOL (vertical take-off and landing) aircraft. Aircraft have been developed specifically for various definite roles. Examples include carrier-based aircraft (the British Buccaneer, the US A6A Intruder and the British Sea Vixen); maritime reconnaissance aircraft (the Canadair and the RAF Nimrod); tactical fighters, fighter-bombers and interceptors (the US F111A, the RAF Hawker Hunter, the USSR MiG 21); tactical bombers (the RAF Canberra Mk 8, the USSR Ilyushin 'Beagle'); strategic bombers (the US Stratofortress B52H, the French Mirage IVA, the RAF Valiant and Vulcan, the USSR Tupolev 'Bear' and 'Blinder'); and multi-role aircraft such as the RAF Lightning, the French Mirage F1, the US F-104G Starfighter and Phantom. Another recent development has been the effort at joint production between allies to reduce costs and to introduce greater interchangeability: an example of such a project is the Anglo-French Jaguar, a single-seat light tactical support aircraft capable of Mach 1·7 at 36,000 feet.

Aircraft carriers In 1906 the German Navy began to take an interest in the Zeppelin *airship* for naval reconnaissance, and in April 1908 definite proposals were made within the German Admiralty for such machines

as scouting vehicles. Interest was also being expressed in Britain and America over the possibilities of heavier-than-air craft to provide the fleet with eyes, to act as a defensive screen. It immediately became apparent that in order to operate at fullest possible effectiveness such aircraft should be provided with a base within the fleet itself. From this realization emerged the aircraft carrier – a vessel which eventually proved capable of asserting local naval superiority and in doing so superseded the *battleship* as the most powerful capital warship. Rather than being a subsidiary of the fleet, the aircraft carrier developed to the extent that it gathered around itself a fleet dependent upon it. The aircraft carrier remains predominant today, despite fears of its vulnerability against missiles; it continues to display its effectiveness in terms of mobility and flexibility, carrying with it the advantage of avoiding the need to establish land bases with their consequent diplomatic entanglements. The first successful flight from platforms rigged on a ship's deck was made by the US airman Eugene Ely in 1911. On 1 January 1912 the British pilot Charles Samson flew his Short airplane from a track constructed on the bows of the cruiser HMS 'Africa'. In 1913 the crude prototype of an aircraft carrier, the converted cruiser HMS 'Hermes', launched her aircraft during trials: 'Hermes' had an abbreviated flying-off deck and 3 aircraft. The same year conversion began on a tanker to give a larger deck space for 10 seaplanes: this warship was commissioned the HMS

'Ark Royal' in 1915. The original 'Hermes' sank after being torpedoed in the Channel in October 1914; her successor, completed in 1919, was the first vessel specially designed as an aircraft carrier. During the First World War the British established the Royal Naval Air Service, merged with the *RFC* into the *RAF* in 1918 but separating again in 1924 as the Fleet Air Arm. The first US carrier was the 'Langley', put into service soon after the First World War. Japan had two aircraft carriers by the time the Washington Naval Treaty of 1921 restricted naval tonnage. Development throughout the inter-war years culminated in the Royal Navy's 'Ark Royal', commissioned in 1938 and incorporating all latest features: arrester wire to halt incoming aircraft, net crash barrier, batsmen to guide pilots in and catapults. The latter system had first been suggested in 1914 and the first successful trial took place in 1917. In September 1939 Britain had 10 carriers, while France and Germany had only 1 each. At the time of *Pearl Harbor*, December 1941, America had 3 carriers in the Pacific – 'Enterprise', 'Lexington' and 'Saratoga' – while Japan had 11. The naval war in the Pacific revolved around these warships and American production soared from 3 carriers in 1942 to over 100 by the end of the war. *Coral Sea*, May 1942, marked the first great carrier battle; *Midway*, June 1942, resulted in the loss of the Japanese main carrier fleet. Post-war developments have included the angled flight-deck, which permits aircraft to land whilst others are taking

off – a British idea but with the Americans incorporating the first angled deck in the training carrier 'Antietam'; the mirror-sight landing device; the steam-powered catapult. The latter two innovations were also British ideas, rapidly taken up by the Americans. Britain herself decided in 1967 that her fixed-wing carrier force would be phased out. By 1973 Britain had only one fixed-wing carrier left in service, plus *commando* carriers equipped with helicopters. The pride of the US fleet was the first nuclear-powered carrier, 'Enterprise', the largest aircraft carrier ever built – standard displacement was 75,700 tons. This vessel was completed in December 1961; cruising range was equivalent to twenty times round the world; the vessel cost about £158,570,000; aircraft complement was up to 100. A second nuclear-powered attack carrier (CVAN), the 'Nimitz', entered service after the 'Enterprise', with two more planned. Russia neglected carrier production until she decided to build one 40,000-ton Kiev-class vessel, probably designed for 25 short/vertical take-off and landing aircraft (S/VTOL) or 36 helicopters; this warship was expected to be in service during 1976–7, with a second vessel being built.

Airship As early as 1852 a steam 'dirigible' managed to fly for a short period, but its speed of only 6 mph meant that it would be unable to counteract even the slightest wind. 'La France', built in 1884 and driven through electric power, obtained a faster speed but exhausted its battery within 5 miles. As with *aircraft*, adequate development had to await the internal combustion engine. In 1898 the Brazilian-born Alberto Santos-Dumont, living in Paris, merged the *balloon* with a petrol-driven machine; in the same year Count Ferdinand von Zeppelin (1838–1917), who had served in the Union Army during the American Civil War and in the Austro-Prussian and Franco-Prussian conflicts, established an airship factory at Friedrichshafen, Germany. In July 1900 the first Zeppelin airship, LZ1, flew at Lake Constance: this, driven by two 15 hp Daimler engines, moved at 16 mph; Zeppelin had constructed the contraption on a solid framework known as a 'rigid', unlike earlier efforts which still resembled balloons. The second rigid airship, LZ2, was completed in 1905 with more powerful engines giving 170 hp: this machine was wrecked on her second flight in June 1906, but had succeeded in reaching a height of 1,800 feet and a speed of 26 mph. Also in 1906 Santos-Dumont flew his craft round Paris in a 30-minute circular tour. LZ3 was completed in October 1906, and stayed airborne for 8 hours during tests. LZ4 appeared in June 1908, built to German Army specifications: she flew over the Alps, but was still too slow and fell victim to a thunderstorm. LZ5 flew a distance of 820 miles in May 1909 and was accepted by the German Army. Progress in Britain proved slower. The Army Balloon factory at Farnborough completed the 'Nulli

Secundus' in 1908, which was non-rigid and ungainly, although managing to fly at 16 mph. *Vickers*, working in conjunction with the British Admiralty, began work on Naval Airship No. 1 or 'Mayfly' in 1909, yet this craft was not completed until 1911 and then proved totally unsatisfactory. The Admiralty rejected the airship idea for a few months, but work started again in 1912. By 1914 the German armed forces had 30 dirigibles, all Zeppelins; the French had 10 and the British 7. The latest Zeppelin, L3, completed in May 1914, had engines totalling 630 hp, an endurance range of 30 hours or 1,500 miles, a crew of 20 and a top speed of just over 47 mph. Zeppelin raids were conducted over France and England in 1915 and early 1916; the heaviest attack took place on London on 13 October 1915, and the last on 5 August 1918. In doing so the Zeppelins initiated a new form of aerial war. Two flights of Zeppelins were flown at the Battle of Jutland, but were unable to have positive influence owing to poor visibility. Fighter *aircraft* soon revealed the vulnerability of airships: the first Zeppelin was shot down over England on 3 September 1916; 2 more were destroyed by ground fire on 26 September, and others soon followed. Sixteen Zeppelins survived the war: 8 were turned over to the allies, 1 was dismantled and the remaining 7 sabotaged in June 1919. The Zeppelin Company was allowed to build 2 small commercial craft, but these were also handed over to France and Italy.

Alamein, El, Battles of, July and October 1942 *Second World War* (Map 14). *Rommel* advanced into Egypt with all possible speed after his victories at Gazala and Mersa Matruh in late spring, but clashed with *Auchinleck*'s 8th Army on 1 July at the hastily improvised El Alamein positions; this, the First Battle of El Alamein, saw the loss of Rommel's initiative in the *desert campaign*. His supply lines were overstretched; the British Desert Air Force was reaching maximum effectiveness – during the battle the RAF flew over 15,000 sorties. The Afrika Korps advanced in the early hours of 1 July only to be stopped by unexpectedly determined artillery fire; Rommel's Italian allies made no progress in a simultaneous thrust farther north. The balance began to shift in Auchinleck's favour on the 3rd, and although the battle continued in varying intensity throughout the month the British commander could claim success by 7 July. Auchinleck introduced improvements into the 8th Army battle-tactics during the battle, which were to become increasingly important: these included more effective use of concentrated artillery fire and deployment of British armour en masse rather than piecemeal, with the tanks drawing the Germans on to their line – a tactic previously used in devastating fashion by the Afrika Korps. *Montgomery* took over command of the 8th Army on 11 August, after Churchill's original choice, General W. H. E. Gott, was killed; *Alexander* took over Auchinleck's other superior role as

GOC-in-C Middle East. Rommel, faced with a growing imbalance in strength, attacked on 31 August in an attempt to break through his enemy's defence at Alam al Halfa. His plan was typically bold: to hold in the north, feint in the centre and punch through the south. Rommel relied on speed and surprise. However, Montgomery had already managed to impose his vigorous will over the 8th Army and he continued the improvements introduced by Auchinleck Deployed in crucial defensive positions at Alam al Halfa ridge, to the rear of the British minefields, was General Sir Brian Horrocks's 13th Corps, preventing Rommel from outflanking the defences. Rommel was obliged to thrust against this ridge; he found the task impossible and started to pull back on 3 September. Montgomery allowed the enemy to retreat, wishing to preserve the 8th Army intact for the decisive Second Battle of El Alamein. By the beginning of October the 8th Army had an awesome preponderance of power: twice as many troops (almost 200,000 to 50,000 Germans and 54,000 Italians), twice as many tanks (1,000 compared to about 500) and similar artillery figures. The Desert Air Force numbered about 530 serviceable aircraft compared with about 150 German and 200 Italian. Montgomery envisaged his infantry breaking two main corridors into the enemy infantry defences: 30th Corps in the north and 13th Corps farther south. British armour would follow the infantry into the breaches to defeat the enemy tanks. Montgomery told his commanders to plan for a 'dog-fight' of a week, with the total battle lasting about 10 days – later amended to 12; this proved correct. At 9.40 p.m. on 23 October, about 800 British guns opened a tremendous barrage in an attempt to blanket the Axis artillery. The battle, code-named operation Lightfoot, moved almost immediately into the infantry assaults. Rommel was away from the area, returning on 25 October from consultations with Mussolini and Hitler. On 28 October, after 6 days of full-scale battle, Montgomery changed his plans: he decided to turn his southern thrust, where the 13th Corps had become bogged down, entirely over to the defensive, thus allowing more divisions to be placed in reserve. These would be used for an attempt to smash through the northern – 30th Corps – area, with this operation code-named Supercharge. Montgomery intended to aim this hammer blow on the faltering Italians. At 1 a.m. on 2 November the offensive began on a 4,000-yards front. By nightfall on 3 November the Afrika Korps had been reduced to a mere 30 tanks. Shortly before dawn, 4 November, Rommel ordered retreat. Only about 36 out of 249 German tanks were left on 4 November and only half the Italian total of 278. Axis killed and wounded probably totalled about 20,000; the 8th Army lost 13,000 and 432 tanks had been put out of action.

Alexander, Sir Harold Rupert, 1st Earl Alexander of Tunis, 1891–1969 British Field-Marshal. Served in France, 1914–18; Northwest Frontier,

India, 1935; Commander, 1st British Division, 1938–40; C-in-C *Burma*, February 1942 to August 1942, replacing *Auchinleck* as C-in-C Middle East. Alexander was appointed Deputy Allied C-in-C North Africa, February 1943, under *Eisenhower* and Supreme Allied Commander Mediterranean, November 1944, responsible for the continued conquest of *Italy*.

Algeria, revolt in, 1954–62 France conquered Algeria after a campaign beginning in 1830, and eventually almost a million French and other Europeans settled in the country. Demands for Algerian autonomy from the French were made soon after the Second World War; the major nationalist organization, the Front de Libération Nationale (FLN), was established in 1951, but the call for independence was countered by the long-held French policy of seeking to integrate the country with metropolitan France. The first major clash between nationalists and security forces took place on 8 May 1948, but not until 1954 did the FLN launch a full-scale *guerrilla war*. French troop reinforcements led to an army of 450,000 in the country, including élite paratroop units. Amongst counter-guerrilla methods was the attempt to close the Algerian borders against FLN incursions from Morocco and Tunisia: along the latter frontier the French established the Morice Line, comprising two rows of electric fencing and barbed wire, separated by minefields and guarded by radar posts. The population was forcibly evacuated

from some adjacent areas, the land being designated as free-fire zones where civilians could be shot at sight. Inside Algeria the French covered large areas with a grid or checkerboard of garrisons and fortified posts, with this system of close territorial control known as 'quadrillage'. In the latter stages of the war about 300,000 troops were committed to territorial defence, either deployed in static positions or in mobile interception roles. One feature of the war was the increasing brutality displayed by both sides, together with the use of torture. In June 1958 the French authorities admitted that security forces had tortured Algerians and clear evidence constantly emerged of widespread atrocities. One colonel in charge of a detainee camp admitted the use of torture, claiming that 'the fight against terrorism makes certain methods of interrogation indispensable as the only way to save human lives and avoid new attacks', and this attitude seemed common. Nevertheless the FLN remained strong, and the war itself became increasingly complicated by other factors. The FLN received support from the Arab states, and French resentment at Egyptian actions contributed to the 1956 *Suez* conflict. In 1958 frustration over failure to put down the FLN led to increasing unrest among the settlers in Algeria. On 13 May there began a revolt by French officers protesting against the political handling of the war and led by the paratroop general Jacques Massau. The French government was overthrown in the subsequent outcry; the

army in Algeria, spearheaded by the paratroop units, was in a virtual state of mutiny, insisting that Algeria must be considered as part of France and that there must be no compromise with the FLN. On 1 June 1958 *De Gaulle* was returned to power, becoming President of the Fifth Republic on 21 December with a new constitution providing him with increased powers. He attempted to organize a referendum on the question of self-determination, but this alienated the extremist settlers, 'ultras', and the Algerians of French descent, 'pieds noirs'. These extremists joined with French military personnel to form the OAS secret army, pledged to keep Algeria under French control, and terrorism reached increasingly brutal proportions. De Gaulle visited Algeria in an attempt to calm the situation, but although he managed to restore French governmental control over the OAS, the FLN terrorism continued. On 22 January 1960 opposers of De Gaulle's policy rioted in Algiers; the riots continued until 1 February when they were put down by loyal French units under General Maurice Challe. The latter himself turned against the central authorities, joining with General Raoul Salan in an army mutiny which broke out on 22 April 1961. This was quietened 4 days later and Salan escaped to the OAS. However, De Gaulle gradually came to terms with the FLN, despite the OAS stance; peace talks began in France on 20 May and negotiations led to the proclamation of a ceasefire on 3 July 1962, with Ahmed Ben Bella the premier. Internal

unrest against Ben Bella led to his overthrow on 19 June 1965, his replacement being the former FLN fighter, Colonel Houari Boumédienne.

Allenby, Sir Edmund Henry, 1st Viscount, 1861–1936 British Field-Marshal. Served in Bechuanaland, 1884–5; Zululand, 1888; and in *Boer War*, 1899–1902. Commanded British 3rd Army in First Battle of the *Somme*, June–November 1916, and in Battle of Arras, April 1917. Allenby relieved General Sir Archibald Murray as commander of British forces in *Palestine*, April 1917; his instructions were to 'take Jerusalem before Christmas'. He defeated the Turks at Beersheba, 31 October, and Junction Station, 13–14 November, entering Jerusalem on 9 December. Allenby resumed his offensive on 18 September 1918 and won a brilliant victory at Megiddo, 19–21 September. He entered Damascus on 1 October and Beirut the following day. Turkey signed an armistice on 30 October.

Alma River, Battle of, September 1854 *Crimean War* (Map 4). British, French and Turkish troops, totalling 52,000 men, began advancing on Sebastopol on 19 September. About 36,500 Russians made a defensive stand on the heights on the south of the Alma River, commanded by Prince Menshikov. The bank of the river was 15 feet high in places, with the hills beyond sloping to the Russian positions on a plateau, from which deadly fire could be directed down on an attempted assault. The offensive

began on the 20th. Menshikov, confident of his positions, had neglected to defend the steepest cliffs southwards on the coast, where a track was discovered and used by French troops. But then the French came under heavy fire from remaining Russian defences in this area; the French commander insisted the British should attack in the centre. Shortly after 3 p.m. Lord *Raglan* therefore gave the order for the advance on the heights. The assault covered a 2-mile front. The advance continued towards the Russian Great Redoubt despite the terrible bombardment. Incredibly, the Russian guns finally ceased to fire; Emperor Nicolas had ordered Menshikov to withdraw Russian artillery before it fell into enemy hands. The Light Division stormed and took the Great Redoubt, but support failed to arrive after the Duke of Cambridge, commander of the second line, delayed while he received more precise instructions from Raglan. During this confusion the Light Division was driven back. The second British line crossed the river, comprising the Brigade of Guards and the Highland Division commanded by Sir Colin *Campbell*. The Guards assaulted the Great Redoubt with the Highlanders on their left, and reached the summit. They then battered through massed Russian infantry to win the battle. The British cavalry, so far inactive, were in an excellent position to destroy the retreating enemy: Raglan refused to give orders for the pursuit, believing the cavalry too precious to be risked. Menshikov withdrew unmolested; the

allies continued the march on Sebastopol prior to the Battle of *Balaklava*. Allied losses at Alma, mostly British, totalled about 3,000; Russian casualties were about 5,700.

American Civil War, 1861-5, general (Map 3) This was a war which spotlighted latest military developments: *rifles*, *breech-loading* and *magazine* infantry weapons including the *machine-gun*, especially the *Gatling*; *railways* and *steam-power*; rifled field artillery, sometimes *breech-loading*; the *torpedo* mine; *ironclad* warships; rudimentary *submarines*; *balloon* observations; *telegraph*. The conflict revealed that the industrial revolution had made the civilian responsible for providing the industrial means of war; the factory became as important as the battlefield. The north achieved victory because it survived the longest; the south collapsed because its war industry had been captured or dislocated. Modern fire power had begun to rob the battlefield of its ability to force the final conclusion: infantry weapons, and especially the machine-gun, had raised the killing range to about 500 yards and had vastly increased the rate of fire, so undermining the ability of the opposing force to overwhelm the enemy through massed bayonet charges. The superiority of defensive warfare had begun to emerge. The war was saved from becoming bogged down because of increased mobility provided by the railroad, and because information could be transmitted through the telegraph. Forces could be shifted

more quickly and with greater effect, and armies were still sufficiently small to be able to penetrate gaps in enemy deployment – and also leave gaps in their own dispositions. Defeat at *Bull Run*, July 1861, meant the north lost the opportunity of ending the struggle in one blow, and the caution of the northern Union generals formed a contrast to *Jackson*'s manoeuvring in the *Shenandoah* campaign, May–June 1862, leading to *Malvern Hill*. The supremacy of the southern Confederate leadership was underlined at the Second Battle of *Bull Run* in August, *Antietam* in September, *Fredericksburg* in December and *Chancellorsville* in May 1863. But Grant had begun to emerge: his leadership, combined with the greater northern resources, started to turn the tide, beginning at *Shiloh* in April 1862. While he built up strength in the west, *Meade* won the devastating victory over the Confederate hero *Lee* at *Gettysburg*, July 1863. Grant's determination resulted in the surrender of *Vicksburg* in the same month. The northern strategic campaign began to find cohesion under Grant and his able lieutenant *Sherman*, with the latter winning his first major victory at *Chattanooga* in November. In March 1864 Grant became Union General-in-Chief, and he planned his gigantic pincer movements which would disembowel the south. These two movements comprised the *Wilderness* campaign striking towards the north and leading to the siege of *Petersburg*, and Sherman's celebrated march to *Atlanta* and then to Savannah. The pincers

were beginning to snap shut when Lee was forced to surrender at *Appomattox*. About 2,210,000 men served in the Union forces during the war; about 140,000 of these died in battle, 281,881 received serious wounds, 224,000 died from other causes. Confederate estimates of men serving ranged from 600,000 to 1,500,000. It has been assessed that about 133,800 Confederates died in the war, plus up to 31,000 dying in Union prisons.

American–Mexican War, 1846–8 Relations between the USA and Mexico deteriorated with the US annexation of Texas, at the latter's request, following the *Texan War of Independence*, 1835–6. Mexico insisted her territory extended to the Nueces River running towards San Antonio, Texas, while the USA claimed an area spreading south to the Rio Grande. US troops under Zachary *Taylor* advanced to the Rio Grande in March 1846, deploying opposite Mexican units at Matamoros. The latter attacked on 25 April prior to a general invasion under General Mariano Arista on 1 May which besieged Camp Texas. Taylor clashed with the enemy on 8 May in the Battle of Palo Alto, which resulted in a Mexican withdrawal. Next day Taylor forced the Mexicans over the Rio Grande in the Battle of Resaca de la Palma. Only on 13 May was war officially declared. Taylor crossed into Mexico 5 days later. He advanced south in August with 6,000 men, storming 10,000 Mexicans under General Pedro de Ampudia at Mon-

terrey, 20–24 September, after which he agreed to a Mexican request for an 8-week truce. This agreement was repudiated by the US President, James Polk, and Taylor continued south to occupy Saltillo on 16 November. Further operations were hampered by disagreement in Washington over strategic plans. The US Army C-in-C, Winfield *Scott*, finally left Washington in late November to establish his HQ at Tampico prior to a move on Vera Cruz. Taylor was meanwhile ordered to adopt a defensive role during Scott's invasion; this was disrupted by the appearance in mid-February of a Mexican army under Santa Anna, advancing from San Luis Potosi. Santa Anna attacked on 22 February but was repulsed in the hard-fought Battle of Buena Vista after stubborn defence by US artillery under Bragg. This victory ended the northern campaigns of the war; the focus shifted to central Mexico. Scott landed on 9 March with 10,000 men and Vera Cruz fell on the 27th; Scott moved west, routing Mexican troops under Santa Anna at Carro Gordo on 18 April and occupying Puebla on 15 May. He advanced on Mexico City in early August, overrunning Mexican defensive positions at Contreras and Churubusco on the 20th. The US offensive resumed on 8 September with a bitter battle at Molino del Rey. Scott's troops took this defensive position, but the US strength was now down to about 7,500 men: Santa Anna had double this number. Scott nevertheless maintained pressure, taking the last major obstacle before Mexico

City, Chapultepec Hill, on 13 September. The garrison at Mexico City surrendered next day. Peace talks led to the Treaty of Guadalupe, 2 February 1848, giving the USA possession of land up to the Rio Grande, including California, Nevada, Utah and large areas of Arizona, New Mexico, Colorado and Wyoming.

American–Spanish War, 1898 US public opinion, incensed by Spain's brutal handling of insurrection in Cuba from 1895 to 1898, was further enraged when the US battleship 'Maine' exploded and sank in Havana harbour, 15 February 1898, with 260 men lost; Spain was accused of blowing up the warship; America declared war on 25 April. On 1 May, Commodore George Dewey's warships attacked the Spanish squadron in Manila Bay: this, 4 cruisers and 3 gunboats under Admiral Patrico Montojo was virtually annihilated. Manila capitulated after the arrival of US troops on 30 June. Meanwhile, Cuba had become the centre of operations. Spanish warships under Admiral Pascual Cervera reached Santiago de Cuba on 19 May; Admiral William T. Sampson, commanding the US Atlantic Fleet, immediately blocked the enemy in the harbour. On 22 June almost 17,000 US troops commanded by General William R. Shafter began landing near Santiago against 35,000 enemy troops commanded by General Arsenio Linares; they met in the Battle of San Juan on 1 July. Fighting centred on two features known as Kettle Hill and El Caney Ridge, taken

at a cost of about 1,500 US casualties, almost double the Spanish total. Admiral Cervera failed to break out of Santiago harbour in a naval engagement on 3 July; Santiago capitulated on 17 July. US troops under General Nelson A. Miles landed at Puerto Rico on 4 August and were engaging in a successful campaign when hostilities ceased with the Treaty of Paris, 10 December. Spain relinquished sovereignty over Cuba, ceded Puerto Rico and Guam to the USA and sold the Philippines to the USA for $20 million. The war, although successful for America, revealed deficiencies in the US armed forces, as did disturbances in the *Philippines* from 1899 to 1902. These failings stimulated reform under Secretary of War Elihu *Root*.

American War of 1812 (1812-15) (Map 2) Britain encroached US neutrality at sea during the seriously naval war against Napoleonic France: over 6,000 US seamen were impressed into the Royal Navy; shots had already been exchanged. War was declared by the USA on 19 June 1812 'to defend the freedom of the seas', although many Americans also saw the conflict as a means of expanding into British Canadian territory. A US attempt to invade Canada in late summer and autumn 1812 failed dismally when US militiamen maintained their constitutional right not to fight outside US territory. An expedition the following year achieved better results, leading to the capture of Detroit on 29 September 1813 and defeat inflicted on 800 British regulars and 1,000 Indians

in the Battle of the Thames, 5 October. Jacob Brown invaded Canada with 3,500 troops on 2-3 July 1814, seized Fort Erie, and 3 days later engaged 1,700 British regulars under General Phineas Riall in the battle of Chippewa. The British were charged down, suffering 236 killed and 322 wounded; US casualties were 61 dead, 255 wounded. Brown continued to push northwards, until Sir Gordon Drummond arrived with reinforcements. The two sides met in the Battle of Lundy's Lane, 25 July, but neither could gain the advantage; Brown retired to Fort Erie, which was abandoned on 5 November, so ending all attempts to invade Canada. Meanwhile, on 31 August 1814 the British in their turn had invaded the USA with 14,000 troops newly arrived from *Wellington*'s army in Europe; these advanced from Montreal under General Augustine Prevost. The target for the invasion was New York, but first Lake Champlain had to be secured. British vessels on the lake were decisively beaten in the Battle of Lake Champlain on 11 September (see naval operations, below); Prevost retreated. Farther south in Alabama the Creek Indians allied themselves with the British and rose in revolt. Militiamen under Andrew *Jackson* marched against them, defeating 900 warriors at Horseshoe Bend, 27 March 1814. Jackson, given command of the Gulf Coast area, moved to New Orleans following rumours of a British invasion. This took place on 13 December 1814, with 7,600 British veterans of the *Peninsular War* landing in the

Lake Borgne area under the command of Major-General Sir Edward Pakenham. Jackson organized efficient defences at New Orleans, although he had only 3,100 trained troops. A full-scale British assault began on 8 January 1815. The British advanced in regular ranks, suicidal against well-positioned defenders, and over 2,000 were killed or wounded with Pakenham among the dead; only 7 Americans died. The British sailed a week later. Land operations in the War of 1812 therefore failed to bring decisive results. Meanwhile, naval operations had been continuing. America had only 14 seaworthy vessels; the Royal Navy employed over 100 ships, including 11 ships of the line and, despite brilliant single-ship actions, the US sailors were unable to break the tight British blockade. The Americans achieved more decisive results on the inland waters, with *Perry*'s victory over a Royal Naval squadron on Lake Erie, 10 September 1813, providing a turning-point of the war in the northwest. (See *Perry*.) The following summer, 1814, the British employed sea power in combination with land forces for a damaging invasion in the Chesapeake Bay area. Admiral Sir John Cockburn's squadron joined 5,400 Peninsular War veterans, under Major-General Robert Ross, and on 19 August this force landed on the Patuxent for an advance on Washington. The British entered the US capital on the 24th, burnt the Capitol and the White House, and marched triumphantly back to their ships. The expedition then sailed north to land

16 miles from Baltimore but this time the local militia successfully defended the town, in an action on 14 September at Fort McHenry during which Ross was fatally wounded; the British withdrew on 14 October. Whilst the Americans were suffering these humiliations the British were dealt an equal disgrace in the most decisive action of the war on Lake Champlain, 11 September. The British had constructed a squadron of 4 ships and 12 armed galleys to support Prevost's advance on New York. The Americans had a squadron of similar size at their Plattsburgh base, commanded by Lieutenant Thomas MacDonough. A ship-to-ship engagement took place on the 11th, during which the Americans outgunned their opponents; the British commander, Captain George Downie, was killed and his squadron surrendered after suffering heavy damage. War ended with the Treaty of Ghent, 14 December – signed before Jackson and Pakenham fought their Battle of New Orleans. The treaty made no mention of basic issues and decided nothing, although the British thereafter ceased violating US maritime neutrality.

Amiens, Battle of, August–September 1918 *First World War* (Map 10). *Ludendorff*'s fifth and final offensive ended at the *Marne* in early August. On 8 August the allies began their counter-attacks, with the British 4th and French 1st Army under *Rawlinson* and Eugene Debeny pushing against the German 18th and 2nd under *Hutier* and Marwitz. Learning from the lesson of *Cambrai*, the allies

avoided a preliminary artillery bombardment and bolstered the attack with 462 tanks. Fog cloaked the initial movement, and allied troops forced a salient 10 miles deep during the first 24 hours, helped by aircraft after the fog lifted. Ludendorff described 8 August as the 'Black Day'. *Haig*, British Commander-in-Chief, paused to regroup; the advance began again on 21 August but depletion of allied reserves eventually enabled the Germans to fall back to their ultimate positions. German casualties were over 100,000, allied about 44,000. The final storming of the *Hindenburg Line* would begin on 26 September after a preliminary US operation against the *St Mihiel* salient.

Anderson, Sir John, 1st Viscount Waverley, 1882–1958 British civil servant. Served in Colonial Office, 1905 onwards; Governor of Bengal, 1932–7; Lord Privy Seal, 1938–9 and Home Secretary, 1939–40 in Neville Chamberlain's government, with duties including those of Home Security; responsible for interning aliens and for air-raid protection – the Anderson shelter was named after him. This construction consisted of two curved walls of corrugated steel bolted to rails; the shelter was sunk 3 feet into the ground and covered with 18 inches of earth. Free issues were provided to those earning less than £250 p.a. On 12 June 1940 Anderson announced the completion of the shelter programme, which he had launched in late 1938; he claimed that 20 million people could now find shelter simul-

taneously. Anderson shelters were later supplemented by the indoor *Morrison* variety. Sir John acted as Lord President of the Council, 1940–3, under *Churchill*; his Lord President's Committee, created June 1940, acquired major influence, dealing with all important domestic, Home Front and economic questions; Churchill called Anderson 'my automatic pilot'. Anderson acted as Chancellor of the Exchequer, 1943 to July 1945.

Angola, guerrilla war in, 1961–75 Fighting broke out in this Portuguese African colony in spring 1961, where tribesmen in the north were influenced by the advent of independence for fellow-Africans in neighbouring *Congo*. Portugal introduced emergency measures in April, sending 15,000 troops. The insurgents were organized into several political and semi-political groups, including the Union of Angolan People (UPA), the Movimento Popular de Libertacao de Angola (MPLA) and the Front for the Unity of Angola (FUA). The guerrillas were helped by the establishment of bases in the Congo. The death of Antonio de Oliveira Salazar in 1970 – Portuguese dictator for 36 years – resulted in the assumption of power by President Caetano, ousted in spring 1974 by General Spinola, a previous commander in Portuguese Africa and a critic of Portuguese policies: during his brief regime Spinola began the proceedings for early independence in the colonies, thus ending the need for insurgency in Angola, Portuguese Guinea – where lower-scale conflict

had begun in 1963 – and in *Mozambique*. Portuguese troop strength before withdrawals began in 1974 had risen to about 55,000 men. Opposition to the Angolan war from inside Portugal had been steadily increasing, on the grounds of the unpopular overseas service and through the high cost: in 1974 Portugal's expenditure on defence amounted to 6·8 per cent of the Gross National Product, at $880 million, and thus represented a higher percentage of the GNP than any other NATO country – the figure for Britain and the USA respectively was 5·2 and 6·0. The new Portuguese government agreed in 1974 for independence for both Angola and Mozambique. Targeted independence dates were respectively 25 June and 11 November 1975. But fighting again broke out in 1975 between rival nationalist groups in Angola, with these factions becoming concentrated around three principal organizations: the National Front for the Liberation of Angola, FNLA, the National Union for the Total Independence of Angola, UNITA, and the MPLA. At the end of the year FNLA forces controlled much of the northern part of the country and UNITA troops held the south; the MPLA managed to cling to a central sector including the capital of Luanda. The situation changed dramatically in the first weeks of 1976 with communist support for the MPLA arriving at Luanda in the form of Cuban troops and Soviet military equipment. The latter included T-34 tanks; multiple rocket launchers and transport vehicles; MiG 19 aircraft were flown into Luanda airfield,

and a Soviet task force including a tank-landing vessel cruised off-shore. Cuban troops, eventually numbering up to 8,000, pushed north and south from the central region and both FNLA and UNITA proved incapable of stemming the advance, despite the presence of about 1,200 South African troops in the far south region. Despite pressure from Secretary of State *Kissinger*, the US Congress blocked the dispatch of aid. By early February the major FNLA and UNITA bases at Carmona and Novo Redondo had been seized, and the MPLA were in control of the country by early March; fears immediately arose that the Cuban troops might move beyond Angola into Zambia or into white Africa.

Anti-aircraft No specific attempts were made to provide protection against air attack in the *First World War* apart from the use of machine-gun fire and crude *balloons*, and theorists in the inter-war years such as *Douhet* and *Mitchell* gave the impression that aircraft in future conflicts would be comparatively safe from ground reprisal. On the basis of misleading figures from bombing in 1917–18 it was estimated in the 1930s that each ton of HE dropped in the next war would cause 50 casualties; perhaps as many as 600,000 people would perish in the first major bombing attack on London. This erroneous concept of the impossibility of finding adequate defence against the bomber stilted development of anti-aircraft weapons. Apart from using other air-

craft, defence against air attack took two main forms up to and during the *Second World War* – balloon and anti-aircraft artillery. Balloon aprons had in fact been constructed for the defence of London during the First World War, but with minimal value. After 1918 some experiments took place in Britain to produce a balloon with cables suitably strong to destroy any aircraft colliding with them, but by 1936 the British Air Staff had come to the conclusion that no immediate prospect existed of perfecting a balloon capable of taking such a cable to the 15,000-feet level; this height was considered to be the minimum required to provide defence against high-flying bombers. Balloons were therefore produced for lower altitudes, of about 5,000 feet, to protect against low-level attacks: by 1940 about 1,500 balloons were deployed in Britain, mainly of this type and organized into 52 squadrons, with future production aimed at 1,200 a month. Such a defensive system was urgently required in view of the acute shortages of anti-aircraft artillery. Until a short while before the start of the Second World War, British artillery defence against low-level attack mainly comprised 3-inch guns and the conventional *Lewis* machine-gun; even by 1940 Britain had only 1,204 heavy and 581 light anti-aircraft guns in the entire country, compared with an estimated required establishment of 2,232 and 1,860 respectively. Britain had, however, an important advantage in her *radar*: information was collected from about 20 main radar stations on the coast and passed from these points and from observers to the Group Operations Room, Fighter Command. In the early stages of the *Blitz* about 200 AA batteries were located in the London area: the number of guns eventually rose above 2,000. The Blitz also revealed that pre-war estimates of the effectiveness of bombers were grossly pessimistic. During the war both strength and weapon power in anti-aircraft systems improved for all major participants. Britain's armoury included the famous 40 mm Bofors, firing 2-pound shells at 120 rpm to a maximum altitude of 12,000 feet; the Oerlikon 20 mm used on shipping, with drum magazines of 60 rounds firing at 650 rpm; and the 3·7-inch gun for high-level defence. The latter weapon was similar to the German 88 mm, which fired 8 rpm to a maximum altitude of over 35,000 feet. US forces adopted the Oerlikon. Later developments concentrated on more effective co-ordination between radar and artillery, as with the 1945 SCR-854 anti-aircraft series, and on the development of surface-to-air *missiles* (SAM). The latter have been produced in both strategic and tactical forms. Strategic anti-aircraft missile systems are designed primarily against opposing missiles, but can be used against aircraft. They include the US Nike Hercules, first becoming operational in 1958, which has nuclear or HE warheads, a range of over 140 km and a ceiling of over 45 km, and the Soviet Griffon, first displayed in public in 1973 and believed to have a range of about 250 km with a ceiling of about

30 km. Tactical SAMs include the US Hawk ('Homing All the Way Killer') which can search out and destroy aircraft travelling at supersonic speeds as low as 30 metres and as high as 11,000 metres; the British Bloodhound and Thunderbird; and numerous Soviet SAM weapons code-named by NATO as Ganef, Goa, Guild and Guideline. The latter has been extensively exported, including to Egypt where it has become a major factor in the Arab–Israeli balance: this has a ceiling of 18,000 metres and a range of about 50 km. Latest postwar advances were incorporated into the NATO Air Defence Ground Environment System, NADGE, a multi-national programme begun in 1967. The system was designed for air defence against aircraft flying at heights up to 100,000 feet, but there was no provision for *anti-ballistic missile (ABM) defence*. Up to 85 sites are envisaged in the NADGE plan, stretching along the NATO front: each is planned to use latest computer and data display equipment to undertake functions of detection, tracking, height-finding, target identification and target-size analysis.

Anti-Ballistic Missile (ABM) defence In the 1960s both the USA and the Soviet Union declared an interest in ABM systems as a means of defence should deterrence fail, and as a possible method of achieving a lead in the arms race. ABM defence generally covers two types of systems: area and terminal defence. The first refers to the interception of missiles above the atmosphere; the latter refers to the interception of any approaching missile which may have pierced the first defences. Thus the Russian Galosh missile is believed to be intended for an area defence, while terminal defence could be provided by either Griffon or the Guideline medium-range anti-aircraft missile. The USA announced plans to build a limited ABM system in 1967, initially to protect the country against Chinese attack. ABM missiles in this Sentinel system would be the Nike Zeus, developed after 1956 as a long-range anti-aircraft missile, and the short-range Sprint for the terminal defence. The Sentinel system was changed in 1969 to the Safeguard system, which had the more limited aim of covering Minuteman ICBM missile sites and small numbers of population centres. Safeguard uses the Spartan missile for area defence – an enlarged version of the earlier Nike Zeus – and the Sprint for terminal defence. The USA also began to research the Site-Defense (originally Hard Site) ABM system for more economical protection of ICBM sites: this would only use short-range missiles. The Interim *Strategic Arms Limitation Talks* (SALT), signed in May 1972 between the USA and the Soviet Union, set restrictions on ABM development. America was allowed to build one Safeguard site; this is now operational at Grand Forks. The Soviet Union continued to develop a more effective ABM missile to replace the Galosh in the Moscow area defence network.

Antietam Creek, campaign and Battle of, September 1862 *American Civil War* (Map 3). Also known as Sharpsburg. Following the Confederate success at *Bull Run*, *Lee* led 55,000 troops over the Potomac at Leesburg on 4 September 1862 to begin his first invasion of the north. Lee's movement was screened by cavalry under *Stuart*. The southern commander aimed to advance north-west into Pennsylvania using protection offered by the Catoctin Mountains; on 9 September he issued orders for *Longstreet*'s 1st Corps to march towards Hagerstown, forming the most northern wing of the Confederate advance; *Jackson*, on the southern wing, would cross the Potomac to seize Harper's Ferry. To face this advance *McClellan* had already moved from Washington with the Army of the Potomac, totalling 97,000 men. On 12 September a copy of Lee's 9 September order fell into McClellan's hands, revealing that the southern army was spread over 25 miles and split by the unfordable Potomac. But the Union Army moved too slowly and McClellan missed his opportunity to strike. Lee concentrated at Sharpsburg while covering forces delayed the Union advance in the so-called Battle of South Mountain. Jackson took Harper's Ferry after sharp fighting on 14–15 September, then rushed to join Lee at Sharpsburg. McClellan still hesitated, delaying his attack until 16 September by which time the Confederates totalled 45,000 men in excellent defensive lines along Antietam Creek near Sharpsburg. Battle began on 17 September – to be the bloodiest one-day clash in the American Civil War. McClellan planned to pin down the Confederate right (southern) wing, while a three-corps attack hammered Lee's left and two more corps struck the Confederate centre over Antietam Creek. Jackson's regiments offered stubborn defence against the Union thrust in the north, especially around the sunken road known thereafter as 'Bloody Lane'. By noon the Union attack against this Confederate left wing had been halted. In the centre, Union troops under General Ambrose *Burnside* managed to seize a bridge over Antietam Creek after desperate resistance by Longstreet's corps. It then took Burnside 2 hours to concentrate his troops for the assault through the Confederate centre, and McClellan hesitated to support Burnside with 20,000 Union troops held in reserve. The Confederates in the centre were starting to give way under Burnside's pressure when more Confederate units rushed to the battlefield: these, under General A. P. Hill, had been left at Harper's Ferry. This division struck Burnside's left flank, driving the Union troops back across the creek and ending the battle. Lee withdrew unmolested across the Potomac. Tactically, he could claim victory, although strategically his invasion of the north had been blocked. McClellan continued to hesitate: he failed to follow Lee until ordered to do so by President Lincoln on 5 October, so beginning the *Fredericksburg* campaign. Union losses at Antietam were about 12,500, Confederate about 13,700.

Anti-tank weapons First attempts to defend against *tanks* were made in the *First World War* by deploying normal field artillery with lowered trajectories: thus the *Hindenburg Line* contained isolated anti-tank positions with dug-in field-guns. Between the World Wars special guns of light construction were produced by all major powers: these were designed with a low silhouette and were given sufficient power to penetrate the armour of every known tank. But the race between armour and power to penetrate armour had already begun, and this accelerated soon after hostilities opened in 1939. Initially the allies seemed to have the advantage. During the Battle of *France* the Germans discovered that their existing 37 mm anti-tank guns were unable to punch through the thick armour of opposing tanks. Moreover, in the campaign against *Russia*, the Germans found that the 76 mm guns on the Soviet KV1 and T34 tanks could penetrate the 30 mm armour on the German vehicles, and an urgent programme was therefore begun both to improve German anti-tank guns and to strengthen panzer armour. The standard size of the gun was raised to a 75 mm minimum; production of the famous 88 mm gun had strong impact – this artillery piece was initially designed as an *anti-aircraft* gun but *Rommel* showed how effective it could be in an anti-tank role. The British 25-pounder gun/howitzer had similar calibre to the German 88 mm, and the same tendency was shown to increase penetration power: the 25-pounder

was developed to replace the old 18-pounder prior to the war; the British 2-pounder was replaced by the 6-pounder in 1940, and the latter was later itself overtaken by the powerful 17-pounder which had a 3,000-yard range. A Russian light anti-tank gun was the Type 32 45 mm with a range of almost 10,000 yards; a comparative US gun was the 37 mm, with a maximum range of 12,800 yards. Japan largely neglected both tank and anti-tank warfare. The Russian and US armies were also equipped with special tank destroyers and self-propelled guns for anti-tank warfare. The most effective Soviet destroyer was the SU-122 built on the T34 hull, carrying a 122 mm gun and with a speed of up to 34 mph: this weapon had a range of 375 miles. The US M10 gun motor carriage was a lighter-weight tank-killer, with a 3-inch gun mounted on a Sherman hull firing armour-piercing shells: these could penetrate 100 mm armour at 100 yards. The Germans embarked on maximum effort to produce a variety of mobile anti-tank weapons, especially after encountering the deadly Soviet T34 tank in 1941: numerous models were produced, including the Hertzer weighing 16 tons and armed with a 75 mm gun. Among Second World War infantry anti-tank weapons was the famous 'Bazooka', a 2·36-inch hand-held rocket launcher developed by the US Ordnance in 1942. The British began the war with the Boys Anti-Tank rifle, in fact already obsolete, which was deployed at platoon level. This was replaced by the Pro-

jector Infantry Anti-Tank (PIAT), with an extremely short range: this weapon weighed only 34·5 pounds and its bomb 2·5 pounds – the user had to approach within 100 yards of the target before a 'kill' could be obtained. Towards the close of hostilities the Germans produced the 'panzerfaust' as a one-man anti-tank rocket; this also had only a short range. The *rocket* became increasingly important as an anti-tank weapon in post-war years, especially those rockets which could be guided manually on to the target. This method was first suggested by the Germans, but was developed after 1945 by the French: the system enabled the operator to pass signals down a thin wire paid out behind the missile in flight. The first such weapon to enter service was the French SS 10 with a range of 1,600 metres; work on the SS 10 began in 1946 and the weapon became operational 10 years later; the SS 11 was introduced as a slightly larger version, with a weight of 65 pounds and able to travel over 2,500 metres to penetrate 600 mm of vertical armour plate. Other modern guided anti-tank missiles include the man-portable French ACL-STRIM, with a calibre of 88·9 mm and an effective range of 400 metres; the German Cobra, also man-portable but with a longer range; the Swedish short-range Bantam, manufactured by Bofors; the British Swingfire which went into service in 1969 and which has a maximum range of over 3,000 metres; and the British man-portable Vigilant. All these and other guided missiles enable accuracies of up to 90 per cent in tests, but this percentage drops substantially in exercise conditions and would presumably be even lower in actual combat.

'Anvil' operation, August 1944
Second World War (Maps 13, 14). Code-named 'Dragoon' in the final phase, this plan for an allied invasion of southern France was the subject of intense Anglo-US debate, with the British anxious to avoid reduction of allied strength in the *Italian campaign*. The US *Joint Chiefs of Staff*, supported by *Eisenhower*, insisted upon the plan as a means of drawing away German forces facing the *Normandy* landings. The operation began on 15 August, undertaken by the US 7th Army under Lieutenant-General Alexander Patch. The assault, between Hyères and Cannes, proved successful: by nightfall nearly 100,000 men were ashore and the meagre German defences – two infantry battalions – had been swamped; the French 2nd Corps under General Jean *Lattre de Tassigny* landed in the second wave. General Frederick Wiese's German 19th Army retreated up the Rhone valley. The allies encountered more determined opposition at Montélimar, 23–28 August, and the bulk of the German forces escaped. The French component captured Toulon and Marseilles, 28 August. Contact between 'Dragoon' forces and *Patton*'s 3rd Army coming down from Normandy was made west of Dijon, 11 September; 4 days later the southern invasion group became the US 6th Army Group under Lieu-

tenant-General Jacob M. Devers, which included the newly created 1st French Army commanded by Lattre de Tassigny.

Anzio Operation, 1944 *Second World War* (Map 14); campaign in *Italy*. The amphibious operation at Anzio, code-named 'Shingle', was designed to speed allied progress by leapfrogging the enemy lines; the movement was to be in conjunction with a thrust by the allied 5th Army south of *Cassino*. Continued deadlock at Cassino resulted in a change of emphasis for the Anzio operation: the latter was strengthened as a full-scale offensive. The landing took place early on 22 January, involving 50,000 British and US troops under US Major-General J. P. Lucas with the spearhead provided by the 1st British and 3rd US Divisions. A bridgehead was secured on the coast 35 miles south of Rome and 60 miles behind the German lines at Cassino. General Lucas now preferred to consolidate his position, believing the mere presence of the Anzio force would draw off the Germans from Cassino. But German reserves were rushed from Rome and north Italy: by the close of January the 3½ allied divisions in the Anzio bridgehead were opposed by 5 German divisions; the enemy counter-attacked on 3 February; by nightfall on the 17th a deep wedge had been driven into the allied lines. The defenders retaliated with sea and air bombardment, and the Germans began to fall back during the night of the 18th. Between 15 and 20 February the

Anzio forces, named the 6th Corps, suffered 3,400 casualties, and a high rate continued. Command was now given to Lieutenant-General L. K. Truscott, who repulsed the next major German thrust on 28–29 February. The bridgehead remained invested throughout March and April. Finally, on 23 May after Cassino had fallen to the allies, the reinforced 6th Corps broke out and joined with 5th Army units on the 25th. Allied battle casualties at Anzio totalled over 25,000, including 7,000 dead. *Kesselring* later claimed total German casualties to have been 40,000, of which 5,000 were killed. *Churchill* commented on the operation: 'We had hoped to land a wild cat that would tear out the bowels of the Boche. Instead we have stranded a vast whale with its tail flopping about in the water.'

Appomattox, campaign and Battle of, 1865 *American Civil War* (Map 3). The year 1865 opened with the Union armies poised to reap the results of *Grant*'s twin turning movements: *Meade*'s advance into the *Wilderness* of North Virginia, and *Sherman*'s advance to *Atlanta* and to the sea. The jaws of the pincer began to close. Jefferson *Davis* attempted to improve the increasingly hopeless Confederate situation on 3 February by appointing *Lee* to supreme command: Joseph Johnston would command the scattered Confederate forces in the Carolinas. Sherman reached Columbia in South Carolina on 17 February and continued north, turning from the coast on 15 March towards Denton-

ville with 60,000 men. Johnston had only 27,000 men with which to oppose him, but attacked on 19 March, hoping to destroy the Union left wing before Sherman could concentrate against him; the Union left was severely mauled but retained cohesion. Johnston withdrew on 20 March having lost about 3,000 men; Union casualties were about half this number. Sherman advanced to Goldsboro on 23 March; he rested for 3 weeks before starting out to join Grant near Petersburg. Meanwhile, General J. Wilson's Union cavalry corps of 13,500 men stabbed into Alabama on 18 March and attacked the Confederate supply base at Selma on 2 August, taking the town; Wilson continued into Georgia. Grant maintained the threat around Petersburg with 90,000 men from the Armies of the Potomac and the James; Lee opposed him with only 60,000, many exhausted and ill-equipped. Lee nevertheless threw forces forward at Fort Stedman on 25 March, but the battle merely weakened him still further, and the next day Grant received 30,000 reinforcements with the arrival of *Sheridan*'s corps. A Union attempt to encircle Lee's flank on 29 March was blocked by Lee's brilliant manoeuvring at Dinwiddie Courthouse and White Oak Road, but an assault by Sheridan's troops at Five Forks on 1 April exposed the entire right of the Confederate Army. Grant launched a full-scale assault on Petersburg on 2 April and by nightfall the Confederates were withdrawing. Lee hoped to be able to join Johnston south of Danville. The

Confederate move south-west began on 3 April; a running campaign continued for the next 6 days. A Confederate delaying action at Sayler's Creek was smashed on 6-7 April, reducing Lee's strength to under 30,000 men. Sheridan outmanoeuvred Lee by reaching Appomattox on 8 April as the Confederates neared Appomattox Courthouse, 2 miles to the north-east. The so-called Battle of Appomattox took place on 9 April: the Confederates attacked Union cavalry, but the position was entirely hopeless with massed Union infantry deploying for battle in overwhelming strength. Lee sought a ceasefire and met Grant at Appomattox Courthouse. The southern commander surrendered his army at 3.45 p.m., 9 April. In the south Johnston surrendered to Sherman on 26 April; all Confederate troops had laid down their arms by 26 May and President Andrew Johnson – Lincoln's successor after the latter's assassination on 14 April – issued his proclamation of amnesty on 29 May.

Arctic convoys, 1941-5 *Second World War* (Map 15). *Hitler*'s invasion of *Russia*, June 1941, soon led to appeals for help from *Stalin*, promptly answered by *Churchill*. Destination ports were Murmansk and Archangel, threatened by U-boats and by aircraft and surface ships based in ports won by the enemy during the *Norway* campaign, 1940. The first convoy sailed from Iceland on 21 August 1941. By the end of 1941 8 convoys had sailed to Russia and 4 had returned;